CW00499824

Second sight

MANCHESTER
1824

Manchester University Press

Second sight

The visionary imagination in late Victorian literature

CATHERINE MAXWELL

Manchester University Press

Manchester and New York

distributed in the United States exclusively by Palgrave Macmillan

Published by Manchester University Press
Oxford Road, Manchester M13 9NR, UK
and Room 400, 175 Fifth Avenue, New York, NY 10010, USA
www.manchesteruniversitypress.co.uk

Distributed in the United States exclusively by
Palgrave Macmillan, 175 Fifth Avenue,
New York, NY 10010, USA

Distributed in Canada exclusively by
UBC Press, University of British Columbia, 2029 West Mall,
Vancouver, BC, Canada V6T 1Z2

British Library Cataloguing-in-Publication Data is available

Library of Congress Cataloging-in-Publication Data is available

ISBN 978 0 7190 7145 4 paperback

First published by Manchester University Press in hardback 2009

This paperback edition first published 2011

Printed by Lightning Source

For Mary Condé
and
Stefano Evangelista

Contents

Acknowledgements

This book was mainly written during periods of leave supported by Queen Mary, University of London and the AHRC. I am happy to acknowledge the assistance of the AHRC, which funded the second part of the leave, and am grateful to Dinah Birch, my referee for the successful application, and to Julia Boffey, an exemplary Head of School.

It gives me great pleasure to acknowledge those friends and colleagues who kindly read and commented on parts of the manuscript: Philip Bullock, Mary Condé, Santanu Das, Stefano Evangelista, Martina Evans, Ana Alicia Garza, Paul Hamilton, Forbes Morlock, Elizabeth Prettejohn, Patricia Pulham, and Sarah Wood. I am deeply grateful for all their thoughtful suggestions and comments. Thanks, too, to Katie Fleming for her Latin translations. Special thanks are due to Patricia Pulham who read the entire manuscript and was a constant source of encouragement.

I am indebted to the Officers of the MHRA for generously giving me presentation copies of the new edition of Rossetti's *Correspondence* and Roger C. Lewis's variorum edition of *The House of Life.* The following libraries have proved indispensable to my research, and I am glad to offer my thanks to their staff: Queen Mary, Senate House, the Courtauld Institute, the British Library, the London Library, Rutgers University Library, and the Miller Library, Colby College.

Some parts of this monograph have already appeared in a different form elsewhere. Fragments of Chapter 3 are taken from my part of the Preface to Vernon Lee's *Hauntings and Other Fantastic Tales* (Peterborough, Ontario: Broadview Press, 2006), 9–27, and from 'Vernon Lee and Eugene Lee-Hamilton' in *Vernon Lee: Decadence, Ethics, Aesthetics*, eds Catherine Maxwell and Patricia Pulham (London and Basingstoke: Palgrave Macmillan, 2006), 21–39. Chapter 4 is a considerably extended version of the essay 'Theodore Watts-Dunton's *Aylwin* (1898) and the Reduplications of Romanticism', from *The Yearbook of English Studies* 37.1 (2007), 1–40, while Chapter 5 reprises part of the essay 'Vision and Visuality', from *A*

Companion to Victorian Poetry, eds Alison Chapman, Richard Cronin and Antony H. Harrison (Oxford: Blackwell 2003), 510–25. I acknowledge Broadview Press, Palgrave Macmillan, the MHRA, and Blackwell Publishing as the original publication source for this material.

A note on the texts

I use throughout the Harvard author–date system of referencing with full publication details given in the References at the end of this book. Where two or more works by the same author have been published in the same year, I have identified them by additional letters e.g. 1974a, 1974b. In the case of Walter Pater and Thomas Hardy where there exist collected multi-volume editions that bear the same date of publication, I have incorporated brief abbreviations to avoid ambiguity. For Pater I have used the 1910 Library Edition (except for *The Renaissance*, preferring in this instance to use Donald Hill's 1980 edition which is designated as Pater 1980, *Ren* 75). The following abbreviations have been used: *App* for *Appreciations*; *GL* for *Gaston de Latour*; *GS* for *Greek Studies*; *ME* for *Marius the Epicurean*; *MS* for *Miscellaneous Studies*; *IP* for *Imaginary Portraits*; and *PP* for *Plato and Platonism.*

Introduction

Second Sight, the title of this monograph, rather than implying a focus on esoteric practices such as spiritualism and clairvoyance in the late Victorian period, denotes the visionary imagination and the way that it either, as Shelley puts it, sees 'the manifestation of something beyond the present & tangible object' (Shelley 1964, 2.47) or imaginatively transfigures that object, as Ruskin puts it, when he states that 'the power of the imagination in exalting any visible object . . . [is], as it were, a spiritual or second sight' (Ruskin 1904, 5.355). A successor to my first monograph, *The Female Sublime from Milton to Swinburne: Bearing Blindness* (2001), this book represents a second opportunity to think about the visionary imagination in the Victorian period, a subject that has received little attention in recent times. *Bearing Blindness* dealt with that form of the visionary imagination known as the sublime, insisting against convention that, far from disappearing in Victorian period, it irradiates the most powerful work of the three leading male poets, Tennyson, Browning, and Swinburne. In *Second Sight*, I move away from this exclusive focus on canonical male poets to concentrate on a range of authors from the late Victorian period, some canonical, some non-canonical, whose works, in addition to poetry, encompass a variety of literary forms such as the essay, the short story, and the novel. The sublime is now treated as only one among a number of forms of imaginative vision used by my chosen writers, all of who are deeply indebted to Romantic influences.

The last forty years or so have seen a variety of critics tackling the subject of visual representation in Victorian literature, but much contemporary work on vision and visuality in literary texts is still dominated by a preoccupation with particulars, with the material and phenomenal world and with material practices that can be traced back to a seminal study, Carol T. Christ's *The Finer Optic* (1975), whose subtitle declares its focus on 'The Aesthetic of Particularity in Victorian Poetry'. Following the lead of Jerome McGann's essay 'Rossetti's Significant Details' (1969), Christ's study noted a Victorian preoccupation with small, often naturalistic, visual details, and explored how, in the poetry of Tennyson, Browning, D. G. Rossetti and Hopkins, such details can signify the poet's sense, sometimes anxious, sometimes celebratory, of 'the world's multitudinousness' (Arnold cited in Christ 1975, 35, 65). While Romantic vision sees beyond the object, or spiritually exalts it as a symbol, detail for these Victorian writers supposedly becomes a preoccupation for its own sake, and epiphany, when it does occur, partakes of 'the possibilities and limits of vision in a world of mere particulars' (Christ 1975, 14). Christ's work inaugurated an interest in visual perception in Victorian poetry that is centred on 'naked particulars', visual objects that clearly and unambiguously present themselves to the view of the reader.

This stress on the optical visible has remained influential, the assumption being that in the face of Victorian anxiety and scepticism the Romantic visionary imagination is de-idealised and replaced by more verifiable certainties of material particularity. Victorian visual studies since Christ have tended to emphasise the empirical visible, crediting emergent optical technologies, cultural spectacle, and the proliferation of mass media forms with responsibility for shaping the visual and perceptual worlds of Victorian literature. While Jonathan Crary's *Techniques of the Observer* (1990) rather carefully attributed the formation of a new kind of observer in the early nineteenth century less to new optical technologies than to a reshaping of subjectivity brought about by processes of modernisation and rationalisation, other accounts have speculated how innovations in optical instruments such as stereoscopes, telescopes, microscopes, and the photographic camera may have altered the nineteenth-century viewer's visual field and played a part in structuring the visual field of various writers. Thus, for example, Lindsay Smith's *Victorian Photography, Painting and Poetry* (1995) explicitly considers how such technologies may have shaped the kind of visual perceptions relayed by Victorian poetry. During the Victorian era, cultural spectacles in the form of theatre, music hall, public art galleries, and exhibitions, promoted and propagated by a new mass media, achieved a greater prominence and, along with the greater availability of illustrations and descriptive text in cheaper books, periodicals, newspapers and posters, can be thought of as helping form the visual imagination. Works such as the collection *Victorian Literature and the Victorian Visual Imagination* (1995), edited by Christ and John O. Jordan, and Kate Flint's more recent *The Victorians and the Visual Imagination* (2000) examine a variety of relationships between literary texts and different kinds of spectacle, illustration or visual technology. The contribution of these influences is undeniable, but is the Victorian imagination formed so exclusively by material culture? Even though Flint proposes that the invisible or the unseen might also be a key Victorian concern (Flint 2000, 20, 22), she makes it clear that for her that non-visibility is a more a matter of sub-visibility, infinitesimal matter or hidden ideological assumptions which can always be rendered visible by emergent technologies or by theoretical speculation about the power relations which condition social interactions and their material consequences (Flint 2000, 63, 273). Her unseen remains part of a broadly empirical tradition. Similar kinds of thinking have overtaken recent treatments of the Victorian supernatural; for, while spectral forms have become popular topics for critical exploration, the tendency has been to read and rematerialise them as 'the ghosts of ideology' – displaced effects of material culture – an approach which seems to me unsatisfactory in that it erases or tries to dispel the sheer uncanniness and strangeness of many texts.

'A certain strangeness, something of the blossoming of the aloe, is indeed an element in all true works of art: that they shall excite or surprise us is indispensable', writes Walter Pater of Michelangelo, adding that 'this strangeness must be sweet also – a lovely strangeness' (Pater 1910, *Ren* 57). Elsewhere, in an essay on Romanticism first published in 1876, Pater stipulates that 'It is the addition of strangeness to beauty which constitutes the romantic character in art' (Pater 1910, *App* 246). Pater is one of a number of late Victorian writers featured in this book whose work is marked by the visionary strangeness of the Romantic imagination, which mediates his own treatment of Hellenism and the Renaissance. Ruskin, lamenting the ugliness of Victorian England, writes that 'The imagination of [beauty], as it was seen in our ancestors, haunts us continually' (Ruskin 1904, 5.325), and, if we acknowledge that the Victorian imagination is partly shaped by the imaginative traditions that precede and haunt it, then we need to look to its immediate Romantic ancestors. Yet, with the exception of a few critics, most notably Harold Bloom, the considerable impact of Romanticism on the latter part of the nineteenth century is still largely unacknowledged. In spite of its title, even *The Last Romantics* (1947), Graham Hough's important study of British Aestheticism, contains virtually no discussion of Romantic influences. In 1972 George Whalley wrote that 'The last part of the history of the word *romantic* in nineteenth-century England is indistinct and has to be inferred, largely from negative evidence', remarking that the second half of the nineteenth century is 'a dead zone where navigation is difficult' (Whalley 1972, 235, 244). Kenneth Daley, in the introduction to his own recent book on the influence of Romanticism on Ruskin and Pater, finds Whalley's verdict still valid, stating his own corrective as the provision of 'a more detailed picture of romanticism's emergence as a literary concept in England' in the later Victorian period (Daley 2001, 4).

Certainly the notion that Romanticism and its visionary concerns got left behind or sidelined by the Victorians should rouse some scepticism, as should the more recent idea propounded by the collection *Nervous Reactions: Victorian Recollections of Romanticism* (Faflak and Wright 2004) that nervousness and ambivalence towards Romanticism represent the predominant Victorian attitude. Reviewing this collection, which focuses mainly on work produced between the Regency and the early 1870s, Kenneth Daley writes: 'in its exclusive focus on the figure of nervousness, the volume ignores those competing, and highly influential, Victorian voices that sought neither to cleanse Romantic voices of their strangeness nor to repudiate their revolutionary aims and emotional excesses, but rather to enthusiastically invoke what they perceive to be the antinomian spirit of Romanticism' (Daley 2006, 553). Certainly during the late Victorian period, when there seems to have been considerable reaction against the growth of materialism, and a concomitant interest in psychic phenomena, spiritualism, and other occult beliefs, literary Romanticism flourished, although this has since been partly obscured by its absorption into Aestheticism and the Symbolist strand of Decadence.[1] Yet in his essay 'Æsthetic Poetry', Pater makes it clear that the poetry of William Morris and Dante Gabriel Rossetti to which he gives this title is 'an afterthought' of 'The writings of the "romantic school"' (Pater 1889, 227, 214; 1974a, 190, 198). In his earliest published essay, 'Coleridge' (1866), Pater had written that Coleridge 'is the perfect flower of the romantic type' (Pater 1973, 26). For Pater, as for the critic Theodore Watts-Dunton, another writer featured in this book, romanticism is pre-eminently a set of characteristics that can be found in the literature of any age, but which flourishes especially in the imaginative literature of the late eighteenth and early nineteenth centuries, with another flowering in the later nineteenth century. In the 1880s Watts-Dunton, one of the most prominent literary critics of the period, gave the name 'the Renascence of Wonder' to a movement that he saw as a revival of the Romantic imagination and which he defined as

> the inevitable expression of the soul of man in a certain stage of civilization (when the sanctions which have made and moulded society are to be found not absolute and eternal, but relative, mundane, ephemeral and subject to the higher sanctions of unseen powers that work behind 'the shows of things') . . . that temper of wonder and mystery which all over Europe had preceded and now followed the temper of imitation, prosaic acceptance, pseudo-classicism and domestic materialism.
>
> (Watts-Dunton 1886, 858)[2]

Watts-Dunton proposed Dante Gabriel Rossetti, whom he regarded as the rightful inheritor of Coleridge's visionary Romanticism, as the instigator of the modern movement: 'Of the true romantic feeling, the ever-present apprehension of the spiritual world and of that struggle of the soul with earthly

1 Pater's formula for Romanticism, 'strangeness and beauty', was adopted as the title of a well-known two-volume anthology of Aesthetic criticism (Warner and Hough 1983).

2 In the Preface to the World's Classics edition of his novel *Aylwin*, Watts-Dunton endorses Robertson Nicoll's more succinct definition of the phrase 'the Renascence of Wonder' as 'aware[ness] of the spiritual world, of the supernatural, of the lifelong struggle of the soul, of the power of the unseen' (Watts-Dunton 1914, xii).

conditions . . . Rossetti's poetry is as full as his pictures' (Watts-Dunton 1886, 860). A more extreme version of this revived Romanticism can be seen in another, more famous admirer of Rossetti, W. B. Yeats, who also loved the visionary and symbolic poetry of Shelley, Coleridge and Blake, and whose *fin-de-siècle* essays wage war against a materialist, empiricist, and positivistic ethos. Yeats's idiosyncratic formulation of Decadence in 'The Autumn of the Body' (1898) envisages a similar contest of spiritual values with 'earthly conditions':

> Writers are struggling all over Europe, though often with a philosophic understanding of their struggle, against that picturesque and declamatory way of writing, against that 'externality' which a time of scientific and political thought has brought into literature. . . . [Man] grew weary when he said, 'These things that I touch and see are alone real,' for he saw them without illusion at last, and found them but air and dust and moisture. . . .The arts are, I believe, about to take on their shoulders the burdens that have fallen from the shoulders of priests, and to lead us back upon our journey by filling our thoughts with the essences of things, and not with things.
>
> (Yeats 1989, 189, 193)

For Yeats, too, Rossetti is part of this Symbolist movement, as we see, when in a slightly later essay, 'The Happiest of the Poets' (1902), he says of him, 'One feels sometimes that he desired a world of essences, of unmixed powers, of impossible purities', and declares that 'Rossetti, drunken with natural beauty, saw the supernatural beauty, the impossible beauty in his frenzy' (Yeats 1989, 53, 64).

Undoubtedly there are large differences between the Romanticism of Watts-Dunton and that of the early Yeats. As an artist Yeats rejected the primacy of Nature and natural forms for the interior 'eternal' language of imaginative symbolism, and strongly distrusted science, seeing it as in league with empiricism, while Watts-Dunton, who as a younger man had nurtured keen scientific interests, venerated Nature as the 'veil' of an immanent spiritual power and beauty, and thought science could be an ally in helping to stimulate appreciation of the wonder of the natural world. None the less, both writers identified Rossetti as the outstanding late Romantic artist, and both would, I think, have identified him as a Symbolist according to the definition of Arthur Symons who, in 'The Decadent Movement in Literature' (1893), asserted that 'The Symbolist . . . flash[es] upon you the "soul" of that which can only be apprehended by the soul – the finer sense of things unseen, the deeper meaning of things evident' (Symons 1925, 99). Certainly both Watts-Dunton and Yeats recognised how in Rossetti's art the female face and form had a central place and profound symbolic significance. Watts-Dunton observes that throughout his life Rossetti had taken an interest in only four subjects, 'poetry, painting, mediæval mysticism, and woman', noting in the same essay that 'to Rossetti the human body, like everything else in Nature, was rich in symbol. Every feature had its suggestive value. To him the mouth really represented the sensuous part of the face no less certainly than the eyes represented the spiritual part' (Watts-Dunton 1883, 416). It is clear from this and the ensuing description of his designs that it always a woman's body that is Rossetti's primary subject. In his essay 'Symbolism in Painting' (1898), Yeats, too, emphasised Rossetti's symbolic purpose: 'If you paint a beautiful woman and fill her face, as Rossetti filled so many faces, with an infinite love, a perfected love, "one's eyes meet no mortal thing when they meet the light of her peaceful eyes," as Michelangelo said of Vittoria Colonna' (Yeats 1989, 150). In 'The Trembling of the Veil' (1922) from *Autobiographies*, Yeats writes of his youthful self and peers: 'Woman herself was still in our eyes . . . romantic and mysterious, still the priestess of her shrine, our emotions, remembering the *Lilith* and the *Sybilla Palmifera* of Rossetti' (Yeats 1955, 302). The poet, essayist, and psychic researcher Frederic W. H. Myers, who noted in Rossetti 'the reaction of Art against Materialism, which becomes more marked as the dominant tone of science grows more soulless and severe', also saw his art as centred predominantly on a spiritualised female beauty: 'The most direct appeals, the most penetrating reminiscences, come to the worshipper of beauty from a woman's eyes' (Myers 1883 in Riede 1992a, 56, 49). For Myers, Rossetti's concentration on the symbolic form of woman marks a larger general tendency towards a special kind of survey of 'the human face and form', and, taking a lead from Pater's 1869 essay on Leonardo, he writes: 'All the arts, in fact, are returning now to the spirit of Leonardo, to the sense that of all visible objects known to us the human face and form are the most complex and mysterious, to the desire to extract the utmost secret, the occult message, from all the phenomena of Life and Being' (Myers in Riede 1992a, 50).

Following Myers, I propose that the visionary Romanticism of the late Victorian era finds a characteristic form of expression in 'the human face and form', and often explicitly in 'a woman's face and form'. While many modern studies pick up on the Victorian preoccupation with the female body, their emphasis is predominantly cultural-historical and ideological, unlike mine, which highlights the visionary treatment of the writers under investigation.[3] For the inspiring figure of a beloved woman haunts all the writers treated in this book, even Pater, who, although he typically favours beautiful young men, none the less epitomises the bloom of youth and beauty in Persephone, an

3 For a selection of influential modern works which examine the Victorian representation of the female body see, for example, Bram Dijkstra's *Idols of Perversity* (1986), Lynda Nead's *Myths of Sexuality* (1988), Lynne Pearce's *Woman/Image/Text* (1991), Elisabeth Bronfen's *Over Her Dead Body* (1992), J. B. Bullen's *The Pre-Raphaelite Body* (1997), and Kathy Alexis Psomiades's *Beauty's Body: Femininity and Representation in British Aestheticism* (1997).

elusive female divinity. Indeed what is noticeable about these various depictions is that they tend to focus on bodies which are lost or elusive, which are inaccessible, ghostly, fragmentary, or incomplete, requiring acts of imaginative recreation. 'Man is in love and loves what vanishes', writes the older Yeats in 'Nineteen Hundred and Nineteen' (Yeats 1982, 234), and his question in his poem 'The Tower' – 'Does the imagination dwell the most / Upon a woman won or a woman lost?' (Yeats 1982, 222) – is often pertinent here, as it suggests that the visionary aspect of the imagination is exercised or stimulated by loss or deprivation, or by what Vernon Lee elsewhere calls 'repression and short commons' (Lee 1908, 4).

My analysis of my chosen writers – Dante Gabriel Rossetti, Walter Pater, Vernon Lee, Eugene Lee-Hamilton, Theodore Watts-Dunton, and Thomas Hardy – centres on the iconic aesthetic image of the human face and form mediated through shadows, spirits, ghosts, corpses, body substitutes, paintings, sculptures, or sculptural fragments, and finds certain repeated motifs such as the *non-finito*, the Michelangelesque incomplete or unfinished body (sculptural or otherwise), the suggestive fragment, and the allied, widely used figure of synecdoche, the part for the whole, which so often acts as stimulus for the visionary imagination. These repeated images or patterns of images illuminate each author's creativity, aesthetic practice, and understanding of the imagination. Other key themes and devices include magnetic or mesmeric power, the refining or essentialising work of death, the hidden, unseen, or unrevealed image or imaging power that none the less asserts its presence in what is seen or felt, and the emergence of what Frank Kermode has called the 'Romantic Image', that master trope of literary Modernism. The fantastic, the mystical, and the supernatural are especially important to these writers, not necessarily as matters of belief, but because they allow a greater range of imaginative and emotional experience. Overall the book reveals how, without abandoning a commitment to material or physical objects or sensations, all of the writers featured, many of them commonly identified as empiricists or materialists and none of them with orthodox religious belief, exercise strong visionary tendencies in their work. These writers certainly have no monopoly on the visionary imagination in the late Victorian period, but they demonstrate interesting overlaps and inter-filiations and were chosen for this reason. If Yeats, who on occasion haunts the margins of this book, receives no chapter in his own right, it is because he is one of the few writers of the period whose treatment of the visionary imagination has already been widely acknowledged and discussed.

The literature of the late Victorian period is currently attracting much critical attention, not least because it occupies the crucial transition between Victorianism and Modernism, anticipating many of the Modernists' thematic concerns and stylistic innovations. As part of this general critical reassessment, much work has focused on reviving supposedly 'minor' writers, in particular women, who had previously dropped out of view, so that, in place of the received, somewhat well-worn narratives of Aestheticism and the *fin de siècle* that previously dominated the understanding of the period, a much wider picture of literary activity can be provided. This monograph also revives some less familiar names, but it at the same time suggests that some of the better-known names are often given lip-service rather than being much read, and that there might be fresh new ways of approaching them.

Famously the canonical male Modernists such as Yeats, Eliot, Pound, and T. E. Hulme rejected 'Romanticism', which they identified with the early nineteenth century and late Victorian poetry that had influenced their own early poems. They cast off Swinburne, Rossetti, and the poets of the 1890s as an 'unvirile' fad and an affair of adolescence. Yet other early twentieth-century writers, especially women like H. D. and Charlotte Mew, far from endorsing the repudiation of Victorian models, showed open and unembarrassed allegiance to Aestheticism and Decadence. Mew, a contemporary of Hardy's and a poet much admired by him, did not publish her first poetry collection till 1916, yet is, justifiably, the subject of the last chapter of Angela Leighton's *Victorian Women Poets* (1992). Hardy, the most popular of my chosen writers, is also a Romantic inheritor. Patronised by Yeats and Eliot, he none the less was admired by Ezra Pound, who regarded him as a sort of Imagist and managed to ignore his Romantic heritage, as did that other later group of anti-Romantics who also championed him, the Movement poets of the 1950s. Yet his formative links with Romanticism counteract the idea that he is somehow an ingenuous chronicler of country life or a mere recorder of material things. Although my chapter on him treats poems published after 1901, he takes his place in this study as the continuator of a Victorian visionary poetic tradition.

Hardy's works are enjoyed by academic and general readers alike, although, unlike his novels, his poetry has attracted relatively few critical studies. This may be a symptom of its very accessibility – his poems are commonly read by ordinary readers as well as schoolchildren and undergraduates, and are frequently anthologised in both academic and non-academic collections. Accessibility is a virtue; however, perceptions such as Philip Larkin's – 'When I came to Hardy it was with the sense of relief that I didn't have to try and jack myself up to a concept of poetry that lay outside my own life' (Larkin 1983, 175) – may mean that readers, and sometimes critics, are content to make only superficial readings, ignoring or resisting the poetry's deeper intellectual demands and imaginative solicitations. Moreover, Hardy's extensive poetic *œuvre* means that there are vast numbers of poems not included in the anthologies and collections that have received little critical examination. My chapter examines a small but varied sample of the poetry, providing an analysis that echoes Virginia Woolf's 1928 verdict on the novels: 'it is no mere transcript of life at a certain time and place that Hardy has given us. It is a vision of the world and of man's lot as they revealed themselves to an astonishing imagination' (Woolf 1986–94, 4.517).

In addition to Hardy, the other two writers featured in this book who could be called canonical are Dante Gabriel Rossetti and Walter Pater, but, while Hardy's work remains perennially in the public eye, Rossetti and Pater, foundational figures in British Aestheticism and the subjects of many valuable critical monographs, are still less appreciated than they should be. While Christina Rossetti, deservedly rehabilitated by feminist scholarship, is now widely known, her brother, who, as Florence Boos (2004) and John Holmes (2005) have recently suggested, exerted a substantial influence over the poetry of the late Victorian period, is still generally underestimated. Anthologies and undergraduate courses in Victorian poetry tend to concentrate on a handful of well-known poems such as 'The Blessed Damozel', 'The Woodspurge', and 'Jenny', while Rossetti's major achievement, the sonnet sequence *The House of Life*, first published in 1870 and reissued in a revised and extended form in 1881, receives relatively little attention outside specialist studies. None the less, recent exhibitions, Jan Marsh's excellent biography (1999), and the magnificent hypertext archive hosted by Virginia University have all gone some way towards raising Rossetti's profile, while editions by Marsh and Jerome McGann have at least ensured that the majority of the poems can be easily accessed.

This is sadly not the case for many of Pater's writings. Although massively influential in his impact on the *fin de siècle* and Modernism,[4] and widely disseminated throughout continental Europe (see Bann 2004), Pater is far more neglected; for, with the exception of Donald Hill's fine edition of *The Renaissance* (1980) and Gerald Monsman's equally fine *Gaston de Latour* (1995), there are no modern scholarly editions of his work available in English.[5] Readers wishing to read major works such as *Marius the Epicurean*, *Appreciations*, *Imaginary Portraits*, *Plato and Platonism*, and *Greek Studies* must either buy poor-value, unannotated, print-on-demand copies, source old

4 Pater has long been established as the prime precursor for literary Modernism. Perry Meisel (1980, 1987) and F. C. McGrath (1986) see him exerting his influence on Woolf, Eliot, Yeats, Joyce, while more recently Cassandra Laity (1996) and Eileen Gregory (1997) have explored his influence on H. D.

5 As Adam Phillips acknowledges (Phillips 1986, xx), his useful, widely used slim World's Classics edition of *The Renaissance* is heavily reliant on Donald Hill's edition, though it lacks the textual apparatus and its annotations are slight in comparison. The same is true of Michael Levey's handy reading edition of *Marius the Epicurean*, now out of print, which is not fully annotated (Pater 1985, 300). Gallingly, scholarly editions of several of the works I mention as unavailable in English are available in a number of other languages including French, Italian and Dutch. See Bann 2004, pp. xxiv–xxvi.

second-hand editions, or download texts from the internet, most of which provide no gloss or contextual commentary – something essential to a writer as allusive and erudite as Pater. It is not surprising that, outside a relatively small though dedicated group of enthusiasts, knowledge of Pater is mainly confined to selected extracts from *The Renaissance.* My chapters on Rossetti and Pater aim to bring new perspectives and new readers to works that occupy a crucial position in the literature of the late Victorian period.

My three non-canonical writers are Vernon Lee, the poet Eugene Lee-Hamilton, and the critic, poet, and novelist Theodore Watts-Dunton. Of these three, the cosmopolitan intellectual Lee (Violet Paget, 1856–1935), author of forty-three books, which include novels, short stories, dramas, biography, travel essays, philosophical dialogues, pacifist polemic, and studies of music, the visual arts, and literary aesthetics, is now undoubtedly the best-known. Her critical fortunes, steadily rising over the last twenty years, have made a meteoric ascent during the last five, so that she is beginning to be acknowledged, along with Pater, as a key name in British Aestheticism and a major influence on Modernists such as Virginia Woolf. The year 2003 saw a new biography by Vineta Colby, a critical monograph by Christa Zorn, and the first international conference on Lee's work, organised by Patricia Pulham and myself. After this came Mary Patricia Kane's short monograph on Lee's fantastic tales (2004) and another conference on Lee, held in her home city of Florence in May 2005, with the proceedings published in 2006 as *Vernon Lee e Firenze settant'anni dopo* (Cenni and Bizzotto 2006). The year 2006 also saw the first critical edition of Lee's supernatural fiction, *Hauntings and Other Fantastic Tales*, and a collection of critical essays, *Vernon Lee: Decadence, Ethics, Aesthetics*, both co-edited by Patricia Pulham and myself, and Pulham's fine monograph on Lee's supernatural tales has recently been published in 2008. Lee has also been the subject of many essays, attracting critics such as Gillian Beer, Angela Leighton, Martha Vicinus, Joseph Bristow, Richard Dellamora, and Dennis Dennisoff. As she may now be deemed to have come of age, my chapter on her dispenses with the standard introduction outlining her biography and listing her many achievements, believing that readers unfamiliar with these details are now well served by existing accounts such as Colby's biography or the prefaces to our edition and critical collection. The chapter aims to go beyond the territory of the standard introductory essay to give an in-depth and wide-ranging analysis of certain recurrent ideas and images in her supernatural tales and aesthetic writings of the same period.

Far less well known is Lee's half-brother, the poet Eugene Lee-Hamilton (1845–1907), although his poems, in particular his sonnets, are often included in anthologies of Victorian poetry. A promising start to a career in the diplomatic service was cut short by illness, and for a substantial period of his adult life Lee-Hamilton was bed-bound with an obscure spinal complaint, probably psychosomatic in origin, and was cared for by his mother and his sister at their home in Florence. Poetry, for which he had already showed some facility, became a mainstay, something he could work on in his head even when he was too ill to dictate to an amanuensis. Vernon Lee proved a loyal sister, promoting her brother's work on trips abroad and negotiating with publishers on his behalf, and during his life he produced a total of seven verse collections. After he finally recovered his health in 1896, there was a brief period of happiness during which he travelled, married the novelist Annie E. Holdsworth, and had a daughter. Sadly this much-loved child died before her second birthday, and he never recovered from this bereavement, dying in 1907 of Bright's disease, the illness that also eventually killed Rossetti. The best of his verse was written during the long period of his first illness, although the posthumously published collection *Mimma Bella* (1909), which commemorates his daughter, is often extremely moving. An accomplished late Victorian practitioner of the dramatic monologue and sharing his sister's predilection for the macabre and for the supernatural, Lee-Hamilton is also a superb sonneteer. Philip Hobsbaum in his *Metre, Rhythm and Verse Form* praises the 'exquisite versification' of Lee-Hamilton's *Sonnets of the Wingless Hours* (1894), declaring it 'The only [Victorian sonnet] sequence to compare with the work of Hopkins' (1996, 163), while, in her obituary review of Lee-Hamilton published in 1907, Edith Wharton wrote that it contained 'some twenty sonnets of exceptional beauty, and four or five which rank after the greatest in the language' (Wharton 1996, 115). The original editions of Lee-Hamilton's poems are now hard to come by, so the selected edition published in 2002 by MacDonald P. Jackson is especially welcome. However, with the exception of Jackson's excellent preface and essays by Alex Falzon and myself, there is little recent secondary work. My section on Lee-Hamilton in Chapter 3 attempts to remedy this situation by providing close readings of three of his dramatic sonnets, with the hope that this will stimulate further interest in his work.

Like Lee-Hamilton, Theodore Watts-Dunton (1836–1914) is now almost entirely unknown in his own right, being reduced to a footnote in the lives of more famous writers such as Rossetti and Swinburne. Again there is virtually no secondary criticism available. However, in his day, he was widely respected as a critic and poet, while *Aylwin*, the novel he had been working on for over twenty years was a bestseller in 1898, enjoying vast success at home and abroad and going through many reprints. As Watts-Dunton is unfamiliar to a modern audience, my chapter on him starts with a preliminary overview of his literary career and reputation that tries to account for his almost complete disappearance from view, before moving into an evaluation of *Aylwin*. Watts-Dunton was highly regarded as a poet, especially as a sonneteer, in his own era, although his poetic talent tends to look rather modest now, especially when set against the work of the more gifted Lee-Hamilton. None the less three of his sonnets are cited and discussed in Chapters 1 and 3, not so much as illustrations of his ability, but more for the influential paradigms they present. His now-neglected critical writing, again much praised by contemporaries, although interestingly eclectic in its range of literary reference and often intelligently perceptive, is not of major importance. But *Aylwin* with its elaborate structure of repetition, its observations on the treatment of trauma and hysteria, and its strange, late Victorian blend of sensation fiction, gypsy lore, the occult, mesmerism, and Romanticism, is very much a novel in keeping with modern critical interests and one well worth reviving.

While my selected writers share many thematic connections, they were in most cases also well known to each other, and in some instances had relationships which had a significant effect on their literary work. Watts-Dunton, one of Rossetti's closest friends and confidants, was one of the few people allowed to visit him during the virtual seclusion of his last decade. After Rossetti's death, he failed to write the widely anticipated biography, but wrote a number of articles about his friend and included a portrait of him under the thin disguise of the artist D'Arcy in *Aylwin*. Rossetti is the subject of an important essay by Pater discussed in Chapters 1 and 2. Pater met Rossetti once when he visited his studio with Swinburne in 1871 (Gosse 1896, 259). Although, according to Watts-Dunton, Rossetti did not take to him (Rothenstein 1931, 232), he none the less admired Pater's writing, warmly praising the essay on Leonardo in a letter to Swinburne of 26 November 1869 (Letter 69.204 in Rossetti 2002–5, 5.324). Pater's feeling for Rossetti was always that of an enthusiast. William Sharp, another of Rossetti's rare visitors, recalls that Pater pumped him for information about the poet when they first met in 1881, and that he named Rossetti as 'the most significant as well of the most fascinating' of the six men then living whom he thought 'certain to be famous in days to come' (Sharp 1894, 803; Seiler 1987, 82).[6] Pater's already-mentioned essay 'Demeter and Persephone', first given as a lecture at the Birmingham and Midland Institute on 29 November 1875 and then published in the *Fortnightly Review* for 1 January 1876, may possibly owe something to Rossetti's sonnet 'Proserpina' (the Latin version of the Greek goddess Persephone), discussed in Chapter 1. Pater is unlikely to have seen any of Rossetti's paintings of Proserpine, but a prose description by Frederic Stephens was published in the *Athenæum* for 14 August 1875, with the English and Italian sonnets published in the same journal a fortnight later on 28 August. Something of the hypnotic melancholy of these pieces may infuse the sombrely magnificent description of Persephone that concludes Pater's essay and is cited at the end of Chapter 2.

6 Vernon Lee identifies the dinner party at which Pater and Sharp first met as occurring on 4 July 1881. Sharp was subsequently invited to stay with Pater in Oxford towards the end of that month (Lee 1937, 96, 109).

Although Lee, Lee-Hamilton, and Hardy never met Rossetti, he seems to have had an impact on their writing. Lee's novel *Miss Brown* (1884b), which lampooned 'Aesthetic' manners and pretensions, cost her her friendship with William Michael and Lucy Rossetti and other members of their circle, for her novel's amoral protagonist, the Aesthetic painter-poet Walter Hamlin, was widely perceived as based on Rossetti (Gunn 1964, 102; Colby 2003, 106). Yet the notion that Hamlin is a portrait of Rossetti should be treated with some caution; according to Lee's intimate friend, the poet Mary Robinson, he also owes much to Lee herself (see Gardner 1987, 366–7). Rossetti has also been suggested by Joan Rees as the original of the poet Philip Trew in Hardy's short story 'An Imaginative Woman' (Rees 1981, 197–8), and more recently by John Holmes as the inspiration for Jocelyn Pearston in his 1892 serialised novel *The Pursuit of the Well-Beloved* (Holmes 2004). Rossetti is mentioned along with Dante, Petrarch, and Shakespeare as one of the great sonneteers in Lee-Hamilton's 'What the Sonnet Is', whose concluding lines describe the sonnet form as 'The dark deep emerald that Rossetti wrought / For his own soul, to wear for evermore'. 'In Memoriam', also from *Sonnets of the Wingless Hours* and dated 14 April 1882, commemorates Rossetti's death five days earlier: 'But he for whom the distant stranger grieves, / Outlives mere life; for men he doth not die' (Lee-Hamilton 1894, 87, 93). Rossetti's secluded life and semi-invalid status combined with his prowess as a sonneteer made him a powerful model for the younger poet, while his sonnet 'Proserpina' seems to be the closest analogue to Lee-Hamilton's own dramatic sonnets.

Pater, Lee, Lee-Hamilton, Hardy, and Watts-Dunton all knew each other either socially or by repute.[7] Hardy transcribed extracts from works by Pater, Lee, and Watts-Dunton into his literary notebooks;[8] Lee wrote on Hardy's

7 For Pater and Watts-Dunton see Rothenstein 1931, 232, and Lee 1937, 96, 152, 223. Pater and Hardy first met in the summer of 1886. Two years later Pater would call on the Hardys when they were spending the summer in Kensington and had Hardy to dinner at his London home. Hardy memorably thought his manner 'that of one carrying weighty ideas without spilling them' (Hardy 1962, 180). Lee first met Hardy in July 1886 while staying in London at the Gower Street home of Mary Robinson (Lee 1937, 223), a house well-known for literary tea-parties and soirées. Hardy and his wife Emma called on Lee and her brother while visiting Florence in April 1887 (Millgate 1985, 282). For Lee's often acid views on Watts-Dunton see Lee 1937, 74, 125, 179.

8 Hardy transcribed extracts taken from Lee's 'The Outdoor Poetry of the Middle Ages and the Renaissance' (1884) and 'A Dialogue on Novels' (1885), both published in the *Contemporary Review* (Hardy 1985, 1.157, 165–6), from Pater's 'Demeter and Persephone', *Marius the Epicurean*, *Appreciations* (Hardy 1985, 1.31, 205–7, 208, 2.17–19), and from Watts-Dunton's 'Poetry' (1885), published in the ninth edition of the *Encyclopædia Britannica* (Hardy 1985, 1.40, 2.66, 69).

prose;[9] Watts-Dunton reviewed Lee-Hamilton's poetry;[10] and Hardy and Watts-Dunton exchanged letters admiring each other's writings.[11] However, the most important of these relationships is that existing between Pater, Lee, and Lee-Hamilton. Pater was a close friend of Lee's, who had been introduced to his writings by her half-brother (Gregory 1954, 23). She stayed with him and his sisters in Oxford during her trips to England when they discussed their work together. His letters to her are among the most interestingly expansive of a slim collection that is otherwise markedly guarded in tone. He reviewed her collection *Juvenilia* (1887), while she wrote about his work on many occasions, dedicating to him her essay collection *Euphorion* in 1884, and commemorating him in the concluding 'Valedictory' of her *Renaissance Fancies and Studies* (1895).[12] Pater also had a warm opinion of Lee-Hamilton's verse, praising *The New Medusa, and Other Poems* as 'A very real and original contribution to poetry' (18 November 1882; Pater 1970, 46) and 'Hunting the King' from *Apollo and Marsyas* as 'a powerful ballad' (4 December 1884; Pater 1970, 56). As shown in Chapter 3, Pater is a key influence on both siblings, especially Lee, and, as will be seen, all three writers share an interest in the classical sculptural relic and the theme of the pagan god as revenant or god in exile.

One effect of bringing these particular writers into conjunction with each other is that one notices certain curious and unanticipated overlaps, not just in terms of themes or imagery, but even, occasionally, in terms of style and voice. While it is not surprising to find Lee sounding like Pater, it is much less

9 'Of Hardy and Meredith' (Lee 1905, 2–3), later collected in *The Handling of Words* (1923). Sent a copy of her essay by J. A. Spender, editor of the *Westminster Gazette*, Hardy thanks his correspondent for 'the article by the accomplished lady Vernon Lee' (27 July 1905; Hardy 1977–88, 3.177).

10 Review of *The New Medusa, and Other Poems* (1882), in the *Athenæum* for 16 December 1882 (Watts-Dunton 1882, 809). Watts-Dunton probably wrote the subsequent reviews of Lee-Hamilton's work that appeared in the *Athenæum*, but I have not been able to verify this. For a list of Lee-Hamilton's reviews see Lyon 1957. The auctioneer's copy of the Sotheby's sales catalogue for Watts-Dunton's library (13 March 1917) held by the British Library lists five books by Lee-Hamilton as lot 598 (p. 55).

11 Hardy mentions 'that masterly essay on Poetry', when thanking Watts-Dunton for his praise of *Wessex Poems* (1898), and, in the same letter refers appreciatively to Watts-Dunton's 'own fine verse, & the rank instantly accorded to "Aylwin" as a novel when it appeared' (26 February 1899; Hardy 1978–88, 2.16). Later Hardy would send Watts-Dunton his *Poems of the Past and Present* (1901) and acknowledge the gift of 'your delightful little *Christmas at the Mermaid*', a poem originally published in 1897 and recently reissued in a new edition (2 December 1901; Hardy 1978–88, 2.304).

12 For more on Lee and Pater see Bini 2004, Bizzotto 2004, Brake 2006, and Evangelista 2006.

expected to find Hardy sounding like both of them as, for example, in a letter to the Editor of the *Daily Chronicle* (28 December 1899), in which he defends his depiction of a phantom in his short poem 'A Christmas Ghost-Story', originally published in the *Westminster Gazette* for 23 December. Protesting against the notion that a ghost should retain physical awareness, Hardy writes: 'In short, and speaking generally, these creatures of the imagination are uncertain, fleeting, and quivering, like winds, mists, gossamer-webs, and fallen autumn leaves; they are sad, pensive, and frequently feel more or less sorrow for the acts of their corporeal years' (Hardy 1966a, 202). In a passage from her essay 'A Dialogue on Novels' (1885), which Hardy transcribed into his Notebooks, Lee had written that 'by the fatality of environment every human being is modified in many different ways; he is rammed into a place until he fits it, and absorbs fragments of all the other personalities with whom he is crushed together' (Lee 1886, 190–1). One of the things that emerges from this study is how Pater, Lee, and Hardy, sharing the same late nineteenth-century environment, generate remarkably sophisticated discourses of the imagination and of creativity, using, in the case of Pater and Hardy, the language of refinement, essence, and death, and, in the case of Lee and Hardy, the language of the supernatural, of hauntings, ghosts, shades, and phantoms which in some cases double for imaginative drives, impulses, and energies, and in others for evocation, memory, and the past. Thus, in an essay first published in 1904 and afterwards collected in *The Handling of Words*, Lee writes that 'Like ghosts, recollections can enter by closed doors, occupy seats already filled, flit about in inappropriate places, baffle our attempts to clutch and scare them; but like ghosts they can only be seen and not touched, only heard and not seen' (Lee 1904a, 378; 1923, 76), while Hardy's speaker in 'In Front of the Landscape' is similarly 'beset' by recollections – 'scenes, miscalled of the bygone' and unruly, undesired presences that 'Show, too, with fuller translation than rested upon them / As living kind' (Hardy 1976, 304). His poem 'The Ghost of the Past' envisages the Past as a spectral companion and housemate:

> We two kept house, the Past and I,
>   The Past and I;
> Through all my tasks it hovered nigh,
>   Leaving me never alone.
> It was a spectral housekeeping
>   Where fell no jarring tone,
> As strange, as still a housekeeping
>   As ever had been known.
>
> (Hardy 1976, 308)

Alternatively the past permeates the present, alerting us to the unseen in the seen, as when Lee writes that 'the present is in itself, however vivid, too transient and thin; like a single bright coat of colour, it requires, in order to remain, a layer or two of the past, unseen, perhaps, but which gives it body, and tone, and stability' (Lee 1887, 69); or when Hardy records 'a needy and illiterate woman saying of another poor haggard woman who had lost her little son years before: "You can see the ghost of that child in her face even now"' (Hardy 1966b, 138).

Literary Modernism, as Helen Sword notes, is now commonly understood as 'a period marked both by a vexed fascination with ghosts and by a persistent foregrounding of the temporal instability that ghostliness calls into play' (Sword 2002, 55). Writers such as Woolf, Joyce, Eliot, and Lawrence evince an attraction to ideas and images of spectrality as representing psychic and imaginative investments and activity, the force of history, memories, and the return of the repressed, and the recurrent visitations of literary and familial parents and ancestors. Both Lee and Hardy, whose writings on ghosts and spectres date back into the nineteenth century, are thus important forerunners. Lee's essay 'Faustus and Helena: Notes on the Supernatural in Art', first published in 1880 in the *Cornhill Magazine*, edited by Woolf's father, Leslie Stephen, is the precursor to Woolf's own essay 'Across the Border' (1918), also known as 'The Supernatural in Modern Fiction'.[13] That Woolf may have read Lee's essay in preparation for her own is suggested by her comment about the 'craving for the supernatural in literature' (Woolf 1986–94, 2.218), which echoes Lee's earlier claim that 'we crave after the supernatural' (Lee 2006, 312).[14] Woolf does not mention Lee directly in the essay but she declares her specific interest in the 'psychical ghost story' epitomised by Henry James's *The Turn of the Screw* (1898–99) (Woolf 1986–94, 2.219). As a reader and reviewer of Lee's works, albeit an ambivalent one, she must have known that Lee was James's precursor in this respect. Indeed *Hauntings* (1890) may have been among the books she recalls Lee giving her father – gifts most likely presented during Lee's regular social visits to the Stephen household (Letter of 23 August 1922 in Woolf 1976, 2.55).[15] Later Woolf would admit with regard to James's ghost stories that 'Henry James was much too fond of the world we know to create one that we do not know. The visionary imagination was by no means his' (Woolf 1986–94,

13 Woolf's essay is a review of Dorothy Scarborough's *The Supernatural in Modern English Fiction* (1917), which does not mention Lee's essay or her supernatural tales.

14 In the same essay Lee writes of 'the essentially modern, passionate, nostalgic craving for the past' and 'To raise a real spectre of the antique is a craving of our own century' (Lee 2006, 315, 319).

15 Lee's published letters mention a number of visits to the Stephens' London house, starting with a dinner party on 23 June 1882 (Lee 1937, 90–1, 94, 156). Woolf's letter recalls Lee in the dining room at Talland House, St Ives, the summer home of the Stephen family till 1895.

3.321) – something that could not be said of Lee. Less ambivalent is the admiration of both Woolf and Lawrence for Hardy; Lawrence producing his idiosyncratic essay *Study of Thomas Hardy* (1914) and Woolf, 'Thomas Hardy's Novels' (1928), in which she wrote: 'His own word, "moments of vision", exactly describes those passages of astonishing beauty and force which are to be found in every book that he wrote' (Woolf 1986–94, 4.509).

This monograph deliberately accents the literary and imaginative dimensions of the various texts considered. As in *Bearing Blindness* my approach is predominantly intertextual. Thus each chapter provides extensive and intensive close readings with an eye to the imagistic and thematic connections between the writings of the selected authors and their individual links with the literary tradition, and, in particular, with Romantic poetry and prose. I have also made selective use of psychoanalysis (Klein, Winnicott) where it offered ways of thinking about loss and creativity that complemented my exploration of the visionary impulse triggered by the lost or elusive woman. Where cultural factors such as the nineteenth-century cult of mesmerism evidently impinge on a text (Chapters 1 and 4), these have been taken into consideration and absorbed into the readings. Individual chapters can be read separately as discrete essays, although each is enhanced by being read in conjunction with the others.

Chapter 1 opens with an analysis of Rossetti's conformation in his last years to a type familiar from *Bearing Blindness*, the type of the hypersensitive, stricken, or wounded male poet, and its analogue the mournful maiden, who manifests herself in his poetry as Proserpine, a grieving prisoner in the Underworld. However, these narcissistic types become charged with an allure or magnetism, something commonly attributed to the poet himself, his poetry, and his images of women, a number of which were identified by Kermode as the origin of the Modernist 'Romantic Image'. Although Rossetti was thought by most of the critics of his own day to be a spiritual, symbolic, or mystical poet, modern critics, taking their lead from Robert Buchanan, have ignored this side of his work in favour of a concentration on 'fleshly' or material concerns. The second part of this chapter revisits the issue of Rossetti's spirituality, by examining the symbolic image of the inspiring female beloved in the love poetry of *The House of Life* (1870, 1881) as a magnetic or mesmeric figure, informed predominantly by Romantic sources. This visionary figure achieves the fusion of the spiritual and material qualities Pater saw in Rossetti's poetry by initiating and enabling spiritual communication and knowledge through the body and physical contact.

Chapter 2 examines how in Pater, a writer heavily associated with sensory relations, there is a strong pull to the visionary or unseen. It explores his obsession with the strange visionary phantasm or trace he calls character, which appears as a refined essence in all perfected form, this process of refinement drawing on Romantic descriptions of literary alchemy. Death and the process of sculptural subtraction present alternative versions of this refinement as, for Pater, this essence is most potently legible in the sculptural body and the beautiful corpse that preserves the marks of life in death. Although most evidently present in comely young men, it is none the less theorised by him as a principle epitomised in Persephone, the young woman snatched away at the height of her youth and beauty to dwell as life-in-death in the Underworld. Such images, again progenitors of the Romantic Image, illuminate the process whereby all aesthetic images stage the uncanny life-in-death and death-in-life of the objects they represent.

Chapter 3 starts by meditating on the Romantic theme of the recovered sculptural relic and the theme of the god in exile derived by Vernon Lee and Eugene Lee-Hamilton from Pater, who had in turn absorbed it from the German Romantic poet Heinrich Heine. It ponders the siblings' joint investment in the figure of the goddess Venus and statues of her, examining their related treatment of a mutilated or fragmentary portion of such a statue in conjunction with Peter Fuller's Kleinian reading of the Venus de Milo. It analyses how Lee's belief in the suggestive power of the fragment allows a late Romantic imaginative sublime to flood through her exploration of supernatural forces in her shorter fiction, and how her brother's similar belief enables the therapeutic compression and release of power in the dramatic soliloquies of his *Imaginary Sonnets* (1888).

Chapter 4 introduces and reconsiders the achievement of Theodore Watts-Dunton, poet, critic, and novelist, before focusing on his best-selling but now neglected novel *Aylwin.* A meditation on the lost woman, the novel offers as part of its end-of-century rearticulation of Romantic values a particularly arresting treatment of woman-as-aesthetic image reduplicated through portraiture and mesmeric therapy, and reinstates the often missing 'pathological' element of the Romantic Image. The chapter traces the uncanny structures of corporeal doubling, repetition and transference which Watts-Dunton allies with Coleridge's 'Christabel' to consider the novel's strategic defence of the Romantic imagination, and shows how it reveals the lines of a Romantic genealogy that extends from Coleridge through Rossetti to writers such as Yeats.

Chapter 5 begins with an examination of what Ruskin would have called Hardy's 'spiritual or second sight', his 'power of the imagination in exalting' visible objects so that they become uncanny, quasi-ghostly versions of themselves. It shows how his imaginative investment in 'the other side' and his profound interest in spectres, shades, and shadows figuratively illustrate his pronouncements on art and literature, and that for him writing, particularly poetry, is a domain especially suited to ghosts and spirits, being a realm of refined essences. The final part of the chapter looks at forms of shadow portraiture in his poetry that bridge the relation between the phenomenal and the visionary, relates these forms of portraiture to the Romantic fragment and synecdoche, and considers their relation to loss, especially the theme of the lost woman, where death acts as a stimulant to vision.

1

'An aching pulse of melodies': Dante Gabriel Rossetti's poetic magnetism

> A sense of power in love, defying distance, and those barriers which are so much more than physical distance, of unutterable desire penetrating into the world of sleep . . . in his later work, makes him speak sometimes almost like a believer in mesmerism.
>
> (Pater 1910, *App* 214)[1]

Anyone who wishes to write about the poetry of Dante Gabriel Rossetti and reads the extant criticism immediately becomes aware how certain specific critical scripts and trajectories present themselves as difficult to avoid. In many respects much criticism still reflects the critical concerns of Robert Buchanan's notorious attack on Rossetti in the two versions of his article 'The Fleshly School of Poetry' (1871, 1872).[2] Countering the favourable initial wave of criticism, which Rossetti had himself orchestrated by asking friends to review his work, Buchanan denied the mystical and symbolic content of the verse, insisting on its 'fleshliness' and earth-bound materiality, its narrow focus, and asserting that Rossetti as a poet was self-absorbed and narcissistic, 'describing his own exquisite emotions', 'a fleshly person, with nothing particular to tell or teach us' (Buchanan 1871 in Riede 1992a, 28, 29); 'poetry', he declared, 'must deal with great issues in which all men are interested, not with the "damnable face-making" of Narcissus in a mirror' (Buchanan 1872, 89). He also attacked what he called Rossetti's 'grotesque mediævalism', his 'affected' use of archaisms, the promotion of style and form over any real content or meaning, and a concomitant lack of sincerity (Buchanan 1871 in Riede 1992a, 31, 35, 31). Moreover the poet was chastised for apparently turning his private life into a literary commodity – 'a husband virtually . . . wheeling his nuptial couch out

1 In keeping with my practice elsewhere, I use the 1910 edition of Pater's work but the essay is also available in David Riede's useful 1992 collection of reprint essays (Riede 1992a, 58–64) and in the online Rossetti Archive: www.rossetti archive.org/.

2 I have cited Buchanan's 1871 article as it appears in Riede 1992a, but the text is also available in the Rossetti Archive.

into the public streets' – while there were hints that the poetry was also informed by his clandestine affair with Jane Morris: 'there is running rampant in English society a certain atrocious form of vice, a monster with two heads – one of which is called Adultery' (Buchanan 1872, ix, 4).[3]

Criticism from the mid-twentieth century onwards has reiterated many of these concerns, albeit in a more sophisticated way. The supernatural and mystical elements of Rossetti's verse have been downplayed or seen as superficial, critics preferring to concentrate on what they see as naturalistic detail rather than symbolism, even arguing that Rossetti resists symbolism, replacing it by perception and sensation. As John Holmes has recently pointed out, Buchanan's charge of lack of meaning or sincerity has been turned about by those who celebrate what they see as Rossetti's absence or annihilation of meaning (Holmes 2005, 13–14). With regard to 'fleshliness', other commentators have focused on Rossetti's depictions of sex and sexuality, particularly in regard to his representation of women, arguing in some cases that his writing has a pornographic or misogynistic content. Rossetti's 'narcissism', his projection of himself into doubles, reflections, into the Romantic epipsyche or female reflecting beloved, has become something of a critical commonplace, although there is often an undercurrent of censure that suggests there is something narrow, limited or self-absorbed about such projections. Inevitably and perhaps more understandably Rossetti's biography also haunts and informs many critical accounts, if in a diluted form. The picturesque, dramatic, and sensational events of his life are hard to resist, especially as there is now available a vast amount of documentation in the form of letters, annotations, commentaries, and memoirs that make it relatively easy to reconstruct particular contexts for specific poems and paintings. Rossetti's major work, the sonnet sequence *The House of Life* (1870, 1881), seems calculated to pique curiosity and arouse speculation about the personal events and circumstances that may have motivated the verse. Indeed Theodore Watts-Dunton, who, after Rossetti's death, was widely anticipated to be his biographer, remarked that any reader might know him 'as intimately as it is possible to know any man whose biography is written only in his works' (Watts-Dunton 1916a, 111).

3 Rossetti had to some degree brought the unpleasant 'nuptial couch' gibe on himself by re-titling the sonnet originally called 'Placatâ Venere' (Venus Appeased) 'Nuptial Sleep'. The date of this sonnet is uncertain, although Jan Marsh suggests it might date to 1859 and Rossetti's sexual relationship with Fanny Cornforth (Marsh 2005, 203, 545). By implying it was an expression of married love, Rossetti unfortunately put himself in the position of a widower betraying his dead wife. In Buchanan's pamphlet, the second of the monster's two heads is 'Dipsomania' (Buchanan 1872, 4), evidently intended to signal Swinburne's alcoholism.

Buchanan's insinuations that personal history informed Rossetti's poetry were fairly quickly supplemented by the potent biographical legend of the reclusive, melancholy poet, who, following his breakdown, spent the last decade of his life virtually immured in his home at 16 Cheyne Walk. 'Melancholy . . . is the invariable shadow of high genius', wrote William Sharp with regard to Rossetti in an article of 1887 (Sharp 1912, 50). As David Riede writes, 'in the years immediately following [Rossetti's] death it seemed as though nearly everyone who knew him rushed into print with memoirs and testimonials' (Riede 1992a, 3). The principal accounts by Sharp and Thomas Hall Caine help make Rossetti into what we now recognise as a type of the sensitive Romantic or Post-Romantic poet, or what Frank Kermode in *Romantic Image*, his classic study of 1957, influentially described as 'the artist in isolation', a figure who still dominates much early twentieth-century poetry. The isolation of Rossetti's later years was compounded by characteristics observable much earlier such as 'a genuine lack of interest in passing events' (Gosse 1882, 724). He evinced little interest in politics and matters of the day. According to Sharp, 'Nor had Rossetti much sympathy with or knowledge of nature. The outer world of things appealed to him but slightly, finding as he did his world of imagination sufficient' (Sharp 1912, 64). In spite of critical accounts that suggest otherwise, the sharply observed natural detail that can be found intermittently in the poems and paintings is, for the most part, symbolic or instrumental (see Maxwell 1993).

Riede suggests that 'much of Rossetti's influence on the aesthetes of the coming generation resulted from what seemed his exemplary, if painful, devotion to an ideal of beauty, his exemplary role as a new type of artist' (Riede 1992a, 7), and he cites Lionel Stevenson's opinion that Rossetti ' "was the first English poet who entirely fulfilled the public image of the *poète maudit* – manic-depressive in temperament, alienated from the mores of his time, sensually self-indulgent, and disintegrating under the influences of sex, alcohol, and drugs" ' (Stevenson 1972, 77, cited in Riede 1992a, 7). Stevenson's take on the legend is itself recognisably more of a later twentieth-century response which emphasises sensuality, addiction, and disintegration, while the immediate post-1882 reminiscences tend to see Rossetti as more spiritualised, tortured by his past, but disabled principally by his unfortunate dependency on chloral. Notably the idea of the sensually degenerate *poète maudit* receives a check from Jan Marsh, Rossetti's most recent biographer, who suggests that he most likely did not lose his virginity until the age of thirty, and that, owing to his hydrocele or testicular ailment, and perhaps impotency, his relationship with Jane Morris was probably unconsummated (Marsh 2005, 202, 351, 331). She also remarks that his later chloral dependency, although severe, never seemed to interfere with his creative life to any great degree, a view corroborated by Edmund Gosse and Rossetti himself (Marsh 2005, 488; Gosse 1882, 725).

This chapter makes no claims to avoid the biography in so far as it has a particular interest and investment in the mythic type of the hypersensitive isolated poet, a type it seems that Rossetti himself deliberately helped cultivate, in spite of having many antithetical traits and characteristics noted by his friends such as an uproarious sense of humour and a 'manly' directness. This self-cultivated tragic aura lends a particular fascination to the verse from which it often seems inextricable. In 'The Song-throe', Sonnet 61 in the 1881 *House of Life*, Rossetti himself had insisted that only deep emotion can generate affecting poetry: 'By thine own tears thy song must tears beget' (Rossetti 1911, 95). As Arthur Symons comments: 'Part of what hypnotises us in his work is, no doubt, that sense of personal tragedy which comes to us out of its elaborate beauty: the eternal tragedy of those who have loved the absolute in beauty too well, and with too mortal a thirst' (Symons 1916, 206). The hypnotic effect that Symons notices is something routinely ascribed by early critics to both Rossetti himself and his writing. This effect is central to my discussion, which none the less aims to transcend mere biographical data to find ways of talking about Rossetti's poetry that restore to it something of the visionary capability once accorded it by the early critics. For, if Buchanan denied the mystical and symbolic content of the verse, criticism that followed Rossetti's death in 1882 would respond by once more reiterating the mystical and supernatural in his poetry. I refer here principally to monographs and essays by William Sharp (1882, 1887), Theodore Watts-Dunton (1883), Walter Pater (1883), F. W. H. Myers (1883), Arthur Symons (1904), and incidental but significant remarks by W. B. Yeats in a number of articles such as 'Symbolism in Painting' (1898), 'The Theatre' (1899), 'The Happiest of the Poets' (1902), and 'Art and Ideas' (1913).[4] Buchanan himself would retract his charges in two poems, and, in a significant essay of reversal published in 1883, singled out Rossetti from among his contemporaries as 'the least objective, the least earthly, and the most ideal' (Buchanan 1887, 153).[5]

Of all these responses the best is Pater's essay, originally written to preface a selection of Rossetti's poetry in Ward's *English Poets* (1883), in that he understands perfectly how Rossetti's verse manages to be simultaneously material and spiritual. No one seems to have noticed that this beautifully considered evaluation, still rightly thought one of the finest pieces of criticism on the poet (McGann 2000, 58), is actually a subtle, extremely cogent, point-by-point correction of Buchanan's earlier charges. Pater stresses Rossetti's exacting, highly individualised but apposite style and vocabulary – these are 'no mere tricks of manner adopted with a view to forcing attention' – which marry 'sincerity' to 'a sort of grandeur of literary worksmanship' (Pater 1910, *App* 206,

4 All these essays are collected in his *Essays and Introductions*. See Yeats 1989.

5 For Buchanan's poems see Caine 1990, 142–3.

210). He reinstates the symbolic purpose of Rossetti's verse, explaining his use of 'sensible imagery', 'concrete definition', and 'abstractions', and relates these to the practice of his precursor Dante (Pater 1910, *App* 207, 208). He re-emphasises Rossetti's central themes as Love and a beauty in which matter and spirit come together – 'all this, conceived with an abundant imagination, and a deep, a philosophic, reflectiveness' (Pater 1910, *App* 212, 213). Besides alluding to Swedenborg's perception of body and soul and the fact that Rossetti in his later work sounds 'sometimes almost like a believer in mesmerism', Pater remarks in his conclusion that Rossetti's work 'was mainly of the esoteric order' (Pater 1910, *App* 214, 218).

Pater aside, the post-1882 critical reaction which emphasises Rossetti's mysticism does not seem to have cut much ice with later critics, who are unaware of its existence, ignore it, or, one assumes, regard it as a form of defensive special pleading. With some notable exceptions such as the Canadian scholar D. M. R. Bentley, critics interested in Rossetti's spiritual and religious influences and intimations are rare.[6] Yet the mystical and symbolic Rossetti deserves reconsideration. There is still much to be said about his use of esoteric sources, including a neoplatonism only too familiar to him through his father Gabriele Rossetti's researches and through his own masterly translations of medieval Italian poetry in his *The Early Italian Poets*, later republished as *Dante and His Circle* (1861, 1874).[7] F. R. Leavis's attack in *The Common Pursuit* on 'Rossetti's shamelessly cheap evocation of a romantic and bogus Platonism' (Leavis 1952, 47) shamelessly ignores what Pater recognised only too well when he effectively grouped together Plato, Dante, and Rossetti (Pater 1910, *App* 212; *PP* 135) for their fusion of material and spiritual, and saw that they were examples of what, borrowing from Rossetti himself, he calls 'Love's lovers' (Pater 1910, *App* 212; *PP* 134–6).[8] F. W. H. Myers also emphasised Rossetti's Platonism in his 1883 essay 'Rossetti and the Religion of Beauty', though, unlike Pater, he thought it was probably unconscious (Myers in Riede 1992a, 48–9).

Henry Treffry Dunn, Rossetti's studio and household assistant, records Rossetti's interest in spiritualism and mesmerism, which included his participation in seances, and remarks that 'He was of a highly imaginative nature, and everything that appertained to the mystic had a strange fascination for

6 See, for example, Bentley 1990a and 1990b.

7 Marsh describes Gabriele Rossetti's highly idiosyncratic five-volume *Amor Platonica*, 'his magnum opus on the secret lore of Platonic love in the Middle Ages', as penetrating 'deep thickets of esoteric knowledge to prove that Dante's writings belonged to a clandestine, anti-Papal alternative to mainstream religion and politics, heavily influenced by freemasonry and gnosticism' (Marsh 2005, 12). For Dante's neoplatonism see Robb 1935, 18.

8 See Sonnet 8: 'Love's Lovers', in *The House of Life* (1881) (Rossetti 1911, 79).

him' (Dunn 1904, 55–61, 55).[9] Some of Rossetti's interest in mysticism probably stemmed from early influences. William Michael's statement about his childhood home indicates its almost palpable atmosphere of arcana: 'Our father, when writing about the *Comedia* or the *Vita Nuova*, was seen surrounded by ponderous folios in italic type, "*libri mistici*" and the like (often about alchemy, freemasonry, Brahminism, Swedenborg, the Cabbala, etc.).' He tells us candidly that the Rossetti children 'were assuredly not much tempted to take up one of his books to see if it would "do to read" ' (W. M. Rossetti 1895, 1.64), a disinclination which none the less may have been reversed as they grew older. The young Rossetti resisted his father's interests and later ridiculed his eccentric theories about Dante, but ended up by developing his own passion for the poet. As he writes in the Preface to *The Early Italian Poets*, 'Thus, in those early days, all around me partook of the influence of the great Florentine; till, from viewing it as a natural element, I also, growing older, was drawn within the circle' (Rossetti 1911, 283–4). Rodger Drew, recalling Watts-Dunton's opinion, reminds us that Rossetti, in spite of his reservations about Gabriele's bizarre and idiosyncratic symbolic system, would, like his sister Christina, inherit his father's 'innate obsession with symbolism' (Drew 2007, 146; Watts-Dunton 1916a, 186). Drew's own recent intriguing monograph *The Stream's Secret: The Symbolism of Dante Gabriel Rossetti* (2007) is a welcome attempt to establish Rossetti's esoteric sources, proposing that his symbolism has its roots in neoplatonism, medieval romance, and alchemy, and in the hermetic magical tradition that developed into Rosicrucianism and Freemasonry. Drew's account is thoughtful and provocative, although one wishes that he had tried more strenuously to anchor his speculations to Rossetti's actual reading, as does Pamela Bickley in her fine article on Rossetti's influence on Yeats, where she assiduously notes his reading of Swedenborg, which 'informs "The Blessed Damozel" and some of the *House of Life* sonnets' (Bickley 2001, 84, 101–2).

This chapter deals less with specific esoteric sources, fascinating though these are, and more with the visual, symbolic, and imaginative dimension of Rossetti's visionary writing. However, as part of this exploration, it draws attention to ideas and images of hypnotic, mesmeric, or 'magnetic' attraction that permeate accounts of Rossetti as a melancholic solitary, and as a dynamic artistic and personal force. It also suggests that ideas of magnetism also play a significant role in Rossetti's poetic understanding of love and creativity, and proposes that this poetic magnetism is inextricably bound up with the figure of woman. The following section opens this exploration with a compelling mythic portrait of Rossetti as a hypersensitive artist, an image articulated by

9 See also Appendix 7: 'Dante Gabriel Rossetti and Spiritualism' in Rossetti 2002–, 5.401–3.

one of the friends who knew and loved him best, the critic, novelist, and poet Theodore Watts-Dunton.

The stricken poet and the weeping maiden

On 19 March 1892, under the general title 'Apparent Pictures', the *Athenæum* published two sonnets by Watts-Dunton, the first of which was titled 'Coleridge':

I see thee pine like her in golden story
 Who, in her prison, woke and saw, one day,
 The gates thrown open – saw the sunbeams play,
With only a web 'tween her and summer's glory;
Who, when that web – so frail, so transitory,
 It broke before her breath – had fallen away,
 Saw other webs and others rise for aye
Which kept her prisoned till her hair was hoary.

Those songs half-sung that yet were all divine –
 That woke Romance, the queen, to reign afresh –
Had been but preludes from that lyre of thine,
 Could thy rare spirit's wings have pierced the mesh
 Spun by the wizard who compels the flesh,
But lets the poet see how heav'n can shine.

(Watts-Dunton 1892, 373; n.d., 251–2)[10]

A few weeks earlier Watts-Dunton had sent 'Coleridge' in manuscript to his friend George Meredith who, in a letter dated 8 March 1892, responded with the following appreciation: 'The Sonnet is pure amber for a piece of descriptive analogy that fits the poet wonderfully; and one might beat about through volumes of essays, and not so paint him. There is Coleridge. But where the source of your story – if anything of such aptness could have been other than dreamed after a draught of Xanadu, – I cannot tell' (Meredith 1970, 2.1071–2).

According to his biographers Thomas Hake and Arthur Compton-Rickett, Watts-Dunton had apparently found his 'story', the image of the web-bound maiden, in 'a paragraph cut from some daily newspaper', but afterwards could not recall from where the story came, 'for he lost the newspaper cutting at the time he was writing the poem; but he had no doubt that it was founded on

10 The second of the sonnets was titled 'Life, the Khan'. Where possible all references to Watts-Dunton's poems refer to his collection *The Coming of Love: Rhoda Boswell's Story and Other Poems*, first published in 1897 but enlarged in subsequent editions. I use the tenth edition, which is undated but must be published after the ninth edition of 1913. Even in the later expanded editions this collection does not contain all the poems published by Watts-Dunton in periodicals or anthologies.

some Eastern tale' (Hake and Compton-Rickett 1916, 1.293). However, as Watts-Dunton would have been aware, Rossetti, discussing Coleridge – 'the poet he admired most' – with Hall Caine, had expressed his dissatisfaction with the conclusion to 'Christabel' with the words 'It hints at infinite beauty, but somehow remains a sort of cobweb' (Caine 1990, 116; 1882a, 155).[11] Moreover, the idea of imprisoning webs may have a source in Rossetti's own sonnet on Coleridge, also discussed in Caine's *Recollections of Rossetti* (Caine 1882, 165–6). 'Samuel Taylor Coleridge', composed in 1880, proposes in its sestet that the six years in which Coleridge produced his poetic masterworks stand out like a beacon from the rest of his troubled life, which was constrained by symbolic 'spider-trammelled prison bars':

> Yet ah! Like desert pools that show the stars
>   Once in long leagues, – even such the scarce-snatched hours
>   Which deepening pain left to his lordliest powers: –
> Heaven lost through spider-trammelled prison-bars.
>   Six years, from sixty saved! Yet kindling skies
>   Own them, a beacon to our centuries.
>
> (Rossetti 1911, 231)

Rossetti's treatment of the suffering Romantic male poet is carried through into Watts-Dunton's sonnet, but, where Rossetti sees a slender yet none the less remarkable legacy emerging from the wreck of Coleridge's life, Watts-Dunton is much more concerned with the loss of potential, the 'might have been' forestalled by the poet's damaged and delusively self-limiting psyche. In his essay 'The Truth about Rossetti' (1883), Watts-Dunton had used another version of the trammelling web to suggest that Coleridge was not fully able to embrace Romance, being held back by other ties: 'Coleridge was enlinked to modern life and thought by a myriad gossamer chains quite unknown to Rossetti' (Watts-Dunton 1883, 415). Yet, for Watts-Dunton and some other critics, Rossetti was the Victorian poet who most resembled Coleridge, a resemblance that will be explored further in Chapter 4. Moreover, if we examine Watts-Dunton's poetic commemoration of Rossetti in 1882, we can see that this earlier symbolic sonnet portrait shows some striking similarities with his later one:

> Thou knewest that island, far away and lone,
>   Whose shores are as a harp, where billows break
>   In spray of music and the breezes shake
> O'er spicy seas a woof of colour and tone,
> While that sweet music echoes like a moan
>   In the island's heart, and sighs around the lake,

11 The 1990 edition of Caine's *Recollections* is a reprint of the revised edition of 1928. Readers should be aware that the 1882 and 1928 editions vary as to content.

Where, watching fearfully a watchful snake,
A damsel weeps upon her emerald throne.

Life's ocean, breaking round thy senses' shore,
Struck golden song, as from the strand of Day:
For us the joy, for thee the fell foe lay –
Pain's blinking snake around the fair isle's core,
Turning to sighs the enchanted sounds that play
Around thy lovely island evermore.

(Watts-Dunton n.d., 187–8)[12]

This sonnet is titled 'A Dead Poet' in Watts-Dunton's collection *The Coming of Love: Rhoda Boswell's Story and Other Poems* (1897), and 'D. G. R.' when it heads the first of the two Appendices added in 1914 to *Aylwin*, his best-selling novel of 1898 (Watts-Dunton 1914, 493). Undoubtedly it was the first of many memorial poems written for Dante Gabriel Rossetti, not least because it was published just before he actually died, appearing under the title 'Heine', in the *Athenæum* for 25 March 1882.[13] Rossetti, dying at Birchington-on-Sea, near Margate in Kent, did not actually pass away till 9 April, when he died in Watts-Dunton's arms. In spite of a title originally commemorating the German Romantic poet Heinrich Heine, who had died, ill and half-blind, in Paris in 1856, Watts-Dunton said that the poem was composed with Rossetti in mind. Hall Caine reprints the poem in the conclusion to his *Recollections of Rossetti* of 1882 when he recalls visiting Rossetti's grave with Watts-Dunton shortly after the funeral and being suddenly struck by the 'extraordinary applicability' of the sonnet 'to him whom we had laid below':

> 'How strangely appropriate it is,' I said, 'to Rossetti, and now I remember how deeply he was moved on reading it.'
> 'He guessed its secret; I addressed it, for disguise, to Heine, to whom it was sadly inapplicable. I meant it for *him*'
>
> (Caine 1882a, 296–7).

In 'A Dead Poet' the motif of the musical island derives from information about Amsterdam Island discovered 'in an old gazetteer'. Hake and Compton-

12 I cite here the slightly revised version included in *The Coming of Love*. For the original see Watts-Dunton 1882a, 380.

13 Samantha Matthews, in a chapter on Rossetti's death and grave, briefly surveys 'a sample of twelve contemporary elegiac tribute-poems invoking Rossetti's burial-place' (Matthews 2004, 38). These poems represent a small portion of the poetry written in commemoration of Rossetti. Thus Matthews does not mention Watts-Dunton's 'A Dead Poet', which does not invoke the burial-place, but she does note his other commemorative poem for Rossetti, 'A Grave by the Sea', a short sequence of four sonnets, whose concluding epigraph reads 'Birchington, Eastertide 1882' (Matthews 2004, 37, n. 61; Watts-Dunton n.d., 189–96).

Rickett explain that 'It was therein affirmed that the Chinese had been familiar with that remote and desolate volcanic rock in the Indian Ocean before its discovery by the Dutch navigator Van Vlaming, and there was a tradition in connection with the island that in certain seasons of the year the shores are surrounded by a ring of music which is caused by waves striking upon the coast.'[14] Quoting the pertinent lines of the sonnet, they add 'it was the fantastic sound of that strange music that appealed to [Watts-Dunton's] imagination and inspired him to sing' (Hake and Compton-Rickett 1916, 292–3). However, what perhaps strikes a modern reader more is the depiction of the poet as a woman, something also true of the poet pictured in 'Coleridge'.

'A Dead Poet' describes in its opening octet a distant island whose shore, washed by the waves, produces sweet music, none the less heard by the heart of the island as moans and sighs. At the heart of the island is a damsel weeping on an emerald throne, watched and apparently imprisoned by a watchful snake. The sestet then compares the island to Rossetti's poetic creativity which, for his readers, produces delightful song but which is ensnared at its core by pain. In the sonnet, Rossetti seems to be figured both by the island itself and by the weeping damsel. This double figuration is present also in 'Coleridge', in whose opening octet the poet is directly compared to an imprisoned sleeping maiden, who wakes and finds the prison gates open and the gateway covered only by a fragile cobweb. However, when she blows the cobweb away, other webs begin to appear in succession, keeping her captive till she is old. By contrast, in the sestet, Coleridge is addressed as a singer whose songs woke the spirit of 'queen Romance', and whose later songs would have been able to break the webs and set her free, had he but managed to fulfil his potential. He has roused sleeping Romance, but he has not been able to secure her release, a task to which he should have been equal.

In these sonnets the two commemorated male poets are identified with women, for the creative core of both seems to be feminine. These representative women are regal – Rossetti's maiden has an 'emerald throne' while Coleridge's awakened maiden is 'Romance, the queen' – but they are, somewhat after the manner of Tennyson's embowered women, in crisis, imprisoned, requiring release, with help unforthcoming. In their guise of imprisoned maidens, Rossetti and Coleridge are portrayed as thwarted in some aspect of their creativity, blocked by obstacles, which, it is hinted, may tragically be of their own making. Both poets are apostrophised by the speaker; more-

14 The island was actually discovered by Juan Sebastian de el Cano in 1522 and named 'New Amsterdam' by Van Dieman in 1633. Willem de Vlamingh (*b.* 1640), a Dutch sea-captain who explored the south-west coast of Australia in the late seventeenth century, made the first landing in 1696. Located three thousand miles from any continent, it is the island most secluded from any inhabited land.

over, Coleridge is gently reproached for not being the rescuer of Romance. Interestingly, in describing the male poet's conflicted creativity, the speaker places him in something like that vexed position which, according to Dorothy Mermin, is supposed to belong to Victorian women poets who, in looking for a subject position, are forced to imagine themselves 'both knight and damsel, both subject and object' (Mermin 1986, 65). Coleridge is queen Romance, but also the male singer who should have released her, while, by implication, Rossetti as distressed damsel is very much in need of a hero who will vanquish the serpent Pain.

The menaced maiden of 'A Dead Poet' recalls Rossetti's Angelica in his double-sonnet poem 'For *Ruggiero and Angelica* by Ingres', written in October 1849 to accompany Ingres's painting (1819), which illustrates a scene from Ariosto's *Orlando furioso*.[15] Ingres paints Ruggiero spearing a dragon at the base of a sea-swept rock to which is chained the naked Angelica; or, as Rossetti describes it in his first sonnet, 'The spear's lithe stem / Thrills in the roaring of those jaws: behind / That evil length of body chafes at fault' (Rossetti 1911, 189). Ingres portrays Angelica with averted face, tilted-back head, and shut eyes. Manacled to the rock, she seems on the verge of swooning. Opening the second of the sonnets, Rossetti's poetic speaker, warning her that the drama has now reached its crisis, issues her with the command: 'Clench thine eyes now, – 'tis the last instant, girl'. Lines 4–8 of the octet give the scene from Angelica's confused perspective, as sensed and imagined by her with her eyes closed:

> Was that the scattered whirl
> Of its foam drenched thee? – or the waves that curl
> And split, bleak spray wherein thy temples ache?
> Or was it his the champion's blood to flake
> Thy flesh? – or thine own blood's anointing, girl?
>
> (Rossetti 1911, 189)

For a moment Rossetti's Angelica is the imaginative architect of the scene, choosing among and perhaps merging possibilities. This moment may have rubbed off on Watts-Dunton's sonnet and a poem as different as Yeats's 'Michael Robartes and the Dancer', first published in 1920, which seems to hold Rossetti's 'Ruggiero and Angelica', and perhaps 'A Dead Poet', in its literary unconscious. Yeats's male speaker Michael Robartes wittily announces to his female interlocutor:

> In this altar-piece the knight,
> Who grips his long spear so to push

15 Rossetti saw the painting at the Luxembourg Gallery, Paris, in 1849. It is now in the Louvre. The sonnets were first published in the Pre-Raphaelite journal *The Germ* no. 4, for 30 April 1850.

That dragon through the fading light,
Loved the lady; and it's plain
The half-dead dragon was her thought,
That every morning rose again
And dug its claws and shrieked and fought.

(Yeats 1982, 197)

Likewise, the implication of 'A Dead Poet' is that the watching damsel produces the mirroring watchful snake.

Watts-Dunton's sonnets on Coleridge and Rossetti, although published separately, portray both poets as displaying similar symptoms of self-delusion, which are possibly drug-induced. In Rossetti's case, the weeping damsel 'watching fearfully a watchful snake' may refer specifically to his chronic insomnia, as well as more generally to the paranoid hypersensitivity and hysteria that isolated him from his public. William Sharp wrote that by the end of his life Rosssetti's 'resolute and dominant nature had become emasculated through the use of chloral' (Sharp 1912, 51). Both of Watts-Dunton's sonnets then present the familiar image of the Romantic artist in isolation, and both choose to present him as a victim of a crippling pathology. The French critic Gabriel Mourey also sees Rossetti as such a victim: 'But for him – his organisation, his temperament, the consciousness of the value of such efforts, and above all his tendency to suffering, to reaction, his acute sensitiveness, all prevented him enjoying the real pleasures of toil' (Mourey 1896, 112). Mourey cites the critic Esther Wood, herself the author of a monograph on Rossetti and Pre-Raphaelitism, who he declares 'has shown an almost clairvoyant penetration in reading Rossetti's character' (Mourey 1896, 112). Her evaluation is worth repeating for its classic summation of the morbid suffering poet:

> There are some temperaments so finely organised, so delicately strung, that even joy is painful to them . . . They cannot lose in the sense of delight the consciousness of what that delight has cost them. They perceive so acutely the realities, the conditions of life, that an hour of rapture makes them more quick to the pain behind and before. Such was Shelley; such were Keats and Byron; such was Dante Gabriel Rossetti. It is the curse of the artistic temperament: it is the blessing of Art.
>
> (Wood cited in Mourey 1896, 112)[16]

In *Adonais* (1821), his elegy for Keats, Shelley sees the young poet as fatally wounded by the critical mauling he received at the hands of his critics for his poem *Endymion* – 'the wound thus wantonly inflicted' (Shelley 1977, 391) is a wound he compares to that suffered by the youthful Adonis, lover of Aphrodite, who was fatally gored by a boar in the groin. Rossetti's wounding was 'wantonly

16 For the French text see Mourey 1895, 186–7. Even allowing for the vagaries of translation, the account cited mirrors but does not exactly replicate a passage in Wood's monograph *Dante Rossetti and the Pre-Raphaelite Movement* (Wood 1894, 277).

inflicted' by Robert Buchanan's famous indictment of him in 'The Fleshly School of Criticism' (1871, 1872), an attack that provoked his nervous breakdown and subsequent withdrawal from public life. In his initial attack Buchanan had implied a want of manliness in Rossetti's verse: his poems have 'nothing virile' about them, 'Jenny' arouses the 'suspicion that we are listening to an emasculated Mr. Browning'; 'it is neither poetic, nor manly, nor even human, to obtrude such things [as sensuality] as the themes of whole poems' (Buchanan in Riede 1992a, 26, 33, 28). In the longer pamphlet version the gibes became more pointed with headings such as 'The Italian Falsetto Singers and their Imitators'. Devastated by the second attack, Rossetti was, as Jan Marsh puts it, 'unmanned', believing he should properly challenge his attacker to a duel, but ' "he had no manhood, he would have to die in shame" ' (Marsh 2005, 437, 438).[17] Buchanan's critical castration of Rossetti no doubt played its part in Watts-Dunton's portrayal of the poet as an isolated, defenceless, and paranoid maiden. William Michael Rossetti testifies that 'the assault produced on Rossetti an effect altogether disproportionate to its intrinsic importance; indeed it developed in his character an excess of sensitiveness and of distempered brooding which his nearest relatives and friends had never before surmised' (W. M. Rossetti 1911a, x).

Yet Watts-Dunton's portrayal of Rossetti is far from wholly negative. The isolated poet, pictured as a remote enchanted island, casts a spell on his readers, entrancing and alluring them with his music. Moreover, as the movement of the poem, which shifts from the outskirts of the isle to its centre, implies, they are equally intrigued and allured by the mournful figure that generates the song, a figure for whom it is not mere delightful music but an articulation of authentic pain and suffering. The portrait of the poet as grieving maiden emphasises, as Wood and Mourey do, the greater sensitiveness and receptivity that help make him a poet who gives joy to his readers. In his article 'The Truth about Rossetti', Watts-Dunton attributes to the poet 'a spontaneous tenderness like that of a woman' (Watts-Dunton 1883, 405).[18] Moreover, the conjoined figures of the distressed maiden and the stricken hypersensitive poet, both bound up in their own emotional dramas, exercise for readers a kind of hypnotic allure.

17 Marsh quotes from a letter of William Bell Scott (8 June 1872) to Alice Boyd published in Fredeman 1971, 278. Fredeman's article is reprinted in an abridged form as Appendix 9 in Rossetti 2002–, 5.207–69. Scott's letter is cited on p. 424.

18 Watts-Dunton seems not to have been the only person among Rossetti's associates to make this identification. Burne-Jones is said by Camille Paglia to have remarked that 'Gabriel was half a woman' (Paglia 1991, 494), although I have not been able to find a source for this comment. For a more recent evaluation of Rossetti's feminisation see Gelpi 1982, 94–114.

As I have shown elsewhere (Maxwell 2001), the feminisation of the male lyric poet has a long historical lineage, and in the nineteenth century the identification of the solitary male poet and the embowered woman, an identification made powerfully in Shelley's 'To a Sky-lark' and the early poems of Tennyson, becomes particularly marked. This identification did not meet with approval by a number of Victorian critics. Lamenting in 1869 the increasing feminisation of literature – that is, a writing that predominantly featured women and their concerns – Alfred Austin had famously bemoaned the fact that 'we have as, novelists and poets, only women or men with womanly deficiencies, steeped in the feminine temper of the times, subdued to what they work in, and ringing such changes as can be rung on what . . . has well been called "everlasting woman"'. He inveighed against the preponderance of female subjects in Tennyson, mocking his 'feminine' muse, though declaring that muse to be 'proper' while Swinburne's was 'improper' (Austin in Hyder 1970, 101, 105). Austin's complaints must have been in Buchanan's mind when, a few years later, he attacked Rossetti, choosing to cast him as a man 'with womanly deficiencies' and to interpret the poet's many female subjects as reductive self-projections:

> Mr. Rossetti is never dramatic, never impersonal – always attitudinizing, posturing, and describing his own exquisite emotions. He is the 'Blessed Damozel,' leaning over the 'gold bar of heaven,' and seeing 'Time, like a pulse shake fierce / Thro' all the worlds'; he is 'heaven-born Helen, Sparta's queen,' whose 'each twin breast is an apple sweet'; he is Lilith the first wife of Adam; he is the rosy Virgin of the poem called 'Ave,' and the Queen in the 'Staff and Scrip'; he is 'Sister Helen' melting her waxen man; he is all these.
>
> (Buchanan 1871 in Riede 1992a, 28–9)

Obviously this characterisation is absurdly simplistic. Nonetheless the self-involved emotionalism of some of Rossetti's heroines, such as Lilith, Helen of Troy, and Sister Helen, oddly prefigures his later self-cultivated, self-consuming poetic identity. Freud notoriously saw narcissism as characteristic of women, especially good-looking ones, whilst also signalling its occurrence in children, 'great criminals and humorists'. He might have added to this list the solipsistic poet in his splendid isolation. Rather than seeing the narcissism of Rossetti's women or his later self-image as in some way deficient, I want to suggest, as Freud does, that it has a particular appeal:

> it seems very evident then that another person's narcissism has a great attraction for those who have renounced part of their own narcissism and are in search of object-love. The charm of a child lies to a great extent in his narcissism, his self-contentment and inaccessibility, just as does the charm of certain animals which seem not to concern themselves about us, such as cats and the large beasts of prey.
>
> (Freud 1984a, 11.82–3)

Both the narcissistic solitary poet and the narcissistic woman have the capacity to draw or attract the rapt gaze of the reader or beholder. Interestingly Rossetti represented himself as irresistibly drawn and absorbed by his own imaginative impulses, as if under the spell of various *femme fatales.* He remarked to William Sharp, '"I do not wrap myself up in my own imaginings . . . it is *they* that envelop *me* from the outer world whether I will or no"' (Sharp 1912, 64). Freud primarily locates the attraction of his narcissistic subjects in their independence, their sense of self-contented integrity, but I would suggest that there are also forms of wounded narcissism that also attract which are manifest in the melancholy poet or in types such as Tennyson's embowered Mariana who luxuriates in her solitary condition.

The next section of this chapter examines a visionary feminine identification by Rossetti that also functions as part of his cultivation of a morbid and isolated poetic self. Watts-Dunton pointed out, 'no poet and no painter has ever before him given so much attention to woman as Rossetti has', but he perhaps means more than he intended when he writes that 'in Rossetti's art the very large part played by woman had a deep psychological meaning. It expressed frankly and fully the man' (Watts-Dunton 1883, 416, 417). That expression certainly would seem to be the case in the poem examined next which relocates the melancholy embowered woman in a dramatically different setting.

Proserpine

A number of Rossetti's major poems seem to narrate their narratives from the woman's point of view, for example, 'The Bride's Prelude', 'Rose Mary', 'Sister Helen', 'Eden Bower', and perhaps most famously 'The Blessed Damozel'. However, with the exception of the late 'The King's Tragedy', spoken by Catherine Douglas or 'Kate Barlass', very few of his poems are written solely in a woman's voice. In 'The Bride's Prelude' and 'Rose Mary' the women's speech is framed by a impersonal narrator, the ballad 'Sister Helen' is focalised through Helen's little brother (especially so in the later 1881 version), while the whole of 'The Blessed Damozel' may be understood as the narration of the bereaved earth-bound male lover. By way of contrast, other poems, such as the dramatic monologues 'A Last Confession' and 'Jenny' specifically exclude the woman's point of view. But one poem, often overlooked, is spoken in a woman's voice, the dramatic sonnet 'Proserpina', written in both Italian and English versions in 1872 to accompany the painting of Proserpine, featuring Jane Morris, which Rossetti had composed the previous year and which he would continue to work on in different painted versions up to his death.[19]

19 The entry on the poem in the Rossetti Archive notes a pastel drawing of Proserpine in the Ashmolean Museum, Oxford, which bears the date 1871. Both the Italian and English sonnets are titled 'Proserpina', but Rossetti elsewhere always uses the English form 'Proserpine', so I have followed his usage.

Proserpine or Proserpina, the Latin name for the Greek Persephone, also known as Kore or the Maiden, is the daughter of Ceres or Demeter, goddess of agriculture. Snatched by Pluto, while gathering flowers in Enna, Proserpine is carried off by him to Hades or the Underworld to be his reluctant bride and queen. Ceres searches in vain for her daughter until she is at last told of her abduction. In her grief and anger, she refuses to cultivate the earth, which lies barren until Jupiter, king of the gods, intervenes, sending Mercury to Hades to petition for Proserpine's return. Pluto agrees, but shortly before she is due to leave, tricks Proserpine into eating one or more pomegranate seeds. Because of this, she is doomed to return to Hades every year to spend time with Pluto as his queen, and at this season Ceres mourns her daughter, bringing winter to the dormant earth. The best-known version of this painting is the one now in the Tate Britain, the so-called 'seventh version', commissioned for Frederick R. Leyland, a Liverpool shipping magnate.[20] In 1878 Rossetti gave a long description of the picture to W. A. Turner, a purchaser of one of the Proserpine paintings:

> The figure represents Proserpine as Empress of Hades. After she was conveyed by Pluto to his realm, and became his bride, her mother Ceres importuned Jupiter for her return to earth, and he was prevailed on to consent to this, provided only she had not partaken of any of the fruits of Hades. It was found, however, that she had eaten one grain of a pomegranate, and this enchained her to her new empire and destiny. She is represented in a gloomy corridor of her palace, with the fatal fruit in her hand. As she passes, a gleam strikes on the wall behind her from some inlet suddenly opened, and admitting for a moment the light of the upper world; and she glances furtively towards it, immersed in thought. The incense-burner stands behind her as the attribute of a goddess. The ivy-branch in the background (a decorative appendage to the sonnet inscribed on the label) may be taken as a symbol of clinging memory.
>
> (Cited in Sharp 1882, 236; also Rossetti 1911, 635)

On 14 August 1875, Frederick Stephens published an essay 'Pictures by Mr Rossetti' in the *Athenæum* that discussed some of Rossetti's most recent artwork and included a lengthy description of the painting *Proserpine*, which 'exhibits, we think, the finest qualities, both technical and inventive, of the artist's genius at their finest pitch. The subject is a new poem in itself, the mode of treatment is finely poetical' (Stephens 1875, 220).[21] Stephens's praise

20 For an interpretation of the complex history of the different versions of the painting see Appendix 2 by Allan Life in Rossetti 2002–, 6.588–604.

21 For this article Stephens drew on notes describing the pictures provided by Rossetti in a letter dated 10 August 1875. See Rossetti hypertext archive. This letter is not included in Doughty and Wahl's 1965–67 edition of Rossetti's letters nor, at the time of writing, has it been published in Fredeman's new edition of the *Correspondence.*

for the painting has been endorsed by successive critics. As Jan Marsh comments: '*Proserpine* is a compelling, haunting image, much admired for its Symbolist power. Its forms and lines have greater gravity than any previous works, and are replete with sombre feeling. . . . To many, this is Rossetti's greatest work, with all the iconic quality Pater had ascribed to the *Mona Lisa*' (Marsh 2005, 460).

A fortnight after Stephens's article appeared, the English and Italian 'Proserpina' sonnets and another painting called 'La Bella Mano' ('the lovely hand') were first published under the general title 'Sonnets for Pictures' in the *Athenæum* on 28 August 1875. The English version of 'Proserpina' is as follows:

> Afar away the light that brings cold cheer
> Unto this wall, – one instant and no more
> Admitted at my distant palace-door:
> Afar the flowers of Enna from this drear
> Cold fruit, which, tasted once, must thrall me here:
> Afar those skies from this Tartarean grey
> That chills me: and afar, how far away,
> The nights that shall be from the days that were.
>
> Afar from my own self I seem, and wing
> Strange ways in thought, and listen for a sign:
> And still some heart unto some soul doth pine, –
> (Whose sounds mine inner sense is fain to bring,
> Continually together murmuring), –
> 'Woe's me for thee, unhappy Proserpine!'
> (Rossetti 1875, 273; 1911, 253 with variants)

Marsh writes that, while at Kelmscott in 1872, Rossetti had asked his lover, Jane Morris, to pose for the painting before she left to return to London:

> The subject had been composed a year past, during the first summer among the flower meadows at Kelmscott, anticipative of Jane's winter return to the dark underworld of London with a husband she had not chosen. It now bore complex layers of symbolism, for Gabriel had signally failed to rescue her from this fate, and was himself now often as gloomy as Dis. (Marsh 2005, 459)

Yet the painting is susceptible of a number of different biographical interpretations. Visiting England from across the Channel, the critic Gabriel Mourey confused the image of Jane Morris as Proserpine with that of Elizabeth Siddal, Rossetti's dead wife:

> he is under the influence of his charming and deeply-mourned Beatrice. But she no more appears to him in the shining raiment of her sweet, gentle beauty. Down there, in the unknown world in which she dwells, she has assumed that air of solemn awe, that look of superhuman knowledge which flashes from the eyes of

Death's guests. She has donned the gloomy mask of Proserpina. For having eaten of the fatal fruit she is henceforth doomed to dwell in the infernal regions. The weight of her heavy hair is a burden to her. Unhappily she is still beautiful, and regret for past joys fills her eyes with melancholy charm. (Mourey 1896, 109–10)

But his mistake seems understandable.[22] Although in Christian iconography the pomegranate is a symbol of resurrection and eternal life, in the mythic associations of Rossetti's painting it is, as Mourey says, echoing Rossetti himself in his prose description of the painting, a 'fatal fruit', which condemns Proserpine to the land of the dead. As Pater, in 'Demeter and Persephone' (1876), an essay to which I shall return in Chapter 2, remarks of the maiden goddess, she is 'a *revenant*, who in the garden of Aidoneus [Pluto] has eaten of the pomegranate, and bears always the secret of decay in her, of return to the grave, in the mystery of those swallowed seeds' (Pater 1910, *GS* 148). Moreover, the emblematic pomegranate with which Proserpine is often pictured is interchangeable with the emblem of the poppy, more evidently symbolic of sleep and death, being the source of the popular Victorian narcotic opium. In classical symbolism the pomegranate is a surrogate for the poppy's narcotic capsule, with its comparable shape, chambered interior, and many seeds (Ruck and Staples 1994, 32).[23] In 1881, when Rossetti republished his poem in *Ballads and Sonnets*, Proserpine's 'Cold fruit' takes on a more sinister meaning, becoming a 'Dire fruit'.

Elizabeth Siddal Rossetti died on 11 February 1862, apparently a suicide, her death the result of an overdose of laudanum, an alcoholic tincture of the drug also known as 'wine of opium'. Swinburne's 'The Garden of Proserpine', probably written in 1865 and included in *Poems and Ballads* (1866), seems to include a reference to laudanum and its fatal properties. In the garden of the Queen of the Underworld, there is

No growth of moor or coppice,
  No heather-flower or vine,
But bloomless buds of poppies,
  Green grapes of Proserpine,
Pale beds of blowing rushes
Where no leaf blooms or blushes
Save this whereout she crushes
  For dead men deadly wine.

(Swinburne 1904, 1.170)

22 Elizabeth Prettejohn points out to me that in the last Proserpine painting, now in Birmingham City Art Gallery, Proserpine has red hair, one of Elizabeth Siddal's famous attributes.

23 Pater writes of depictions of Persephone holding in her hand a poppy, 'emblem of sleep and death by its narcotic juices, of life and resurrection by its innumerable seeds' (Pater 1910, 148–9).

Generally read as a yearning for oblivion, an escape from the stresses and strains of desire, Swinburne's poem seems to entertain the idea of suicide as such an escape, with the 'wine' crushed from poppy buds, Proserpine's 'green grapes', offering one solution.[24] Perhaps Swinburne, who had been devoted to Elizabeth, had dined with her and Rossetti on the eve of her death, and was obliged to testify at her inquest, may even have identified her with Proserpine, goddess of death, herself:

> Pale, beyond porch and portal,
> Crowned with calm leaves, she stands
> Who gathers all things mortal
> With cold immortal hands;
> Her languid lips are sweeter
> Than love's who fears to greet her
> To men that mix and meet her
> From many times and lands.
>
> (Swinburne 1904, 1.170)

In Rossetti's painting of Elizabeth as *Beata Beatrix*, Dante's Beatrice in her mystic rapture, which he worked on between 1864 and 1870, a bird drops a poppy, symbolic of her coming death, between her hands. The sonnet 'Proserpina' could thus be a prosopopeia, a personification which, in this case, brings the dead to life, being spoken by Rossetti's deceased wife, prematurely doomed to the Underworld and leaving the world behind her: 'Afar the flowers of Enna from this drear / Dire fruit, which, tasted once, must thrall me here.' In the sestet of the sonnet, Proserpine 'listen[s] for a sign' that she is missed and mourned, fancying that she can hear someone continually lamenting her: ' "Woe's me for thee, unhappy Proserpine!" ' In the original myth, this lamenting voice would be that of Ceres, her mother; in Rossetti's reworking of the myth, this voice might be his own, mourning his lost wife or the distant Jane Morris. Certainly we know that in the years after her death Rossetti tried to communicate with his wife through seances, asking her questions and apprehending her voice through rapped messages. Proserpine in the Underworld is a figure of Life-in-Death; in Rossetti's painting and poem she is a figure held in suspension between two realms, belonging to both and neither, and tantalised by the gleam of light which finds its way into her subterranean palace.

With reference to the painting's 'complex layers of symbolism', Marsh writes of Rossetti, 'His own mood seems expressed through Proserpine's. '*Oimè per te, Proserpina infelice*!' he wrote in a sonnet, in Italian sent to William "to pick holes in" on 7 November [1872]' (Marsh 2005, 459; Letter 72.109 in Rossetti 2002–, 5.316). 'Woe's me for thee, unhappy Proserpine', to give the last line of

24 Opium is produced by milking the latex from the unripe fruits (or seed pods) of opium poppies.

the English sonnet, is an odd formulation, which already implies a strongly empathetic identification. Indeed Proserpine or Kore, that archetypal mourning maiden, could also be Rossetti himself after his breakdown following the publication of the longer pamphlet version of *The Fleshly School of Poetry* on 12 May 1872. In the early June of that year, driven to mania by Buchanan's insults repeated in the popular press, he, too, had tried to commit suicide by an overdose of laudanum. He had then hovered between life and death for a number of days, but had been successfully revived by his anxious brother and friends. Pre-dating this incident he had from 1870 onwards become increasingly dependent on another narcotic – chloral – washed down with alcohol as a remedy for his insomnia and the 'fear-filled thoughts' that dogged him at night (Marsh 2005, 442). 'Proserpina' could then be Rossetti's personification of himself as a grieving imprisoned maiden, reprising the Tennysonian embowered maiden who doubles with the solitary poet, and providing a precedent for the grieving maiden of Watts-Dunton's sonnet.

Truly the poem does offer 'strange ways in thought'. In an editorial commentary, Jerome McGann writes that 'The sestet develops an uncanny sense that Proserpine is listening for the sounds and signs of the very poem she appears to be authoring, and hence that the final line is giving us, as it were, Rossetti's own words, here reported back to us from the underworld' (McGann 2003, 397). This peculiar sense of circularity is even more acute if we understand that Rossetti inhabits Proserpine, who listens for the sympathetic voice of mourning which Rossetti as poet inscribes for her in that last line. Her none the less apparently inexplicable sense that she is, as she says, 'afar from mine own self', gives us the clue that her identity has been shared with another. This circle of narcissistic mourning and self-consolation is oddly hypnotic, its repeated chant of 'Afar, Afar, Afar', in spite of its reference to distance, working only to draw the reader further into the narcotic dusk of the poem.

McGann mentions as 'one of Rossetti's most cherished convictions: that works of art involve transrational powers of awareness'. This means that works that were originally impersonal are able to become 'intensely, bizarrely personal'. He explains that, as Rossetti knew from his reading of Dante's *Vita Nuova*, 'Poems have meanings that are "Dictated from Eternity," beyond the knowledge or control of the artist', and that 'In his painting and writing alike, Rossetti regularly reworked earlier materials in order to reveal their concealed, premonitory meaning' (McGann 2000, 64, 65, 64). Written in late 1872, 'Proserpina' is hardly an impersonal or innocent work, but it certainly becomes ever more loaded as, during his last decade, depressed and reclusive, Rossetti would increasingly immure himself in his gloomy house at Cheyne Walk. The unhappy maiden of the painting, who hypnotises us with her melancholy beauty, is conjoined with the gloomily isolated and morbidly introspective poet. Both figures have a strong allure and, as mentioned earlier, wounded narcissism has its own appeal. Hall Caine, visiting the reclusive Rossetti, thought that he 'was one of the most magnetic of men, but it was not more his genius than his unhappiness that held certain of his friends by a spell' (Caine 1882a, 235).[25]

Narcissus

Considering Rossetti's breakdown, Jan Marsh debates the proposition 'that late-onset breakdowns are more common in those with high degrees of narcissism, as the sense of mortality and failure impends in middle life', stating that 'Rossetti was self-absorbed, though not therefore unself-critical' (Marsh 2005, 451). 'Narcissistic', a word frequently applied to Rossetti and his poetry, interestingly shares the same Greek root as 'narcotic', where νάρκη (*narkē*) means 'numbness' or 'stiffness'. When the beautiful youth Narcissus falls in love with his reflection in the water, he seems numbed, arrested, lulled into a stupor by its narcotic powers. As Ovid, relating the story in his *Metamorphoses* relates:

> *astupet ipse sibi vultuque immotus eodem*
> *haeret, ut e Pario formatum marmore signum.*
> (Ovid 1946, 152–4; *Metamorphoses* 3.418–19)

> He was astonished at himself and, immobile, with that same expression
> He was stuck there like a statue carved out of Parian marble.[26]

Narcissus remains transfixed, rooted to the spot, by the image, unable and unwilling to leave the object of his passion, and eventually pining away by the water's edge. When he dies, he is transformed into the narcissus flower, so named for the narcotic stupor it supposedly induces.[27] Even after he has entered the Underworld, Ovid tells us, 'he kept on looking at himself in the Stygian waters' (*tum quoque se, postquam est inferna sede receptus, / in Stygia spectabat aqua* (Ovid 1946, 158)). Although we think Narcissus the archetypal narcissist because he falls in love with himself, he does so, at least at first, unwittingly, not realising the youth he loves is his own reflection. For Narcissus, we might say, it is the youth he loves in vain who seems narcissistic – that is, narcissistic and alluring at the same time, for there is something about the spectacle of narcissism that is arresting, that stops one in one's tracks.

25 In the 1928 revised version of his *Recollections*, Caine writes 'it was not so much his genius as his unhappiness that held me as by a spell' (Caine 1990, 67).
26 My thanks to Katie Fleming for this and the subsequent translation.
27 In the Homeric Hymn to Demeter, Persephone is snatched as she pulls at the bulb of a large narcissus flower, which in symbolic terms hints that her journey to the Underworld may be narcotically induced. The Persephone/Proserpine story, as Rossetti may have intuited, is suffused with narcotic detail.

While some will remain immune to its charms, narcissism, as Freud suggested, can be oddly attractive, hence his description cited earlier detailing what Naomi Schor calls the 'magnetic effects of narcissism' (Schor 1987, 38). Rossetti himself acknowledged these magnetic effects. Apropos his painting *Lady Lilith*, whose protagonist he famously described in the accompanying sonnet 'Body's Beauty' as 'subtly of herself contemplative' (Rossetti 1911, 100), he wrote to Thomas Gordon Hake noting 'that self-absorption by whose strange fascination such natures draw others within their own circle' (21 April 1870; Letter 70.110 in Rossetti 2002–, 4.450). Later he would stipulate to William Bell Scott in another letter that 'Absorption is not annihilation' (10 September 1871; Letter 71.144 in Rossetti 2002–, 5.141). He might, unconsciously perhaps, have been speaking of himself when he wrote about *Lady Lilith*, for, with regard to his own narcissistic appeal, W. J. Stillman noted his 'frank egotism which made him see everything and everybody purely in relation to him'; 'he had been so spoiled by all his friends and exercised such fascination on all around him, that no one rebelled at being treated in his princely way for it was only with his friends that he used it. He dominated all who had the least sympathy with him and his genius' (Stillman 1901, 80, 85).

The narcissistic look or gaze may be both arresting and hypnotic as viewers of Rossetti's paintings of *femmes fatales* may know. F. W. H. Myers alludes to the 'haunting beauty' of his female portraits, which unite 'strange and puissant physical loveliness with depth and remoteness of gaze', while he characterises Rossetti's life as 'absorbed in Art' (Myers in Riede 1992a, 52, 53, 56). 'I loved ere I loved a woman, Love' writes Rossetti in a verse fragment addressed 'To Art' (Rossetti 1911, 240), and Art is his first mistress, refracted in the hypnotic women of his paintings. The female beauties sought and admired by the Pre-Raphaelites were known by them as 'stunners', possessing the kind of beauty that hits the viewer between the eyes and knocks him out, leaving him pleasurably dazed and confused. Narcissus was stunned, love-struck by his reflection, and many of the words that denote the effects wrought by an alluring beauty suggest the influence of some kind of magical hold over the viewer; it casts a spell so that the viewer is bewitched, charmed, entranced, enslaved, or fascinated. 'Her gaze struck awe', remarks Rossetti of the spiritual 'Beauty enthroned' in his sonnet 'Soul's Beauty', while in the partner sonnet, 'Body's Beauty', Lilith, who embodies the physical, narcissistic beauty,

> subtly of herself contemplative,
> Draws men to watch the bright web she can weave,
> Till heart and body and life are in its hold.
>
> The rose and poppy are her flowers; for where
> Is he not found, O Lilith, whom shed scent
> And soft-shed kisses and soft sleep shall snare?
>
> (Rossetti 1911, 100)

In casting its spell, narcissistic beauty in particular has some kind of narcotic component that draws in the viewer, stupefies him, and brings him to a standstill. 'To fascinate', from Latin *fascinare*, is specifically 'to cast a spell over a person or animal by a look' (*OED*), and is specifically used of serpents, who are said to deprive their prey or victim of the power of escape or resistance by their hypnotic numbing look. Rossetti, who knew Goethe's *Faust* from childhood (W. M. Rossetti 1895, 1.58) and was also familiar with the translation by Shelley (1822), must have been struck by the description of a beautiful girl Faust sees on the night of the witches' Sabbath who reminds him of his first love Margaret. Mephistopheles warns him off with the words:

> it is an enchanted phantom,
> A lifeless idol; with its numbing look,
> It freezes up the blood of man; and they
> Who meet its ghastly stare are turned to stone,
> Like those who saw Medusa.
>
> (Shelley 1970, 761)

This absorbing Medusan stare numbs and petrifies, a fatally all-absorbing version of the magnetic or mesmerising gaze of the entrancing being. Rossetti's own anxieties about being absorbed to the point of paralysis, and thus perhaps even 'annihilation', seem to surface in his short poem 'Aspecta Medusa'. The Greek hero Perseus saved and won Andromeda from the predations of a sea-monster by showing the beast the severed Medusa head, which he carried with him in a special wallet. In Rossetti's poem Perseus satisfies Andomeda's curiosity about the Medusa head and protects her from its adverse effects by showing her its reflection in a pool:

> Andromeda, by Perseus saved and wed,
> Hankered each day to see the Gorgon's head:
> Till o'er a fount he held it, bade her lean,
> And mirrored in the wave was safely seen
> That death she lived by.
>
> Let not thine eyes know
> Any forbidden thing itself, although
> It once should save as well as kill: but be
> Its shadow upon life enough for thee.
>
> (Rossetti 1911, 209)

Art here is the reflective surface which functions as did Perseus' gleaming shield, allowing him to see the Medusa reflection or 'shadow' at a remove rather than directly and thus avoid its paralysing gaze. Art has the power to neutralise things that are ugly or threatening, even masking or containing them within a formal beauty. As Shelley writes in *A Defence of Poetry*, 'Poetry is a mirror which makes beautiful that which is distorted' (Shelley 1977, 485). In Freudian terms the Medusa head represents the 'castrated' female genitals, a threat to the integrity of the male (Maxwell 2001, 83–4). Art turns the fatally paralysing feminine into the attractive narcissism of the *femme fatale*, although in Rossetti's poem the Medusa head, made safe in the reflective waters of the 'fount', is still not shown to us even at a remove. We are left to imagine for ourselves that censored or occluded face appearing as it were in the blank space that separates the two parts of the poem. Ideally in Rossetti's poetry or paintings, as in much other Aesthetic or Decadent art, woman's difference, her 'castration', potentially a threat to the male viewer or reader and always subliminally present in the *femme fatale*, is masked by beauty, so that she fascinates or mesmerises, but not to the point of paralysis. A certain pleasurable disturbance may be apparent but should be kept in check by the taming, pacifying powers of art. Yet, it should be added, this ideal is far from incontrovertible; for art may not always pacify, nor woman's danger always be contained.

Rossetti's magnetism

Recalling Schor's description of the 'magnetic effects of narcissism' and Rossetti's own magnetically narcissistic beauties, we should be aware that he was himself frequently spoken of as 'magnetic', a word that in the nineteenth century denotes mesmeric power. 'Animal magnetism' or 'mesmerism', made famous by the eighteenth-century German physician Anton Mesmer (1734–1815), was the forerunner of what was later more commonly known as hypnosis. As Alison Winter explains, in a mesmeric seance of the kind widespread by the 1840s, the magnetiser or mesmerist could, by gazing into his subjects' eyes and passing or skimming his hands over their bodies, induce states of trance or coma, thereby establishing a strange communion with them in which they might then speak his thoughts or echo his movements or sensations. In deeper states 'subjects might claim to see events occurring in the future, inside the body, in distant lands, and even in the heavens' (Winter 1998, 3–4). The mesmeric trance had also a more serious medical use in that it could be used therapeutically to administer pain relief or as a means of alleviating or even removing physical or mental symptoms of disease. In common with many other Victorians, Rossetti was familiar with mesmeric spectacles. In a review of modern continental paintings exhibited at Lichfield House published in the *Spectator* for August 1851, he praises the contributions of the French painter François-Auguste Biard, singling out as his best work the painting 'A Performance of Mesmerism in a Parisian Drawing-room' (Rossetti 1911, 578). Moreover he had attended such events himself, inviting his brother William earlier that same year (9 May) to join him, Millais, and Hunt 'to have another shy at seeing the Electro-biology', that is, a hypnotic exhibition (Letter 51.10 in Rossetti 2002–, 1.173). During 1870 he also organised for friends two mesmeric performances in a tent in the garden at Cheyne Walk during which two young women were mesmerised by a Mr Bergheim (Dunn 1904, 56–61; Rossetti 2002–, 5.402–3).[28]

Rossetti's own personal magnetism, as noted by his friends and associates, describes his compelling character, his powerful influence, and his ability to dominate others and bend them to his will. In his 'Autobiographical Notes', Watts-Dunton described Rossetti's face as possessing 'an imperious magnetism', while his voice 'awakened an eagerness on the part of the listener to catch the sound; it seemed to draw one towards him' (cited in Hake and Compton-Rickett 1916, 1.82). In his biography of Rossetti, written and published in the same year as the poet's death, the young William Sharp described Rossetti as 'a man who exercised an almost irresistible charm over most with whom he was brought into contact. His manner could be particularly winning, especially with those much younger than himself, and his voice was alike notable for its sonorous beauty and for a magnetic quality that made the ear alert where the speaker was engaged in conversation, recitation, or reading' (Sharp 1882, 36). In the same year, the young Hall Caine described Rossetti as 'one of the most magnetic of men' (Caine 1882a, 235), while Edmund Gosse, who had also known Rossetti personally, opened a commemorative article with the words: 'Those whose privilege it was to meet the late Mr. Gabriel Rossetti at once in the plenitude of his powers and in the freshness of their own impressions, will not expect to be moved again through life by so magnetic a presence' (Gosse 1882, 718).[29] The critic and dramatist J. W. Comyns Carr similarly attested 'that potent spell which he wielded over all who came within the sphere of his influence', and that 'magical and inspiring was the spell he exercised over us all' (Carr 1914, 48, 53), while Sidney Colvin wrote that 'His voice was magical in its mellow beauty of *timbre* and quality and in its power to convey the sense of a whole world of brooding passion and mystery, both human and elemental, behind the words' (Colvin 1921, 65). In the first of the Appendices attached to Watts-Dunton's *Aylwin* in 1914, the anonymous author, clearly reliant on Watts-Dunton's personal testimony, writes of Rossetti, 'As to his personal fascination, among all the poets of England we have no record of anything equal to it.' And he continues:

> To describe the magnetism of such a man is, of course, impossible. Much has been written on what is called the *demonic* power in certain individuals – the

28 Apparently J. S. Bergheim, a civil engineer and member of the Spiritualism Committee of the London Dialectical Society.

29 In the revised version of his *Recollections of Rossetti* (1928), Hall Caine would assert that, to him, Rossetti was 'the most fascinating, the most affectionate, and the most magnetic of men' (Caine 1990, 67).

power of casting one's own influence over all others. Napoleon's case is generally instanced as a typical one. But Napoleon's demonic power was of a self-conscious kind. It would seem, however that there is another kind of demonic power – the power of shedding quite unconsciously one's personality upon all brought into contact with it. The demonic power of Rossetti . . . was quite unconscious.

(Watts-Dunton 1914, 496).[30]

Arthur Symons declared that Rossetti was 'intensely sensitive; and this made him a sort of medium to forces seen and unseen. So he fascinated women; so did the supernatural fascinate him' (Symons 1929, 13).

Rossetti's magnetism and especially his magnetic voice also carry through into assessments of his work. Echoing the poet-painter's own words about *Lady Lilith*, Symons wrote that in his work 'there is an actually hypnotic quality which exerts itself on those who come within his circle at all; a quality like that of an unconscious medium, or like that of a woman against whose attraction one is without defence. It is the sound of a voice, rather than anything said; and when Rossetti speaks, no other voice, for the moment, seems worth listening to' (Symons 1916, 202). Gabriel Mourey wrote that 'In the rhythms of his verse and in the creations of his dreams runs a strain of soothing intoxicating charm' (Mourey 1896, 93); William Sharp, that 'a powerful and magnetic imagination is his highest characteristic' (Sharp 1912, 64–5). More recently Adrienne Munich has drawn our attention to how, like his women, Rossetti desired his poems to 'stun' and how he was perpetually on the look out for 'stunning words' to use in his poetry (Munich 1989, 86). Yet clearly to another sort of reader, such as F. R. Leavis, such efforts are simply 'a wordy pretentiousness' (Leavis 1952, 48). In his essay of reversal, 'A Note on Dante Rosssetti' (1883), Buchanan wrote:

But let me confess at the outset that, to understand poems like these, the reader must bring something of the sympathy he receives. If he approaches in the wrong mood, or in an antipathetic one, the poems may at first repel him. The magnetism is for magnetic people, under what the mediums call 'test' conditions. I myself, being then in a non-receptive mood, once regarded Rossetti's verse balefully, disliked his subjects and his workmanship.

(Buchanan 1887, 154)

Buchanan, I think, has identified something important here about Rossetti: that his work can summon up in the reader a strong ambivalence, which can even spill over into repulsion. For some readers and viewers Rossetti's art does not

30 This Appendix may be written by Watts-Dunton himself, or by Thomas St E. Hake, author of Appendix 2, friend of Rossetti, and friend, secretary, and biographer to Watts-Dunton.

always check, control, or tame the aggressive, threatening, or grotesque aspects of his subjects, especially his female subjects, as effectively as might be expected, something that becomes more evident in many of the later paintings. Vernon Lee, viewing Rossetti portraits of Marie Spartali Stillman and Jane Morris at Frederick R. Leyland's house in July 1883 thought them 'coarse & repulsive', and was 'afflicted' by 'the frightful discrepancy between the morbid coarseness of his painting & the Danteseque delicacy of his poems' (Lee 1937, 126). Even an admirer of Rossetti such as Jerome McGann, for example, can refer to some of the later paintings as 'repellent', or at least 'self-consciously repulsive' (McGann 2000, 150, 151). James Richardson, one of Rossetti's best critics, writes persuasively about the compression of his language and syntax in *The House of Life*, which can lead to an effect the reverse of magnetic attraction: 'Compression implies crowding, and indeed readers unsympathetic to Rossetti's sonnets often seem to be *repelled* – not merely morally or aesthetically, but almost literally pushed out and away' (Richardson 1988, 112). Rossetti's intense imaginative circle or inner world can seem close and stifling, and, while poems and paintings work to draw and attract, readers and viewers may find themselves reacting against a feeling of envelopment or claustrophobia, a sensation of crowding and intrusion perhaps heightened by spiritual things taking on material presences. Browning famously objected to a verse he found '*scented* with poetry', resisting the encroaching personification of Love as 'a lubberly naked man putting his arms there and his wings here about a pair of young lovers' (Letter to Isa Blagden, 19 June 1870, in Browning 1951, 336, 337). Buchanan similarly complained that 'the fleshly feeling is everywhere . . . it is generally in the foreground, flushing the whole poem with unhealthy rose-colour, stifling the senses with overpowering sickliness, as of too much civet' (Buchanan 1871 in Riede 1992a, 28).

It may have been his unwilling envelopment in the intense heady atmosphere of 'Nuptial Sleep' (originally 'Placatâ Venere') that made Buchanan reject it as 'simply nasty' (Buchanan 1871 in Riede 1992a, 28):

At length their long kiss severed, with sweet smart:
   And as the last slow sudden drops are shed
   From sparkling eaves when all the storm has fled,
So singly flagged the pulses of each heart.
Their bosoms sundered, with the opening start
   Of married flowers to either side outspread
   From the knit stem; yet still their mouths, burnt red,
Fawned on each other where they lay apart.

Sleep sank them lower than the tide of dreams,
   And their dreams watched them sink, and slid away.
Slowly their souls swam up again, through gleams
   Of watered light and dull drowned waifs of day;

> Till from some wonder of new woods and streams
> He woke, and wondered more: for there she lay.
>
> (Rossetti 1911, 76)[31]

Rossetti defended his sonnet as 'embodying . . . a beauty of natural universal function', justifying it as a 'passing phase of description' in *The House of Life*, and not 'his own representative view of the subject of love' (Rossetti in Riede 1992, 41), but he seems to have written a deeper poem than he here admits. For while the octet puts the accent predominantly (but not exclusively) on physical effects as the couple leave off their lovemaking, the sestet concentrates on the psychical and spiritual sequel. Here the couple fall into what is eventually a deep and dreamless sleep. After a time they move back into the lighter dream-sleep which precedes waking. The male lover finally surfaces from dreams of a wondrous Edenic landscape to find the greater mystery of his beloved lying beside him. Jerome McGann argues that 'following an experience of ecstatic physical union – the beloved appears to the eyes of the lover as a unique identity, wholly individuated despite the previous moments of mutual absorption. The lover's (actual) "wonder" is thus reduplicated, or realized, in the rhetoric of the speaker, who is spellbound before his imagination of the separate lovers' (McGann 1988 in Riede 1992a, 182). There is much to be said for this view, including 'absorption is not annihilation', but perhaps more emphasis should be placed on Rossetti's evocation in the sestet of Milton's *Paradise Lost* Book 8, in which Adam relates to Raphael how God put him to sleep so that he might create Eve from his rib and thus satisfy his longing for a companion. Adam explains that 'Mine eyes he closed, but left open the cell / Of fancy my internal sight' (Milton 1971, 420; 8.461–2), enabling him to see God's creation of Eve:

> Under his forming hands a creature grew,
> Manlike, but different sex, so lovely fair,
> That what seemed fair in all the world, seemed now
> Mean.
>
> (Milton 1971, 421; 8.470–3)

After admiring this fair creature, Adam finds that

> She disappeared, and left me dark, I waked
> To find her, or for ever to deplore
> Her loss, and other pleasures all abjure:
> When out of hope, behold her, not far off,
> Such as I saw her in my dream, adorned
> With what all earth and heaven could bestow
> To make her amiable.
>
> (Milton 1971, 422; 8.478–84)

31 Sonnet 5 in the 1870 *House of Life*, but then omitted in the 1881 expanded version. W. M. Rossetti restored it as Sonnet 6a in Rossetti 1911.

Rossetti surely recalls Keats's famous remark in his letter to Benjamin Bailey: 'The Imagination may be compared to Adam's dream – he awoke and found it truth' (22 November 1817; Keats 1958, 1.185).[32] The physical consummation with its wedding of bodies here ushers a kind of conception followed by a psychical or spiritual rebirth. The mutual deep sleep of the lovers suggests a submersion in the depths of the unconscious, a kind of dream-womb from which they will surface as new or transformed beings, emerging from sleep irrevocably changed by the experience they have gone through together. In Milton the body of Adam is divided into the separate identities of Adam and Eve. Shortly after seeing Eve, Adam persuades her to consummate their bond so that they again become 'one flesh'. Rossetti starts with the couple forming a 'nuptial body', and thence their new identities as partners – identities which by implication will be reinforced by further physical union. Certainly to the awakened male lover the female beloved has the distinctness of a new creation, and he wonders at her as Adam does at Eve. But as Eve was born of Adam's body, so the woman is by virtue of their shared lovemaking the man's 'nuptial' partner, and, at a deeper level, the fulfilment of a visionary longing, born of his desiring imagination. This fleshing-out of the imagination reminds us that even in this supposedly sensual sonnet the beloved woman emerges as an inspiring agent of wonder.

With regard to the male lover's 'wondering' gaze over the woman, we should note that for Theodore Watts-Dunton the word 'wonder' had a particular significance in relation to Rossetti. Watts-Dunton would coin the phrase 'the Renascence of Wonder' to describe the revival of the Romantic spirit in the latter part of the nineteenth century, and in his 1886 *Encyclopædia Britannica* article on Rossetti, he wrote:

> The goal before the young Rossetti's eyes . . . was to reach through art the forgotten world of old romance – that world of wonder and mystery and spiritual beauty which the old masters knew and could have painted had not lack of science, combined with slavery to monkish traditions of asceticism, crippled their strength. . . . [I]n that great movement of man's soul which may be appropriately named 'the Renascence of the Spirit of Wonder in Poetry and Art' – he became the acknowledged protagonist before ever the pre-Raphaelite brotherhood was founded, and down to his last breath at Birchington.
>
> (Watts-Dunton 1886, 857–8)[33]

In Rossetti that 'world of wonder and mystery and spiritual beauty' is characteristically reached through his treatment of women and love, where at its most ideal it is realised in a language of magnetic communication that manages to be

32 Riede also briefly notes the allusions to Milton and Keats (Riede 1992b, 124–5).

33 These remarks are repeated with slight variants in the revised entry found in the 11th edition of 1911 (Watts-Dunton 1911, 749).

simultaneously physical and spiritual. In Rossetti's verse it is women who are magnetisers and who exert their powers over men. In an essay on 1868 Swinburne picks up the word 'draw' from 'Body's Beauty' to write of Lilith in the picture that partners the sonnet: 'She is indifferent, equable, magnetic; she charms and draws down the souls of men by pure force of absorption . . . and because of this she attracts all men at once in body and in spirit' (Swinburne 1875a, 375–6). In Rossetti's love poetry, we tend to move from the stunning impact of the blow of beauty, from the narcissistic *femme fatale* or siren, to the gentler but no less mesmerising beloved, whose 'wonder' is that she is an imaginative and visionary agent, opening up the channels of spiritual and physical communication. This can be seen a few sonnets before 'Nuptial Sleep' in 'Love's Redemption', Sonnet 2 of the 1870 *House of Life*, where the woman magnetically 'draws up' the male lover out of his depression by her gaze, granting deliverance to his 'prisoned spirit'.

O Thou who at Love's hour ecstatically
   Unto my lips dost evermore present
   The body and blood of Love in sacrament;
Whom I have neared and felt thy breath to be
The inmost incense of his sanctuary;
   Who without speech hast owned him, and intent
   Upon his will, thy life with mine hast blent,
And murmured o'er the cup, remember me!

O what from thee the grace, for me the prize,
   And what to Love the glory, – when the whole
   Of the deep stair thou tread'st to the dim shoal
And weary water of the place of sighs,
And there dost work deliverance, as thine eyes
   Draw up my prisoned spirit to thy soul!

(Rossetti 1961, 105–6)

The sonnet plays with the idea of perfect communication, where 'to communicate' is also in the language of the church 'to receive holy communion'. In his pamphlet Buchanan identified this poem as 'blasphemy' (Buchanan 1872, 59), evidently balking at the identification of the beloved's physical and spiritual presence in sexual union with the real presence of Christ in the Eucharistic bread and wine. Yet, consonant with the multiple meanings and identities of Rossetti's poetry, the beloved's physical and spiritual presence, because given in absolute love, cannot be other than Love's own presence. In 'Heart's Hope', Sonnet 5 in the 1881 *House of Life*, the lover will declare to his beloved how he is unable to tell 'our love from God' (Rossetti 1911, 76). Moreover, marriage, no less than holy communion, is in Catholic theology a sacrament, the 'outward sign of an inward grace', which, properly, the couple rather than the priest are understood to administer to each other and which technically requires no set ecclesiastical rite. Rossetti's use of language is daring, but reflects his belief in the sacramental power of love. None the less Buchanan's charge of blasphemy clearly gave him anxiety and must have been behind his decision to tone down the sacramental language of the octet when, in 1881, he re-presented this poem as Sonnet 3: 'Love's Testament' (Rossetti 1911, 75; see also Rossetti 2007, 42–4). Yet elsewhere in *The House of Life*, the woman's presence communicates a magical strength that the male lover drinks in. In 'True Woman: I. Herself' (Sonnet 56, 1881), she is 'an essence more environing / Than wine's drained juice' (Rossetti 1911, 93), while in the conclusion to the elegiac sonnet quartet 'Willowwood' (Sonnets 24–7, 1870; Sonnets 49–52, 1881), the male lover imbibes his beloved as a source of inspiration, when, watching her watery image disappear, he leans low 'and drank / A long draught from the water where she sank, / Her breath and all her tears and all her soul' (Rossetti 1911, 92).

The beloved woman of *The House of Life*, while she undoubtedly has her origins in Rossetti's personal history, is in his verse transformed into an iconic figure who serves as the speaker's muse and inspiratrice and helps him, through his love of her, to engender Art – the creative relationship between Love and Art being one of the key themes of the sequence. Thus it seems besides the point to reprove Rossetti, as some have done, for showing little interest in her as an independent being. She is a presence rather than a personality. And while she certainly owes much to the beloved woman of medieval Italian poetry, she has particular magnetic powers of her own. Her power, absorbed by her lover, helps him become an artist whose work, centred on her, exerts its own magnetic attraction. To emphasise a word important in the love poetry, she draws him to her so that he can limn or draw her, and, in doing so, draw others to view his designs.

Admittedly Love is only one theme, if a very important one, in *The House of Life*, which, composed ultimately from over a hundred sonnets, many of which were incorporated from other contexts, could hardly be read as a unified sequence. Thus the ideal of Love and the beloved is offset or counterpointed, particularly towards in the latter stages of the sequence, by expressions of loss, separation, disillusion, and despondency. Yet for many readers Love is still the predominant emotion or experience of *The House of Life*, and Rossetti reinforced this by making the last poem of both the 1870 and 1881 sequences 'The One Hope', a sonnet which, as D. M. R. Bentley suggests, 'constitutes a particularly condensed and important statement of the hope that characterized the poetry and painting of his last years – the hope for an afterlife founded on eternal love' (Bentley 1990b, 153). Thus while the negative expressions of emotion are undeniable, and contribute to and corroborate the mythic spell of the melancholic poet, they need not be seen to obliterate or cancel the ideal of 'Love's spell' ('A Day of Love', Sonnet 12, 1870; Sonnet 16, 1881), which still holds its own, intimately informing, as we shall see, Rossetti's ideal of creativity and infusing his language and imagery with a characteristic charge.

Magnetic communication

> Mesmerism Rossetti had a reasonable faith in. (Dunn 1904, 56)

As Alison Winter has shown with reference to Wilkie Collins's *The Woman in White*, the sensation novel, which held readers in rapt attention with its thrilling content and absorbing plots, mirrored the experience of a mesmeric trance (Winter 1998, 322–31).[34] We may assume that the language of mesmeric communication and entrancement itself entered many such works, as it certainly pervades *Gabriel Denver* (1873), a novel by the young Oliver Madox Brown, the son of Rossetti's former teacher, the painter Ford Madox Brown, and the brother of Lucy, his future sister-in-law.[35] Rossetti, who pointed out some of the faults of the novel in a letter to the author, none the less described it as 'suprisingly accomplished and even' and 'quite a wonder' (10 November 1873; Letter 73.331 in Rossetti 2002–, 6.321–2). In this melodramatic tale, the eponymous hero, engaged to his cousin Deborah, falls passionately in love with a beautiful young woman named Laura Conway, whom he had met once previously when she was a lovely child. Glimpsing the adult Laura for the first time, after he has tracked the sound of her singing, Gabriel

> was left staring up at the empty casement like a bird fascinated by a snake, his heart beginning to throb and his nerves to thrill as though under the influence of some wild burst of music – as, indeed, on first hearing her voice he had been. Such subtle and mesmerical magic seemed instilled into his brain, that he still remained as though stupefied, with his face turned up to the blank window, which with its gilded carving looked like a frame from which some wonderful picture had been withdrawn.
> (Brown 1873, 30–1)

However, the primary literary influence for Rossetti's magnetic metaphors was not the sensation novel but poetry. Rossetti admired at least two contemporary poets who had written about animal magnetism: Browning, whose strange and troubling love poem 'Mesmerism' appeared in *Men and Women*, his best-known collection of 1855, and Thomas Gordon Hake (1809–95), the only poet Rossetti ever reviewed. In his review of Hake's *Madeline and Other Poems* (1871), originally published in the *Academy* (1 February 1871), Rossetti

34 *The Woman in White* first appeared in serial form in 1859–60, the work of a novelist who had himself experimented with mesmerism.

35 Oliver Madox Brown died of septicaemia on 5 November 1874 aged nineteen, exactly a year after the publication of *Gabriel Denver*. William Rossetti and Lucy Madox Brown married on 31 March 1874.

suggested that, in 'Madeline', 'there is an evident intention . . . to make hysterical and even mesmeric phenomena in some degree the groundwork of his conception' (Rossetti 1911, 626), a supposition borne out by Hake's admission in his *Memoirs* that the origins of the poem lie in a lecture he gave in Boston in 1853 'on "Sleep, Dreams, Sleep-walking, Sleep-talking and the Mesmeric State" which last I explained by the facts of hypnotism' (Hake 1892, 233, 193). But the Romantic poets Coleridge and Shelley were an equally powerful if not a greater influence. Nigel Leask attributes an interest in mesmerism to John Polidori (1795–1821), author of *The Vampyre* (1819), Byron's physician, and Rossetti's maternal uncle, who pursued his medical training at Edinburgh (1810–15), where he completed and afterwards published a dissertation on somnambulism (Leask 1992, 55).[36] Polidori's diary, which records his time spent with Byron during the eventful year 1816, was not published until 1911, but William Michael Rossetti, its editor, had already published extracts in the Memoir which prefaces his 1870 edition of Shelley's poems. We can be therefore be confident that Dante Gabriel Rossetti with his strong Romantic interests would have been familiar with Polidori's account, cited by his brother (W. M. Rossetti 1870, 1.lxxxix), of the famous house party of the Shelleys, Clair Clairmont, and Byron at the Villa Diodati, Lake Geneva, in 1816, and the incident which, according to Leask, would have constituted Shelley's first mesmeric experience, brought about by hearing Byron recite verses from Coleridge's 'Christabel'. Looking at his wife while listening to the description of Geraldine disrobing, Shelley's overwrought imagination was overpowered by the image of a woman 'who had eyes instead of nipples', which made him rush screaming from the room (Polidori 1911, 128; Leask 1992, 56–7). Leask also cites Coleridge's description, in the concluding chapter of the *Biographia Literaria* (1817), of the effects of impassioned recitation on the entranced auditor as a form of 'Animal Magnetism' (Leask 1992, 61). As Tim Fulford, following others, has noted, Coleridge's own Ancient Mariner has the ability to entrance his listeners: 'the mariner himself acquires magnetic power and has the ability to mesmerize others who are prepared to believe in him. And the mariner's involuntary methods follow accounts of magnetists' methods quite closely; spellbound by the mariner's "skinny hand" and "glittering eye" . . . the wedding guest is entranced' (Fulford 2004, 74). Coleridge's uncanny Geraldine is another mesmerist, entrancing Christabel with eyes that 'gan glitter bright', and, as Fulford explains, the description of her trance also closely 'follows Coleridge's understanding of mesmerism's effects' (Fulford 2004, 75–6).

36 In a letter of 21 March 1855 to William Allingham about Polidori, Rossetti defends his uncle, remarking 'He was my mother's favorite [*sic*] brother, and I feel certain her love for him is a proof that his memory deserves some respect' (Letter 55.15 in Rossetti 2002–, 2.28).

Shelley was supposed to have been introduced to 'animal magnetism' or mesmerism by Thomas Medwin in December 1820, but, as P. M. S. Dawson and Leask suggest, he almost certainly knew about it before this date from the detailed account in Southey's *Letters from England* (1807), which he read in 1810–11, and again in 1815 (Dawson 1986, 16; Leask 1992, 55, 65). Mesmeric and magnetic images and effects can be detected in works pre-dating 1820 such as *Prometheus Unbound* (written 1818–19, published 1820) and 'The Witch of Atlas' (written August 1820) as well as in works which follow such as *A Defence of Poetry* (written February–March 1821), *Epipsychidion* (1821) and *Hellas* (1822). 'The Magnetic Lady to her Patient' (written 1822), and a key source for Rossetti, is, however, the only poem which explicitly foregrounds the mesmeric process. In December 1820 Medwin mesmerised Shelley in order to relive his painful nephritic spasms, and, as Richard Holmes, his biographer reports, Shelley continued the practice throughout 1821, finding it 'especially efficacious when the "magnetiser" was a woman' (Holmes 1987, 627). Standard mesmeric practice involved a male therapist who generally worked on female subjects, so Shelley's willingness to reverse conventional gender relations and submit himself to a woman's control is unusual, although his submission was, in some instances at least, probably motivated by a strong element of sexual attraction such as we find in 'The Magnetic Lady to her Patient' which describes the mesmeric ministrations of the married Jane Williams.

Interestingly, when in August 1876 Rossetti was given 'medical orders' to abstain from chloral for two nights and underwent a formal magnetic cure to help his insomnia and to alleviate pains in his limbs, his practitioner was also a woman whom William Michael Rossetti identifies as 'a Miss Chandos' (W. M. Rossetti 1895, 1.339). Unnamed in Oswald Doughty's biography of Rossetti and unmentioned in Marsh's, Miss Chandos is undoubtedly Chandos Leigh Hunt (*b.* 1854), grand-niece of Leigh Hunt, the poet and political revolutionist, and thus, like Rossetti, possessed of Romantic antecedents. Trained by the healer and advocate of vegetarianism James Wallace, whom she later married, she had, by the time she treated Rossetti, when she was still only twenty-two, built up an extremely successful London practice, had her own trained staff and, according to the cultural historian Alex Owen, had 'evolved into a truly holistic healer who used herbal remedies, dietary control, hydropathy, physical manipulation, and mesmerism' (Owen 1990, 127). She was also a popular and gifted public lecturer and, in 1876, published the expanded text of one of her lectures as *A Treatise on All the Known Uses of Organic Magnetism, Phenomenal and Curative*. In a chapter titled 'A Lady Mesmerist' in his survey *Mystic London* (1875), the Reverend Charles Davies gives a light-hearted account of attending a public mesmeric seance led by Chandos Leigh Hunt at James Burns's Spiritual Institution, Southampton Row, in the mid-1870s, presumably just before she became well-known. Confessing to be nervous 'because lady mediums and mesmerisers are so apt to run to eighteen stone, or be old and frumpish', he was 'agreeably surprised' to find 'a very pretty young lady indeed, of not more than eighteen or twenty years of age', 'a tall active young lady' with a 'mystic crop of long black curls, which waved about like the locks of a sibyl' (Davies 1875, 262, 263, cited in Owen 1990, 124). Considering the susceptibilities of the forty-eight-year-old Rossetti, he too must have been delighted. The experiment seems to have been successful, resulting in 'better nights and no pain in the limbs' and a reduced intake of chloral (W. M. Rossetti 1895, 1.339, 2.337). Owen reports Leigh Hunt's belief that 'the mesmerist must possess a "great and good spirit, great powers of mental concentration, and a powerful Magnetic Gaze" ', and indicates that she, 'unlike the majority of healers, lay great stress on what she called the "magnetic Will" and her ability to subdue the will of others' (Owen 1990, 128). Thus the reversal of conventional gender relations noted in Shelley's preference for a female mesmerist is further accentuated in Leigh Hunt's implicit demand that her male patients submit to her will. Rossetti's treatment by Leigh Hunt post-dates much of the verse discussed here, but his choice of a female mesmerist is in line with both 'The Magnetic Lady' and the gender relations of his own amatory verse in which the woman is implicitly a magnetic agent. In this verse the love element is dominant and the woman's magnetism more implicit and symbolic than in Shelley's poem, finding typical expression in words such as 'draw' – 'thine eyes / Draw up my prisoned spirit to thy soul!' – and 'spell', a word which also occurs in Shelley's poem (l. 37).

'The Magnetic Lady to her Patient' is an evident influence on the short poem 'Song and Music', originally written in 1849 under the title 'Lines and Music', but first published in 1881. Less rarefied than later *House of Life* sonnets such as 'Love's Redemption', 'Song and Music' none the less provides a striking presentation of the woman as the magnetic agent of physical and spiritual communication:

O leave your hand where it lies cool
  Upon the eyes whose lids are hot:
Its rosy shade is bountiful
  Of silence, and assuages thought.
O lay your lips against your hand
  And let me feel your breath through it,
While through the sense your song shall fit
  The soul to understand.

The music lives upon my brain,
  Between your hands, within mine eyes;
It stirs your lifted throat like pain,
  An aching pulse of melodies.
Lean nearer, let the music pause:
  The soul may better understand

Your music, shadowed in your hand,
  Now while the song withdraws.

(Rossetti 1911, 192)

The similarity to the first verse of Shelley's poem, where it is the ministering woman who speaks, is particularly marked:

'Sleep, sleep on! forget thy pain;
  My hand is on thy brow,
My spirit on thy brain;
My pity on thy heart, poor friend;
  And from my fingers flow
The powers of life, and like a sign,
  Seal thee from thine hour of woe;
And brood on thee, but may not blend
  With thine.'

(Shelley 1970, 667)

Shelley's Lady, identified as 'Jane' in the final verse, is specifically using 'magnetic' or mesmeric power to calm the physical and mental pain of the male 'sleeper', whom she pities but does not love, her heart being given elsewhere. Although she does not sing, the incantatory 'spell' (l. 37) of the poem suggests a kind of music, while she declares to her patient that her 'soul . . . breathes mute music on thy sleep' (Shelley 1970, 667). In Rossetti's poem it is, we assume, the male lover, who addresses his beloved and asks for her soothing hand on his brow while she sings to him. While her touch is not explicitly mesmeric or hypnotic, it is implicitly so, reminding us of Pater's perception that Rossetti can sound 'almost like a believer in mesmerism' (Pater 1910, *App* 214). We might note, however, that the image of the woman's breath passing through her hand on to her lover's brow may allude to 'magnetic breathing', a technique known as 'insufflation', which Alex Owen describes as the 'most common type of contact' practised by mesmeric healers on the patient's body, and 'considered an important aspect of mesmeric healing . . . thought to increase the organism's vitality and . . . recommended as an antidote to the loss of life force' (Owen 1990, 129). This practice may also inform Shelley's image of the 'soul's breath'. However, while in Shelley's poem, the Lady's 'powers of life . . . may not blend' with those of the male sleeper, in Rossetti's poem, the male lover is directly looking for a communication of souls, wanting the words of what is presumably his lady's love song to be channelled through her assuaging hand into his spirit. He puns brilliantly on 'sense', evoking the actual 'meaning' of her song, his powers of understanding, and her touch. The song is thus especially 'touching', as physical intimacy apparently acting as a conduit to the spiritual becomes inseparable from it, or as Rossetti will put it in 'Heart's Hope':

For lo! in some poor rhythmic period,
Lady, I fain would tell how evermore
Thy soul I know not from thy body, nor
Thee from myself, neither our love from God.

(Rossetti 1911, 76)

In her essay 'Mesmerism and Agency in the Courtship of Elizabeth Barrett and Robert Browning', Alison Chapman states that it was 'reported as extremely common for the patient in a trance to be in sympathy with the mesmerist's physical and even emotional sensations. Such a phenomenon was widely reported and termed as "en rapport"' (Chapman 1999, 305). In corroboration she cites William Gregory's *Animal Magnetism* (1877):

> The sleeper acquires the power of perceiving every sensation, bodily and otherwise, of his mesmerist . . . Indeed there appears to be no difference between the two. He feels what is felt by the person *en rapport* with him, as truly as if the original impressions were made upon himself. He forms, for the time, a part of the person on whom the direct impressions are made, and all sensations, or many sensations, are common to both parties.
>
> (Gregory, cited in Chapman 1999, 305)

Such a community of physical sensation and spiritual perception also seems to exist in Rossetti's poem, although it is debatable whether all sensations and perceptions have their origin in the woman. Rossetti rather implies a blending or reciprocal exchange. We assume the 'soul' mentioned in 'Song and Music' to be the speaker's, but, of course, it could also be the beloved's, or even the couple's joint soul. Through the singer's physical contact with the speaker, and her tactile communication of her song, his soul, her soul, or their joint soul, will 'better understand' or intuit the deeper meaning of the song, even when it is over. Like Shelley's poem, Rossetti's is deeply synaesthetic: music is felt through touch, and touch perhaps may even be enhanced by colour or 'rosy shade'. There is that blending of the senses which induces a spiritual effect, with the senses being those of both parties. As the woman's song links the bodies of the couple, the physical sensations of the speaker get mixed with those of his beloved:

The music lives upon my brain,
Between your hands, within mine eyes;
It stirs your lifted throat like pain,
An aching pulse of melodies.

While the music is channelled by the woman to the speaker, both might be able to feel a pulse beating in her covering hands or his covered eyes, which it would be hard confidently to ascribe to one or the other. This pulse becomes one with the 'aching pulse of melodies'. Moreover, is the speaker's perception that the song stirs his beloved's 'throat like pain' something that she actually feels or something that he feels for her? The 'aching pulse of melodies', the physical and emotional intensity of the song, seems to be felt by the heightened physical and mental consciousness of both of them.

The scholarly commentary on 'Song and Music' in the Rossetti hypertext archive says rather surprisingly that it 'is more an intellectual exercise than anything else'. In fact, like many short lyrical verses, the poem is concerned with the nature of lyric itself, something traditionally associated with mixed emotions such as mingled joy and pain (Maxwell 2001, 12, 31–2, 44–5). Indeed Rossetti's sonnet 'Transfigured Life' talks of how the singer's blended 'Joy' and 'Pain' are 'parents' to his 'Song' (Rossetti 1911, 94). The classical lyric poet Sappho (*c.* 630 BC) was celebrated for being the first to represent the emotional nature of relationships in her verse, with various of her poems – sung to the accompaniment of the lyre – dealing with the mixed emotions of love, which she famously describes as γλυκύπικρον (*glukupikron*) or 'bittersweet' (Maxwell 2001, 32). In the case of her poem now best known as Fragment 31, the mixed emotions of love present themselves as physical symptoms such as the feeling of being on fire, breaking into a sweat, the drumming of pulses, and a feeling of chill.[37] Rossetti's poem with its 'aching pulse of melodies' continues in that tradition, although, rather than the love symptoms being felt by the speaker alone, as is the case in Sappho's poem, both lover and beloved are here involved as they seem communicate their feelings magnetically to each other through touch. However, if we imagine, after the pattern of Sappho, the female singer as voicing an emotionally charged song, we might note that, true to a poetic tradition in which male poets re-voice Sappho, she is to a degree absorbed by the speaker, just as his own poem effectively absorbs her song.[38] Her song lies not just 'shadowed' in her assuaging hand, but vibrates still, shadowed or contained in the speaker's own music. Breathed through her hand on to his brow and into his 'brain', her song seems literally to 'inspire' his. Like Swinburne and Yeats, two other superb lyrical poets, Rossetti had no great feeling for actual music, his musicality expressing itself in his verse.[39] However, throughout his work we encounter the metaphor of music as a symbol for the harmonies of life, or for the ineffable nature of love, especially that communicated by the beloved woman. In the sonnet 'True Woman: I. Herself' (Sonnet 56, 1881) the beloved woman is described as 'a music ravishing / More than the passionate pulse of Philomel' (Rossetti 1911, 93), and it is this, her own superior 'passionate pulse', which Rossetti symbolically absorbs into his lyrical celebration of her.

37 See the recent acclaimed translation by Anne Carson (Carson 2002, 63).

38 Rossetti's translation of two fragments from Sappho, originally titled 'One Girl' and later 'Beauty (A Combination from Sappho)' (Rossetti 1911, 544), concluded his *Poems* (1870).

39 On Rossetti's 'indifference to music' see Dunn 1904, 28–9.

Clearly 'Song and Music' was significant to Rossetti as an early expression of the way in which the beloved exerts her inspiring and magnetic powers on her lover. Indeed he reprises the poem in his later sonnet 'Mid-rapture', Sonnet 26 in the 1881 *House of Life*. In this sonnet, where the beloved's gaze 'absorbs within its sphere / My worshipping face', we see the mixed sense impressions of the early lyric condensed and chiasmatically transposed into yet another level of figurative meaning. Thus the beloved's

voice attuned above
All modulation of the deep-bowered dove,
   Is like a hand laid softly on the soul;
   Whose hand is like a sweet voice to control
Those worn tired brows it hath the keeping of.

(Rossetti 1911, 83)

Her voice is like a hand that touches the soul, while her hand is like a voice that commands the body. Another *House of Life* sonnet that slides effortlessly between physical and spiritual registers is 'The Love-letter' (Sonnet 9, 1870; Sonnet 10, 1881), where the woman's loving presence is on this occasion felt as a pulse transmitted through her written words. The magnetic love-missive penned by the beloved absorbs and communicates her original sensory and tactile presence, and, through that, her soul:

Warmed by her hand and shadowed by her hair
   As close she leaned and poured her heart through thee,
   Whereof the articulate throbs accompany
The smooth black stream that makes thy whiteness fair, –
Sweet fluttering sheet, even of her breath aware, –
   Oh let thy silent song disclose to me
   That soul wherewith her lips and eyes agree
Like married music in Love's answering air.
Fain had I watched her when, at some fond thought,
   Her bosom to the writing closelier press'd,
   And her breast's secrets peered into her breast;
When, through eyes raised an instant, her soul sought
My soul, and from the sudden confluence caught
   The words that made her love the loveliest.

(Rossetti 1911, 78)

In 'Love-Lily', the first of the additional songs that accompanied *The House of Life* of 1870, the opening stanza associates the 'hands', 'brows', and 'lips' of the beloved with intense physical attraction, while the second stanza connects her 'voice', 'heart', and 'mind' with spiritual communion. The concluding stanza brings together all these attributes to underline how in true love these experiences are properly inseparable. Throughout the sonnets of *The House of Life*, there is particular emphasis on the woman's hands, lips, eyes, and voice as magnetic conductors of her saving and inspiring presence, even when they are represented in painting, as in 'Genius in Beauty' (Sonnet 18, 1881) which praises 'this sovereign face, whose love-spell breathes / Even from its shadowed contour on the wall' (Rossetti 1911, 80). This may also be the case in the sonnet 'Life-in-love' (Sonnet 15, 1870; Sonnet 36, 1881), which, in recent years, has received a good deal of attention for its possible multiple identities:

Not in thy body is thy life at all,
  But in this lady's lips and hands and eyes;
  Through these she yields thee life that vivifies
What else were sorrow's servant and death's thrall.
Look on thyself without her, and recall
  The waste remembrance and forlorn surmise
  That lived but in a dead-drawn breath of sighs
O'er vanished hours and hours eventual.

Even so much life hath the poor tress of hair
  Which, stored apart, is all love hath to show
  For heart-beats and for fire-heats long ago;
Even so much life endures unknown, even where,
  'Mid change the changeless night environeth,
  Lies all that golden hair undimmed in death.

(Rossetti 1911, 86)

As various commentators have observed, it is ambiguous who is signified by 'thy', 'thee', and 'thyself' – is this the poet-speaker, a former (dead) love, or a current love? Similarly, who is signified by 'this lady' and 'she' – the present or the former love?[40] The sestet with its allusion to the 'tress' of hair and the 'golden hair' that lies 'undimmed in death' also pushes the reader towards the biographical identity of the dead auburn-haired Elizabeth Siddal, whose body, when she was exhumed, was somewhat cryptically described as 'quite perfect'.[41] Such a manoeuvre inevitably then positions her against the later love, Jane Morris, whose presence may be understood as signalled in the preceding octave. As has also been noted, it is unclear whether the octave points us towards an actual woman or to paintings or drawings of her.

One side-effect of this visionary swirl of identities has been to lose sight of one of the most compelling statements of the beloved's power. Let us take it then that the poet-speaker addresses himself. The magnetic communication of the beloved woman clearly vivifies her lover, redeeming him from an impris-

40 McGann 2000, 52–3, lists the principal possibilities. Other critics who comment on this sonnet's ambiguities include Hersey 1986, 39, and Holmes 2005, 18.

41 For the exhumation and a gloss on Charles Howell's report that 'all in the coffin was found quite perfect' see Marsh 2005, 375. Hall Caine describes Rossetti showing him 'a long thick tress of rich auburn hair' (Caine 1990, 133).

oning and deadening bereavement. If we take it that she is also his muse and the subject of pictures he has made and now surveys, then she reinvigorates him, giving him new life through his art. The inspiring, soulful 'lips and hands and eyes' of the beloved – all features that have a characteristic expressiveness in Rossetti's pictures with the capacity to touch the viewer – when translated into his paintings, communicate her power channelled through his artistry, touching him repeatedly when he reviews his own work. The first three lines of the sestet effect a comparison between the speaker's former bereaved self and the relic of the tress. Lacking the beloved's inspiration, he would resemble the 'poor tress' of hair, a sad remnant of his former dead love and their long-ago once-passionate romance. Yet the last three lines effect a more positive comparison, allowing for the possibility that just as he now is 'vivified' or has a new life, just so much life may 'endure unknown' for the dead love, whose encoffined golden hair tellingly bears no sign of corruption.

Rossetti will return to the theme of inspiration and deeply felt emotion in his sonnet 'The Song-throe' which, as Sonnet 61, follows 'Transfigured Life' in *The House of Life* (1881). Here addressing the Singer, he declares that all truly moving song must arise from the speaker's own emotional pain: 'By thine own tears thy song must tears beget' (Rossetti 1911, 95). Hall Caine in his *Recollections of Rossetti* recalls the poet reading to him from the 'new sonnets' of the 1881 *House of Life*, and noticing how on several occasions 'the emotion of the written words had broken up his voice' (Caine 1990, 53). A 'throe' is a spasm of pain that convulses the body or the mind, being physical, or emotional, or both simultaneously. In 'The Song-throe', Apollo, god of poetry, 'Song-god' as well as 'Sun-god', does not serve but pursues the poet:

> The Song-god – He the Sun-god – is no slave
>   Of thine: thy Hunter he, who for thy soul
>   Fledges his shaft: to no august control
> Of thy skilled hand his quivered store he gave:
> But if thy lips' loud cry leap to his smart,
> The inspir'd recoil shall pierce thy brother's heart.
>
> (Rossetti 1911, 95)

Just as Cupid's dart arouses love, Apollo's arrow inflicts poetry, with 'inflicts' being the key word. The shock of being wounded makes the poet recoil so that the arrow glances aside to find and wound another victim. Poetry is worthy of the name only if it makes the poet feel his pain, this being the sign that it will move others.

Although the imagery is explicitly of arrows and wounding, the chain of affect and inspiration here reminds one of the magnetic chain of poetic inspiration presented by Plato's Socrates in the *Ion*. Starting with an image of physical magnetism, Socrates then moves to a metaphorical application:

> For this stone not only attracts iron rings, but also imparts to them a power whereby they in turn are able to do the same thing as the stone . . . In the same manner also the Muse inspires men herself, and then by means of these inspired persons the inspiration spreads to others, and holds them in a connected chain.
> (Plato 1962, 421)[42]

Magnetised by the beloved woman or by other mesmerising female forces, Rossetti endeavours to pass on the experience. His ideal readers are wounded by what wounds him, are drawn and attracted by what draws and attracts him. This magnetic attraction and communication are typically expressed and experienced through a language at once physical and emotional. We saw the loaded use of the word 'sense' in 'Song and Music', a use that recurs in the sestet of 'Heart's Hope', where, as proof of his feelings, the speaker wants to produce from his heart

> such evidence
> As to all hearts all things shall signify;
> Tender as dawn's first hill-fire, and intense
> As instantaneous penetrating sense,
> In Spring's birth-hour, of other Springs gone by.
> (Rossetti 1911, 76)

Here 'intense', 'instantaneous', and 'penetrating' immediately give us the vigorous thrust of a physical sensation, which then unexpectedly opens out into the pathos of an emotional memory or recollection. 'Tender', too, has various physical applications such as 'young, newborn', while in terms of visual sensation it suggests hues that are pale, soft-tinted, or blush-coloured. It also hints at physical and emotional sensitivity or vulnerability. Such tender meanings are common throughout Rossetti's work. Like 'throe' and 'sense' is 'pang', a word used in the early sonnet 'For *An Allegorical Dance of Women* by Andrea Mantegna (In the Louvre)':

> Scarcely, I think; yet it indeed *may* be
> The meaning reached him, when this music rang
> Clear through his frame, a sweet possessive pang,
> And he beheld these rocks and that ridged sea.
> But I believe that, leaning tow'rds them, he
> Just felt their hair carried across his face
> As each girl passed him; nor gave ear to trace
> How many feet; nor bent assuredly
> His feet from the blind fixedness of thought

42 'The Song-throe' was composed in April 1880. Rossetti may possibly have known the *Ion*, from Benjamin Jowett's translation *The Dialogues of Plato* (1871; 2nd ed., 1875). See Plato 1875, 1.237–57; 247.

> To know the dancers. It is bitter glad
> Even unto tears. Its meaning filleth it,
> A secret of the wells of Life: to wit: –
> The heart's each pulse shall keep the sense it had
> With all, though the mind's labour run to nought.
>
> (Rossetti 1911, 188–9)

Richard Stein identifies the painting as Mantegna's *Parnassus* (*Mars et Vénus dit le Parnasse*, 1497) from the Louvre, and the 'he', the spectator, as the Mercury who stands beside the winged horse Pegasus to the right of the scene (Stein 1975, 137). But Mercury seems more interested in gazing at his winged companion. The 'he' is more likely to represent the artist, imagined as he beheld the visionary scene that became his painting. He stands in as proxy for Rossetti and the reader, mediating the experience as we enter that scene through his notional visionary gaze. In his editorial commentary William Michael Rossetti reproduces a note his brother wrote for the original 1850 publication in *The Germ*: 'It is necessary to mention that this picture appears to have been, in the artist's mind, an allegory, which the modern spectator may seek vainly to interpret' (Rossetti 1911, 665). Although the sonnet title tells us that the painting depicts an allegorical dance, the sonnet itself refuses to decipher the allegory, concentrating rather on the imaginative impact of the scene. The scene may have communicated an intellectual meaning to the artist as viewer, but the speaker prefers to believe that the primary means of communication was sensory and intuitive. The viewer is magnetically drawn to what he sees and absorbed by it.

Unsurprisingly at the visionary heart of this scene is a spectacle centred on women. As in 'Song and Music', which featured a mesmerising female singer, the viewer is entranced, hypnotised by the movement of graceful women who dance to music. Gazing on these mesmeric dancers, he does not try to identify them but drinks it all in, narcotically suspended in 'the blind fixedness of thought'. If the intellectual meaning of the scene strikes him at all, it happens instantly when the scene first dawns on his sight and when the 'music rang / Clear through his frame, a sweet possessive pang'. Similar to a throe, a 'pang' is a sudden sharp spasm of pain that pierces or shoots through the body or mind. If so affected, the viewer would be suddenly possessed by the intellectual meaning of the allegory in a manner more akin to physical sensation and epiphanic revelation. Moreover, a 'sweet possessive pang' sounds reminiscent of orgasm in intercourse, as if for the artist, as for the imaginative viewer or reader, intellectual meaning should be more like the erotic knowing of a sexual partner, something communicated or conferred by an intense all-immersing experience rather than by a coolly calculated act of decipherment. As the speaker tells us in the last five lines of the sonnet, the scene's meaning cannot be detached from its constituents but instead saturates them: 'Its meaning filleth it, / A secret of the wells of Life'. When Rossetti tells us that this secret meaning is 'bitter glad / Even unto tears', he reminds us of Sappho's influential oxymoronic description of erotic love as 'bittersweet'. Thus we should not be surprised when we finally we encounter again Rossetti's key word 'sense', signifying an ineradicable physical and intuitive knowledge, which is absorbed by the body and the memory, and is opposed to purposeless speculation and analysis: 'The heart's each pulse shall keep the sense it had / With all, though the mind's labour run to nought.' For Rossetti, creativity is a kind of knowledge best compared with erotic knowledge, which is why it is communicated in the magnetic, simultaneously spiritual and physical language of love.

As in Socrates' metaphor of the magnetic transmission of inspiration, such creative knowledge is contagious. If, as suggested, the sonnet proposes Mantegna as the first viewer of this scene, 'frame' refers both to his own body and to his painting, which communicates the substance of his vision, even its 'unheard music', to others. The artist's notional vision is taken up by Rossetti, who enacts it in his sonnet, passing it on to his readers. One reader who clearly absorbed it was Yeats, whose poem 'Her Vision in the Wood', from *A Woman Young and Old* (1929), integrates elements of Rossetti's scene into its verse.[43] In this altogether darker erotic fable, Yeats's visionary female spectator sees 'bodies from a picture or a coin', who shoulder 'a litter with a wounded man':

All stately women moving to a song
With loosened hair or foreheads grief-distraught,
It seemed a Quattrocento painter's throng,
A thoughtless image of Mantegna's thought.

(Yeats 1982, 312–13)

The mangled body on the litter is revealed as the woman's former lover and, in the gaze that he turns on her, she finds 'love's bitter-sweet had all come back' and realises the vision is no allegory: 'That they had brought no fabulous symbol there / But my heart's victim and its torturer'. Rossetti's dancers, here translated into 'stately women moving to a song', must also have been attractive to Yeats, who would make the figure of the self-absorbed dancer into what Kermode calls the 'Romantic Image' and an icon for literary Modernism.

Erotic knowledge and the artist's creative knowledge fuse once more in 'The Portrait' from *The House of Life* (Sonnet 9 1870; Sonnet 10, 1881), where the artist is once more a magnetiser:

O Lord of all compassionate control,
  O Love! let this my lady's picture glow
  Under my hand to praise her name, and show

43 Kermode briefly signals the link between these two poems in his *Romantic Image* (Kermode 1986, 62).

Even of her inner self the perfect whole:
That he who seeks her beauty's furthest goal,
  Beyond the light that the sweet glances throw
  And refluent wave of the sweet smile, may know
The very sky and sea-line of her soul.

Lo! it is done. Above the enthroning throat
  The mouth's mould testifies of voice and kiss,
    The shadowed eyes remember and forsee.
Her face is made her shrine. Let all men note
  That in all years (O Love, thy gift is this!)
    They that would look on her must come to me.

(Rossetti 1911, 78)

At first sight we might well assume that the 'glow' is the natural radiance of the woman's soul, as in 'True Woman: I. Herself' (Sonnet 56, 1881) – 'her soul's purest depth and loveliest glow' (Rossetti 1911, 93). We might also assume that the speaker wants the 'glow' of the woman's inspiring presence to illuminate his picture of her, which we primarily imagine as a painting but which is also his verse portrait. However, the sonnet makes it clear that he hopes her 'glow' will be conjured by his hand, which, as it writes or paints his subject, not only magnetically illuminates her but also caressingly confers an erotically animating warmth and bliss. The lover's hand that has known and touched her, should, when it is engaged on her portrait, arouse or startle her image into life, infusing it with intimate knowledge. Thus, for example, when successfully executed, 'The mouth's mould testifies of voice and kiss'. It is this fusion of erotic and artistic knowledge that will enable the artist to present 'Even of her inner self the perfect whole'. Ideally the viewer will see beyond the superficial sweetness of physical detail into the impressive vista of her spirit: 'The very sky and sea-line of her soul'.

While the magnetic woman is the original inspiring agent who imprints herself on her lover's creative consciousness, it is his magnetised creative agency, made effective by Love, that will pass her presence on to future viewers and readers. This is why the sonnet is addressed to Love and not directly to the lady. Love's gift is twofold: firstly, that the speaker becomes the guardian and transmitter of her ideal image, which he can then communicate to future generations – 'They that would look on her must come to me'; secondly, that his image alone carries his unrivalled lover's knowledge of her as body and soul. A simple photographic image, for example, would not be able to communicate the same kind of intimate soul-revealing knowledge. But by inference the portrait reveals the artist's soul too, something implicit in the conclusion to the sonnet. The apparent narcissism of the last line, partly mitigated by a full understanding of 'Love's gift', is made more explicable by the fact that the portrait brings together artist and subject, an identification that will become even stronger when both are dead.

The sonnet 'Threefold Homage', written three years later in 1871 and recently included in Appendix Eight of Roger Lewis's excellent new edition of *The House of Life* (1881), is a related poem which also speculates on what the speaker hopes to transmit to subsequent readers and viewers. This sonnet, however, is more modestly tentative in its claims:

Was I most born to paint your sovereign face,
  Or most to sing it, or most to love it, dear?
  Full sweet the hope that unborn eye and ear
Through me may guess the secret of your grace.
Yet ah! neath every picture might I trace,
  And note beside each song, – 'Let none think here
  To breathe indeed this beauty's atmosphere,
To apprehend this body and soul's embrace.'

Faint shadow of you at best I weave, except
  That innermost image all unseen, which still
Proves me at heart your beauty's crowned adept.
  Yet was this nought, our hope's high day to fill, –
  That o'er us, while we kissed, with answering thrill,
Two Muses held Love's hand, and smiled, and wept?

(Rossetti 2007, 292)

Addressing his beloved, the speaker wonders whether he best pays her homage through painting, poetry, or the love that he bears her. Although the hope is that future generations 'Through me may guess the secret of your grace', he knows that his paintings and poems will always fall short of her ideal. Crucially viewers and readers are debarred from a truly intimate knowledge of the beloved and should not believe that in these works inspired by her they actually see 'this body and soul's embrace'. By implication it is only he who has this vital eroticised knowledge of her, which he is unable and perhaps even reluctant to pass on. For while his best outward representations of her are but 'Faint shadow' of her reality, the private image he holds of her in his heart distinguishes him as the artist who does full justice to her beauty. None the less referring back to the 'sweet hope' of line 3, he ends by wistfully recalling the special promise of their love, which, when first born, seemed consecrated by Love's partnership with the Muses of poetry and painting – that is, a great romance destined to be immortalised in picture and in song.

The ambition of the speaker seems to be that one day he will be able to translate 'That innermost image all unseen' into his art, yet at the same time the achievement of this sonnet seems to lie in that visionary unseen image which becomes precious in proportion to the extent that it is held back, kept private, not given to our view. Resisting the ostensible drive towards public recognition, 'That innermost image all unseen' representative of the intimate communication between lover and beloved, is withheld from us, while none the less functioning as a hypnotic focus, which gives the poem its appeal. As we shall see in Chapter 5, this privacy, which allures us by being out of reach, is more characteristic of the visionary tactics of another poet, Thomas Hardy. However, here 'That innermost image all unseen', which draws our gaze, is the heart-held source of the eroticised knowledge and inspirational power that gives Rossetti's love poetry its magnetic energy, its enduring capacity to draw the unborn eye and ear.

2

Walter Pater's 'strange veil of sight'

> Through Leonardo's strange veil of sight things reach him so.
>
> (Pater 1980, *Ren* 87)

No one, I think, would deny that, like Florian Deleal, his youthful counterpart in 'The Child in the House' (1878), that semi-autobiographical essay he called 'the germinating, original, source, specimen, of all my *imaginative* work' (Pater 1970, xxix), Pater possessed 'a passionateness in his relation to fair outward objects, an inexplicable excitement in their presence' (Pater 1910, *MS* 186). Yet his visual presentation of those 'fair outward objects' is anything but straightforward. His all-important sense of the material world and our relation to it can be found in the famous Conclusion to *The Renaissance*, which originally appeared as the second half of a review, 'Poems by William Morris', published anonymously in the *Westminster Review* in 1868.[1] The Conclusion presents in its first two paragraphs two separate examples of 'modern thought', both of which have an impact on our understanding of the object world. The Greek epigraph, which translates as 'Heraclitus says "All things are in motion and nothing at rest"' (Pater 1980, *Ren* 186, 451), suggests that both views can be seen as modern variants of the Heraclitean idea of perpetual flux.[2] In the first, which relays the scientific view of our physical life, all material objects, especially our own bodies, are in a constant state of flux as they are composed and eventually decomposed by the forces of change. In the second paragraph, which deals with the sceptical speculations of modern relativist philosophy, Pater examines the 'inward world of thought and feeling' where mental forces

1 'Poems by William Morris', *Westminster Review* 34 (October 1868), 300–12. For a useful modern reprint of this article see Pater 1974b, 105–17. All references to the Conclusion are to *The Renaissance* (Pater 1980, *Ren*).

2 The epigraph, a saying of the philosopher Heraclitus (*c.* 535–475 BC), is repeated by Socrates in Plato's *Cratylus*, 402A. Pater's editor, Donald L. Hill, uses the translation of his Oxford contemporary, Benjamin Jowett (Pater 1980, *Ren* 451). According to Heraclitus, all things are in a perpetual state of flux, being differentiations produced by strife of a single mobile principle – fire.

acts out a similar process: 'external objects' seem to press 'upon us with a sharp importunate reality . . . But when reflexion begins to play upon [them] they are dissipated under its influence; the cohesive force seems suspended like some trick of magic; each object is loosed into a group of impressions – colour, odour, texture – in the mind of the observer' (Pater 1980, *Ren* 187). As Billie Andrew Inman and Carolyn Williams have persuasively argued, Pater should not be understood as necessarily endorsing both or either of these views (Inman 1981; Williams 1989). Williams explains that 'in the "Conclusion" Pater briefly but painstakingly outlines the material and epistemological conclusions drawn by "modern thought," and then he devotes the full force of his rhetorical, figurative, and philosophical energies to proposing an alternative stance. His formulation of aestheticism is that alternative stance.' She also remarks that Pater's Aestheticism 'can be fully understood only if we see it in its role as a dialectical response, operating both within and against the forces he outlines' (Williams 1989, 12, 13).

Pater's antidote to the depressing views of modern science and philosophy is to develop a strategy of compensation. He doesn't attempt to refute the two positions he has outlined, but he refuses to allow either of them to dictate a *modus vivendi*. Against the deductions of modern science and sceptical philosophy he pits his own innate and deeply felt sense of the beauty he finds in the physical world. Later he will restate his own position in the person of his hero Marius in his novel *Marius the Epicurean* (1885) who similarly rebels against the stranglehold of sceptical philosophy:

> Conceded that what is secure in our existence is but the sharp apex of the present moment between two hypothetical eternities, and all that is real in our experience but a series of fleeting impressions . . . then, he, at least, in whom those fleeting impressions – faces, voices, impressions – were very real and imperious, might well set himself to the consideration, how such actual moments as they passed might be made to yield their utmost, by the most dexterous training of capacity.
> (Pater 1910 *ME* 1.146; 1985, 117)[3]

The second half of the Conclusion takes up the theme of movement from its opening paragraphs, along with certain other key images, to fight fire with fire. Modern, sceptical, relativist philosophy brings disillusionment, but any philosophy worth living by should enliven our existence. It is the task of the individual subject in the short time he has available to rouse himself, to be alert and attentive to those privileged moments in the ever-evolving passage of life in which the beauty of form perfects itself. His full participation in these moments of beauty temporarily sets him free from the trammels of existence,

3 References are to 1910 Library edition followed by Michael Levey's 1985 Penguin Classics edition of the novel.

and it is his business to seek out as many of these moments as possible; thus he should be careful not to become habituated to certain kinds of experience nor to be guided by any narrow creed or system of thought which sets limitations upon him. Art, an especially concentrated form of perceptual experience dwelling on the beauty of form, is particularly satisfying. The 'love of art for its own sake' is one of few passions guaranteed to provide the 'fruit of a quickened, multiplied consciousness'. 'While all melts under our feet', and against the blaze of the all-devouring Heraclitean bonfire, the individual must grasp at every opportunity to get 'as many pulsations as possible into the given time'; he must cultivate his own intense light of heightened perception and, famously, 'burn with this hard, gem-like flame' (Pater 1980, *Ren* 189–90).

While art has the capacity to stay the moment and present seemingly eternal lovely forms for our attention, art objects themselves, like the material world around them, are dynamic both in their creation and in their effects, being, as the Preface to *The Renaissance* proposes, 'receptacles of so many powers or forces', or, to use the words of the Conclusion, examples of a 'focus where the greatest number of vital forces unite in their purest energy' (Pater 1980, *Ren* xix, 188). Moreover, the Preface, with its famous distortion of Matthew Arnold's precept, makes it evident that that it is the individual's own 'impression' of the art object and not the object in itself that is important to Pater:

> 'To see the object as in itself it really is,' has been justly said to be the aim of all true criticism whatever; and in æsthetic criticism the first step towards seeing one's object as it really is, is to know one's own impression as it really is, to discriminate it, to realise it distinctly. The objects with which æsthetic criticism deals – music, poetry and accomplished forms of human life – are indeed receptacles of so many powers or forces: they possess, like the products of nature, so many virtues or qualities. What is this song or picture, this engaging personality presented in a life or in a book, to *me*? Does it give me pleasure? And if so, what sort or degree of pleasure? How is my nature modified by its presence, and under its influence? (Pater 1980, *Ren* xix–xx)[4]

Subjected to analysis, art objects, those complex gatherings of energies, can be further dissolved into what the aesthetic critic sees as their constituent 'virtues or qualities', or made the focus of his own webs of association and impression (Pater 1980, *Ren* xix). This goes some way to explaining why Pater issued *Studies in the History of the Renaissance* (1873), five of whose original ten essays consider named Renaissance artists and a major critic of Hellenic sculpture, with no illustrations, including as the frontispiece in the second and successive editions one minor drawing of doubtful provenance, supposedly by Leonardo.[5]

4 For Arnold's precept 'To see the object as in itself it really is' see 'On Translating Homer' (1861) and 'The Function of Criticism at the Present Time' (1865).

Pater's own impressionistic descriptions of art objects, of which the Mona Lisa is the most famous and the most extreme example, give us not documentary accounts of paintings and sculptures but rather a suggestive imagery that evokes his mood or feeling, an imagery that vies with, estranges, replaces or distorts the familiar or recognisable image we might expect to see. Thus Camille Paglia writes of Pater's 'obscuring of the visible just when we eagerly turn toward it' (Paglia 1991, 482) while Adam Phillips observes 'Once the critic begins to realize his impression the object might begin to disappear' (Phillips 1986, xvi).

Certainly, reading Pater's *Renaissance*, we often are aware that the evident visual content of a picture is undercut or overtaken by some strange subliminal energy, which wells up disturbing the surface imagery, and the reader is directed to look elsewhere, to look beyond the immediate images. Thus Botticelli, for example, 'if he painted religious incidents, painted them with an under-current of original sentiment, which touches you as the real matter of the picture through the veil of its ostensible subject' (Pater 1980, *Ren* 39). In Leonardo's painting of St John the Baptist, 'We recognise one of those symbolical inventions in which the ostensible subject is used, not as matter for definite pictorial realisation, but as the starting-point of a train of sentiment, subtle and vague as a piece of music' (Pater 1980, *Ren* 93). Indeed Leonardo uses 'incidents of sacred story . . . as a cryptic language for fancies all his own' (Pater 1980, *Ren* 97).

One might also notice, rather surprisingly, in a writer so much associated with sensory relations, that there is also a distinct pull towards the visionary and the unseen. Even in the Greeks, who seem so much concerned with the visible world, Pater declares that 'we detect in that primitive life . . . a certain mystical apprehension, now almost departed, of unseen powers beyond the material veil of things'. Indeed, 'the religious imagination of the Greeks' welds together 'the whole range of man's experiences of a given object, or series of objects – all their outward qualities, and the visible facts regarding them – all the hidden ordinances by which those facts and qualities hold of unseen forces, and have their roots in purely visionary places' (Pater 1910, *GS* 20, 29). The visionary tendency is also present in major Renaissance artists and thinkers: Pico della Mirandola 'explains the grades or steps by which the soul passes from the love of a physical object to the love of unseen beauty, and unfolds the analogies between this process and other movements upward of human thought' (Pater 1980, *Ren* 36); Botticelli is 'a visionary painter, and in his visionariness he resembles Dante . . . the genius of which Botticelli is the type usurps the

5 The third edition (1888) of *The Renaissance* adds the essay on 'The School of Giorgione', first published in the *Fortnightly Review* in October 1877. For more comments on the drawing, referred to in the essay on Leonardo as 'a face of doubtful sex, set in the shadow of its own hair' (Pater 1980, *Ren* 90), see Donoghue 1995, 68.

data before it as the exponent of ideas, moods, visions of its own' (Pater 1980, *Ren* 41–2); while Michelangelo 'is always pressing forward from the outward beauty – *il bel del fuor che agli occhi piace*, to apprehend the unseen beauty; *trascenda nella forma universale* – that abstract form of beauty, about which the Platonists reason' (Pater 1980, *Ren* 69). Poets, too, can manifest a visionary intensity that melts away the purely visible world. In *Appreciations*, we learn that, for Wordsworth,

> as he dwelt upon those moments of profound, imaginative power, in which the outward object appears to take colour and expression, a new nature almost, from the prompting of the observant mind, the actual world would, as it were, dissolve and detach itself, flake by flake, and he seemed to be the creator, and when he would the destroyer, of the world in which he lived.
>
> (Pater 1910, *App* 55)

At other times, the thought of 'a spirit of life in outward things . . . lifted him above the furrow, above the green turf of the Westmoreland churchyard, to a world altogether different in its vagueness and vastness, and the narrow glen was full of the brooding power of one universal spirit' (Pater 1910, *App* 56).

Pater seems to suggest that this visionary faculty is endemic in certain kinds of contemporary writing. In 'Æsthetic Poetry', included only in the first edition of *Appreciations* (1889), we learn that the new phenomenon of 'æsthetic poetry' (originally the poetry of William Morris, but here perhaps more generally the world of Pre-Raphaelite poetry) refers to 'no actual form of life'.[6] If all other poetry 'projects above the realities of its time, a world in which the forms of things are transfigured', then 'Of that transfigured world this new poetry takes possession, and sublimates beyond it another still fainter and more spectral, which is literally an artificial "earthly paradise." It is a finer ideal, extracted from what in relation to any actual world is already an ideal' (Pater 1889, 213; 1974a, 190). In a later essay on Dante Gabriel Rossetti (1883), Pater decides that 'his characteristic, his really revealing work, lay in the adding to poetry of fresh new poetic material, of a new order of phenomena, in the creation of a new ideal' (Pater 1910, *App* 218). Prose, too, can manifest the visionary impulse. Pater's own novel *Marius the Epicurean* is set in the reign of the Emperor Marcus Aurelius in the second century AD, but its meditative protagonist wrestles with religious and philosophical questions relevant to the late nineteenth century and close to its author's heart. In his novel Pater revisits the

6 Originally the first half of the review 'Poems by William Morris' (1868), 'Æsthetic Poetry' was printed in a revised form in the first edition of *Appreciations* (1889), 213–27, but dropped in subsequent editions and not reinstated in the 1910 Library edition. For references to 'Æsthetic Poetry', I have used the 1889 text followed by its reprint in Pater 1974a. For the earlier 'Poems by William Morris' text see 1974b.

language and imagery of the Conclusion, as can be seen in the chapter titled 'The Will as Vision', when Marius experiences an epiphanic 'privileged hour' in which 'The purely material world, that close, impassable prison-wall, seemed just then the unreal thing, to be actually dissolving away all around him' (Pater 1985, 212; 1910, *ME* 2.70). And in his essay 'Style' (1888), which focuses on prose writing, Pater keeps gesturing towards the 'vision within' (Pater 1910, *App* 9, 10, 23, 29, 36) and 'that other world the mind sees so steadily within' (Pater 1910, 31).

The 'sensible imagination'[7]

It is the contention of this chapter that, although Pater is deeply invested in the visible world and visible objects, the visual field or web of his writing is complicated by an inwoven visionary layer or 'strange veil of sight' which consists of precipitated traces of abstract things given a fleeting spectral materiality. At its most elementary level this is a bodying-out of abstract things or processes in order to make them vivid and intelligible. Just so, Florian in 'The Child in the House', relishing 'beautiful physical things', finds that he needs 'a sensible vehicle or occasion' to make abstractions real to him:

> In later years he came upon philosophies which occupied him much in the estimate of the proportion of the sensuous and the ideal elements in human knowledge, the relative parts they bear in it; and, in his intellectual scheme, was led to assign very little to the abstract thought, and much to its sensible vehicle or occasion. Such metaphysical speculation did but reinforce what was instinctive in his way of receiving the world, and for him, everywhere, that sensible vehicle or occasion became, perhaps only too surely, the necessary concomitant of any perception of things, real enough to be of any weight or reckoning, in his house of thought. There were times when he could think of the necessity he was under of associating all thoughts to sight and touch, as a sympathetic link between himself and actual, feeling, living objects; a protest in favour of real men and women against mere grey, unreal abstractions.
>
> (Pater 1910, *MS* 186–7)

In a very simple and obvious way we see the tendency towards embodiment at work in the opening paragraphs of the Conclusion to *The Renaissance*. In describing the implications of 'modern thought' Pater imports a vivid illustrative imagery, giving essentially abstract processes a kind of poetic illustration. While, as Billie Inman has shown, some or indeed much of this imagery has its origins in scientific or philosophical sources (Inman 1981), Pater's language, cadences, and rhythms invest it with the metaphorical grace of poetry, liturgy, or scripture:

7 The phrase occurs in *Gaston de Latour* (Pater 1910, 151; 1995, 77).

Like the elements of which we are composed, the action of these forces extends beyond us; it rusts iron and ripens corn. Far out on every side of us those elements are broadcast, driven in many currents; and birth and gesture and death and the springing of the violets from the grave are but a few out of ten thousand resultant combinations. (Pater 1980, *Ren* 186)[8]

Or if we begin with the inward world of thought and feeling, the whirlpool is still more rapid, the flame more eager and devouring. There it is no longer the gradual darkening of the eye, the gradual fading of colour from the wall – movements of the shore-side, where the water flows down indeed, though in apparent rest – but race of the midstream, a drift of momentary acts of sight and passion and thought. (Pater 1980, *Ren* 187)

In Pater's writing, ideas, concepts, abstractions, accounts of mental processes have a visual imagery or visible presentation of their own. One suspects this presentation is immediate, that the relevant images arose naturally in Pater's mind as he thought about abstractions. Such images arise in the earliest of his known writings, the short essay 'Diaphaneitè', apparently given as a paper to the Old Mortality Society in February 1864, but not published until after Pater's death, when his friend Charles Shadwell collected it in the posthumous *Miscellaneous Studies* (1895). 'Diaphaneitè' describes Pater's notion of the ideal character, a subject that intrigued him throughout his life, as he endeavoured to isolate, name, and analyse the dominant characteristics in the artists and writers he studied. What one notices in this early essay where he tries to identify this 'rare' and 'precious' type is the way in which this elusive character acquires a faint but determinable visible presence, even though Pater seems to situate it on the borders of vision by using images of transparency and white light. Indeed 'diaphaneitè', a word Denis Donoghue identifies as coming into French in the fourteenth century and English in the seventeenth, means 'the state of being pervious to light' (Donoghue 1995, 110).[9] Although one of the 'higher forms of inward life', the diaphanous character has an 'entire transparency of nature' which means that 'as he comes nearer and nearer to perfection, the veil of an outer life not simply expressive of the inward becomes thinner and thinner' (Pater 1910, *MS* 250, 251, 249). Moreover the translucent image of the crystal, a favourite Paterian image of purity, appears here for the

8 The image of the violets springing from the grave is, of course, in any case poetic, deriving from Shakespeare's *Hamlet* and Laertes's words at Ophelia's grave: 'Lay her i' th' earth, / And from her fair and unpolluted flesh / May violets spring' (Donald Hill's commentary in Pater 1980, 454).

9 As Anne Varty points out, the grave accent on Pater's use of the word suggests that it is not French but Greek. Transliterated into ancient Greek, 'it assumes the form of a second-person plural imperative verb: "[You shall] become transparent!' or "shine through!" This reinforces the sense of the essay as a manifesto or imperative command for the future' (Varty 1991, 258, note 2).

first time in the mention of 'this clear crystal nature' (Pater 1910, *MS* 253). Yet other images in the essay suggest that the diaphanous character can be thought of as some kind of beautiful, buried, classical artefact, brought to the surface and to view by chance: 'It is like the reminiscence of a forgotten culture'; 'Such a character is like a relic from the classical age, laid open by accident to our alien modern atmosphere. It has something of the clear ring, the eternal outline of the antique' (Pater 1910, *MS* 250, 251).

These last images are interesting for a number of reasons: in the first place because the image of the excavated classical relic is itself an emblem for the Renaissance, the subject of Pater's first monograph, and a period when, 'in the midst of a frozen world, the buried fire of ancient art rose up from under the soil' (Pater 1980, *Ren* 146) and a 'forgotten culture' was revived. The image of the classical relic thus forges a link between this early essay and *The Renaissance*, also hinting that the diaphanous character is himself a force for cultural rebirth, as in fact is suggested by the last sentence of 'Diaphaneitè': 'A majority of such [types] would be the regeneration of the world' (Pater 1910 *MS* 254). Secondly, as other critics have noted before, a number of key images and specific phrases from 'Diaphaneitè', including the images of the classical artefact, actually find their way into the essay on the eighteenth-century classicist Johann Winckelmann, first published in 1867 and afterwards included in *The Renaissance* (Roellinger 1965; Varty 1991). Thus Winckelmann 'seems to realise the fancy of the reminiscence of a forgotten knowledge', possesses the 'key to the understanding of the Greek spirit . . . in his own nature, itself like the relic of classical antiquity, laid open to our alien, modern atmosphere', while his sense of the classical tradition has 'the clear ring, the eternal outline, of the genuine antique' (Pater 1980, *Ren* 155, 175, 144). Winckelmann thus understands and appreciates classical culture because he himself partakes of its character. Finally, in its presentation of the classical relic or artefact as a symbol for the diaphanous character, 'Diaphaneitè' anticipates the focus in 'Winckelmann', and in other essays in *The Renaissance*, on sculpture, which Pater regards as the best artistic treatment of human form, and arguably, of pure form in itself. This last point is significant for we shall return later in this chapter to the issue of sculpture's handling of form and character.

Unsurprisingly then, in view of Pater's own use of visual symbols and metaphors for abstractions, this tendency is something he valued in others, finding a foundational historical source in the ancient Greeks for whom, he believes, it was a habitual and authentic form of expression. In 'The Myth of Demeter and Persephone', first published in 1876, Pater finds, that while for the most part, 'The personification of abstract ideas by modern painters or sculptors . . . [is] a mere transparent allegory, or figure of speech, which could please almost no one', there are instances, in Giotto, say, for example, or William Blake, which are more than mere symbolism, being 'a "survival" from a different age, with the whole mood of which this mode of expression was much more congruous than it is with ours'. This age is when the ancient Greek myth 'of Demeter and Persephone was first created', being a 'very poetical time', in which 'every impression men received of the action of powers without or within them suggested to them the presence of a soul or will, like their own – a person, with a living spirit, and senses, and hands, and feet' (Pater 1910, *GS* 98–100).

Pater is therefore always alert to manifestations of this form of genuine symbolic power in other writers and artists. Plato is the prime example of the individual who carries 'an elaborate cultivation of the bodily senses . . . into the world of intellectual abstractions; seeing and hearing there too, associating for ever all the imagery of things seen with the conditions of what primarily exists only for the mind, filling that "hollow land" with delightful colour and form' (Pater 1910, *PP* 139–40). Dante, too, has this gift, and, praising his highly particularised visual detail, Pater observes:

> the modern artist, the modern student of art, of Dante's art, while he demands it in any record of the external world, will value this minuteness, this minute perfection, even more perhaps in the treatment of mental phenomena, when the intelligence which touched so finely the niceties of visible colour and outline turns to the invisible world, noting there also with a like subtlety the intimacies of the soul.
>
> (Pater 1892, xviii–xix)

Of Dante Gabriel Rossetti, he writes, 'Like Dante, he knows no region of spirit which shall not be sensuous also, or material', observing elsewhere that his 'delight in concrete definition is allied with another of his conformities to Dante, the really imaginative vividness, namely, of his personifications – his hold upon them, or rather their hold upon him, with the force of a Frankenstein, when once they have taken life from him' (Pater 1910, *App* 213, 208).[10] In his essay 'Raphael' (1892), Pater praises the artist's 'transmission to others of complex and difficult ideas', explaining how 'By him theoretic conceptions are addressed, so to speak, to the intelligence of the eye', and commenting 'Plato, as you know supposed a kind of visible loveliness about ideas' (Pater 1910, *MS* 56, 57).

These writers and artists, like Pater himself, have a fluid sense of the relation of internal to external things and qualities. We have already seen how the transparency of the ideal diaphanous character allows what is inward to shine through or be easily traced through its ever-thinning 'veil of outer life'. At best, there is a perfect match or correspondence between inside and outside as the ideal character manifests itself transparently in the external world.

10 Pater here makes the common slip of confusing Mary Shelley's inventor Victor Frankenstein with his 'creature' or monster.

Alternatively images from the external world help embody abstract ideas. We also see that in 'Dante Gabriel Rossetti' Pater renders the internal/external binary in terms of 'spirit' and 'matter', and he goes on to tell us that 'Spirit and matter, indeed, have been for the most part opposed, with a false contrast or antagonism by schoolmen, whose artificial creation those abstractions really are. In our actual concrete experience, the two trains of phenomena which the words *matter* and *spirit* do but roughly distinguish, play inextricably into each other'. To Dante, the medieval precursor of Rossetti, 'in the vehement heat and impassioned heat of his conceptions, the material and the spiritual are fused and blent: if the spiritual attains the definite visibility of a crystal, what is material loses its earthiness and impurity. And here again, by force of instinct, Rossetti is one with him' (Pater 1910, *App* 212–13). Pater evidently relished this particular formulation as it recurs in *Plato and Platonism.* For Plato, 'as for Dante, in the impassioned glow of his conceptions, the material and the spiritual are blent and fused together. While, in that fire and heat, what is spiritual attains the definite visibility of a crystal, what is material, on the other hand, will lose its earthiness and impurity' (Pater 1910, *PP* 135). Notably the essay on Rossetti stresses as much the poet's ability to give material things a spiritual significance – 'lifeless nature . . . translated to a higher service, in which it does but incorporate itself with some phase of strong emotion' (Pater 1910, *App* 211), as it does his instinct to give spiritual ideas a material or physical presence, which is more the tendency of Plato, 'a seer who has a sort of sensuous love of the un-seen', who is the possessor of 'an instinctive imaginative power – a sort of *visual* power, but causing others also to see what is matter of original intuition for him' (Pater 1910, *PP* 143, 142).

Pater also intimates that Plato, Dante, and Rossetti share this characteristic of fusing material and spiritual by virtue of the fact that they all are or have been lovers (Pater 1910, *App* 212; *PP* 134–6), and thus 'associated themselves pre-eminently with the power and bloom of living persons' and a discipline which involves 'an exquisite culture of the senses' (Pater 1910, *PP* 134–5). Such cultivated lovers (of whom Plato is the leading type) naturally carry forward their highly developed sensibilities

> into the world of intellectual abstractions . . . as if now at last the mind were veritably dealing with living people there, living people who play upon us through the affinities, the repulsion and attraction, of *persons* towards one another, all the magnetism, as we call it, of actual human friendship or love:– There, is the *formula* of Plato's genius, the essential condition of the specially Platonic temper, of Platonism. And his style, because it really is Plato's style, conforms to, and in its turn promotes in others, that mental situation.
>
> (Pater 1910, *PP* 140)

Such a formula takes up Florian's 'protest in favour of real men and women against mere grey, unreal abstractions', by treating abstractions as if they were men and women.[11] One obvious example of this is Leonardo's Mona Lisa, who 'might stand as the embodiment of the old fancy, the symbol of the modern idea', the 'old fancy' being, as Pater has previously explained, 'the fancy of a perpetual life, sweeping together ten thousand experiences', while the 'modern idea' is 'the idea of humanity as wrought upon by, and summing up in itself all modes of thought and life' (Pater 1980, *Ren* 99). Pater, too, one suspects, classes himself as one of the lovers he describes – this perhaps accounting for the fact that, in his search for beauty in art and literature, he approaches it through named persons, artists, and authors, attempting in each encounter to gauge or determine each individual's particular character or personality.[12] Moreover, as we shall see, he on occasion also shows, like a lover, an erotic attraction to the fair forms or persons he writes about, or an erotic identification with them.

Pater recognises that, like Dante Gabriel Rossetti, outstanding artists such as Leonardo are capable of making material things spiritually significant. Thus the related images that illustrate 'Leonardo's type of womanly beauty', which Pater calls the 'Daughters of Herodias', possess 'all those finer conditions wherein material things rise to that subtlety of operation which constitutes them spiritual, where only the finer nerve and the keener touch can follow' (Pater 1980, *Ren* 91). Statements such as these elevate or spiritualise materiality, offering a view at odds with the Pater who is often conventionally understood as a mere sensate empiricist, revelling in a world of material objects.

'The Child in the House' offers a foundational account of how material things acquire spiritual resonance, as Pater brilliantly describes the way in which the child's emotionally charged, early impressions of material things become an integral part of 'the story of his spirit . . . that process of brain-building by which we are, each one of us, what we are.' The adult Florian finds

11 According to Pater, Robert Browning was 'one of my best-loved writers' (Pater 1970, 70). Notably *Men and Women* (1855) is the title of his most celebrated volume of poetry, possibly inspired by his second letter to Elizabeth Barrett (13 January 1845) and his outburst 'You speak out, *you*, – I only make men & women speak – give you truth broken into prismatic hues, and fear the pure white light, even if it is in me' (Kintner 1960, 1.7). Clearly Pater admired the way Browning made 'men & women speak' and body out complex moral, intellectual, and psychological ideas.

12 Significantly Pater makes two women only the actual subject matter of an essay, these two being his friends Vernon Lee and Mary Ward, although references to notable women authors such as Sappho, Margaret Cavendish (the Duchess of Newcastle), Madame de Staël, Emily Brontë, George Sand, and George Eliot can be found scattered throughout his essays. While there is an undoubted homoerotic element in Pater's attraction to his non-fictional male subjects, a number of whom – such as Michelangelo, Leonardo and Winckelmann – have evident homosexual tendencies, arguably these subjects are less interesting to him as biographical figures than as embodiments of certain ideas and forces.

that the remembered house in which he lived as a child becomes a container for, indeed part of, his nascent identity:

> In that half-spiritualised house he could watch the better, over again, the gradual expansion of the soul which had come to be there – of which indeed, through the law which makes material objects about them so large an element in children's lives, it had actually become a part; inward and outward being woven through and through each other into one inextricable texture – half, tint and trace of homely colour and form, from the wood and bricks; half, mere soul-stuff, floated thither from who knows how far.
>
> (Pater 1910, *MS* 173)

The child is in the house but the house is also inside the child, and he will carry it with him when he leaves its physical walls and makes his journey into the adult world.[13] This perhaps explains why Pater originally called the essay 'The House and the Child', and why in the essay on style, Pater can use the architectural image of house-building for the labour of the writer as he works on his composition, yet suddenly change his metaphor when he signifies the writer's completion of the task, so that 'The house he has built is rather a body he has informed' (Pater 1910, *App* 24). For Pater, house and body are to a certain degree interchangeable, both being domiciles for the informing soul, yet both bound up with and inextricable from it.

In 'Style', Pater, analysing the formation of the creative mind, again complicates the distinction between what is within or without, although he does hint at the priority of 'that other world within', clothed, as it then must be, in 'visible vesture' borrowed from the world without:

> Into the mind sensitive to 'form,' a flood of random sounds, colours, incidents, is ever penetrating from the world without, to become, by sympathetic selection, a part of its very structure, and, in turn, the visible vesture and expression of that other world it sees so steadily within, nay, already with a partial conformity thereto, to be refined, enlarged, corrected, at a hundred points.
>
> (Pater 1910, *App* 31)

Thus in addition to the substitutive imagery that Pater imports into the text when he describes art objects, the visual field of his writing is also infiltrated by the sometimes subliminal, sometimes overt, visual activity of metaphorised abstract processes, with these making another kind of demand on his reader's attention. But I also want to suggest that, over and above the more specific senses of symbolic realisation, embodiment, allegory, and personification, there are other less immediate, less concretely realised kinds of abstraction which have a kind of spectral presence in his texts, which none the less can be glimpsed, haunting the body of his writing. Time after time Pater seems to be

13 Pater's later male protagonists Marius, Emerald Uthwart, and Gaston de Latour are also shaped and informed by their passionate love of their childhood home.

trying to catch or arrest the elusive phantasm of an essence or the ghost of an abstraction. The phantasmal essence is something Pater looks for over and over again in his many analyses of artists and writers as he attempts to envisage in each case what he names 'character'. A closely related spectre is the ghostly abstraction sometimes glimpsed obliquely at the heart of the artist's actual work as a visionary creative power, but properly outside the field of ordinary vision. In order to try and gain some focus on these elusive topics, we begin at a place, which for Pater is already over-determined, that is to say the conceptual boundary line which marks one thing off from another, but which for Pater, so often, is permeable, a point of mergence and fusion.

Fusion and synthesis

In 'Coleridge' Pater tells us how, 'in modern times', the 'sciences of observation . . . reveal real types of life evanescing into each other by inexpressible refinements of change. Things pass into their opposites by accumulation of undefinable quantities' (Pater 1910, *App* 66; 1973, 2).[14] A little later, he remarks 'experience gives us, not the truth of eternal outlines ascertained once for all, but a world of fine gradations and subtly linked conditions, shifting intricately as we ourselves change' (Pater 1910, *App* 67–8; 1973, 2, with variant punctuation). We have already witnessed how Pater sees the fluid relation between what is internal and external, and criticises the 'false contrast or antagonism' between matter and spirit. Like Swinburne, one of his most important literary precursors, Pater has a habit of collapsing boundaries, of erasing the lines separating ideas and qualities commonly held to be distinct, even in some instances turning one thing into what looks like its opposite.[15] To give a few obvious examples: in the opening paragraphs of 'Style', Pater quickly dismantles the distinction between poetry and prose to concentrate on 'the literature of the imaginative sense of fact' (Pater 1910, *App* 8), while in the Postscript to *Appreciations*, originally titled 'Romanticism' (1876), where he explores the distinctions between the romantic and the classical character, he is at pains to point out that 'all critical terms are relative', and that what may start out romantic, 'after a very little while becomes classical in its turn' (Pater 1910, 258). Elsewhere he shows that what starts as 'classical' in the historical sense of the word, can become romantic. In 'Winckelmann', his growing dissatisfaction

14 'Coleridge', in *Appreciations*, revises and amalgamates two earlier essays on the poet dating from 1866 and 1880. As Pater overlaps here with 'Coleridge's Writings' published in the *Westminster Review* in January 1866, this is indicated by a reference to its 1973 reprint.

15 For critical analysis of Swinburne as a breaker of boundaries see Maxwell 2001, 193–207, and Maxwell 2006a, 20–6.

with the Arnoldian ideal of Greek life as a bright, untroubled joyousness means that, when he contrasts ancient Greek and later Christian cultures, he begins increasingly to bring them together to discover their shared interest in the '"worship of sorrow"', itself a 'preparation for the romantic temper' (Pater 1980, *Ren* 180, 178).[16] As Stefano Evangelista has shown, Pater's 'romantic Hellenism' means that he envisages Greek culture as already marked and mediated by the romantic imagination with its characteristic 'addition of strangeness to beauty' (Pater 1910, *App* 246).[17] And throughout Pater's work Christianity and the Hellenic and Roman religions have moments of *rapprochement*, linked as they are, he believes, by 'a universal pagan sentiment, a paganism which existed before the Greek religion, and has lingered far onward into the Christian world, ineradicable, like some persistent vegetable growth' (Pater 1980, *Ren* 160). In *Marius the Epicurean* the narrator remarks of 'the saint and the Cyrenaic lover of beauty', 'Carry their respective positions a point further, shift the terms a little, and they might actually touch', adding 'Perhaps all theories of practice tend, as they rise to their best, as understood by their worthiest representatives, to identification with each other' (Pater 1910, *ME* 2.20; 1985, 184).

Or, to take a major chronological example, no one can have failed to notice that Pater's idea of the Renaissance is remarkably elastic, stretching back to the French Middle Ages and forward to embrace the eighteenth-century German classicist Winckelmann (1717–68). Pater declares that his 'theory of a Renaissance within the middle age . . . heal[s] that rupture between the middle age and the Renaissance which has so often been exaggerated'. Such theories, he remarks, 'which bring into connexion with each other modes of thought and feeling, periods of taste, forms of art and poetry, which the narrowness of men's minds constantly tends to oppose to each other, have a great stimulus for the intellect, and are almost always worth understanding' (Pater 1980, *Ren* 2). Pater's justification for including Winckelmann is that his pioneering work on Greek sculpture continues the spirit of the Renaissance as a revival of classicism, but, as suggested above, his own romantic Hellenism accompanies and frames the views he attributes to Winckelmann. Pater's sense of the advantage to be gained by bringing disparate things into 'connexion' with each other is nicely clarified by Jeffrey Wallen, in his fine essay on *The Renaissance*, when he notices how

16 See Arnold's characterisation of 'early Greek genius' in his Preface to *Poems* (1853) as 'the calm, the cheerfulness, the disinterested objectivity' (Arnold 1979, 654). The phrase 'worship of sorrow', which Pater uses earlier in 'Winckelmann' without quotation marks (Pater 1980, 162), is originally Goethe's.

17 See Evangelista 2002 and 2003. See also Evangelista, *Aestheticism and the Greeks*, forthcoming.

> Throughout the book, Pater is fascinated by moments of contact and transmission, by possibilities of combination and reconciliation, and especially, by instances of re-vitalization. These moments let us enter into the experiences of others (by breaking the rigid frames of our contemporary world), or they let us bring together that which has been separated by our reified categories of understanding (the body and the intellect, the pagan and the Christian, the strange and the sweet), or they let us explain the borders between the living and the dead, the animated body and the corpse.
>
> (Wallen 1999, 1037)

The Paterian process of synthesis or unification has its own characteristic symbolism, or embodiment of this abstract process, manifested in a critical language borrowed from esoteric alchemy.[18] This language of dissolution, of dissolving, melting, fusing and blending, combined with images of purification and refinement, light and gold, can be seen throughout the essays that comprise *The Renaissance.* Dating from antiquity, alchemy is a process of refining base substances and unifying opposed elements in a *coniunctio* or 'marriage' to make an end product commonly identified either as gold or as a substance known as 'the Philosophers' Stone' with the power to transmute other things to gold.[19] Another miraculous substance produced by the process is the *Elixir Vitae*, or 'the Elixir of Life', believed to confer immortality. Lyndy Abraham writes, 'It is generally thought that the elixir and the philosopher's stone are the same essence, the elixir being in liquid form, the stone being in solid or powder form' (Abraham 1998, 147). The elaborate alchemic process is described in a heavily symbolic pictorial language that the would-be alchemist must master to achieve his goal. Esoteric or mystical alchemy is a spiritual and psychological process of refinement, which uses the pictorial and symbolic language as a spiritual text of self-discovery, and realises the end product of the process as the perfected self or soul. Pater borrowed his alchemical vocabulary from Swinburne (see Maxwell 2001, 209–10, and 2006a, 91–4) and from earlier Romantic writers such as Coleridge and Shelley, who used it to illustrate the process of refinement by which the literary artist turns or 'transmutes' raw materials into lasting imaginative creations. Both Swinburne and Pater undoubtedly share a debt to Shelley, whose 'A Defence of Poetry' (1820) provides one of the loveliest descriptions of literary alchemy. For Shelley, poetry enables the *coincidentia oppositorum*, the coming-together of opposites, which makes the successful fusion, *coniunctio*, *hieros gamos*, or 'sacred marriage':

18 In his discussion of Pater's 'chemical' metaphors of artistic creativity, Perry Meisel mentions 'alchemy' once (Meisel 1980, 55), but does not seem to register the extent to which the alchemical analogy permeates Pater's work.

19 The Latin is *lapis philosophorum* with the philosophers in the plural, but frequently rendered in English in the singular.

> Poetry thus makes immortal all that is best or most beautiful in the world . . . [It] turns all things to loveliness; it exalts the beauty of that which is most beautiful, and it adds beauty to that which is most deformed; it marries exultation and horror, grief and pleasure, eternity and change; it subdues to union under its light yoke all irreconcilable things. It transmutes all that it touches, and every form moving within the radiance of its presence is changed by wondrous sympathy to an incarnation of the spirit which it breathes; its secret alchemy turns to potable gold the poisonous waters which flow from death through life.
>
> (Shelley 1977, 505)[20]

Throughout Pater's work it is easy to see how many of his characterisations of artworks, artists, or key concepts are the distilled product of 'alchemic' marriages or syntheses. Paul Barolsky observes of Pater's most famous image: 'The Mona Lisa is the essential synthesis of antitheses. Nature and art, myth and history, body and soul, paganism and Christianity, all, she personifies life and death, eternity and change, combined in their total sweep' (Barolsky 1987, 36). Thus, too, Michelangelo, possessing 'a lovely strangeness', is 'sweetness and strength' and Leonardo, 'beauty and terror', or 'Curiosity and the desire for beauty' with that 'curiosity often in conflict with the desire of beauty' (Pater 1980, *Ren* 57, 82, 86). Both men then, are, like so many of Pater's favoured types, 'Romantic' artists *avant la lettre*, because, as the Postscript to *Appreciations* tells us, 'It is the addition of strangeness to beauty, that constitutes the romantic character in art; and the desire of beauty being a fixed element in every artistic organisation, it is the addition of curiosity to this desire of beauty, that constitutes the romantic temper' (Pater 1910, *App* 246). Notice how, following shortly after this characterisation of 'the romantic temper' in the Postscript, Pater refines upon it in an explicit alchemical metaphor that carries an echo of Shelley:

> With a passionate care for beauty, the romantic spirit refuses to have it, unless the condition of strangeness be first fulfilled. Its desire is for a beauty born of unlikely elements, by a profound alchemy, by a difficult initiation, by the charm which wrings it even out of terrible things; and a trace of distortion, of the grotesque, may perhaps linger, as an additional element of expression, about its ultimate grace.
>
> (Pater 1910, *App* 247–8)

In 'Demeter and Persephone', published in January and February 1876, the same year as 'Romanticism' (the Postscript to *Appreciations*), Pater wrote that

> the most important artistic monuments of that legend sufficiently prove that the Romantic spirit was really at work in the minds of Greek artists, extracting by a kind of subtle alchemy, a beauty, not without the elements of tranquillity, of dignity and order, out of a matter, at first sight painful and strange.
>
> (Pater 1910, *GS* 111)

20 See the very similar passage in Chapter 14 of Coleridge's *Biographia Literaria* (1817) in Coleridge 1975, 173–4.

Leonardo, perhaps the most 'Romantic' of Pater's Renaissance men, is himself explicitly pictured as an alchemist, the strong atmosphere of mystery which enshrouds this essay deriving in part from a sense that this artist had unrivalled occult knowledge and powers:

> Poring over his crucibles, making experiments with colour, trying, by a strange variation of the alchemist's dream, to discover the secret, not of an elixir to make man's natural life immortal, but of giving immortality to the subtlest and most delicate effects of painting, he seemed to them rather the sorcerer or the magician, possessed of curious secrets and a hidden knowledge, living in a world of which he alone possessed the key. What his philosophy seems to have been most like is that of Paracelsus or Cardan; and much of the spirit of the older alchemy still hangs about it, with its confidence in short cuts and odd byways to knowledge.
>
> (Pater 1980, *Ren* 84)[21]

And we have already seen how Plato, Dante, and Rossetti bring about a fusion in their work which, when examined, is evidently alchemical: 'in the vehement heat and impassioned heat of [their] conceptions, the material and the spiritual are fused and blent: if the spiritual attains the definite visibility of a crystal, what is material loses it earthiness and impurity' (Pater 1910, *App* 212). In the Postscript to *Appreciations*, Pater uses a similar image of heat, fusion, and purification, when he describes the

> born romanticists, who start with an original, untried *matter*, still in fusion; who conceive this vividly, and hold by it as the essence of their work; who, by the very vividness and heat of their conception, purge away, sooner or later, all that is not organically appropriate to it, till the whole effect adjusts itself in clear, orderly, proportionate form.
>
> (Pater 1910, *App* 257–8)

However if artists like Leonardo and Dante are alchemists, subtly refining their work, then critics, in so far as they too participate in the alchemical process of creativity, their own and that of others, are also alchemists. The analytic process urged as the work of 'the æsthetic critic' in the Preface to *The Renaissance* also seems heavily inflected by alchemical imagery:

> To [the æsthetic critic], the picture, the landscape, the engaging personality in life or in a book, *La Gioconda*, the hills of Carrara, Pico of Mirandola, are valuable for their virtues, as we say, in speaking of a herb, a wine, a gem, for the property each has of affecting one with a special, a unique, impression of pleasure. . . . And the

21 Paracelsus is the pseudonym of the Swiss Philippus Aureolus Theophrastus Bombastus von Hohenheim (1493–1541), famous sage, doctor, and alchemist; Geronimo or Girolamo Cardano (1501–1576) was an Italian physician, mathematician, and astrologer.

function of the æsthetic critic is to distinguish, to analyse, and separate from its adjuncts, the virtue by which a picture, a landscape, a fair personality in life or in a book, produces the special impression of beauty or pleasure, to indicate what the source of that impression is, and under what conditions it is experienced. His end is reached when he has disengaged that virtue, and noted it, as a chemist notes some natural element, for himself and others.

(Pater 1980, *Ren* xx)

Pater is using the word 'virtue' in its Paracelsist sense, which, as Charles Nicholl explains, 'has more in common with Latin *virtus* (manliness, strength, excellence) than with our morally flavoured definition'. He elaborates: '"Virtue" is the hidden power, spiritual and concentrate, contained in all bodies – plants, metals and man – and has specific curative effects when extracted. It is closely connected to the alchemical quintessence, to which Paracelsus often likens it' (Nicholl 1980, 57–8).[22] Pater uses the word 'virtue' as 'essence' or, as he will gloss it, 'active principle', and the 'chemist' he mentions in this extract from the Preface is not the contemporary Victorian chemist but his forerunner, the alchemist. Only he would describe the properties of a herb, a wine, a gem, as 'virtues'. The critic as alchemist, who tries to distil the essence of each of the many beautiful things so that he can pinpoint what it is that gives the impression of pleasure, is like the poet-speaker in Shakespeare's sonnets who tries to distil the young man's beauty into his verse and preserve it for future generations.[23] The dissolve or dissolution of the object into a web of impressionistic imagery can be seen as the critic's attempt to break down, distil, and extract the essence of the object as it seems to him. However, as Pater makes apparent, because of the stringent demands of the creative process, most art objects contain an amount of dross that needs to be separated out from the parts of real value:

Often it will require great nicety to disengage this virtue from the commoner elements with which it may be found in combination. Few artists, not Goethe or Byron even, work quite cleanly, casting off all *débris*, and leaving us what the heat of their imagination has wholly fused and transformed. Take, for instance, the writings of Wordsworth. The heat of his genius, entering into the substance of his work, has crystallised a part, but only a part, of it; and in that great mass of verse there is much which might well be forgotten. But scattered up and down it, sometimes fusing and transforming entire compositions, like the Stanzas on *Resolution*

22 Paracelsus founded his medicine on four 'pillars': Philosophy, Astronomy, Alchemy, and Virtue. For 'Virtue' see also *OED*, section 11: 'A particular power, efficacy or good quality inherent in, or pertaining to something.'

23 See, in particular, Sonnet 5. For references to 'virtue' in the sonnets see Sonnet 81 in which the speaker declares: 'You still such live – such virtue hath my pen – / Where breath most breathes, ev'n in the mouths of men.' See also Sonnet 93. 'How like Eve's apple doth thy beauty show, / If thy sweet virtue answer not thy show' (Shakespeare 1977, 71, 80).

> *and Independence*, or the *Ode on the Recollections of Childhood*, sometimes, as if at random, depositing a fine crystal here or there, in a matter it does not wholly search through and transmute, we trace the action of his unique, incommunicable faculty, that strange, mystical sense of a life in natural things . . . Well! That is the *virtue*, the active principle in Wordsworth's poetry; and then the function of the critic of Wordsworth's is to follow up that active principle, to disengage it, to mark the degree in which it penetrates his verse.
>
> (Pater 1980, *Ren* xxi–xxii)[24]

Most artists as alchemists do not work 'cleanly' so it is the job of the critic as alchemist to extract what is of value. Although William Sharp noted Pater's attraction to gold and what he called 'the chemic action of golden light' (Sharp 1894, 806, in Seiler 1987, 86), here in the Preface he uses a favourite image, the luminous crystal rather than gold, to represent the desired end product of the creative process.[25] Yet the crystal, too, may have an alchemical significance and the accompanying imagery of fusion and transmutation is clearly alchemical.[26] The essence or active principle of imaginative creativity in its purest unadulterated form, when properly treated, may result in a perfect and immortal crystal. In the creations of some disciplined artists this 'active principle' can

24 Pater's remarks on Wordsworth's only partial transmutation of his matter recall Shelley's remarks on poetic inspiration in his 'Defence': 'The parts of a composition may be poetical, without the composition as a whole being a poem. A single sentence may be considered as a whole, though it may be found in a series of unassimilated portions' (Shelley 1977, 485–6).

25 Pater told Sharp that 'the chemic action of golden light' is '"the primary color [*sic*] of delight" throughout nature and in nearly all art', and that '"Through all writing, too, that is rare and distinctive and beautiful . . . there is a golden thread."' He read aloud to Sharp 'The School of Giorgione', 'chosen because of the allusions in it to that very alchemy of light of which he had spoken' (Sharp 1894, 806, in Seiler 1987, 86).

26 Referring to different stages in the alchemical process, Lyndy Abraham writes: 'Crystal is the name for the philosopher's stone or elixir at both the white stage, or albedo, and the red stage or rubedo' (Abraham 1998, 50). In her study of alchemical imagery in the work of Andrew Marvell, Abraham writes of 'the philosopher's stone which transforms gross matter into a pure, crystal body' (Abraham 1990, 233). She also cites Sir Thomas Browne, one of Pater's literary subjects, who writes in his *Religio Medici*: 'Philosophers that opinioned the worlds destruction by fire, did never dreame of annihilation, which is beyond the power of sublunary cases; for the last and proper element is but vitrification or a reduction of a body into Glasse; and therefore some of our Chymicks [i.e. alchemists] facetiously affirm, that at the last fire all shall be crystallized and reverberated into glasse, which is the utmost action of the element' (cited Abraham 1990, 219–20). Such references inform perhaps Pater's interest in the Heraclitean fire-flux and his fascination with crystalline images or images of transparency, all of which come together in the 'hard gem-like flame' of the Conclusion.

be seen almost immediately, as in the works of the ancient Greek sculptors, who sought 'the type in the individual, to abstract and express only what is structural and permanent' so that 'In this way their works came to be like some subtle extract or essence, or almost like pure thoughts or ideas' (Pater 1980, *Ren* 51).

Throughout his *œuvre* Pater tries to pinpoint the 'active principle' of each artist, school, culture, or period he treats, by distilling and extracting from their works or cultural artefacts an essence that, in many cases, will not be a simple quality but a synthesis of often seemingly opposite qualities. The qualities he discovers are then projected back on to the respective artist, school, or culture. For, although Pater seems to be much taken with interesting 'personalities', arguably these personalities are embodied abstractions. He is interested in specific persons only in so far as they are the initiating source of the intriguing qualities he discovers in their work; that is to say he is primarily interested in artists *as artists*, the makers of beautiful things, employing biographical data only in as much as it complements and enhances the patterns he finds in each person's art.[27] The artist, in addition to being the source of the work and the store or repository of certain unique characteristics, infuses and energises the successful work with its recognisable essence. However, as his 'personality' is in sum the projection of the typical 'character' or essence we see displayed in his work, it is thus curiously 'impersonal' in a way that anticipates 'impersonality' in the Modernist thought of T. S. Eliot, who, as Perry Meisel and others have shown, was deeply influenced by Pater.[28] At the end of his essay on Michelangelo, Pater suggests that the 'qualities of the great masters in art or literature', artists such as he examines in *The Renaissance*, provide us with

27 Quoting Pater, Paul Barolsky notes, 'the "true outlines" of Giorgione's own life and person are "obscured"; he is thus like Abelard, Pico, Botticelli, and Leonardo, all living lives either colorless or in shadow' (Barolsky 1987, 46).

28 For Eliot on 'impersonality' see 'Tradition and the Individual Talent' (1919) (Eliot 1920, 47–59). See also 'Repression and the Individual Talent' in Meisel 1987, 71–86. We might notice too, how in 'Tradition and the Individual Talent', the essay in which Eliot defines 'impersonality', he makes a pointed attempt to modernise or trump Pater's alchemical symbolism with the modern scientific analogy of 'the action which takes place when a bit of finely filiated platinum is introduced into a chamber containing oxygen and sulphur dioxide' (Eliot 1920, 53). But, the alchemical symbolism will out: 'For it is not the "greatness," the intensity, of the emotions, the components, but the intensity of the artistic process, the pressure, so to speak, under which the fusion takes place, that counts' (Eliot 1920, 55). And, as the rest of the essay shows, Eliot cannot get away from Pater's influence, with other Paterian language, some of it markedly alchemical, creeping back in the words 'peculiar essence' (48); 'transmute' (54); 'receptacle', 'unite' (55); 'fusion of elements', 'combine' (56); 'combination of positive and negative emotions' (57); 'formula', 'concentration' (58); 'surrendering' (59). See also 'Shakespeare and the Stoicism of Seneca' (1927)

'typical standards, or revealing instances of the laws by which certain æsthetic effects are produced'. He continues:

> The old masters indeed are simpler; their characteristics are written larger, and are easier to read, than the analogues of them in all the mixed, confused productions of the modern mind. But once we have succeeded in defining for ourselves those characteristics, and the law of their combination, we have acquired a standard or measure which helps us put in its right place many a vagrant genius, many an unclassified talent, many precious though imperfect products of art.
>
> (Pater 1980, *Ren* 76)

The 'components of the true character of Michelangelo . . . sweetness and strength', can be found, for example, in William Blake and Victor Hugo, 'who though not of his school, and unaware, are his true sons, and help us to understand him, as he in turn interprets and justifies them'. The 'old masters' then constitute a kind of canon of 'character', which is not prescriptive, but rather an identificatory and interpretative aid. 'Perhaps', concludes Pater tentatively, 'this is the chief use in studying old masters' (Pater 1980, *Ren* 76).

I would propose that in reading Pater the interest lies less in determining a particular essence or character for an artist than in tracing the actual process of its production, refinement, and extraction. If, as seems to be the case, many of Pater's specific findings have a generic likeness, heavily inflected by the Romanticism through which he self-consciously views his subjects, this in itself suggests that he is seeking not this or that particular result or outcome, but ultimately a kind of archetypal creative character, the essence of an essence, and the conditions in which it visibly flourishes.

Pater and form

Essence or character is what is primarily revealed in each artist's specific style or form. Although in 'The School of Giorgione' Pater famously proposes that '*All art constantly aspires towards the condition of music*', that is, towards a synthesis of form and matter, the same essay also implies that matter is far less important. (We should not automatically assume that Paterian syntheses are static or fixed or that both terms have equal value.) If it is 'the constant effort

Footnote 28 *(Cont.)*
for another Paterian alchemical formulation of impersonality: 'what every poet starts from is his own emotions . . . Shakespeare, too, was occupied with the struggle which alone constitutes life for the poet – to transmute his personal and private agonies into something rich and strange, something universal and impersonal' (Eliot 1932, 137). Less surprisingly, alchemical imagery can also be found in Yeats's critical writing. See especially 'The Autumn of the Body' (1898), in Yeats 1989, 193.

of art to obliterate' this distinction between matter and form, it ideally achieves this by having form subsume matter:

> That the mere matter of a poem, for instance, its subject, namely, its given incidents or situation . . . should be nothing without the form, the spirit, of the handling, that this form, this mode of handling, should become an end in itself, should penetrate every part of the matter: this is what all art constantly strives after, and achieves in different degrees.
>
> (Pater 1980, *Ren* 106)

Pater provides examples of this in relation to both painting and poetry:

> And hence the superiority, for most conditions of the picturesque, of a river-side in France to a Swiss valley, because, on the French river-side, mere topography, the simple material counts for so little.
>
> And the very perfection of [lyrical] poetry often appears to depend, in part, on a certain suppression or vagueness of mere subject.
>
> (Pater 1980, *Ren* 107, 108)

And he concludes: 'Art, then, is thus always striving to be independent of the mere intelligence, to become a matter of pure perception, to get rid of its responsibilities to its subject or material' (Pater 1980, *Ren* 108). The tale of Aucassin and Nicolette, described in 'Two Early French Stories' is 'to be entertained not for its matter only, but chiefly for its manner' (Pater 1980, *Ren* 14), while Joachim's du Bellay's verse and indeed the whole Pléiade school of poetry has 'a certain silvery grace of fancy, nearly all the pleasure of which is in the surprise at the happy and dexterous way in which a thing slight in itself is handled' (Pater 1980, *Ren* 140). In the essay on Leonardo we learn that 'No one ever ruled over the mere *subject* in hand more entirely than Leonardo, or bent it more dexterously to purely artistic ends' (Pater 1980, *Ren* 93). And we have already seen how ancient Greek sculpture, because it tended to suppress individual particularity in favour of the universal type, also elevated form over content; indeed, as Pater says in 'Winckelmann', 'threw itself upon pure form' (Pater 1980, *Ren* 169). In such comments on the pre-eminence of form we see Pater's Aestheticism, his own version of 'art for art's sake'. And in these works in which form predominates, which Pater suggests are among the best of their kind, essence or character must necessarily communicate through style or form – the artists who created them being, like the Greeks, disciplined and conscientious stylists and craftsmen, artists who work 'cleanly' leaving the critic relatively little to perform in the way of alchemical extraction.

Although music serves Pater with an ideal of synthesis, he displays little interest in it as an art-form. Sculpture with its emphasis on pure form attracts him far more. As a means of embodiment, sculpture seems able to translate abstract ideas into concrete form without loss, as well as portraying natural forms effectively. In 'Demeter and Persephone' Pater remarks on 'the art of sculpture, humanising and refining man's conceptions of the unseen' (Pater 1910, *GS* 144), while in 'The Age of Athletic Prizemen' he admires the naturalism of the statues of athletes, seeing the *Discobolus*, or quoit-player, as

> embodying (say, in one perfect flower) all one has ever fancied or seen, in old Greece or on Thames's side, of the unspoiled body of youth, thus delighting itself and others, at that perfect, because unconscious, point of good-fortune, as it moves or rests just there for a moment, between the animal and spiritual worlds.
> (Pater 1910, *GS* 288)

As we saw earlier, whether as abstract or naturalistic embodiments, the Greeks' sculptural 'works came to be like some subtle extract or essence, or almost like pure thoughts or ideas' (Pater 1980, *Ren* 51). Admiring the *Discobolus*, Pater wonders, 'Was it the portrait of one much-admired youth, or rather the type, the rectified essence, of many such, at the most pregnant, the essential, moment, of the exercise of their natural powers, of what they really were?' (Pater 1910, *GS* 289–90). A 'rectified essence' is one that is purified or refined by repeated distillation. Sculpture, as an ideal art-form that reveals essence, involves, like alchemy, a lengthy process of refinement, but, as we shall see, sculptural refinement has its own process which will provide Pater with another means of description for the realisation of form.

When we study Pater's interest in style or form, we encounter two more of his key critical terms that describe the labour of disciplined artists. In the first place, the Greek *ascêsis*, or 'discipline', which for the modern reader can have a rather unpleasant savour of monastic austerity, but which for Pater, one suspects, has a pleasurable, even slightly erotic edge in that it describes the energetic discipline of Greek athletes training in the *palaestra*, young men stripped for strenuous exercise or, as he puts in the Preface to *The Renaissance*, 'the charm of *ascêsis*, of the austere and serious girding of the loins in youth' (Pater 1980, *Ren* xxiii). In 'Style', *ascêsis* is invoked as the artist's necessary discipline, a practice that will help him exercise discrimination in word choice and placement:

> Self-restraint, a skilful economy of means, *ascêsis*, that too has a beauty of its own; and for the reader supposed there will be an æsthetic satisfaction in that frugal closeness of style which makes the most of a word, in the exaction from every sentence of a precise relief, in the just spacing out of word to thought, the logically filled space connected always with the delightful sense of difficulty overcome.
> (Pater 1910, *App* 17)

(One cannot help but notice that this sentence, with its judiciously chosen phrase 'frugal closeness', and its elegantly organised clauses, which carefully separate out its refinements of meaning, beautifully enacts the precision it describes. Pater is a master of such deliciously satisfying self-reflexive sentences.)

The toning and discipline of the body, which is originally the meaning of *ascêsis*, links it to Pater's second term, which has an application to the formation of the sculptural body or the body of a writer's work. This term is 'surplusage', denoting the superfluous or extraneous stylistic matter the writer must remove:

> Surplusage! He will dread that as the runner on his muscles. For in truth all art does but consist in the removal of surplusage, from the last finish of the gem-engraver blowing away the last particle of invisible dust, back to the earliest divination of the finished work to be, lying somewhere, according to Michelangelo's fancy, in the rough-hewn block of stone.
>
> (Pater 1910, *App* 19–20)

The artist must faithfully body out the initiating conception, being careful not to distort it by importing additional and unnecessary elaborations. Pater's reference is to one of Michelangelo's best-known sonnets. Famously Michelangelo himself has a poetic style that is extremely condensed, as if he were trying to cut out superfluous verbiage to get at the essence of his meaning, and this highly compressed sonnet is no exception, opening with the lines

> *No ha l'ottimo artista alcun concetto*
> *c'un marmo solo in sé no circonscriva*
> *col suo superchio, e solo a quella arriva*
> *la man che ubbidisce all'intelletto.*
>
> (Michelangelo 1991, 302)

One of Michelangelo's more recent commentators, James M. Saslow, translates these difficult lines as following:

> Not even the best of artists has any conception
> that a single marble block does not contain
> within its excess, and *that* is only attained
> by the hand that obeys the intellect.
>
> (Michelangelo 1991, 302)

In his essay on 'The Poetry of Michelangelo', Pater had alluded approvingly to John Addington Symonds's translation of Michelangelo's sonnets, which first appeared in the *Contemporary Review* in 1872.[29] Symonds rendered these lines as

> The best of artists hath no thought to show
> which the rough stone in its superfluous shell

29 In *Studies in the History of the Renaissance*, Pater cited three of the translated sonnets entire, but omitted them in subsequent editions, praising Symonds's translations in a footnote. For detailed account of Pater's use of Symonds and a comparison of their views see Alex Potts, 'Pungent Prophecies of Art: Symonds, Pater and Michelangelo' (Potts 2000, 102–21). For other critical remarks on Pater and Michelangelo see 'Pater and Ruskin on Michelangelo' (Bullen 1981, 55–73), and the fine monograph on the reception of Michelangelo by Østermark-Johansen (1998).

> doth not include; to break the marble spell
> is all the hand that serves the brain can do.
>
> (Michelangelo 1950, 47)

Symonds's translation describes the marble that surrounds the *concetto* as a 'superfluous shell', emphasising the 'surplusage' that the artist must remove to liberate his conception. Pater's use of this image suggests that the *concetto*, 'conception', or 'earliest divination of the finished work to be', is 'pure perception' (Pater 1980, *Ren* 108), and not to be confused with the subject, matter, or content of the work of art. Michelangelo's imagery in this sonnet is, as Saslow puts it in his commentary, 'most important for his revelations of Neoplatonic artistic theory', adding that lines 1–4

> express M's sculptural theory of subtraction, by which the artist physically removes excess outer mass in order to reveal the preexisting form-idea already present within; the term *concetto*, 'conception,' is complex, and of central importance in Neoplatonic and Cinquecento art theory . . . Several poems expound on the basic theme that this conception, or mental inspiration, precedes and guides the physical labor of carving.
>
> (Michelangelo 1991, 302, 303)

Pater, too, notes in 'The Poetry of Michelangelo' how 'Michelangelo is always pressing forward from the outward beauty – *il bel del fuor che agli occhi piace*, to apprehend the unseen beauty; *trascenda nella forma universale* – that abstract form of beauty, about which the Platonists reason' (Pater 1980, *Ren* 69). And in the preceding 'Luca della Robbia', an essay which seems to be as much about Michelangelo as its ostensible subject, Pater writes: 'To him [Michelangelo], . . . work which did not bring what was inward to the surface . . . was not worth doing at all' (Pater 1980, *Ren* 52). The art historian Paul Barolsky has observed that 'it goes unnoticed even by his admirers that Pater's suggestions were the first general indications of the extreme Neoplatonism in Renaissance theology, philosophy, poetry, painting, sculpture and architecture', adding that

> *The Renaissance* prefigured and influenced the more detailed historical account in Nesca Robb's *Neoplatonism in the Italian Renaissance* (1935), a work which in turn stimulated the most distinguished art-historical scholars of Renaissance Neoplatonism, Erwin Panofsky, Edgar Wind, and E. H. Gombrich, all of whom followed, if distantly in the wake of Pater, and much of whose work depends on his implicit historical formulation.
>
> (Barolsky 1987, 17)

While Pater may be the first critic to identify the significance and range of Renaissance neoplatonism, he is, Barolsky points out, one of its last practitioners. Having singled out Pater's own characterisation of Platonism as '"not a formal theory or body of theories, but a tendency or group of tendencies"',

Barolsky remarks, 'Pater's *Renaissance* is permeated by an abiding concern with this Platonic "tendency" of vision toward "pure form," and it is, along with Pater's other writings, one of the last sustained expressions of Platonism in the Western tradition' (Barolsky 1987, 143).[30]

It is primarily an artist's use and realisation of form that gives us his essence or character. Outward form is, at its purest, a reflection of an inner form or vision, or, to use Pater's Platonic formulation, 'the unseen beauty, that abstract form of beauty'. As we saw earlier, for Pater, the sensible imagination, though like other cerebral processes constituted out of an accumulation of multiple sensory experiences, none the less still seems to clothe something pre-existing, being 'the visible vesture and expression of that other world [the mind] sees so steadily within' (Pater 1910, *App* 31). The critic who appraises form may then experience a pull away from the simply visible towards the visionary, when, seeking to find the essence of the work, dissolving it into its associations and impressions, he glimpses something of the *concetto*, the visionary 'unseen beauty', at the core of the work, which the artist intuited as he created it. For Pater, form, which the artist realises by *ascêsis* and the subtraction of surplusage, is good or effective to the extent that it gives the viewer a sense of a powerfully directed energy arising from the generative matrix of a properly unseen internal form or vision.

Life, death and character

Paradoxically, by way of visual analogy to his 'sculptural theory of subtraction', Michelangelo tended to leave his sculptures comparatively rough-hewn or unfinished, and has even left us a number of apparently incomplete sculptures, known collectively as the *non-finiti*. Some of these sculptures go under the name of *The Prisoners, The Captives*, or *The Slaves*, for, in each of them, the sculpted figure seems to be still in the process of emerging from the rock, even trying to struggle free from it.[31] In 'Luca della Robbia', Pater is fascinated by Michelangelo's studied lack of finish, commenting how he gains an effect of vitality 'by leaving nearly all his sculpture in a puzzling sort of incompleteness, which suggests rather than realises actual form'. Pater knows that Michelangelo's incompleteness is a strength, in that, like the Romantic fragment, it has a wonderful power of imaginative suggestion:

> Many have wondered at that incompleteness, suspecting however, that Michelangelo himself loved and was loath to change it, and feeling at the same time that they too would lose something if the half-realised form ever quite emerged

30 Pater's characterisation of Platonism occurs at the beginning of Chapter 7, 'The Doctrine of Plato' in *Plato and Platonism* (1893). See Pater 1910, 150.

31 See the fine example provided by Saslow, titled *Awakening Slave*, in Michelangelo 1991, 304.

> from the stone, so rough-hewn here, so delicately finished there; and they have wished to fathom the charm of this incompleteness. Well! That incompleteness is Michelangelo's equivalent for colour in sculpture; it is his way of etherealising pure form, of relieving its stiff realism, and communicating to it breath, pulsation, the effect of life. . . . And it was in reality perfect finish. In this way he combines the utmost amount of passion and intensity with the sense of a yielding and flexible life; he gets not vitality merely, but a wonderful force, of expression.
> (Pater 1980, *Ren* 53)

The art of the effective removal of surplusage seems to be knowing when to stop. It is not a matter of trying to pare the image down into some perfected essential form. Indeed that kind of realisation is impossible. Less can suggest more: by not finishing his works, Michelangelo leaves them in a dynamic process of becoming, and keeps them in contact with the generative energy of the *concetto* apparently welling up within the stone, engaging the viewer in the creative process of imaginative projection.[32] In 'The Poetry of Michelangelo', Pater returns to this topic:

> As I have already pointed out, he secures that ideality of expression . . . by an incompleteness, which is surely not always undesigned, and which, as I think, no one regrets, and trusts to the spectator to complete the half-emergent form. And as his persons have something of the unwrought stone about them, so, as if to realise the expression by which the old Florentine records describe a sculptor – *master of live stone* – with him the very rocks seem to have life. They have but to cast away the dust and scurf that they may rise and stand on their feet. . . . on the crown of the head of the *David* there still remains a morsel of uncut stone, as if by one touch to maintain its connexion with the place from which it was hewn. (Pater 1980, *Ren* 59–60)

Michelangelo's refusal to 'finish' his statues gives them an air of partial unsculpture. In 'Mont Blanc', Shelley, another writer influenced by Plato, describes 'the sweep / Of the etherial waterfall, whose veil / Robes some unsculptured image' (Shelley 1977, 90).[33] As I have suggested elsewhere, 'the "unsculptured image" can mean a shape in the rocks not made by man, but it can also suggest an image, not fully formed or visible, caught in the process of its emergence or disappearance' (Maxwell 2001, 77).[34] The emergent 'unsculptured image', the Shelleyan version of the Michelangelesque *concetto*,

32 As Bullen points out, Ruskin criticises 'what he calls Michelangelo's "bad workmanship" – the lack of finish and the incompleteness of some of the sculpture' (Bullen 1981, 56). Østermark-Johansen comments: 'The *non-finito*, so heavily criticized by Ruskin, becomes in Pater's view a positive and creative feature' (Østermark-Johansen 1998, 102). Potts indicates that Symonds disagreed with Pater on this point (Potts 2000, 112).

33 For Shelley's Platonism see Notopoulos 1969.

34 Leonardo is famous for leaving his works incomplete and Pater seems to find a painterly equivalent to Michelangelo's *non-finito* or Shelley's 'unsculptured image'

is the dynamic, energising, 'pure' or latent form inside the stone (properly, of course, within the artist's mind), which the sculptor strives to liberate. But arguably an attempt at full liberation or delivery in the form of 'too finished' an image cuts off, severs the sculpture from its source of power, allowing the artist and viewer no further participation in the creative process and condemning the image to a death-like stasis.

For one of the threats which sculpture must defend against is the appearance of death. In a chapter, in his book on late Victorian sculpture, which explores the '"hard realism"' of Edward Onslow Ford's *Shelley Memorial*, the art critic David Getsy writes:

> The corpse is anathema to sculpture. For centuries, sculptors have resisted the immotility of sculpture in order to imbue their works with life. The most biting criticism of figurative sculpture has been to call it cold and lifeless. Sculptors have used such methods as contrapposto, naturalism, facial expression, and implied movement in order to convince the viewer that these blocks of stone or chunks of bronze are not material objects but living, breathing things. 'Inertia,' as the sculpture critic Agnes Rindge once wrote, 'is death.'
>
> (Getsy 2004, 134)

Yet, as Getsy also reminds us, 'In art-historical terms, the corpse is the logical conclusion of realism. The paintings of the dead Christ by Caravaggio or Manet, for example, remind us that one of the most forceful matters for realism is death' (Getsy 2004, 134). It is Pater who provides Getsy with the phrase 'hard realism', which occurs in a passage he cites from 'Luca della Robbia':

> [The] limitation [of sculpture] results from the material, and other necessary conditions, of all sculptured work, and consists in the tendency of such work to a *hard realism*, a one-sided presentment of mere form, that solid material frame which only motion can relieve, a thing of heavy shadows, and an individuality of expression pushed to caricature. Against this tendency to the hard presentment of mere form trying vainly to compete with the reality of nature itself, all noble sculpture constantly struggles; each great system of sculpture resisting it in its own way, etherealising, spiritualising, relieving, its *stiffness, its heaviness, and death.*
>
> (Pater 1980, *Ren* 50–1; cited Getsy 2004, 134, with emphasis)

Michelangelo's *non-finiti*, his slaves and captives, struggle against death in the confines of finished form. For, as we have seen, 'incompleteness is

Footnote 34 *(Cont.)*
in his *Last Supper*, and especially in the 'central head' of Jesus: 'Vasari pretends that the central head was never finished. But finished or unfinished, or owing part of its effect to a mellowing decay, the head of Jesus does but consummate the sentiment of the whole company – ghosts through which you see the wall, faint as the shadows of the leaves upon the wall on autumn afternoons. This figure is but the faintest, the most spectral of them all' (Pater 1980, *Ren* 94, 95).

Michelangelo's . . . way of etherealising pure form, of relieving its stiff realism, and communicating to it breath, pulsation, the effect of life'. And in 'The Poetry of Michelangelo', Pater insists that 'This creation of life – life coming always as relief or recovery, and always in strong contrast with the rough-hewn mass in which it is kindled – is in various ways the motive of all his work . . . and this, although at least one-half of his work was designed for the adornment of tombs' (Pater 1980, *Ren* 59).

Yet, in the same essay, Pater also tells us that, for Michelangelo, 'pity, the pity of the Virgin Mother over the dead body of Christ, expanded into the pity of all mothers over all dead sons, the entombment, with its cruel "hard stones": – this is the subject of his predilection. He has left it in many forms . . . but always as a hopeless, rayless, almost heathen sorrow – no divine sorrow, but mere pity and awe at the stiff limbs and colourless lips' (Pater 1980, *Ren* 74). And, when Pater insists on Michelangelo's ability to imbue his sculptures with life, his qualification 'life coming always as relief or recovery', like his proposition that 'all noble sculpture struggles' against a death-like realism, suggests that death is already present as an antithesis, being an integral part of the sculptural body. Implicitly then for Pater, the successful figurative sculpture is a synthesis of death and life, though preferably with life more immediately present to the eye.

This bodily synthesis of death and life recurs elsewhere in Pater's writing, being something to which he was much attracted. We have already seen how Paul Barolsky detected its presence in the Mona Lisa, 'the essential synthesis of antitheses', who, although she 'has been dead many times, and learned the secrets of the grave', also embodies 'The fancy of the perpetual life' (Pater 1980, *Ren* 99). Jeffrey Wallen sees Pater fascinated by images of life-in-death, singling out the image of Pico della Mirandola who, 'while his actual work has passed away, yet his own qualities are still active, and himself remains, as one alive in the grave, *caesiis et vigilibus oculis* [his eyes grey, and quick of look], as his biographer describes him, and with that sanguine, clear skin, *decenti rubore interspersa* [intermingled with comely reds], as with the light of morning upon it' (Pater 1980, *Ren* 38; cited by Wallen 1999, 1042, with parenthetical translation). Pico is partnered by Winckelmann, who, in his intellectual discovery of Greek sculpture, with its idealisation of youthful male beauty, joys in 'finding the ideal of that youth still red with life in the grave'. Furthermore, in the essay on Pico, Pater chooses to end his long citation from Heinrich Heine's *Gods in Exile* with the words 'But they found the grave empty'; words that imply that the missing body of the recently executed Apollo has also been 'alive in the grave' (Pater 1980, *Ren* 167, 25; Wallen 1999, 1042–3).[35] Wallen, too, notes Pater's

35 Pater uses a similar image when in his essay 'Demeter and Persephone', he discusses the former site of Demeter's temple at Cnidus: 'It is one of the graves of that old religion but with much still fresh in it' (Pater 1910, *GS* 142).

'fascination with sculpted figures, "purged of the commonness of the world"', and later observes that 'Greek sculpture offers Pater the opportunity to gaze on the living body, but turned to stone; life and death are united in art' (Pater 1980, *Ren* 172; Wallen 1999, 1047). We might interpolate here the figure of Trypho, '"the son of Eutychus"', whom Pater fondly describes from a memorial preserved in the British Museum:

> With all the suppleness, the delicate musculature, of the flower of his youth, his handsome face sweetened by a kind and simple heart, in motion, surely, he steps forth from some shadowy chamber, *strigil* in hand, as of old, and with his coarse towel or cloak of monumental drapery over one shoulder. But whither precisely, you may ask, and as what, is he moving there in the doorway? Well! In effect, certainly, it is the memory of the dead lad, emerging thus from his tomb, – the still active soul, or permanent thought, of him, as he most liked to be.
>
> (Pater 1910, *GS* 272)

Responding to the evident homoerotic surveillance of such images of beautiful young men, Wallen comments, 'Moreover, sculpture allows Pater to contemplate the naked male physique, yet without fear of response, and without the uncanniness of gazing at corpses' (Wallen 1999, 1043, 1047).

As we saw earlier, implicit in the Conclusion to *The Renaissance* is the idea that art, a concentrated form of perceptual expression dwelling on the beauty of form, is an especially effective means of offering us those peak moments of experience that justify our existence. Moreover, art objects, as opposed to natural objects, have the seeming capacity to arrest the moment and freeze form, allowing us to return repeatedly to admire their lasting beauty: 'For ever wilt thou love, and she be fair', as Keats observes of the figures of the lovers on the Grecian Urn (Keats 1970, 535). Art offers a seeming permanence, so that the moments when we engage with art are moments of contemplative stasis in the flux of time. Sculpture, in particular, when it treats natural forms such as the human body, has this evident advantage over its model: the beautiful body it portrays will endure while the model is subject to change and decay. However, as we have just seen, sculpture's freezing of form is problematic in that it can suggest death, and it may be the case that death cannot be wholly expunged from sculpture. Moreover some sculptors do indeed sculpt dead bodies, which, as sculptures, have the advantage of non-corruption and permanence. And even the corpse, albeit temporarily, shares with sculpture the power to arrest beauty, and there are a number of common beliefs about what we might call 'the aesthetic powers of death'; that is, death's powers to refine or make beautiful the bodies of the dead. In his essay on Michelangelo, Pater, in discussing the preoccupation of the Florentines with death, rehearses one of these, when he proposes that

> They must often have leaned over the lifeless body, when all was at length quiet and smoothed out. After death, it is said, the traces of slighter and more superficial

> dispositions disappear; the lines become more simple and dignified; only the abstract lines remain, in a great indifference. They came thus to see death in its distinction.
>
> (Pater 1980, *Ren* 74)

Here death emulates the idealisation of sculpture described by Pater in the essay on Winckelmann: 'it unveils man in the repose of his unchanging characteristics. That white light purged from the angry, bloodlike stains of action and passion, reveals, not what is accidental in man, but the tranquil godship in him, as opposed to the restless accidents of life.' A little later in the same essay, he affirms, 'the type, the general character of the subject to be delineated, is all-important.' And later still, in contrast to the Hellenic ideal of impassivity, he notes that 'Men and women, again, in the hurry of life, often wear the sharp impress of one absorbing motive, from which it is said death sets their features free' (Pater 1980, *Ren* 170, 172, 173).

The source from which Pater may have taken his notion of the aesthetic powers of death is Sir Thomas Browne's 'Letter to a Friend', a short essay in which he describes for a colleague the last days of a mutual friend. In his own essay on Browne (1886) in *Appreciations*, Pater writes of 'the deep impression he received during those visits, of a sort of physical beauty in the coming of death, with which he still surprises and moves his reader'. As a doctor, Browne is present 'to assist as it were at the spiritualising of the bodily frame by natural process; a wonderful new type of a kind of mortified grace being evolved by the way. The spiritual body has anticipated the formal moment of death; the alert soul, in that tardy decay, changing its vesture gradually, and as if piece by piece' (Pater 1910, *App* 152–3).[36] Interestingly Pater compares Browne's 'attitude of questioning awe on the threshold of another life with 'the delicate monumental sculpture of the Tuscan school'. Alluding to the shared sympathy of Browne and 'those unsophisticated Italian workmen', Pater writes: 'with them, and with the writer of the *Letter to a Friend* . . . – so strangely! the visible function of death is but to refine, to detach from aught that is vulgar' (Pater 1910, *App* 153). This sentiment is already present in *The Renaissance*, where Pater declares that the Virgin Mary, in Fra Angelico's *Coronation of the Virgin*, is 'corpse-like in her refinement', and that, in his portrait of Beatrice d'Este, Leonardo catches 'some presentiment of early death, painting her precise and grave, full of the refinement of the dead' (Pater 1980, *Ren* 163, 88); while in 'Luca della Robbia', an essay focusing on the Tuscan sculptors of the fifteenth century, Pater praises 'the careful sepulchral portraits of particular persons . . . monuments

36 Regarding Pater's meditations on the bodily effects of death, it is worth remembering that his father, whom he lost aged three, was a surgeon, a fact that may also have a bearing on his recapitulation of the post-mortem of Emerald Uthwart in *Miscellaneous Studies.*

. . . inexhaustible in suggestions of repose, of a subdued sabbatic joy, a kind of sacred grace and refinement' (Pater 1980, *Ren* 54). Death then is a type of subtraction of surplusage, sharing with ideal figurative sculpture the ability to refine away all the petty everyday accidentals, the superficial traits, habits, and accretions, and to present man 'in his unchanging characteristics', the human subject in his essential character. Like alchemy, death and sculpture refine form to offer the abstraction of essence.

If death refines character or essence, this may help explain Pater's fascination with death, which, as many critics have observed, is a persistent theme in his writing. Death, for Pater, is nearly always accompanied by or contrasted with beauty. This is evident as early as 'Poems by William Morris', afterwards 'Æsthetic Poetry', where he observes:

> One characteristic of the pagan spirit these new poems have which is on their surface – the continual suggestion, pensive or passionate, of the shortness of life; this is contrasted with the bloom of the world and gives a new seduction to it; the sense of death and the desire of beauty; the desire of beauty quickened by the sense of death.
>
> (Pater 1974b, 113; 1889, *App* 277; 1974a, 198, with variants)

Here the threat of death, the threat of eventual oblivion, is seen as the enemy of beauty which, like our lives, is transient, and thus provokes us to value and desire beauty all the more. Florian, in 'The Child in the House', possessed by a great love of beauty, feels this contrast and inducement acutely: 'For with this desire of physical beauty mingled itself early the fear of death – the fear of death intensified by the desire of beauty' (Pater 1910, *App* 189–90). 'Poems by William Morris' and the Conclusion to *The Renaissance* also make beauty the compensation for our transient lives, for 'we are all *condamnés*, as Victor Hugo says: we are all under sentence of death but with a sort of indefinite reprieve' (Pater 1980, *Ren* 190; 1974, 116 with variants). Beauty is a 'bloom', a sign of life, which is contrasted and intensified by its juxtaposition with death, but death has the potential to stop beauty temporarily in its tracks and to increase its loveliness by refining it of its subjection to everyday necessity. 'Death is the mother of beauty', as Wallace Stevens remarks in 'Sunday Morning', that most Paterian of poems (Stevens 1984, 68).[37] In the idealised sculpture of the beautiful young man, or in his lovely dead body from which the imperfect petty accidentals of life have been purged, beauty and death can come together as one in a strangely potent synthesis of life-in-death, revealing the essence of character, and one which, when embodied in Pico, 'alive in the grave', and in Winckelmann's unearthed classical sculptures, 'still red with life in the grave', could also be said to be the character of the Renaissance itself.

37 For Stevens and Pater see Bates 1985, 111–14.

Pater's Romantic Images

Pater's maverick early biographer Thomas Wright tells how, whether deliberately or not, Pater was omitted from the invitations to the unveiling at University College, Oxford, of Edward Onslow Ford's *Shelley Memorial*, the subject of David Getsy's chapter on '"hard realism"' (Wright 1907, 2.193–4). As Getsy explains, in his sculpture of the poet Ford chose to ignore the fact that Shelley's body, when recovered from the sea, had suffered much decomposition and was identifiable only by 'the surviving possessions and tattered clothes' (Getsy 2004, 136). In Ford's memorial the body is presented whole and naked, but is unmistakably a frail and lifeless body. To modern eyes the sculptured corpse of Shelley still looks idealised, but, in company with other critics of the day (see Getsy 2004, 138), Wright was perturbed by its naturalism and speculates that Pater would not have admired it, remarking of the domed space in which the statue is housed: 'You feel in that chamber as if you were in a morgue, only worse. The poet is represented just as his poor naked body was taken from the water, and we can't help thinking that, although the statue is a work of genius, it would have been far better buried' (Wright 1907, 2.194). But Pater by no means shuns the morgue and, in spite of Wallen's remark that sculpture saves him 'from the uncanniness of gazing at corpses', does not show compunction on this score elsewhere. The adult Florian in 'The Child in the House' famously visits

> the *Morgue* in Paris, or . . . that other fair cemetery at Munich, where all the dead must go and lie in state before burial, behind glass windows, among the flowers and incense and holy candles – the aged clergy with their sacred ornaments, the young men in their dancing-shoes and spotless white linen – after which visits, those waxen, resistless faces would always live with him for many days, making the broadest sunshine sickly.
>
> (Pater 1910, *MS* 190)

Commenting on 'Pater's preoccupation with death', John Rosenberg remarks on this passage: 'However briefly, the spotless dancers have become perfect works of art, frozen into immobility . . . Their "resistless" faces reflect the expressionless passivity of death, a passivity always erotically charged for Pater. But "resistless," through a cunning transposition, also means *irresistible*.' Rosenberg also recalls Frank Kermode's 'striking connection between Pater's aestheticized image of the Munich dancers and the later life-in-death, death-in-life imagery of Yeats' (Rosenberg 2005, 196), a connection made nearly fifty years earlier. If we turn back to Kermode, we find him pronounce on the Munich cemetery scene: 'This is the simple form of that cult of the dead face which late, separated from all obvious pathological interest, turns up in Yeats, and in Vorticism.' Directly after this, he then moves into a direct recapitulation of the conclusion to Pater's 'Emerald Uthwart' (1892), a story that offers a more complex treatment of the fair male corpse:

> At the end of that very odd story, 'Emerald Uthwart', a hardened medical man expatiates upon the beauty of the corpse from which he is removing a ball of shot, speaking of 'the extreme purity of the outlines, both of face and limbs,' and of 'the flesh . . . still almost firm as that of a living person'. 'This expression of health and life, under my seemingly merciless doings . . . touched me to a degree very unusual in persons of my years and profession . . . The flowers . . . were hastily replaced, the hands and the peak of the handsome nose remaining visible among them; the wind ruffled the fair hair a little; the lips were still red. I shall not forget it'.
> (Pater 1910, *MS* 245–6, cited in Kermode 1986, 64)

Kermode then comments:

> Here is the life-in-death, death-in-life of the Romantic Image, almost essential to the understanding of some of Yeats's poems (and incidentally, anticipating the tone of Thomas Mann.) The beauty of Emerald Uthwart, unimpaired by the shifting distracting motions of life, is a reflection of an aesthetic assumption. The Image has nothing to do with organic life, though it may appear to have; its purity of outline is possible only in a sphere far removed from that in which humanity obtrudes its preoccupations. We look back, once more, to the arbitrary, aniconic, contours of a neoplatonic emblem, and forward to abstraction and the cult of Byzantium.
> (Kermode 1986, 64)

Kermode's Romantic Image has a certain overlap with the treatment of the aesthetic image we find in the work of the French writer and philosopher Maurice Blanchot. Blanchot, like Browne and Pater, is smitten by the conceit of the refinement of death, the disappearance in the corpse of 'the traces of slighter and more superficial dispositions', but he gives this trope a highly idiosyncratic expression, using the figure of the corpse to explain the way in which the aesthetic image of an object suspends and subsumes that object's value and signification in the object world. The after-life of the image, its independence and self-realisation, when it has contained and transformed the object is like the corpse, in which, Blanchot suggests, at a certain point after death, 'the lamented dead person begins to resemble *himself*':

> Himself designates the impersonal, distant, and inaccessible being that resemblance, in order to be resemblance to someone, also draws towards the day. Yes, it is really he, the dear living one; but all the same it is more than him, he is more beautiful, more imposing, already monumental and so absolutely himself that he is in some sense *doubled* by himself, united to the solemn impersonality of himself by resemblance and by image. This large-scale being, important and superb, . . . may recall, because of his sovereign appearance, the great images of classic art. . . . The cadaver is its own image. He no longer has any relations with the world, in which he still appears, except those of an image, an obscure possibility, a shadow which is constantly present behind the living form and which now, far from separating itself from that form, completely transforms itself into a shadow. The cadaver is reflection making itself master of the reflected life, absorbing it,

> substantially identifying itself with it by making it lose its value in terms of use and truth and change into something incredible – unusual and neutral.
> (Blanchot 1981, 82, 83)

The refined reflection that is the image (and the corpse) absorbs the object (and the deceased) and attains a strange primacy. Such a formulation has evident analogies in Romantic and Aestheticist theory. Shelley's sense of the idealisation that occurs in mirroring (and hence the mirror of art) parallels Blanchot's sense of the object as purified ideal held within the reflection that absorbs it:

> Why is the reflection more beautiful than the objects it reflects? The colours are more vivid, yet blended with more harmony; the openings from within into the soft and tender colours of the distant wood, and the intersection of the mountains, surpass and misrepresent truth. (Shelley 1988, 337)

> doesn't the reflection always seem more spiritual than the object reflected? Isn't it the ideal expression of that object, its presence freed of existence, its form without matter? And artists who exile themselves in the illusion of images, isn't it their task to idealize beings, to elevate them to their disembodied resemblance? (Blanchot 1981, 81)

Pater's apprehension of poetry's 'transfigured world' and his assertion of the subsumption of matter or subject by artistic form seem pertinent, as does his idealisation of certain beings who though embodied, when dead, vigorously assert their character in what Blanchot would call a 'disembodied resemblance'.

Blanchot's analysis applies to all aesthetic images – all of them, if you like, in the way they subsume, suspend, and idealise the object, stage a kind of uncanny life-in-death and death-in-life – while Kermode's notion of the Romantic Image remains quite specific. None the less one might speculate that the powerful and alluring Romantic Image, which 'has nothing to do with organic life' and whose 'sphere' is 'far removed from that in which humanity obtrudes its preoccupations' – qualities especially evident in writers who are concerned with Aestheticism, with versions of art for art's sake – that this Image, like Pater's images of the beautiful dead who offer us their purified essence to our gaze, solicits our attention by making conspicuous something that may be common to all images but which is normally hidden from us. This may go some way to explaining the obsessive interest of Pater and other Aesthetic writers in such images.

We should note that 'Emerald Uthwart' stages a careful build-up to the realisation and display of the final Image. Although Kermode does not comment on this, readers will be aware that Emerald's death, rather that like that described in Sir Thomas Browne's 'Letter to a Friend', had been some time in moving towards its eventual close; indeed his last years might be described as a 'death-in-life'. Some years before, when serving as officers in the British army in Flanders, he and a close friend, James Stokes, had been sentenced to die by military firing-squad for a rash initiative regarded by the military courts as a desertion. In a nightmarish scene, the men prepare to die, with their coffins and their graves open before them. Stokes is shot, but Emerald is spared at the last moment, being deemed less responsible for the crime. He is instead publicly disgraced and dismissed from the army. Penniless, humiliated, and broken-hearted, he makes his way back to his much-loved home in Sussex to die among his family, carrying with him 'The memory of the grave into which he had gazed so steadily on the execution morning, into which, as he feels, one half of himself had then descended'. From the moment of reprieve Emerald starts evolving into the Romantic Image he will eventually become. His gentle decline at his Sussex home, peacefully set amid woods and lovely gardens, allows him to 'drink in here the last sweets of the sensible world'. Like Sir Thomas Browne's dying friend, he seems refined, spiritualised by death, 'a kind of mortified grace being evolved by the way', with his essential character manifesting itself in the process: 'The original softness of his temperament, against which the sense of greater things thrust upon him had successfully reacted, asserted itself again as he lay at ease' (Pater 1910, *MS* 240). While he is dying, he hears that there is a reversal of judgement concerning his supposed crime and is offered a commission, and so, finally, dies, with 'a kind of odd satisfaction and pride', his death at the last the result of an 'old gun-shot wound', honourably sustained in battle and 'wrongly thought to be cured' (Pater 1910, *MS* 243, 242). There is, however, a hint that this physical injury, exacerbated by Emerald's distress at his cruel treatment, is the manifestation of the wound inflicted by the cancelled yet fantasised shot of execution. Removing the ball from Emerald's heart, the surgeon writes, 'such mental strain would of course been aggravated by the presence of a foreign object in that place' (Pater 1910, *MS* 244).

Emerald's experience of looking into his grave, and his anticipation of his demise which makes his life a death-in-life, are presaged in the earlier male protagonists of Pater's *Imaginary Portraits* (1887). Sebastian van Storck, consumed by his philosophic, nihilistic desire for the absolute, attempts to 'die to self', purging his life of all other desires to escape the finite object world, and only too glad to give up his life in the act of saving a child. Like Emerald, his mental state produces an allied physical condition: 'the body, following, as it does with powerful temperaments, the lead of the mind and the will, the intellectual consumption (so to term it) had been concurrent with, had been strengthened by, a vein of physical *phthisis*' (Pater 1910, *IP* 109, 112). Antony Watteau, also stricken by consumption, and afflicted by 'the restlessness which . . . is itself a symptom of this terrible disease', is pronounced on his death to have been 'a sick man all his life . . . a seeker after something in the world that is there in no satisfying measure, or not at all' (Pater 1910, *IP* 40, 44). In medieval Auxerre, Denys, the symbolic actor of the myth of Dionysus, subdued and melancholy, continually looking into the grave, retreats into the monastery of St Germain. Having twice escaped death, he comes out of retirement and seemingly submits to his fate when he takes the lead role in a festival pageant 'in which the person of Winter would be hunted blindfold through the streets': 'The old, forgotten player saw his part before him, and, as if mechanically, fell again into the chief place, monk's dress and all.' Inevitably 'The pretended hunting of the unholy creature became a real one, which brought out, in rapid increase, men's evil passions', and the body of Denys is ripped apart in a Dionysian *sparagmos* (Pater 1910, *IP* 75, 76). Duke Carl of Rosenmold, repelled by death, decides to pre-empt it by fabricating his own demise and attending his own funeral. Shortly afterwards he 'returns to life', determining that 'He would never again be quite so near people's lives as in the past – a fitful, intermittent visitor – almost as if he had been properly dead; the empty coffin remaining as a kind of symbolical "coronation incident," setting forth his future relations to his subjects' (Pater 1910, *IP* 140). Ironically the coffin and funeral rites also have to do duty for the Duke's own accidental death which occurs not long after, the place of his actual decease and his remains being unknown.

The sometimes bizarrely literal death-in-life experiences of the *Imaginary Portraits* are themselves preceded by *Marius the Epicurean*, a novel much possessed by death. Marius, who from a young age takes the honouring of the dead seriously, as a young man shares the deathbed of his friend Flavian to keep his dying companion warm. Later, shortly before his own death, he revisits his family home, drawn towards the place by 'the dead before him': 'It was as if they had been waiting for him there through all those years, and felt his footsteps approaching now, and understood his devotion, quite gratefully, in that lowliness of theirs, in spite of its tardy fulfilment.' On arrival, he enters his family tomb and contemplates the many mortuary urns. 'With a vain yearning, as he stood there, still to be able to do something for them, he reflected that such doing must be, after all, in the nature of things, mainly for himself.' And so he undertakes to bury the dead, 'deep below the surface, to be remembered only by him' (Pater 1910; *ME* 2.204–5, 207; 1985, 286, 287).

Just as the dead allure Marius towards his family sepulchre, so do these extended death-in-life narratives draw us ineluctably towards their inevitable conclusions. As incomplete adumbrations of the Romantic Image, they show us the formation of these young men's characters in a process of refinement that takes its cue from the death they incline towards. Their lives are evolving works of art whose character will finally be determined at the fixed point of death. As we have seen, these many examples of death-in-life are counterpointed by the explicit images of life-in-death found in Emerald's coffin and in the beautiful young men of *The Renaissance*, 'alive in the grave'. Yet Pater's most famous Romantic Image in *The Renaissance* and indeed all his work – a key one for Yeats[38] – is, of course, a woman: the Mona Lisa, who owes her life-in-death death-in-life qualities to the fact that 'like the vampire, she has been dead many times, and learned the secrets of the grave' (Pater 1980, *Ren* 99).[39] She is an Image, which, as Kermode declares, 'owes much to Rossetti' (Kermode 1986, 62). Kermode does not comment on the fact that the Munich cemetery scene and the post-mortem of Emerald Uthwart feature specifically masculine and homoerotic versions of the Image, although he does remark a little earlier (in a language conditioned by his time), that, in relation to 'the investigation of pathological sexuality' in Catullus, Verlaine, and Baudelaire, 'the cult of the Image and that of abnormality and estrangement are found in association' (Kermode 1986, 63). However, Kermode seems to have no problem *per se* with Pater's masculine Romantic Images. Although, on account of its beauty and passivity, the Image is typically feminine, its constitution, its synthesis of these qualities along with those of life and death, make it potent regardless of gender. John Addington Symonds, another homosexual writer alert to male beauty, none the less lights on a feminine Romantic Image as a leading symbol for his *Renaissance in Italy*, and when, in 1875, Pater reviewed the first volume, *The Age of the Despots*, published that same year, we should hardly be surprised that the sole excerpt he cites from the book as 'a specimen of Mr Symonds's style' is centred on that compelling Image. In this excerpt, Symonds retells a story by the anti-papal humanist lawyer Stefano Infessura of the discovery in 1485 of a Roman sarcophagus inscribed 'Julia, daughter of Claudius':

> and inside the coffin lay the body of a most beautiful girl of fifteen years, preserved by precious unguents from corruption and the injury of time. The bloom of youth was still upon her cheeks and lips; her eyes and mouth were half open, her long hair floated round her shoulders. She was instantly removed to the Capitol; and then began a procession of pilgrims from all the quarters of Rome to gaze upon this saint of the old Pagan world. In the eyes of those enthusiastic worshippers her beauty was far beyond imagination or description; she was far fairer than any woman of the modern age could hope to be. At last Pope Innocent VIII. feared lest the orthodox faith should suffer by this cult of a heathen corpse. Julia was

38 Yeats famously printed Pater's description of Mona Lisa arranged in the form of free verse as the opening poem in his *The Oxford Book of Modern Verse 1892–1935* (Yeats 1936, 1).

39 Pater's description of the painting of the Medusa, then ascribed to Leonardo, is another feminine or possibly androgynous Romantic Image, combining beauty and horror, stasis and motion, and life and death. In the first edition of *The Renaissance*, Pater's description of the Medusa carries an explicit reference to Shelley's poem on the same painting which notes the same syntheses (see Donald Hill's textual note in Pater 1980, *Ren* 230). For a treatment of Shelley's poem see Maxwell 2001, 80–7.

> buried, secretly and by night by his direction, and naught remained in the Capitol but her empty marble coffin.
>
> (Symonds cited in Pater 1980, *Ren* 199–200)[40]

Interestingly in this story it is the actual corpse of Julia, embalmed, and therefore not subject to decay, that preserves her 'bloom of youth', her vital essential beauty in death. It is this body with its curious life-in-death that captures the imagination of quattrocento Rome, rather than the recovered beautiful classical sculpture, the usual relic of antiquity and symbol of the Renaissance. As Pater had himself imagined beautiful young men 'alive in the grave' as embodying the character of the Renaissance, he cannot but have been struck by Symonds's declaration that 'What foundation for the legend may really have existed need not here be questioned. Let us rather use the mythus as a parable of the ecstatic devotion which prompted men of that age to discover a form of unimaginable beauty in the tomb of the classic world' (Symonds cited in Pater 1980, *Ren* 200).

Edith Cooper and Katherine Bradley, the Victorian lesbian couple who wrote as Michael Field, were probably familiar with all these life-in-death images, as they had well-developed interests in both European art and Italy. They were both admirers of Pater. When in 1895, the year after Pater's death, Edith Cooper records a dream about herself and Katherine ('Michael'), it is evidently Pater's youths 'alive in the grave' who are her influence:

> Michael & I were in an Italian Duomo, visiting a Tomb on which was the Effigy of a beautiful youth, painted to look like life. The board-floor was shaky round the tomb, but treading lightly we came close: then the Effigy turned over from supine to prone, & we saw the rich-long lashes of oaten-gold lift & pale mocking eyes opened on us, while a fine, smiling tremour [*sic*] quickened the mouth, & I cried out *I have seen the Renaissance*!
>
> (Cooper cited in Leighton 2003, 225)[41]

Yet, of course, what Cooper sees is not so much the Renaissance, but Pater's *Renaissance*, or rather his highly idiosyncratic image for it, an epitome of all the Romantic 'strangeness and beauty' he found in the subject and presented for contemplation in his famous study of 1873.

40 Donald Hill includes this review (Pater 1980, *Ren* 196–202), along with another on Sidney Colvin's *Children in Italian and English Design* (1872), in his edition. See the recent edition of Vernon Lee's *Hauntings* for comment on the influential appeal of Infessura's story for a number of Aesthetic writers (Lee 2006, 238).

41 Extract taken from the unpublished journal of Michael Field for 1895, British Library Add. MS 46783, fol. 13a. Leighton, who gives a longer extract, suggests that Cooper responds to Pater's Mona Lisa (Leighton 2003, 225). In context the dream refers obliquely to Bernard Berenson, another scholar of the Renaissance, but the imagery is clearly Paterian.

Death and the maiden

If, with a few notable exceptions, the feminine Romantic Image is relatively rare in Pater's works, we might note that the figure of the female mourner, often a mother, a woman present at death, especially a man's death, is recurrent. We see her first in 'The Poetry of Michelangelo', where, having spoken of the all pervading atmosphere of death in fifteenth-century Florence, which gave the great Florentines their seriousness, Pater discusses Michelangelo's sentiment of pity which always accompanies his treatment of death:

> *Pietà*, pity, the pity of the Virgin Mother over the dead body of Christ, expanded into the pity of all mothers over all dead sons, the entombment, with its cruel 'hard stones':– this is the subject of his predilection. He has left it in many forms, sketches, half-finished designs, finished and unfinished groups of sculpture . . . There is a drawing of his at Oxford, in which the dead body has sunk to the earth between the mother's feet, with the arms extended over her knees.
>
> (Pater 1980, *Ren* 74)

At the other end of Pater's *œuvre*, in what is perhaps his most striking example, the doctor, commissioned to carry out Emerald Uthwart's post-mortem, reports that

> The mother of the deceased was present, and actually assisted my operations, amid such tokens of distress, though perfectly self-controlled, as I fervently hope I may never witness again. . . . The expression of health and life, under my seemingly merciless doings, together with the mother's distress, touched me to a degree very unusual, I conceive, in persons of my years and profession.
>
> (Pater 1910, *MS* 245–6)

In between these figures we have the mother of Marius, a widow, whose young son is 'sincerely touched and awed by his mother's sorrow', her 'sustained freshness of regret' for his father dead ten years before: 'The life of the widow, languid and shadowy enough but for the poignancy of that regret, was like one long service to the departed soul; its many annual observances centering about the funeral urn' (Pater 1910, *ME* 1.17; 1985, 45). Indeed the 'cloistral' atmosphere of his home

> made the whole place seem to Marius, as it were, *sacellum*, the peculiar sanctuary, of his mother, who, still in real widowhood, provided the deceased Marius the elder with that secondary sort of life which we can give to the dead, in our intensely realised memory of them – the 'subjective immortality,' to use a modern phrase, for which many a Roman epitaph cries out plaintively to widow or sister or daughter, still in the land of the living. . . . And Marius the younger, even thus early, came to think of women's tears, of women's hands to lay one to rest, in death as in the sleep of childhood, as a sort of natural want.
>
> (Pater 1910, *ME* 1.20, 21; 1985, 47)

The atmosphere of austere, tranquil beauty with which Marius' widowed mother surrounds his childhood is revived much later in the novel, when Marius encounters Cecilia, a 'wealthy Roman matron' and widow of Cecilius, whose house serves as a meeting place for a congregation of the early Christian Church. The grounds of the house encompass a crypt, originally 'the family burial-place of the Cecilii', but now expanded underground into a 'vast *necropolis*, a whole township of the deceased', to house the dead of the Christian community (Pater 1910, *ME* 2.105, 98, 99; 1985, 233, 239). Cecilia, who is thus the guardian of the dead, and whose 'temperate beauty' reminds Marius of 'the serious and virile beauty of the best female statuary of Greece', is also a maternal icon, first seen carrying 'a little child at rest in her arms', with another small child accompanying her, 'the fingers of one hand within her girdle'. After becoming a regular attender at services, Marius, struck by 'the sympathy of that pure and elevated soul', for a while entertains the thought of marrying her: 'in this woman, to whom children instinctively clung, he might find such a sister, at least, as he had always longed for'. Our final glimpse of Cecilia, a somewhat shadowy figure always seen at a distance, is when Marius arrives one day to find her 'occupied with the burial of one of the children of her household', a burial which seems to coincide with the interment of his hopes: 'And now perusing intently the expression with which Cecilia assisted, directed, and returned afterwards to her house, he felt that he too had had to-day his funeral of a little child' (Pater 1910, *ME* 2.105, 186, 187, 188; 1985, 233, 276, 277).

After *Marius*, we find the unnamed diarist of 'A Prince of Court Painters' (identified historically with Marie-Marguerite Pater, the sister of the painter Jean-Baptiste Pater), who, tied to her domestic female sphere, does not directly witness Watteau's death, but none the less follows the reports of his dying and expresses sorrow and pity for him. Commenting on his at last taking comfort in 'matters of religion', she remarks:

> Ah! It was ever so with me. And one *lives* also most reasonably so. – With women, at least, it is thus, quite certainly. Yet I know not what there is of a pity which strikes so deep, at the thought of a man, a while since so strong, turning his face to the wall from the things which most occupy men's lives.
>
> (Pater 1910, *IP* 43)

And, in 'Hippolytus Veiled: A Study from Euripides' (1889), there is the Amazon Antiope, the rejected mistress of King Theseus, who, living in retirement in one of the 'doomed, decaying villages . . . within the Attic border', makes the care of their son Hippolytus the chief concern of her life, while always foreboding his death. As a young man, the chaste and handsome Hippolytus, a victor of the chariot-race, attends his father's court where he unwittingly inspires a mad lust in his stepmother Phaedra. When he resists her advances, she falsely accuses him of assault, and he is cursed by his father the King. Returning home, he soon after falls ill, with a sickness his mother fears is fatal:

> As if for the last time, she presses on him the things he had liked best in that eating and drinking she had found so beautiful. The eyes, the eyelids are big with sorrow; and, as he understands again, making an effort for her sake, the healthy light returns into his; a hand seizes hers gratefully, and a slow convalescence begins, the happiest period in the wild mother's life.
>
> (Pater 1910, *GS* 163, 184)

She nurses him back to health, puts her misgivings to one side as he resumes his passion for racing, only to find his body brought home horribly broken and disfigured, 'entangled in the trapping of the chariot', after his horses are scared by a freak wave on the shore. We glimpse her at the end, 'counting the wounds, the disfigurements, telling over the pains which had shot through that dear head now insensible to touch among the pillows under the harsh broad daylight' (Pater 1910, *GS* 186).

We might observe that in the main these sorrowing or pity-filled women are tied to the domestic sphere and, on the whole, are obliged to live their lives through those of men, who may be living, but are often dead, dying, or doomed to die. These women too, like the men they so often mourn, enact the script of a death-in-life narrative. Pater's use of Greek myth helps us locate an archetype of this female mourner, who is a kind of mother or midwife to death, although in her case it is a maiden that she mourns. It is in the early essay 'Winckelmann', in which Pater first proposes that the Greeks had their own '"worship of sorrow"', that the name of the goddess Demeter first appears: 'Greek religion has not merely its mournful mysteries of Adonis, of Hyacinthus, of Demeter' (Pater 1980, *Ren* 162, 180, 178).

The essay 'Demeter and Persephone', published three years after the first edition of *The Renaissance*, is a sustained treatment of the myth of Kore. (The Kore, Persephone, or Proserpine myth was also, as we saw in Chapter 1, a myth that haunted Rossetti.) For Pater, Demeter is, in the first instance, 'the goddess of the fields and originator and patroness of the labours of the countryman, in their yearly order' (Pater 1910, *GS* 93). He opens his essay with a translation of the Homeric Hymn to Demeter, the 'central expression . . . of the story of Demeter and Persephone', which tells how, with the consent of Zeus, king of the gods, Persephone, while gathering flowers apart from her mother, is snatched by Aidoneus, ruler of the Underworld, who carried her away weeping to be his consort. Demeter, hearing her cry, searched high and low for her child, to no avail, until she is finally told what had happened by the Sun who had witnessed the abduction. In her grief, Demeter forsook the assembly of the gods and lived among men in the form of an aged woman, full of regret for daughter, and laying waste the earth which normally was in her care. Finally, at the intervention of Zeus, Hermes, messenger of the gods, is sent to the Underworld, the kingdom of the dead, to entreat Aidoneus to let Persephone return to her mother. Aidoneus agrees but, before Persephone departs, persuades her to eat a little of a pomegranate, 'designing secretly thereby, that she should not always remain upon earth, but might some time return to him' (Pater 1910, *GS* 82, 90). The women are finally united but Zeus orders that Persephone must remain two parts of the year with her mother and one part with her husband in the Underworld.

In its earliest forms the myth seems intended to explain 'the earth in its changes, the growth and decay of all things born of it' (Pater 1910, *GS* 97). The myth presents the natural cycle of the year in terms of loss and mourning. Thus when Persephone is with her mother the earth is fertile, but when she returns to her husband, her mother mourns, winter falls, and the earth is dormant and barren. Twice, in his ensuing discussion of the myth and its religious significance, Pater reminds us of his earlier remarks in 'Winckelmann' when, with regard to Demeter's sufferings and the mournful nature of her story, he tells us that 'the "worship of sorrow," as Goethe called it', is erroneously supposed to have no place in classical religious sentiment (1910 Pater, *GS* 110, 134).

In his explanation of the complexities of the evolving identities of Demeter and Persephone, Pater, as ever, is conscious of mergence and fusion:

> The gods of Greek mythology overlap each other; they are confused or connected with each other, lightly or deeply, as the case may be, and sometimes have their doubles, at first sight as in a troubled dream, yet never, when we examine each detail more closely, without a certain truth to human reason.
>
> (Pater 1910, *GS* 100)

Broadly following Ruskin, Pater distinguishes three phases of myth.[42] In the first phase, the 'instinctive, or mystical, phase', myth exists as a mutable 'unwritten legend', an attempt to make sense of 'certain primitive impressions of the phenomena of the natural world'. Thus in this phase, Demeter and Persephone come into being 'at first in a sort of confused union'. In this second phase, 'the poets of a later age' take possession of this earlier 'conception': 'they create Demeter and Persephone as we know them in art and poetry . . . the mother and the daughter define themselves with special functions, and with fixed, well-understood relationships'. Thus Demeter is 'the goddess of agriculture, of the fertility of the earth' and 'the guardian of married life, the deity of the discretion of wives . . . the founder of civilised order, . . . the patron of travellers' (Pater 1910, *GS* 91, 92, 103, 108). Lastly, in what Pater calls the 'third' or 'ethical phase', 'the myths of the Greek religion become parts of an ideal, visible embodiments of the susceptibilities and intuitions of the nobler kinds of souls' (Pater 1910, *GS* 91, 92–3, 137). In this third or ethical phase Demeter becomes 'the type of divine grief', 'the weary woman, indeed, our Lady of Sorrows, the *mater*

42 For the links with 'Ruskin's schematization' of myth in *The Queen of the Air* see Evangelista 2002, 109.

dolorosa of the ancient world, but with a certain latent reference, all through, to the mystical person of the earth', or 'Demeter *Achæa*, Ceres *Deserta*, the *mater dolorosa* of the Greeks, a type as not yet recognised in any other work of ancient art' (Pater 1910, *GS* 114, 144–5). It is in the ethical phase that these types of sorrow get embodied in sculptural form.

First seen gathering flowers and, thus, associated with them, Persephone is called 'the flower-like girl' in the Homeric Hymn to Demeter, or, more strictly, 'καλυκῶπις (*kalukoupis*) – like the budding calyx of a flower'. Rising from the Underworld every spring, she heralds and embodies summer, 'the flowery splendour and consummated glory of the year', ushering in autumn when she is obliged to return once more to the land of the dead (Pater 1910, *GS* 83, 117, 109). While in 'the mythical conception . . . the mother and daughter are almost interchangeable', Persephone, 'always at the side of Demeter and sharing her worship', gradually becomes detached from her, 'going and coming, on her mysterious business'.

> From being the goddess of summer and the flowers, she becomes the goddess of night and sleep and death, confuseable [*sic*] with Hecate, goddess of midnight terrors, – Κόρη ἄρρητος (*Korē arrētos*) the mother of the Erinnyes . . . She is a twofold goddess, therefore, according as one or the other of these two contrasted aspects of her nature is seized, respectively. A duality, an inherent opposition in the very conception of Persephone, runs through all her story, and is part of her ghostly power. There is ever something in her of a divided or ambiguous identity: hence the many euphemisms of later language concerning her.
>
> (Pater 1910, *GS* 108, 109, 109–10)[43]

Towards the end of his essay, Pater comments that 'as sorrow is the characteristic sentiment of Demeter, so awe of Persephone'. While the conception of Demeter is 'chiefly human, and even domestic', Persephone 'is wholly unearthly . . . *Despœna*, the final mistress of all that lives . . . She is compact of sleep, and death, and flowers, but of narcotic flowers especially' (Pater 1910, *GS* 148).

Clearly as a woman bereaved of a beloved child, a type, then, of grief, a *mater dolorosa*, an original domestic goddess, shrouded by death-in-life, Demeter is behind the mourning, pitying women of Pater's funereal texts; but always implicit as the object of sorrow and loss, is Persephone, goddess of summer, of the bloom of flowers, but also of death itself. Pater, surveying a small sculptural representation of her in her deathly aspect, sees 'the fine shadows of the little face, and of the eyes and lips especially, like the shadows of a flower – a flower risen noiselessly from its dwelling in the dust' (Pater 1910, *GS* 150). Thus, too, we recall from 'Poems by William Morris', Pater's early characterisation of

43 Pater translates this Greek phrase later in his essay as 'the maiden whom none may name' (Pater 1910, *GS* 129).

'beauty' as 'the bloom of the world', his young men 'alive in the grave', and Emerald, dead, with the bloom of youth still on him, 'the body . . . almost hidden under very rich-scented cut flowers . . . The extreme purity of the outlines, both of the face and limbs . . . such is usually found only in quite early youth . . . The flesh . . . still almost as firm as that of a living person' (Pater 1910, *MS* 245). Pater tells us directly that the myth of Persephone is an archetypal myth of loss, containing within itself all other stories of beautiful young people who die, or fall into a death-like sleep, in their prime or bloom of life: 'Her story is, indeed, but the story, in an intenser form, of Adonis, of Hyacinth, of Adrastus – the king's blooming son, fated, in the story of Herodotus, to be wounded to death with an iron spear – of Linus, a fair child who is torn to pieces by hounds every spring-time – of the English Sleeping Beauty' (Pater 1910, *GS* 109). With that last reference one thinks also of Symonds's 'Julia, daughter of Claudius', with 'The bloom of youth still upon her cheeks and lips'. Thus in all Pater's accounts of women pitying or mourning the deaths of comely young men, not only Demeter but, by implication, Persephone is present too in the uncanny bloom of beauty which gives the appearance of life-in-death.

Towards the end of 'Demeter and Persephone', we notice that in describing the three sculptures found in the excavated 'sacred precinct of Demeter at Cnidus', Pater makes a number of analogies with Renaissance works of art. One statue of Demeter has 'something of the wasted pity of Michelangelo's *mater dolorosa*', while another has qualities including 'a certain weight of over-thoughtfulness in the brows', which 'recall the manner of Leonardo da Vinci, a master, one of whose characteristics is a very sensitive expression of the sentiment of maternity'. This same work 'reminds one especially of a work by one of his scholars, the *Virgin of the Balances*, in the Louvre'. Such analogies with these well-known icons not only heighten the value of the mutilated statues, but also suggest that the statues are themselves anticipations of the sentiments and ideals modern viewers find in Renaissance art. Pater reminds us that not only is the myth of Demeter and Persephone the founding myth of maternal loss, but that antique sculptures such as those found at Cnidus are the founding stones in an artistic tradition that stretches to the present day, providing sources for artists like Michelangelo and Leonardo (Pater 1910, *GS* 140, 145, 147). What is more is that in the descriptions of the last few pages we also pick up echoes of Pater's famous portrait of Mona Lisa. Demeter, for example, 'is not without a certain pensiveness, having seen the seed fall into the ground and die, many times' (Pater 1910, *GS* 147), like Mona Lisa, who 'has been dead many time, and learned the secrets of the grave' (Pater 1980, *Ren* 99). But it is Persephone who seems most definitely intended as a classical prevision of Mona Lisa. Not only that, she anticipates *La Gioconda* as *femme fatale* and as a Romantic Image of death-in-life and life-in-death:

> She is compact of sleep, and death, and flowers, but of narcotic flowers especially, – a *revenant*, who in the garden of Aidoneus has eaten of the pomegranate, and bears always the secret of decay in her, of return to the grave, in the mystery of those swallowed seeds; sometimes in later work, holding in her hand the key of the great prison-house, but which unlocks all secrets also; (there, finally, or through oracles revealed in dreams;) sometimes, like Demeter, the poppy, emblem of sleep and death by its narcotic juices, of life and resurrection by its innumerable seeds, of the dreams, therefore, that may intervene between falling asleep and waking. Treated as it is in the Homeric hymn, and still more in this statue, the image of Persephone may be regarded as the result of many efforts to lift the old Chthonian gloom, still lingering on in heavier souls, concerning the grave, to connect with it impressions of dignity and beauty, and a certain sweetness even; it is meant to make men in love, or at least with peace, with death. The Persephone of Praxiteles' school, then, is *Aphrodite-Persephone, Venus-Libitina.* Her shadowy eyes have gazed upon the fainter colouring of the under-world, and the tranquillity born of it, has 'passed into her face'; for the Greek Hades is, after all, but a quiet, twilight, place, not very different from that *House of Fame* where Dante places the great souls of the classical world.
>
> (Pater 1910, *GS* 148–9)[44]

Thus Persephone functions for Pater as the archetypal image of death-in-life and life-in-death, underlying all other such images, and present in all images of dead youth mourned by a Demeter, a sorrowing mother figure. In *Gaston de Latour*, his last unfinished novel, part of which was published after his death, Pater tells us that for the young Gaston 'sorrow came along with beauty, a rival of its intricate omnipresence in life' (Pater 1910, *GL* 23; 1995, 11). Yet Demeter is not so much a rival as an inseparable companion to the deathly bloom of beauty that is Persephone, and a witness to the visionary essence or character that she precipitates in the faces of the dead. Source of those 'women's tears' which Marius 'came to think of . . . as a sort of natural want', the goddess of sorrow brings awareness too of what Gaston intuits as 'the great stream of human tears falling always through the shadows of the world' (Pater 1910, *GL* 23; 1995, 12).

44 Donald Hill mentions that Pater's 'visionary meditations on Demeter and Persephone (1876) . . . are of the same genre' as the Mona Lisa (Pater 1980, *Ren* 380), while Richard Dellamora finds Persephone 'close to the nineteenth-century image of the *femme fatale*' (Dellamora 1990, 175). The quoted phrase '"passed into her face"' recalls Wordsworth's 'Three years she grew in sun and shower': 'And beauty born of murmuring sound / Shall pass into her face' (Wordsworth 1997, 71).

3

Of Venus, vagueness, and vision: Vernon Lee, Eugene Lee-Hamilton, and 'the spell of the fragment'

For a thousand years I lay,
Deep imbedded in the clay;
And the ground above the sleeper
Grew unnoticed ever deeper,
Day by day.

Men and women
Overhead
Lived their little life
Of an hour,
Like the flower
And the herb.
Beauties courted and superb
Felt decay
And passed away,
Like a breath;
Knowing nothing of the beauty,
Ever radiant,
Underneath.

(Eugene Lee-Hamilton 1878, 95–6)

It happened that in digging the ground for a fresh piece of vineyard, a spade struck upon an uncommonly large round stone, which being uncovered, disclosed itself to be a full-length woman, carved in marble, and embedded in the clay, face upwards. The peasants fled in terror, some crying out that they had found an embalmed Pagan, and some, a sleeping female devil. But Eudæmon merely smiled, and wiped the earth off the figure, which was exceeding comely, and set it up on a carved tombstone of the ancients, at the end of the grass walk through the orchard, and close to the bee-hives.

(Vernon Lee 1904b, 181)

Both the writers Eugene Lee-Hamilton and his half-sister Vernon Lee were given to images of burial and submersion, disinterment, emergence and discovery. If those images connected with burial suggest repression or storage, those associated with disinterment commonly have archaeological function, suggesting the coming-to-light or excavation of lost or broken objects, and offering the reader depth-models of the past or the psyche. In a sonnet titled 'Sunken Gold', from *Apollo and Marsyas, and Other Poems* (1884), later collected in *Sonnets of the Wingless Hours* (1894), Lee-Hamilton pictures submerged treasure representing the 'wasted gifts, the long-lost hopes' lying 'Beneath the now hushed surface of myself, / In lonelier depths than where the diver gropes' (Lee-Hamilton 1884, 131; 1894, 52), a cruelly apt illustration of his abilities and ambitions frustrated by the long illness that afflicted him for over twenty years. Another sonnet by Lee-Hamilton, 'Roman Baths' from *Sonnets of the Wingless Hours*, describes how one day rich mosaic pavements are found beneath the turf that has overgrown the site of some ancient baths:

> So, underneath the surface of To-day,
> Lies yesterday, and what we call the Past,
> The only thing which never can decay.
>
> Things bygone are the only things that last:
> The Present is mere grass, quick-mown away;
> The Past is stone, and stands for ever fast.
>
> (Lee-Hamilton 1894, 94)

Vernon Lee, no less than her brother, was particularly sensitive to the artefacts of classical antiquity, and the way that, in Italy, they appear at once exotic and utterly commonplace, almost incidentally punctuating the landscape of the present with a mark of the distant past. In her essay 'Old Italian Gardens' (1895), she comments how, in the outskirts of Rome,

> from underground, everywhere, issues a legion of statues, headless, armless, in all stages of mutilation, who are charitably mended, and take their place, mute sentinels, white and earth-stained, at every intersecting box hedge, under every ilex grove, beneath the cypresses of each sweeping hillside avenue, wherever a tree can make a niche or a bough a canopy.
>
> (Lee 1897, 121–2)

From 'Among these inhabitants of the gardens of Cæsar, Lucullus, or Sallust, who, after a thousand years' sleep, pierce through the earth into new gardens', she singles out those anonymous, battered, and disfigured statues that now serve as garden Hermes, and wonders if they were once busts of Cæsars, hastily made and hastily adapted to suit successive emperors, or philosophers 'once presiding over the rolls of poetry or science in some noble's or some rhetor's library', or even sometime works of genius by sculptors such as Phidias or Praxiteles (Lee 1897, 122–3). Though they 'pierce through the earth into new gardens', these fragments of an earlier age, although endlessly suggestive, can offer no hard and fast answers to the question of their identity.

This question of a statue's identity is central to one of Lee's later stories 'Marsyas in Flanders', from *For Maurice* (1927), set in the Middle Ages but told to a modern narrator by a local antiquary. An effigy, presumed to be a figure of the crucified Christ but lacking its arms and cross, is cast up by the sea on the Flemish coast. Adopted by the local people, the image is mounted on a cross and erected in a nearby church, but is found on successive occasions to have shifted its position and broken free from the cross. Finally, after strange events witnessed by the church warder, who subsequently goes mad, the authorities privately make and install a substitute crucifix, while they bury the effigy beneath a nearby outhouse vault, having '"run an iron stake through his middle, like a vampire, to prevent his rising."' The Antiquary shows the narrator the recovered effigy, which turns out to be not an image of Christ, but '"an antique satyr, a Marsyas awaiting his punishment"'(Lee 1927a, 91, 92). Thrown up from the sea, which perhaps acts as a kind of reservoir of unconscious or submerged images, this relic of the pagan past violently resists the Christian interpretation placed upon it, and is then deliberately repressed by burial. Disinterred after many centuries, it is not allowed to come to public view, but is kept below ground in the darkness of the cellar, and shown only to select visitors. Indeed there is a strong sense that it still retains some of its danger. Something of the effigy's pagan nature seems to permeate the church with its 'gargoyle wolves', its curious suggestions of 'preparations for a witches' sabbath' and 'shrill quavering sound as of pipers inside'. As the Antiquary asks the narrator, '"There – have you ever known such a wild, savage church before?"' (Lee 1927a, 74, 75) The story concludes with the Antiquary's remark: '"I think the Abbot and the Prior were not so wrong as to drive the iron stake through him when they removed him from the church"' (Lee 1927, 92).

The image of something strange that emerges from the depths or from the deep is one which, as we shall see, will reappear in the writing of both Lee and Lee-Hamilton, recalling Pater's brilliant image of the Renaissance, when, 'in the midst of a frozen world, the buried fire of ancient art rose up from under the soil' (Pater 1980, *Ren* 146). In Lee-Hamilton's sonnet 'The Waifs of Time',

> So ever and anon the soundless sea
> Which we call Time, casts up upon the strand
> Some tardy waif from lost antiquity:
>
> A stained maimed god, a faun with shattered hand,
> From Art's great wreck is suddenly set free,
> And stands before us as immortals stand.
>
> (Lee-Hamilton 1894, 36)

In her essay on association, 'The Lake of Charlemagne' in *Juvenilia* (1887), Lee directly figures the process by which 'association gather[s] the past to the present, assimilating for ever new impressions to old ones' through a picture of the mind as the deep whirl of a witches' brew:

> Within the mind of all men for whom or through whom the beautiful exists, there has thus come to exist a perpetual coming and going, submerging and rising to the surface of fragments of thought, and feeling, and perception; a chaotic whirl of atoms, of broken-down fragments of works of art, of shreds dyed with some strange sky or wave tint of nature, of mere imperfect silhouettes, and of most heterogeneous dabs of colour; moreover, faces and voices of persons, branches of trees, bars of melody, snatches of verse, little shreds of mysterious and momentary feelings, of love and hate and hopefulness and sorrow; a perfect witches' caldron full, and seething like a witch broth, each atom seeking the atoms most akin to itself, uniting with them, but usually to be swept back again into the common whirl.
>
> (Lee 1887, 62–3)

One image powerfully connected with the beautiful that whelms up in the work of both Lee and Lee-Hamilton is the figure of the Venus, goddess of love, born of the foam of the sea. Eugene Lee-Hamilton had a long-standing interest in Venus and sculptural images of her, and his first volume of verse, *Poems and Transcripts* (1878), contains two poems about statues of the goddess – 'The Song of the Plaster Cast' and 'Venus Unburied' – the first of these providing the epigraph for this chapter. What his biographer Harvey T. Lyon calls his 'Venus-worship' (Lyon 1955, 104) meant that Lee-Hamilton included one or more poems about Venus in five out of the six collections of his verse published between 1878 and 1894.[1] Vernon Lee, who, as I have argued elsewhere (Maxwell 2006b), was deeply influenced by her older half-brother, seems to have absorbed his passion for Venus which appears most prominently in her stories 'Dionea' (1890) and 'St. Eudæmon and His Orange-tree' (1904), but also arguably constitutes a latent force in all her early tales.

Both writers were fascinated by the theme of revenants from the pagan past. Lee, in particular, would explore this theme in a number of texts: apart from the three stories already mentioned – 'Dionea', 'St Eudæmon', and 'Marsyas in Flanders' – it recurs in a number of her other tales and essays such as 'Pictor Sacrilegus' (1891), collected in *Renaissance Fancies and Studies* (1895), 'Dionysus in the Euganean Hills' (1921a), 'Dom Sylvanus' (1921), and 'The Gods and Ritter Tanhûser' (1927), from *For Maurice*. However, Venus has a special prominence in the work of both writers. Although this chapter does not treat Lee's later tale 'St. Eudæmon' in any detail, it traces the origins and development of both writers' interest in Venus, focusing attention on their treatment of a particular image of a Venus cast up from the deep and its significance for

1 The exception is *The New Medusa, and Other Poems* (1882), although, as will be seen, the title poem contains motifs that link it to other works that do treat Venus.

their work. The appearance of this specific image has an affinity with Lee's presentation of the supernatural and her aesthetic interest in the fragment and the incomplete, both of which belong to a Romantic and Post-Romantic visionary tradition. Ideas and images rehearsed in this opening, such as the often-fragmentary classical artefact, and its excavation, discovery, and mutilation are also important. The chapter ends with an examination of three of Eugene Lee-Hamilton's poems, showing how he too uses ideas similar to his sister's for the visionary projections of his *Imaginary Sonnets* (1888).

Venus rising

There are various key literary and cultural references that underpin and foster both siblings' passion for Venus. In the first instance, the discovery of the Venus de Milo, one of the most significant Greek classical sculptures, had been relatively recent in 1820, when a Greek peasant named Yorgos, digging his land in a mountainous part of the island of Melos, saw the ground subside to reveal a niche containing the Venus. News of the find came first to the French, who determined to acquire the statue for their nation. In his study *Venus Disarmed: The Story of the Venus de Milo*, Gregory Curtis, the most up-to-date commentator on the history of the sculpture, has indicated how the complex story of that acquisition is still dogged by its own mythology such as an apparently spurious pitched battle between the French and the Turks for possession of the statue, a story which till recently was accepted by many authorities (Curtis 2005, 109–12; 115–17). Indeed the art critic Peter Fuller, in his fascinating essay on the history and significance of the Venus de Milo, is inclined to endorse the story of the battle as explaining what he believed to be injuries sustained by the statue after its discovery; an alternative explanation being that this damage may have been the result of the rough handling and transport of the Venus. In any case, according to Fuller, 'there is no doubt that the statue arrived in Paris bearing the signs of relatively recent injuries' (Fuller 1980, 77). He indicates that the precise condition of the Venus, when first discovered, remains unclear, as does that of the fragments found with her, and gives a detailed account of how, 'For much of the 19th century, the dating, attribution and reconstruction of the statue were matters of vigorous controversy' (Fuller 1980, 73).

An early letter of Lee-Hamilton's, sent from Paris to his mother and dated 14 August 1870, shows that he was fascinated by this controversy, writing: 'Tell Baby [Violet] that I heard the Comte de Sortigio . . . say that he was told in Greece by the man who dug up the Venus de Milo (now in the Louvre) that when she was found her arms were with the statue, . . . and are now lost' (cited in Lyon 1955, 104). One noticeable feature of this letter is that Eugene Lee-Hamilton specifically requests that the information about the statue should be passed on to his thirteen-year-old sister; that is, he assumes that she will share his interest and excitement. Much later on, we see Lee-Hamilton participating in the debate about possible reconstructions of the statue in two sonnets paired under the title 'To the So-called Venus of Milo', published in *Sonnets of the Wingless Hours* (1894). As Fuller explains, many different art-critics of the period tried to imagine what the undamaged sculpture would have looked like. Many were of the opinion that she was holding an apple, symbolising her victory in the Judgement of Paris (and, indeed, this is the view held today by Gregory Curtis).[2] Some believed that she may have been holding a spear; others thought that she was holding or supporting a shield, perhaps even looking at herself in its polished surface, while 'Boehm thought she was actually depicted writing on the inside of the shield' (Fuller 1980, 86–7).[3] In the first sonnet Lee-Hamilton takes up the idea of the goddess writing on the shield, but goes so far as to deny the statue is a Venus, instead seeing it more as an inspiring Niké or goddess of Victory made to inspire men before battle:

> No Venus thou; but nurse of legions steeled
> By Freedom's self, where rang her highest note,
> And never has thy bosom felt a kiss:
>
> No Venus thou; but on the golden shield
> Which once thy lost left held, thy lost right wrote
> 'At Marathon and briny Salamis.'
>
> (Lee-Hamilton 1894, 37)

In the second sonnet, more romantic in nature than its predecessor, Lee-Hamilton returns to one of his favourite themes: the buried artefact. The poetic speaker wonders where the statue's missing arms are lying: whether they are tangled in the roots of an old olive tree, or in a corn field, or at the bottom of the sea, or pounded to lime to make mortar, or strewn as dust, 'as was the hand which wrought them in an hour' (Lee-Hamilton 1894, 38).

After its installation in the Louvre, the Venus de Milo became a Romantic icon. Fuller writes:

> Not only Chateaubriand, Lamartine, Victor Hugo and Saint-Victor were seduced by it, but so were much younger Romantic writers: Gautier and Alfred de Musset were among those who had been children when the statue arrived in Paris who wrote poems about it as adults. In Germany, Heine proclaimed the Venus as 'Our

2 'The Venus de Milo was holding up the apple in her left hand as she serenely contemplated the symbol of her victory over Juno and Minerva' (Curtis 2005, 191). Curtis also explains that the apple has a local significance: the shape of the island where the Venus sculpture was found, to the Greeks, resembled an apple, and was thus called Melos, from the Greek μῆλον [*mēlon*] for apple.

3 Probably Sir Joseph Edgar Boehm (1834–90), sculptor-in-ordinary to Queen Victoria.

> Lady of Beauty', and even the English responded without letting their jealousy get the better of them.
>
> (Fuller 1980, 82)[4]

There is a famous story of the last visit to the Louvre of the ill and aged poet Heinrich Heine (1797–1856) to see the Venus de Milo whom he had worshipped throughout his life. Prostrating himself before her, he wept, while she looked at him as if saying 'I have no arms. What do you want from me? What could I do for you?'[5]

Heine was, of course, the author of *Les Dieux en Exil* or *The Gods in Exile* (1853), that influential text which had such a powerful effect on Walter Pater and, after him, Lee-Hamilton and Lee. Heine's essay is a serio-comic account of the clash between Christian and pagan classical culture in the medieval period as told by old fables and ballads. Using these, he narrates how, after the triumph of Christianity, the Olympian gods were forced to go into exile and to hide or disguise themselves, with some of them taking humble jobs to earn their living. Pater introduces his essay 'Pico della Mirandola', first published in 1871, and then collected in *Studies in the History of the Renaissance* (1873), with several paragraphs of translation from *The Gods in Exile*, focusing chiefly on Apollo's return in the Middle Ages.[6] In his fictional stories in the 'gods in exile' vein, 'Denys L'Auxerrois' (1886) and 'Apollo in Picardy' (1893), it is male deities, Dionysus and Apollo respectively, who engage his attention. However, in Heine's text, the first of the pagan deities to be discussed is Venus.[7] The 'most fascinating legends', he writes, are based on the belief that the gods, who 'have lost their majesty by the victory of Christ, and are now sheer devils . . . hide by day in gloomy wreck and rubbish, but by night arise in charming loveliness to bewilder and allure some heedless wanderer or daring youth' (Heine 1892, 307). Outlining an example of this genre, he gives a standard plotline, favoured, he says, by 'popular belief, and our more recent German poets':

> Italy is generally the scene selected, and the hero some German knight who, on account of his youthful inexperience or his fine figure, is ensnared by the beautiful uncanny belles who seek him for his prey. He wanders forth on a fair autumn

4 Fuller cites a long passage from Thackeray's novel *The Newcomes* (1853–54) in which Clive Newcome describes his first visit to the Louvre and the Venus de Milo in the 1830s (Fuller 1980, 82–3).

5 This much-repeated story is mentioned by Lyon in his thesis on Lee-Hamilton (Lyon 1955, 100). It is also the subject of the sonnet 'Venus of the Louvre' by the American poet Emma Lazarus.

6 Pater's editor, Donald L. Hill (Pater 1980, 322), points out that Pater translates not from the French version of Heine's text but from the revised German translation of the essay published in 1853–54.

7 Heine acknowledges as his chief source Heinrich Kornmann's *Mons Veneris* (Frankfurt, 1614).

> day with his solitary fancies . . . But all at once he stands before a marble statue, at the sight of which he stops, startled. It may be the Goddess of Beauty, and he regards her face to face, and the heart of the young barbarian is secretly seized by the sorcery of the olden time.
>
> (Heine 1892, 308)

Heine then tells how, having fallen in love with the fair form depicted, the young man neglects his own friends and pastimes to visit the statue, giving rise to 'strange tales current as to his deeds among the ruins of heathen days. But one morning he burst with pale distorted features into his inn, pays his reckoning, buckles his knapsack, and hastens over the Alps. What has happened to him?' (Heine 1892, 309). It seems that one day, strolling in the ruins after sunset, he is unable to find the usual location of the statue, and eventually, at midnight, finds himself outside a villa. Invited in by the servants, he finds in the brilliantly lit hall a lady resembling his beloved statue. She takes him through many beautiful apartments to the dining hall where she presents him with the choicest delicacies. The wine she offers him gives him confidence to express his love and, finally, he falls asleep 'on the bosom of his tender hostess'. He is then troubled by terrible dreams.

> At last he dreamt that his beautiful hostess had changed to a hideous monster, and that he, in reckless fear of death, had drawn his sword and cut her head off!
>
> It was not until a late hour, when the sun was high in the heaven, that the knight awoke. But instead of the splendid villa in which he thought he had passed the night, he found himself amid the well-known ruins, and he saw that the beautiful statue, which he so dearly loved, had fallen from its pedestal, and its head, broken from the body, lay at his feet!
>
> (Heine 1892, 311)

It is this story which is the basis for 'The Last Love of Venus' in Eugene Lee-Hamilton's collection *Gods, Saints, and Men* (1880), described by him in his Preface to the volume as 'my own development of one of the legends of the Tannhäuser cycle collected or invented by Heinrich Heine' (Lee-Hamilton 1880, vi). The poem, set in the Middle Ages, opens with an encapsulation of Heine's thesis – 'The Gods of beauty and of gladness / Lived on; but exiled and in sadness' – and the narrator subsequently casts himself as emulating Heine: 'I love the legends that relate / To these strange exiles and their fate' (Lee-Hamilton 1880, 1, 3). The poem's rather jaunty metre picks up on the somewhat arch, serio-comic, and tongue-in-cheek quality of Heine's essay, as when, detailing the later employments of the gods, Lee-Hamilton's narrator reminds us of Venus' hiding place in the Venusberg:

> Thus in a mountain's deep recess,
> In undiminished loveliness,
> Dwelt Venus in the middle ages,

Decoying some stray knights and pages,
And cheering exiles' endless leisure
With mortal loves and earthly pleasure.

(Lee-Hamilton 1880, 1)

Like Heine's essay, the poem explores the tension between medieval Christian culture and pagan Hellenism. It focuses on Wolfram, a Swabian Christian in Italy as part of group of knights acting an escort, 'When, to be crowned by Papal hand / Imperial Otho came to Rome' (Lee-Hamilton 1880, 4). Alone of his fellow-countrymen, Wolfram loves to wander among the ancient ruins. He finds a subterranean shrine among the ruins containing a beautiful statue of Venus: ''Twas Venus such as from the wave, / She rose to conquer and enslave' (Lee-Hamilton 1880, 8). Charmed by her beauty, he visits her daily. The main action of the poem, however, takes place on St John's Eve:

For, on that eve beyond a doubt,
All evil spirits were about.
It was the eve on which 'twas said,
The fallen Gods might raise their head,
Emerging from deep hidden mines
To haunt once more their ancient shrines.

(Lee-Hamilton 1880, 10–11)

On this Eve, Wolfram returns to the shrine where, among a pagan festal throng, he meets Venus herself. He pledges his loyalty to her and she gives him a cup of enchanted wine, which makes him dream he is flying with her in a chariot pulled by doves. As they travel, Venus shows him exotic paradisal lands but, when night falls, Wolfram finds he is flying on a broomstick with an ugly old witch who makes him witness horrible and disturbing sights. Seemingly his latent Christian guilt and fears have permeated his reverie. Finally, when he gets the opportunity,

He seized his sword, and with one stroke
Cut off her head, – and then awoke.

'Twas night no more, but early day.
With wondering eyes he looked around:
A lately fallen statue lay
Beside him, headless, on the ground;
The head – that head whose pagan beauty
Had lured him from his Christian duty,
Some paces further off had rolled.

(Lee-Hamilton 1880, 30)

Wolfram also finds that a laurel wreath, which Venus had placed on his head as a sign of his devotion to her, is now branded on his brow. The motif of the statue's mutilation, in this case by decapitation, will prove a significant one for Lee-Hamilton.

In *The Gods in Exile*, Heine discusses the Venusberg, mentioned in this poem, as another of the legends associated with Venus:

> Among the German race rings most exquisitely romantic the legend of the goddess Venus, who, when her temple was destroyed, fled into the heart of a hidden mountain, where she leads the gayest, strangest life with a mad and merry mob of fairy, airy sprites, beautiful nymphs of forest and of stream, and many a famous hero who has suddenly vanished from the world.
>
> (Heine 1892, 315)

By means of old ballads reproduced in his essay, Heine relates the famous story of Tannhäuser, a German knight who is seduced and detained by Venus in her palace under the mountain. This story in the nineteenth century would inspire among other things Swinburne's 'Laus Veneris' (published in *Poems and Ballads* 1866) and Richard Wagner's opera *Tannhäuser*, completed and first performed in 1845. In an essay published in 1872, 'Two Early French Stories', also collected in *Studies in the History of the Renaissance*, Pater briefly refers to Venus who, for him, typifies the antinomianism, the rebellion of the medieval Renaissance against 'the moral and religious ideas of the time': 'It was the return of that ancient Venus, not dead, but hidden for a time in the caves of the Venusberg, of those old pagan gods still going to and fro on the earth, under all sorts of disguises' (Pater 1980, *Ren* 18, 19).

The other story concerning Venus, related by Heine, deals with a

> young knight who once by playing at ball with some friends, finding that the ring on his finger was in the way, drew it off, and to keep it in safety, put it on the finger of a marble statue. But when the game was over, and he went to the statue, which was that of a heathen goddess, he saw with terror that the marble finger on which he had placed the ring was no longer straight as before, but bent so he could not reclaim the ring without breaking the hand, from which a certain feeling of sympathy restrained him.
>
> (Heine 1892, 311–12)

Heine then relates how the knight is troubled by the unwanted attentions of a woman resembling the statue and how he finally rids himself of her. Another source for this story, not mentioned by him, is a medieval tale by William of Malmesbury. William Morris's version of this tale, which he titled 'The Ring given to Venus', appears in his poetic cycle *The Earthly Paradise* (1868–70), but its most famous nineteenth-century incarnation is Prosper Mérimée's macabre tale 'Venus d'Ille' (1837), which uses only part of the original legend with the addition of the unfortunate bridegroom apparently crushed to death by a vast bronze Venus. In the Preface to *Hauntings: Fantastic Stories* (1890), Lee, as part of an ironic discussion about what constitutes an 'authentic' ghost story, briefly refers to the story about Venus and the ring: 'the tale of the finger of the bronze Venus closing over the wedding ring, whether told by Morris in verse patterned like some tapestry, or by Mérimée in terror of cynical reality, or droned by the original mediæval professional storyteller' (Lee 2006, 38). She would herself draw on the legend of Venus and the ring in her story 'St. Eudæmon and his Orange-tree', in *Pope Jacynth and Other Fantastic Tales* of 1904, but it does not play a part in *Hauntings*, her first and best-known collection of supernatural tales. Mérimée does influence Lee but, as we shall see, it is his allusive style and not so much the content of his story 'Venus d'Ille' that has an impact on her.

The malign or sinister power of Venus does, however, filter through into two influential nineteenth-century impressionistic descriptions of *femmes fatales* that had a palpable effect on the strange and elusive spectres that figure in *Hauntings*. In the first instance Swinburne famously describes a drawing by Michelangelo of a snake woman as 'the deadlier Venus incarnate' (Swinburne 1875b, 320; Appendix A in Lee 2006, 280). Secondly, the opening lines of Pater's celebrated impressionistic portrait of Leonardo's Mona Lisa – 'The presence that rose thus so strangely beside the waters, is expressive of what in the ways of a thousand years men had come to desire' (Pater 1980, *Ren* 98; Appendix C in Lee 2006, 288, with variants) – recall the rising of the ever-desirable Venus from the foam. Influenced by both Heine and Swinburne, Pater's description of this beautiful but sinister *femme fatale* renders her, in the words of Denis Donoghue, 'a pagan god in exile' (Donoghue 1995, 135).

The French translation of various of Lee's collected writings, a collection which includes *Hauntings* (*Hallucinations*), is entitled *Au Pays du Vénus* (1894a) – a title which bears witness to the fact that we are in territory ruled by the goddess. Certainly the uncanny beings of the four *Hauntings* stories – the *femmes fatales* Dionea, Medea da Carpi, and Alice Oke and the *homme fatal* Zaffirino – are marked by a cluster of associations that link them to Venus via Swinburne's snaky Venusian *femme fatale* and Pater's mysterious Mona Lisa with her 'unfathomable' smile.[8] Thus the most obvious Venus figure in *Hauntings*, the eponymous Dionea, has 'an odd, ferocious gleam in her eyes, and a still odder smile, tortuous, serpentine, like that of Leonardo da Vinci's women' (Lee 2006, 84). In 'Amour Dure', Spiridion Trepka's arresting description of the portrait of Medea da Carpi with its cool, detached, enigmatic smile evokes Pater's Mona Lisa (see Zorn 1997, 2003; Maxwell 1997). Alice Oke, too, in 'Oke of Okehurst', has a much remarked-on 'irrelevant and far-off smile', and the narrator comments of her: 'That woman would slip through my fingers like a snake if I attempted to grasp her elusive character' (Lee 2006, 122, 147). Finally, in 'A Wicked Voice' the

8 Mona Lisa is herself genetically linked to Leonardo's snaky-haired Medusa in the same essay (see Pater 1980, *Ren* 83). In her excellent article 'Serpentine Rivers and Serpentine Thought: Flux and Movement in Walter Pater's Leonardo Essay' (2002), Lene Østermark-Johansen shows how the serpentine figure pervades Pater's essay.

eighteenth-century castrato singer Zaffirino with his 'odd smile, brazen and cruel', and 'wicked woman's face' bears an undoubted likeness to Swinburne's snake lady, specifically reminding the narrator Magnus 'of my boyish romantic dreams when I read Swinburne and Baudelaire, the faces of wicked, vindictive women' (Lee 2006, 162, 163, 162). Moreover Zaffirino seems aligned with Satan, represented in old paintings as 'the demon with his woman's face' (Lee 2006, 156); that is, in the familiar guise of a serpent with a woman's head. In her preface to 'Winthrop's Adventure' (1881), the early version of 'A Wicked Voice' (1887), Lee tells us that the painted image of the castrato singer Farinelli that inspired both stories was called 'a wizard, *serpent*, sphinx' by the young John Singer Sargent and her youthful self (Lee 1927a, xxx; my emphasis). Intriguingly, one of the descriptions of Zaffirino's voice in 'A Wicked Voice' has a strangely serpentine quality: 'The voice wound and unwound itself in long languishing phrases, in rich, voluptuous *rifiorituras*, all fretted with tiny scales and exquisite, crisp shakes; it stopped ever and anon, swaying as if panting in languid delight' (Lee 2006, 179).

It is, however, 'Dionea' that remains my chief interest here. The story features a beautiful but uncanny young woman, cast up on the Ligurian shore as a child and raised by nuns, whose behaviour puts her at odds with the local community. While the superstitious local peasant community mainly shuns her, she fascinates and enthrals a succession of more educated and well-to-do men such as the local priest Father Domenico, her employer Sor Agostino, a sculptor Waldemar, and the elderly narrator Dr Alessandro De Rosis, who, after the example of Heine, is writing his own study of the pagan gods in exile. All, excepting De Rosis, come to an untimely end on account of their feelings for her. The pious and ascetic Father Domenico, unable to conquer his passion for her, commits suicide; Sor Agostino, who pesters her, is struck by lightning; while Waldemar, unable to capture her beauty in a sculpture, finally falls victim to a pagan religious frenzy, sacrifices his wife Gertrude, and throws himself off a cliff. De Rosis, fascinated by the 'gods in exile' theme, subtly allows it to inform the continuing story of Dionea he is relaying to his patron Lady Evelyn Savelli. Throughout his narrative, he hints that Dionea may be from another sphere and repeatedly draws our attention to her likeness to Venus-Aphrodite, goddess of love. While he comes to the conclusion that there is no historical evidence to support his mythographical thesis, the substance of what he has narrated to Lady Evelyn seems to be a personal verification and can be seen as a substitute version of his abandoned project. De Rosis himself seems spared by Dionea on account of his past kindness to her and because he increasingly feels a 'religious awe' (Lee 2006, 100) in her presence. Her most important conquest is Waldemar, whose exclusive (and perhaps homoerotic) interest in male subjects for his sculptures at first makes him reluctant to use Dionea, as Gertrude

9 For a reading of Waldemar's homoerotic art see Evangelista forthcoming.

proposes, as a model.[9] But, as if rising to the challenge, Dionea accepts Gertrude's proposal and, Waldemar, magnetised by her, changes his mind. Thereafter his previous disdain for the female form is punished by his inability to capture Dionea's growing beauty, and his obsession with his model, which is no simple sexual attraction, makes him into her devotee.

Significantly Dionea opens in 1873, the year of publication of Pater's *Studies in the History of the Renaissance*, bearing his influential allusions to Heine.[10] Lee may partly have identified De Rosis, an elderly scholarly man, fascinated by Heine's tale of the gods in exile, with Pater, although I suspect her narrator may owe more to her friend the novelist Giovanni Ruffini (1807–81), who, like De Rosis, had in his earlier years supported the cause of a Italian Unification and, as a result of his political sympathies, had been obliged to live abroad in exile.[11] De Rosis writes his first letter to his patron, Lady Evelyn Savelli, on 29 June, approximately a week after a storm has washed ashore the orphan Dionea, lashed to a plank. This means that she is likely to have appeared on 23 June, in ancient times the feast day of Venus. As Lee knew, this feast coincides with the Christian feast day of St John's Eve, or the Vigil of the Birth of St John the Baptist, mentioned by Eugene Lee-Hamilton in 'The Last Love of Venus' as the day when the Christian knight Wolfram meets the goddess. This same Christian and pagan feast day also figures in Lee's story 'St. Eudæmon and his Orange-tree' (Lee 1904b, 182, 183, 184) and in other of her tales.[12] The text of 'Dionea' is crammed with suggestive detail alluding to Venus: the name of the village to which Dionea comes is Montemirto Ligure, the first word meaning literally 'myrtle-mountain', and myrtle, a shrub dedicated to Venus, is mentioned frequently in the tale, as are roses – Venus's signature blossom – and white doves or pigeons which are her birds. Lee sets her tale near the actual coastal town of Porto Venere, meaning 'Port of Venus', whose name derives from a nearby former temple site (Lee 2006, 77). The shrine and statue found in Lee-Hamilton's 'The Last Love of Venus' also recur in Lee's story;

10 In Pater's *Marius the Epicurean* (1885), published five years before 'Dionea', Marius's boyhood home at Luna is located near 'Port of Venus', or Porto Venere, which figures significantly in 'Dionea'.

11 In later life, Ruffini, like De Rosis, returned to Italy to live in his native village of Taggia, in Liguria, from which he corresponded with Lee. Similarly De Rosis' (fictional) village Montemirto Ligure, from which he carries on his correspondence with his patron, Lady Evelyn Savelli, is situated in Liguria. See Beatrice Corrigan's article 'Giovanni Ruffini's Letters to Vernon Lee 1875–9' (1962).

12 The feast day of Venus or St John's Eve, 23 June, proves to be a significant date not only in 'Dionea' and 'St. Eudæmon' but also in 'A Wedding Chest' (Lee 2006, 233) and 'Winthrop's Adventure' (Lee 1927b, 179). The narrator of 'Winthrop's Adventure' is told by one of the peasants that, on St John's Eve, 'dead people . . . walk about' (Lee 1927, 185).

Waldemar's studio, where he sculpts his Venus using Dionea as a model, is located on the site of a pagan temple dedicated to the goddess.[13]

'Dionea' may also owe something to Lee-Hamilton's dramatic monologue, 'The New Medusa', from his collection *The New Medusa, and Other Poems* (Lee-Hamilton 1882, 12–27). In this poem, set in 1620, the male narrator also gives in to his suspicions about his mistress whose long, snake-like coils of hair seem to wrap round his throat at night. (Indeed Lee-Hamilton's pervasive snake imagery, here associated with enigma, is another contributing factor to the mysterious serpentine spectres of Lee's *Hauntings* stories.) Like De Rosis in 'Dionea', the narrator of 'The New Medusa' suspects that his mistress's true identity derives from Greek myth; however, in this case, his suspicion brings about her demise. His story begins properly when he tells how, following a terrible storm, he helped rescue from the sea a mysterious and beautiful woman, lashed to a mast, who, like Dionea, seems to be of Greek origin. Bought by him as a slave, she becomes his mistress and accompanies him on his travels. Like Dionea, she is strong and self-contained, and possesses mysterious powers. While the narrator loves her, he also begins to fear her, suspecting she may be a Medusa in disguise. The poem suggests that his suspicion may well be the product of an obsessional delusion, which, allowed to grow, finally brings about the woman's death. Having cut off her head with his sword – an ending that reprises the decollation of the statue in 'The Last Love of Venus' and Heine's essay – he is then filled with terrible misgiving. Lee's Dionea, on the other hand, suffers no such grisly fate. Rather she seems to wreak havoc on those who would resist or molest her, and, having exacted a ritual sacrifice in her honour, sails away into the dawn.

Three years after the publication of *Hauntings*, Eugene wrote his sister a letter (27 August 1893) in which he warmly praised her story 'Dionea' whilst adding some scathing criticisms:

> I have been reading *Dionea*. It is a splendid piece of work – as beautiful as myrtle & olive & doves & sunshine round a treacherous sea. The end especially – the vision of Dionea sailing away – haunts one like a wizard-show glimpse of antique loveliness and terror. But there is too much of 'dearest Excellency' in the story, and one gets tired of the constant see-saw between 'dear Lady Evelyn' and 'dear Donna Evelina'. If I could have read the thing in manuscript I would have made you alter that. Also in your method of telling through allusion you are often bewildering and half your readers won't understand you. I noticed the same fault in your Dialogues, plus the involution & length of the sentences; and I should not wonder if this were enough in itself to explain why you are not more popular than you are.[14]

13 In 'St. Eudæmon', Eudæmon sites his chapel on just such a spot.

14 ELH to VL, Letter of 27 August 1893, Vernon Lee Archive, Colby College, Maine.

Eugene's delay in responding to her collection had been due to his poor health, which, at its worst, had prevented him from reading on his own, and Lee takes this into account in her reply:

> As regards obscurity in the narrative, I think that if you read it three months hence that would not strike you; for you will regain a habit of twigging suggestions and of easily following tortuosities of narrative which is the result of the habit of consecutive reading. You will then, I think, agree with me that such a story requires to appear & reappear & disappear, to be baffling, in order to acquire its supernatural quality. You see there is not real story; once assert the identity of Dionea with Venus, once show her clearly, & no charm remains. The *Venus d'Ille* of Prosper Merimée (there are improper passages, so read it to yrself) by far the finest story of the *Dionea* sort, is quite as obscure and baffling, at least I think so in remembering it. The sort of straight on end mystery as in Gauthier's *Avatar* & *Morte Amoureuse* is very boring. I think stories in which adventure preponderates, like Stevenson's, cannot be too clear in narrative, or stories of the supernatural too allusive.
>
> (31 August 1893; Lee 1937, 363–4)

Definition here is the enemy of the supernatural. The identity of Dionea with Venus, once made plain, would diminish the power of the story. Lee had explored this in more detail in a fine early essay on the supernatural, 'Faustus and Helena' (1880), in which she explains that ghostly effects are brought about only by suggestion and not embodiment: 'paint us that vagueness, mould into shape that darkness, modulate into chords that silence – tell us the character and history of those vague beings . . . What do we obtain? A picture, a piece of music, a story; but the ghost is gone' (Lee 2006, 310).

In the letter she writes to Eugene, we also see Lee confidently reversing the dynamic of the tutorial relationship she had with her brother who, when she was an adolescent, had called her by the pet name of 'Baby' and directed her youthful reading, and who, even in his recent letter, still shows pretensions to correcting what he thinks of as her errors. In her letter, Lee somewhat magisterially reminds her brother about how one reads. She also instructs him to read, for its power of allusion, Mérimée's *Venus d'Ille*, a text which, considering his 'Venus-Worship', he must surely have known well. It is interesting that the jostle for authority that takes place between siblings in this exchange is provoked by a text that demonstrates their shared interest in Venus, an interest which Lee absorbed from her brother. While Lee-Hamilton does not lay claim to the Venus topos in his letter, the detail that he 'would have made' Lee alter salient features of her narrative suggests that he still sees himself as owning her and rewriting her text. Her response undercuts this by suggesting it will take him time to become a properly sophisticated reader and referring him back to the primary material. None the less this tussle between siblings can't really be described as 'Venus envy'; one of the striking details of Lee and Lee-Hamilton's creative relationship is the way in which brother and sister share ideas and interests and borrow from each other. In fact an earlier example of Venus surfacing in the writings of both siblings is the specific result of a find Lee made efforts to share with her brother. It is also a find that perhaps explains something of their joint fascination with the sculptured Venus.

'But doth suffer a sea-change / Into something rich and strange'

Eugene Lee-Hamilton, restricted by his illness to a very limited sphere, had little opportunity to seek out new sights for inspiration. His sister, with a feeling for what might interest him, seems to have kept a look-out for suitable subjects.[15] In a letter written to her mother from Paris on Saturday 23 June 1883, she writes:

> I saw at the Louvre a very beautiful & singular thing, which I recommend to Eugène as a possible sonnet subject. It is a torso, half draped, of a Venus, found on the seashore at a place in Africa called Tripoli Vecchio – somewhere near Carthage, I presume. It has evidently been rolled for years & years in the surf, for it is all worn away, every line & curve softened, so it looks exquisitely soft and strange & creamy, hand, breasts & drapery all indicated clearly but washed by the sea into something soft, vague & lovely. (Lee 1937, 117)

Obviously inspired by his sister's suggestion, Eugene quickly produced a fine sonnet, published the following year in his *Apollo and Marsyas, and Other Poems* (1884). Titled 'On a Surf-rolled Torso of Venus, Found at Tripoli Vecchio, and Now in the Louvre', the sonnet, which shows Eugene's own strong imaginative characterisation, is none the less in its sestet still clearly indebted to Lee's description:

> One day in the world's youth, long, long ago,
>   Before the golden hair of Time grew grey,
>   The bright warm sea, scarce stirred by the dolphins' play,
> Was swept by sudden music soft and low;
> And rippling, as 'neath kisses, parted slow,
>   And gave a new and dripping goddess birth,
>   Who brought transcendent loveliness on earth,
> With limbs more pure than sunset-tinted snow.
> And lo, that self-same sea has now upthrown
>   A mutilated Venus, rolled and rolled
> For ages by the surf, and that has grown
>   More soft, more chaste, more lovely than of old,
> With every line made vague, so that the stone
>   Seems seen as through a veil which ages hold.
>
> (Lee-Hamilton 1884, 133)

15 See, for other examples, Maxwell 2006b, 27.

However, in the manner of the smoothing action of the sea he had described, Eugene continued over time to smooth and polish the poem, producing another version which he included in *Sonnets of the Wingless Hours* of 1894, now titled 'On a Surf-rolled Torso of Venus. Discovered at Tripoli Vecchio':

One day, in the world's youth, long, long ago,
  Before the golden hair of Time grew gray,
  The bright warm sea, scarce stirred by dolphins' play,
Was swept by sudden music strange and low;

And rippling with the kisses Zephyrs blow,
  Gave forth a dripping goddess, whose strong sway
  All earth, all air, all wave, was to obey,
Throned on a shell more rosy than dawn's glow.

And, lo, that self-same sea has now upthrown
  A mutilated Venus, roll'd and roll'd
For centuries in surf, and who has grown

More soft, more chaste, more lovely than of old,
  With every line made vague, so that the stone
Seems seen as through a veil which Ages hold.

(Lee-Hamilton 1894, 44)

This slightly more sophisticated version notably omits the title reference to torso's location in the Louvre, which the invalid Eugene could not have visited in his own right, and thus somewhat diminishes the ostensible debt to his sister's first-hand account. Apart from details such as smoothing out the rhythm by removing the superfluous 'the' in line 3, or changing 'soft' (one of Lee's words) to the more magical and Paterian 'strange' in line 4, Eugene strengthens the portrait of the goddess Venus by evoking in lines 5–8 images from Botticelli's *The Birth of Venus* (*c.* 1485–86) in the Uffizi Gallery, Florence – a well-known picture he could easily have seen in reproduction or viewed before his illness. Part of the work of refinement was to stamp Eugene's own poetic personality more firmly on the poem.

Eugene's use and evocation of his sister's prose inevitably calls to mind Willliam Wordsworth's use of his sister Dorothy's Journal, the difference being that in this instance Lee quite deliberately chose to describe a specific subject expressly for her brother's use. That she was so readily able to identify and describe a subject that would appeal to him and that he could easily develop indicates the degree of creative sympathy that existed between them. Thus although, on this occasion, Lee sparks her brother's writing by her own short text about a Venus sculpture, her own increasing interest in the subject was undoubtedly stimulated by his example.

There are some striking aspects of these texts that cast light on the shared aesthetic preferences of both siblings. Peter Fuller's analysis of reaction to the

Venus de Milo is helpful here because, although Lee and Lee-Hamilton are referring to a different artefact, some aspects of what Fuller says are still relevant to consideration of the Venus torso. In my analysis I shall be referring to the second (1894) version of Eugene's sonnet. Both the texts by the siblings suggest that the Venus torso, the work of human hands, is improved by the work of time and nature. In a comparison with the mythic birth of Venus, implicit in Lee but made explicit by Lee-Hamilton, the Venus torso, 'upthrown' on the shore by the sea in which it has lain for years, undergoes a 'rebirth' in which it appears improved, far more beautiful than when it was first made and first appeared on earth. Its time in the watery womb of the sea is like a second gestation, except that, rather than gaining in features and definition in the manner of a normal developing embryo, the torso loses its finished identity, as the seawater, blurring and softening the original lines of the sculpture, produces a lovelier artefact. In fact, if we refer this to the exchange about 'Dionea' between the two siblings cited earlier, we might say that the sculpture is now more enigmatic, less simple to read; its softened lines making it an 'allusive' rather than a clear text, and, by virtue of that, a more satisfying one in that it doesn't reveal its secrets too easily.

One of the most striking phrases used to describe the sculpture is Lee-Hamilton's 'A mutilated Venus'. Although Lee does not use this or an analogous expression in her prose description, she does, however, use the expression 'mutilated Venus' to describe a broken image of the goddess in her essay 'Symmetria Prisca', first published in 1879, and then collected in *Euphorion* (1884a, 1.171), a coincidence that suggests that Eugene may have borrowed his sister's coinage.[16] Moreover, as has been noted before, the mutilated naked body of a woman is a key image in her work, appearing in 'A Wedding Chest' (1904) in the naked corpse of Maddalena, who has been stabbed through the neck, and at the end of 'Prince Alberic and the Snake Lady' (1896), where the persons employed to clean the prison cell formerly belonging to Prince Alberic discover 'the body of a woman, naked, and miserably disfigured with blows and sabre cuts' (Lee 2006, 237, 227).[17] As we have seen, the figure of a mutilated woman occurs also in Lee-Hamilton's work, in the decapitations that conclude 'The New Medusa' and 'The Last Love of Venus', where, in this last instance, we see another 'mutilated Venus'. However, in the Venus torso texts, the

16 'Symmetria Prisca' was first published as 'The Artistic Dualism of the Renaissance' in the *Contemporary Review* 36 (September 1879), 44–65, and then collected in *Euphorion* (1884), where the phrase 'mutilated Venus' occurs at 1.45. Lee uses the words 'mutilation' or 'mutilated' with regard to broken statues in a number of places such as 'Old Italian Gardens', in *Limbo* (Lee 1897, 121, 123).

17 See the editors' Introduction to *Hauntings* (Lee 2006, 17). Both these stories appeared in Lee's collection *Pope Jacynth and Other Fantastic Tales* (1904).

mutilations endured by this female sculptural body are deemed to constitute its aesthetic charm. Indeed, the torso is likely to have been twice mutilated, firstly by becoming fragmented from an original full-length statue, and secondly by the process of erosion that has occurred during its long stay in the sea. It is significant that, when Fuller comes to discuss the aesthetic appeal of the Venus de Milo, he lists the various kinds of damage to the sculpture, and comments: 'The form with which the observer is confronted today is that of a *mutilated woman*' (Fuller 1980, 96). This form, he asserts, would have been intolerable to the sculpture's original viewers, the Greeks, for one of the distinctions between contemporary and classical appreciation of sculptures is that: 'The Greeks abhorred any evidence of mutilation in their sculptures. (They would not have been able to attend to the Venus in its present state at all, let alone to have derived a deep aesthetic experience from it)' (Fuller 1980, 128). This is in contrast to contemporary taste, which, as Fuller notes, 'commonly prefers Michelangelo's unfinished figures to those that he completed' (Fuller 1980, 128), and he adds that the nineteenth-century cult of the Venus de Milo undoubtedly flourished because of Romanticism and 'the cult of the fragment . . . central to it' (Fuller 1980, 97).

In its original complete state, the Venus de Milo would have conformed to a specific type, but, as Fuller notes, 'Fragmentation physically stripped the Venus out of its original signifying system'. With the loss of its arms, 'the statue was no longer locked so firmly into this intricate set of ideological relations. Its meaning became more ambiguous, and hence more open to annexation by subsequent signifying systems' (Fuller 1980, 108, 109). For Fuller, while appreciation of the damaged Venus de Milo does seem relative in that it involves a Post-Romantic aesthetic of fragmentation, the loss of her arms gives the mutilated statue a rare transcendent and universal quality in that it detaches or disengages her from the specific cultural context of her creation and purpose. I would suggest that, for Lee-Hamilton in particular, something similar happens to the Venus torso. Thus, in the conclusion to his sonnet, the erosion wrought by the sea on the stone makes it seem as if it were 'seen as through a veil which Ages hold'; that is, the erosive effects of time on the torso blur the more defined identity given it by the sculptor, removing it from its specific cultural and historical moment of execution.

However, there may be also a secondary alternative meaning here. An earlier poem by Lee-Hamilton, 'The Song of the Plaster Cast', from *Poems and Transcripts*, has a prose Preface in which the poet explains his intention:

> In the following poem I have attempted to tell the story of a Greek statue; not of this or of that individual copy of it, – for of nearly every great antique, antiquity alone has given us four or five copies, which in modern times have been reproduced indefinitely in marble or plaster, – but of that which constitutes the identity of the statue – which makes us say, in the presence of a plaster cast, or

> merely of a drawing, 'This is the Discobolus of Myron,' 'This is the Faun of Praxiteles,' – in short, of the *form* of the conception which arose in the mind of the sculptor, and which he, first, embodied, but which may be indefinitely repeated – *the form* which corresponds in the statue to that purely intellectual identity which makes the *Iliad* the *Iliad, Paradise Lost Paradise Lost,* in whichever of a hundred different editions it may be seen . . . This abstract *form* and not its individual embodiments in stone or in metal, is *the statue*; and my object has been to trace the many changes of substance through which the form of a renowned Greek Venus has been handed down in all its identity.
>
> (Lee-Hamilton 1878, 87)

Lee-Hamilton is influenced here by notions of Platonic form and by Pater's insistence on the priority of form over matter or material. (Thomas Hardy is of a similar mind when he writes that the 'essence and soul', or 'form', or 'aesthetic phantom' of a building is independent of 'the particular blocks of stone or timber that compose it' (Hardy 1966c, 213–14).) Clearly 'On a Surf-rolled Torso of Venus' and 'The Song of the Plaster Cast' are two distinct poems, but Lee-Hamilton's notion of the sculptor's '*form* of the conception', 'This abstract *form*', inherent in the many different embodiments of the statue, has an application to the Venus sonnet. Both Lee and Lee-Hamilton suggest that the surf-rolled Venus is an improvement on the original sculpture, but there is also the sense that the torso in its current state is now the fulfilment of a long artistic process started by the sculptor but perfected by the sea – a process that evokes Michelangelo's famous notion, mentioned in Chapter 2, that the block of stone already contains with it a form which the sculptor must then release. Thus the erosion wrought by time and the sea does not ruin the sculpture, but rather strips it down and brings it closer to a latent abstract form, the dynamic Shelleyan 'unsculptured image' or Michelangelesque *concetto*, always present in the stone, possibly intuited or intended by the sculptor, but only now able to communicate its power, revitalised by its lack of definition and finish. Thus, in Lee-Hamilton's words, 'the stone / Seems seen as through a veil which Ages hold' *because* the blurring caused by the lapse of time makes the sculpture take on an idea of form always present in the work but only now successfully abstracted from it by time and nature.

We might note, however, that Lee-Hamilton does impose something on the sculpture which could be seen be a symptom of his own time or of his own pathology. He claims that the image of Venus, who, after all, is primarily the goddess of erotic love, is now in its eroded form 'more chaste'; that is, the sea has washed away any obvious voluptuousness, has toned down its sexual appeal or blunted or effaced its specifically sexual characteristics. Interestingly, in Lee's prose description, the 'breasts' of the goddess are still visible, if blurred, and, although she repeats the word 'soft' three times, suggesting a more acceptable taming or domestication of sexual power, her Venus does have its own eroticism, possessing a more evidently tactile and sensuous quality – 'exquisitely soft and strange & creamy' – than her brother's. Does Lee-Hamilton's treatment of the Venus torso thus figure an opportunity to exercise censorship in which he deletes or cancels the threatening self-assertive sexuality of the goddess? Does this treatment form a parallel to 'The New Medusa' where the narrator, subconsciously menaced by his mistress's enigmatic self-containment and confident sexuality, decapitates her? Are these defensive or aggressive manoeuvres a more general symptom of late Victorian prudishness or the specific tactics of a heterosexual man whose disability has removed him from pursuing any kind of sexual relations with women?

While there is doubtless some truth in these propositions, there may be a larger issue at stake. In considering further the issue of a specific aggression directed at the sculpture which is none the less part of a process that also softens and repairs injuries, it is helpful to look at the second part of Peter Fuller's essay on the Venus de Milo, where he draws on psychoanalytic theory associated with the Freudian therapist Melanie Klein in order to account for the statue's appeal. He specifically uses the Kleinian model, formulated by one of Klein's best-known followers, Hannah Segal, who believed that artistic creativity involved a working through of the emotions experienced by the infant as it developed. During its earliest months of life, the infant passes from an initial 'paranoid schizoid' position, characterised by 'splitting', to a 'depressive position'. In the first position, the infant, as Segal expresses it,

> lives in a world of part objects: the mother's breasts, hands, eyes, holding arms. These objects are not only anatomically part objects; they are also split in his mind into very good and very bad ones. The very young infant sways between states of blissful satisfaction where he feels united or fused with his ideal objects and states of hatred and persecution when he feels his objects are totally bad. His love is directed to his ideal objects and his hatred to the bad objects conceived as the sources of all his pain and fear.
>
> (Segal 1975, cited in Fuller 1980, 114–15)

According to Segal, in the succeeding 'depressive position', the infant, formerly aware of 'part objects', now

> perceives complete persons; instead of 'split' objects – ideally good or overwhelmingly persecuting – he sees a whole object both good and bad. The whole object is loved and introjected and forms the core of an integrated ego. But this new constellation ushers in a new anxiety situation.
>
> (Segal 1952, cited in Fuller 1980, 115)

Now the infant fears loss of his loved object in both the external world and its introjected form. With the infant still prevalent to 'uncontrollable greedy and sadistic impulses', which express themselves in phantasy, the external and internal love objects are subject to attack and destruction, causing 'the whole internal world to feel 'destroyed and shattered as well':

> Bits of the destroyed object may turn into persecutors, and there is a fear of internal persecution as well as a pining for the lost loved object and guilt for the attack. The memory of the good situation, where the infant's ego contained the whole loved object, and the realization that it has been lost through his own attacks, gives rise to an intense feeling of loss and guilt, and the wish to restore and recreate the lost love object outside and within the ego.
>
> (Segal 1952, cited in Fuller 1980, 115)

Fuller explains that it is this experience of desolation that provokes reparative impulses and the desire to reinstate the lost object in both its external and internal forms. In Segal's opinion, such impulses constitute '"a fundamental drive in all artistic creativity"' (Segal 1975, cited in Fuller 1980, 116) in that the artist who, in effect, is working through his infantile depressive position again, using his artistic agency, seeks to repair the internal world that he lost through his own aggression. Not only must he seek compensatory re-creation in his inner world, but, in Fuller's words, 'He has also to externalise the completed object, and to give it a life of its own in the external world' (Fuller 1980, 116). Fuller also cites another Kleinian, the art critic and painter Adrian Stokes, who differed from Segal in believing that 'the artist was not just working through the depressive position, but necessarily expressing that sense of fusion with the mother (breast), and sadistic attack upon her, characteristic of the earliest stage' (Fuller 1980, 117) and that 'negative expressions can figure successfully in art only if there is present, as well "a reparative nucleus"' (Stokes 1955, 410, cited in Fuller 1980, 117).

This preamble is necessary in order to appreciate Fuller's important claim with regard to the Venus de Milo that now

> we are . . . in a position to explain the apparent aesthetic superiority of the present mutilated version over its original . . . For the millions who have enjoyed the statue since 1821, she is a representation of the internal 'Mother' who has survived the ravages of a phantasised attack. Despite her fragmentation, the reparative element remains dominant: it is expressed through the fact that the Venus *has* endured throughout the centuries; in the still-evident idealisation in the midst of naturalism; and, above all, . . . through the richness and excellence which the classical sculptor so manifestly attributed to his medium.
>
> The injuries which the statue has sustained have simultaneously rendered it, in Segal's terms, a work which we must complete internally, or at least one which refuses to give us all the answers: this, too, seems to increase our aesthetic enjoyment of it.
>
> (Fuller 1980, 120)

I would contend that something analogous is at stake in both Lee's and Lee-Hamilton's treatment of the Venus torso. Both of them focus on a broken female body but envision it as renewed and perfected by the sea which has smoothed out the rawness of its injuries and made it into something soft and pleasing to the eye. The smoothing process can, however, also be seen as a continued low-level form of aggression in that it erodes the definition of the sculpture; yet both brother and sister insist that such erosion is beneficial, even reparative, as it makes the sculpture lovelier, possibly realising the latent ideal form within the stone. Notably, Lee-Hamilton is more candid about the aggression directed at the sculpture, calling it 'a mutilated Venus', and his finished version seems to have erased more of the sculpture's female sexuality. Lee is less aggressive, giving the image a more specific female eroticism. We might observe too that, for Lee-Hamilton, there is a specific reversal of power in that Venus who was once omnipotent – 'All earth, all air, all wave, was to obey' – becomes subject to the influence of the waves she once mastered.

In most successful artworks the processes of attack on and reparation of the mother's body would be integral to the aesthetic of the work and not immediately visible or obvious. However, in this instance, like the Venus de Milo, the texts or artworks of both siblings have a special fascination in that they directly foreground what we can identify as an image of the mother's wounded and repaired body; the particular nature of the subject matter gives us an allegory of the creative impulses. Certainly here the figure of Venus, an ideal representation of mature female sexual beauty, which also represents the mother, is absorbed or taken into the subject's womblike unconscious where she is reshaped or reformed in a process that can last for years. In this process in which she moves only to the rhythm of the waves or impulses of the unconscious – waves which also gently deface her – we can see that 'sense of fusion with the mother (breast), and sadistic attack upon her' which Adrian Stokes believed could co-exist in a work of art. In her essay 'The Lake of Charlemagne' in *Juvenilia*, Lee raises the question of whether the definition of an art object might not be effaced by the constant wash of the waves of associative or impressionistic thought (Lee 1887, 1.54).[18] We might note that the French word for 'wave', as the polyglot Lee would have known, is 'la vague'. The unrelated English word 'vague', a particular favourite of Lee's, means, of course, 'lacking precision or sharp definition', and, in her description of the Venus torso, the sculpture is 'washed by the sea into something soft, vague & lovely'. The allusive waves of association that soften and efface definition might be called the waves of vagueness or the waves of the vague. In her essay Lee counters the notion of obliteration with the alternative proposal that it is in fact the waves of association that make up 'the firm soil of our mind', by steadily collecting and composing a fabric out of the flotsam and jetsam of consciousness (Lee 1887, 1.55). In fact it is perfectly possible, as I think Lee realises herself, for both models to co-exist as a process of effacement and cumulative growth.

18 See Catherine Wiley's sensitive reading of this essay in Maxwell and Pulham 2006a, 62–7.

Obviously a Kleinian analysis sees the working through of maternal attack and reparation as common to all art, but, although I am not interested in making a specifically psycho-biographical interpretation of the Venus torso texts, one can't fail to notice that for both these siblings their relationship with their own mother was of the utmost importance. Lee-Hamilton's obscure paralytic illness seems heavily determined by his desire not to be separated from his mother and his recovery accelerated rapidly after her death. Having given up many pleasures to become totally dependent on her, he might well have experienced unconscious resentment. Lee too, as she said, 'adored' her mother (Lee 1923, 301), writing to her from Rome in 1890, 'I think constantly, here in Rome, of all that you did for me while we lived here, & how completely you *made* me intellectually' (Lee 1937, 316); yet, as a child, she had to compete for her mother's affection and attention with her brother, knowing that Eugene would always come first. It is hard not to suspect that the siblings' shared preoccupation with the figure of Venus owed something to their own relations with their unusually dominant mother, added to which it may be that Lee eagerly took up her brother's theme, as she did many of his other intellectual views and interests, in emulation of the son favoured by the mother.

Moreover, with regard to Lee and her own sexuality, as Patricia Pulham has indicated (Pulham 2006, 138–9), various psychoanalytic models of lesbianism draw in different ways on the mother–child dynamic. One or more of these, as she suggests, may be relevant to Lee, and, certainly, Lee's continued association of her second female partner, the boyish but nurturing Kit Anstruther-Thomson, with the Venus de Milo, is striking.[19] We might notice too that the disturbing images of mutilated naked women mentioned as occurring in Lee's work are also maternal figures: along with Maddalena's naked corpse is found her dead newborn child, while the mutilated woman discovered at the end of 'Prince Alberic and the Snake Lady' is, we assume, the Snake Lady herself, Prince Alberic's beloved godmother. We can also add the (presumably clothed) body of Gertrude, a mother, pregnant with her third child, who is found slaughtered on the altar to Venus at the denouement of 'Dionea'. Other of Lee's mutilated dead women include Alice Oke, shot through the heart by her deranged husband, and the spectral Monna Filomena, in the Renaissance supernatural tale 'Ravenna and Her Ghosts' (1894), who, naked, is hunted through the woods by the vengeful ghost of her former lover, transfixed with a spear, and her heart cut out and thrown to the hounds.[20]

19 See the description of Althea, based on Kit, in *Althea* (Lee 1894b, 3) and Lee's discussion of Kit, in her Introduction to *Art and Man* (Lee 1924, 7, 8).

20 Later reprinted in *Limbo and Other Essays to which is now added 'Ariadne in Mantua'* (1908b).

However, it is possible, I think, to acknowledge that the figure of Venus and indeed the mutilated woman may carry an extra weight for Lee and Lee-Hamilton in terms of a maternal symbolism without reducing their work to a simple reflection of their biographies. What is more interesting is how, say, a wider Kleinian reading might be able to account for some of the peculiarities of their work. Indeed, acts of violence and mutilation are common in both Lee and Lee-Hamilton's work, occurring to men as well as women, although the violence meted out to women tends to be more shocking because it breaks more of a taboo. Both siblings were noted for their prudishness (Maxwell 2006b, 36), yet one senses a pleasure in their use of violence to shock the reader, with that violence often coolly narrated as if it was simply an element of design in a larger aesthetic whole. Putting aside the more limited psycho-biographical application and looking at the larger picture of their textual artworks, it may be that such outbreaks of violence and grotesquerie that punctuate the stories and poems could be read as both siblings' exercise of their destructive impulses which partner the more reparative, aesthetic qualities of their texts – the fluent, elaborate, elegant passages of description, the experiments with style and register – say, Lee's imitation of the Renaissance chronicler in 'Ravenna and Her Ghosts' and 'A Wedding Chest' – and Lee-Hamilton's witty and ingenious use of rhyme and metre. Often random and inexplicable, the violent shocks and outbreaks also have an enigmatic function, exposing us to what it is in the story that 'won't tell'. As such, they resemble those fractures and breakages in the body of the statue which, in Fuller's words, 'refuse to give us all the answers', a quality, he says, which can enhance 'aesthetic enjoyment of the work' (Fuller 1980, 120).

The haunting of the Incomplete[21]

The eroded Venus torso, although it might be described as 'perfected' by the sea, is not finished or complete. Indeed, as a renovated piece of art it thrives on its very incompletion. Lovely as a thing in itself, it still possesses enough definition to summon up the idea of Venus to which it refers. While Fuller intimates that pleasure can be derived from uncertainty and enigma, he also suggests that the injuries sustained by the Venus de Milo render it, 'in Segal's terms, a work which we must complete internally', and that such internal completion can also 'increase our aesthetic enjoyment' (Fuller 1980, 120). In 'Symmetria Prisca' (1879), the essay in which she used the phrase 'mutilated Venus', Lee had already envisaged the effects of such internal completion on 'the man of the Renaissance' who discovers a broken antique torso:

21 See Robert Browning's line 'Artistry's haunting curse – the Incomplete', from *The Ring and the Book*, 11.1561 (Browning 2001, 700), and repeated in 'Beatrice Signorini' (Browning 1981, 2.900).

> Look at this: it is corroded by oxides, battered by ill-usage, stained with earth: it is not a group, not even a whole statue, it has neither head nor arms remaining; it is a mere broken fragment of antique sculpture, – a naked body with a fold or two of drapery; it is not by Phidias nor by Praxiteles, it may not even be Greek; it may be some cheap copy, made for a garden or a bath, in the days of Hadrian. But to the artist of the fifteenth century it is the revelation of the whole world, a world in itself. We can scarcely realize all this; but let us look and reflect, and even we may feel as must have felt the man of the Renaissance in the presence of that mutilated, stained, battered torso. He sees in that broken stump a grandeur of outline, a magnificence of osseous structure, a breadth of muscle and sinew, a smooth, firm covering of flesh, such as he would vainly seek in any of his living models; he sees a delicate and infinite variety of indentures, of projections, of creases following the bend of every limb; he sees, where the surface still exists intact, an elasticity of skin, a buoyancy of hidden life such as all the colours of his palette are unable to imitate; and in this piece of drapery, negligently gathered over the hips or rolled upon the arm, he sees a magnificent alternation of large folds and small plaits, of straight lines, and broken lines, and curves. He sees all this; but he sees more: the broken torso is, as we have said, not merely a world in itself, but the revelation of a world. It is the revelation of antique civilization, of the palæstra and the stadium, of the sanctification of the body, of the apotheosis of man, of the religion of life and nature and joy.
>
> (Lee 1884a, 1.192–3)

Lee's masterly description of the Renaissance spectator's consciousness makes it clear that this kind of 'completion' is not just a matter of supplying missing limbs; rather the spectator is startled into recognition of the superiority of the Greek sculptural body and Greek sculptural techniques, thereby gaining access to the past and a culture whose ideals are so very different from his own. This Renaissance spectator then is also a particularly skilled and imaginative reader who knows how to get the most out of a text. Intriguingly Lee's Renaissance spectator precedes Pater's modern spectator of Greek art, described in his essay 'The Beginnings of Greek Sculpture', first published a few months after Lee's essay in the *Fortnightly Review* in February and March 1880. 'Greek art is for us, in all its stages,' writes Pater, 'a fragment only; in each of them it is necessary, in a somewhat visionary manner, to fill up empty spaces, and more or less make substitution' (Pater 1910, *GS* 205). Pater's modern spectator, although pleasingly visionary, seems still outstripped by Lee's Renaissance spectator, whose ability to conjure up the ancient world from a broken torso makes him comparable to her reader of the supernatural who has the 'habit of twigging suggestions and of easily following tortuosities of narrative', and knows how to work an allusive text.

Lee's exchange with her brother about how one reads such a text evokes the famous exchange of letters between Ruskin and Browning in 1855 in which Ruskin complains that Browning's 'Ellipses are quite Unconscionable';

Browning retorts: 'I *know* that I don't make out my conception by my language; all poetry being a putting the infinite within the finite. You would have me paint it all plain out, which can't be; but by various artifices I try to make shift with touches and bits of outlines which *succeed* if they bear the conception from me to you' (Browning 1996, 256, 257). George Santayana, in a tirade against Browning in 'The Poetry of Barbarism' (1900), was clearly not the kind of reader who favoured imaginative reconstruction, complaining 'Even his short poems have no completeness, no limpidity. They are little torsos made broken so as to stimulate the reader to the restoration of their missing legs and arms' (Santayana 1968, 1.111). As we have just seen demonstrated by Lee's 'man of the Renaissance', a truly imaginative reader does not try to guess at the correct appearance and placement of restored limbs, but opens his mind to a deeper knowledge of creative power which radiates from the fragment – an attempted restoration being, in the case of the Venus de Milo, incapable of resolution and irrelevant to an appreciation of its beauty. This kind of illumination prefigures that seen in Rilke's poem 'Archaic Torso of Apollo', written in early 1908:

> Though we've not known his unimagined head
> and what divinity his eyes were showing,
> his torso like a branching street-lamp's glowing,
> wherein his gaze, only turned down, can shed
>
> light still. Or else the breast's insurgency
> could not be dazzling you, or you discerning
> in that slight twist of loins a smile returning
> to where was centred his virility.
>
> (Rilke 1960, 2.143)

For Rilke, the torso of Apollo is a beautiful object in itself, yet it still emanates the luminous gaze, the radiance that belonged to the complete if unimaginable statue, giving the viewer a sense too of that original power. Elsewhere, in an analysis of Browning's poetry, I have suggested that he

> typically uses a poetic technique which calls up an imaginative sublime by a few select suggestive details and by the blanks, tensions and fractures in his language. The language of Browning's texts, which is often apparently dramatic, is shot through with small hesitations, lacunae, divergences which run counter to the overt dramatic intention and allow something else to happen. These moments have the capacity to function as lyric epiphanies allowing access to what he called the infinite.
>
> (Maxwell 2001, 150)

From her many references to him in her writing, it would seem that Browning was Lee's favourite poet, a detail which seems hardly surprising when we consider that both of them shared a passion for reanimation, for raising the ghosts of the past.[22] As Browning remarked to Mrs FitzGerald, 'poetry, if it is to deserve the name, ought to create – or reanimate something – not merely reproduce *raw* fact taken from somebody else's work' (Browning 1966, 157), and, in the first canto of *The Ring and the Book*, he experiments with images of the poet as a mage, alchemist, or prophet who can conjure up ghosts or resurrect the dead (Maxwell 2006b, 140). Both Browning and Lee are conscious inheritors of the Romantic cult of the suggestive fragment. Browning uses the sketch rather than the fully defined picture as a cue that evokes the model all the more effectively. Thus in Browning's *Men and Women* (1855), the woman speaker of 'Any Wife to Any Husband' says, 'That is a portrait of me on the wall – / Three lines, my face comes at so slight a call' (Browning 1981, I.563), while in her essay on the supernatural in art, 'Faustus and Helena', Lee fixes upon the idea of the sketch as the preferred visual means for conjuring up spectres. First of all she examines and dismisses Raphael's *Lo Stregozzo*, a picture of a witch riding through a marsh on a chariot of bones, 'a master-piece of drawing and of pictorial fancy' (Lee 2006, 307), but a failure as a means for representing the supernatural, in that it tries to realise the subject too distinctly, being ultimately 'clear, harmonious, and beautiful in treatment'. In contrast she describes from memory a nameless sketch she recalls seeing at a picture-dealer's in Rome, a sketch of a dramatic scene by some 'German smearer of the early sixteenth century; very ugly, stupid, unattractive: ill drawn, ill composed of a uniform hard, vulgar brown' (Lee 2006, 308), and concludes that it nevertheless does have supernatural quality.

> Why can this nameless smearer succeed where Raphael has failed? Because he is content to suggest to the imagination and lets it create for itself its world of the

22 Lee knew Browning personally and corresponded with him, and Browning famously mentions her name in his poem 'Inapprehensiveness', from *Asolando* (1889). See Gunn 1964, 79, 126; Colby 2003, 81–2. Browning's *The Ring and the Book* was a favourite poem of Lee's. See the allusions in *Baldwin*, especially with regard to the discussion of Caponsacchi's defence of Pompilia (Lee 1886, 231–3; 285–9), and in *Althea* (Lee 1894b, 43–5). For a small sample of Lee's literary references to Browning see also her references to *Pippa Passes*, in 'On Modern Travelling', in *Limbo* (Lee 1897, 101–2). In *Althea* (Lee 1894b, 5), Browning is mentioned along with Turner and Ruskin as an example of genius. In 'The Use of Beauty' in *Laurus Nobilis*, he is given a special place among the great lyric poets (Lee 1909, 15), while he is mentioned with Goethe as an example of the highest kind of literary artist in the conclusion to *The Handling of Words* (Lee 1923, 315). In a letter dated 7 August 1893, Lee writes how Mabel Price has introduced her to Browning's *Fifine at the Fair*: 'It is full of magnificent things' (Lee 1937, 358). Lee remarks in the same letter (written only a very short time before the exchange of letters about 'Dionea'): 'I don't think Eugene would appreciate it *yet*. But some day he must read it; & although parts of it will always be distasteful to him, it may suggest a widening out of his own style. But it wd be a pity to embark prematurely on reading an obscure, difficult thing.'

> supernatural . . . because he suggests everything and shows nothing, while Raphael creates, defines, perfects, gives form to that which is by its nature formless.
>
> (Lee 2006, 309)

In 'Faustus and Helena', Lee suggests that for modern individuals ghosts are pervasive moods, feelings, atmospheres, generated by certain potent clusters of associations. A ghost is 'a vague feeling we can scarcely describe, a something pleasing and terrible which invades our whole consciousness, and which, confusedly embodied, we half dread to see behind us, we know not in what shape, if we look round' (Lee 2006, 310). However, such a characterisation does not seem to erase the more conventional notion of the ghost as a personified presence of the dead, which reveals itself to the living or impresses itself upon their consciousness. Lee's use of the sketch in 'Faustus and Helena' as a means for conjuring up spectres implies that, in spite of seeing most artistic forms as too finished and defined to convey supernatural effects, she believes that there are representational ruses by which the supernatural can come into play. How then does she tackle the problem of representation when, during the 1880s, she writes the four supernatural stories collected and published as *Hauntings* (1890), which are visited briefly earlier in this chapter? She was certainly aware of the inherent difficulties of writing a supernatural tale, anxious that the textual bodying-out of her stories might in some way deprive them of their power. Her stories often started as oral narratives told to friends and, in the preface to the third story in *Hauntings*, 'Oke of Okehurst', she addresses her dedicatee Count Peter Boutourline, reminding him of when he first heard her tell it to him at Florence: 'You thought it a fantastic tale, you lover of fantastic things, and urged me to write it out at once, although I protested that, in such matters, that to write is to exorcise, to dispel the charm; and that printers' ink chases away the ghosts that may pleasantly haunt us, as efficaciously as gallons of holy water' (Lee 2006, 105).

If finished forms and definition belong to a practice of art which excludes the supernatural, we might start by noticing how all the stories in *Hauntings* are structured around incompletion – an incompletion which makes their protagonists susceptible to revenants and which also marks their projects and outcomes with inconclusion. All four stories are told by men who evidently have concerns and interests of their own which make them partial and, in some cases, not wholly reliable narrators. In 'Amour Dure', Spiridion Trepka, a young disaffected Polish historian, comes to Italy to write a history of Urbania, but soon finds himself taking an interest in Medea da Carpi, a fascinating sixteenth-century political intriguer, and starts planning a revisionary history of her parallel to his official project. His diary records his growing obsession and his belief that she has begun to communicate with him. The story ends abruptly with Trepka's official and unofficial histories incomplete, his diary ambiguous, and the mystery of his strange romance and its consequences unresolved. The eponymous heroine of 'Dionea' disturbs but also fascinates both the elderly narrator, Dr Alessandro De Rosis, as he is writing his history of the gods in exile, and the visiting sculptor Waldemar, who, initially disdainful of women as models, agrees to sculpt her. Unable to capture her beauty, which seems constantly to outstrip his efforts, he becomes increasingly obsessed, eventually perishing in macabre circumstances while Dionea disappears. At the end of the story there is still a mystery about Dionea, her origins, involvement in the tragedy, and current whereabouts, and Waldemar's statue is unfinished, as is De Rosis's mythological project, which, he has decided, lacks foundation. A similar lack of resolution also characterises 'Oke of Okehurst' in which a young painter, recovering from a recent artistic failure, is engaged to paint the portrait of Alice Oke, wife of a country squire. While staying with the couple he finds himself frustrated and tantalised by his inability to capture the likeness of the elusive Alice. He also watches Alice frustrate and tease her adoring and vulnerable husband with her tales of her romance with the ghost of a Caroline poet. In the end events conspire to prevent the completion of the painting which remains 'a huge wreck . . . merely blocked in, and seems quite mad', that none the less 'has something of her' (Lee 2006, 106). Finally in 'A Wicked Voice' the young Norwegian composer Magnus, who has come to Venice to finish his Wagnerian opera *Ogier the Dane*, insults the memory of Zaffirino, a famous eighteenth-century singer, and then finds himself unable to complete his opera when he is overwhelmed and possessed by Zaffirino's voice. After a period of illness, his creative block persists when he finds he can compose only in the eighteenth-century style he despises.

Three of the stories are thus haunted by enigmatic, elusive yet compelling women who defy being fixed and defined by those around them, even seeming to cross the boundaries of time and space. The fourth, 'A Wicked Voice', features a 'confusedly embodied' male ghost whose appeal and danger comes through a partial feminisation which makes his extraordinary voice seem indefinable: 'there was no agreement on the subject of this voice: it was called by all sorts of names and described by all manner of incongruous adjectives; people went so far as to dispute whether the voice belonged to a man or to a woman; every one had some new definition' (Lee 2006, 310, 170). Femininity in all these stories is fused with the spectral to suggest something that resists simple categorisation and which leaves everything open and without resolution. As the young painter in 'Oke of Okehurst' comments of the failure of even great artists to capture female beauty: 'Something – and that the very essence – always escapes, perhaps because real beauty is as much a thing in time – a thing like music, a succession, a series – as in space' (Lee 2006, 114–15). 'Something always escapes' could be the watchword of these stories. Certainly Medea and Dionea do appear to escape the situations that imprison them; the elusive Alice Oke, too, seems to have given her husband the slip – when she lies dead, 'her wide-open white eyes seemed to smile vaguely and distantly' (Lee 2006, 152) – while Zaffirino's tantalising voice lives on, escaping burial in the past.

As we saw from Lee's reply to her brother concerning 'Dionea', stories of the supernatural need to be 'allusive', and the spectral efficacy of her ghostly characters seems to derive directly from the kinds of allusion and suggestion, from ideas, images, and descriptions Lee employed in 'Faustus and Helena', as can be seen in the following three examples. First of all, as we have seen, the idea of gods-as-ghosts or revenants which pervades 'Dionea', and arguably touches the other *Hauntings* stories, is heavily influenced by Heine, but 'Faustus and Helena' also traces a link between the most ancient pagan conception of divinity and later ideas of ghosts through what Lee calls 'the imagination wrought upon by certain kinds of physical surroundings', or 'the effect on the imagination of certain external impressions' (Lee 2006, 296). Thus the god Pan is 'the weird, shaggy, cloven-footed shape which the goat-herd or the huntsman has seen gliding about among the bushes' but 'Pan is also the wood, with all its sights and noises, the solitude, the gloom, the infinity of rustling leaves and cracking branches; he is the greenish-yellow light stealing in amid the boughs' (Lee 2006, 297). In 'Dionea', De Rosis seems directly to echo this passage: 'Who knows whether [the Pagan divinities] do not exist to this day? And, indeed, is it possible they should not? For the awfulness of the deep woods, with their filtered green light, the creek of the swaying, solitary reeds, exists, and is Pan' (Lee 2006, 91). To the susceptible or impressionable mind, and thus perhaps the primitive mind still latent in us all, the suggestive quality of certain atmospheric stimuli help project the 'confusedly embodied' ghost.

Secondly, in explaining how the original supernatural legend of Faustus and Helen is superior to the literary versions by Goethe and Marlowe, Lee uses a musical analogy: the legend in its original state 'does not give the complete and limited satisfaction of a work of art; it has the charm of the fantastic and fitful shapes formed by the flickering firelight or the wreathing mists; it haunts like some vague strain of music, drowsily heard in half-sleep' (Lee 2006, 292). This analogy prepares us for the haunting song of Zaffirino, also described as 'veiled . . . in a subtle, downy wrapper' or possessing a 'downy vagueness' (Lee 2006, 167, 170), and first heard by Magnus in a kind of waking dream. The essay gives us not only a premonition of the kind or quality of music Magnus will hear but also something about the state of consciousness in which subjects are most disposed to experience supernatural phenomena. Moreover, the word 'vague' occurring frequently in both the essay and the stories is Lee's favourite indicator of the supernatural.

Thirdly, continuing the theme of suggestion that excites the fancy as epitomised in the sketch, the painter in 'Oke of Okehurst' tells the visitor viewing his studio, that, while he never succeeded in completing Alice Oke's portrait, he none the less has hundreds of sketches of her: 'Mere scratches, but they may give some idea of her marvellous, fantastic kind of grace' (Lee 2006, 106). This inability to paint her is matched by his inability to describe her in words. His language, too, is only ever a sketch: 'how is it possible to give even the vaguest notion with mere wretched words – words only possessing a wretched abstract meaning, an impotent conventional association?' (Lee 2006, 115). There is something about her that 'always escapes', perhaps because she is never fully there; for she is frequently described as being 'absent' (Lee 2006, 122, 125, 136, 145), 'distant' (Lee 2006, 122, 124, 127, 130, 141, 150), engaged or taken up by 'that unseen something' (Lee 2006, 119, 144). In such descriptions Lee reminds us of her essay and the sketch by the 'nameless smearer' that succeeds where the polished picture of Raphael fails.

In her privileging of the rude unfinished sketch over the highly finished picture, Lee aligns herself to a lengthy tradition that sees incompletion as a cue for, if not the supernatural, then the sublime. Edmund Burke in his *Philosophical Enquiry into the Sublime and the Beautiful* (1757) discusses how

> The spring is the pleasantest of the seasons; and the young of most animals, though far from being compleatly fashioned, afford a more agreeable sensation than the full grown; because the imagination is entertained with the promise of something more, and does not acquiesce in the present object of the sense. In unfinished sketches of drawing I have often seen something which pleased me beyond the best finishing.
>
> (Burke 1987, 77)

John Keats in December 1818 admires engravings from the frescos in the Campo Santo at Pisa 'even finer to me than more accomplish'd works – as there was left so much room for Imagination' (Keats 1958, 2.19). Ruskin in *Modern Painters* is eloquent on the importance of suggestive incompletion in pictures:

> It follows evidently from the first of these characters of the imagination, its dislike of substance and presence, that a picture has in some measure even an advantage with us in not being real. The imagination rejoices in something to do, springs up with all its willing power, flattered and happy . . . And thus it is, that, for the most part, imperfect sketches, engravings, outlines, rude sculptures, and other forms of abstraction, possess a charm which the most finished picture frequently wants.
>
> (Ruskin 1903–4, 5.184–6)

In Nathaniel Hawthorne's *The Marble Faun* (1860), a novel much beloved by the young Vernon Lee, the narrator describes the power of certain Old Master sketches:

> The charm [of these designs] lay partly in their very imperfection; for this is suggestive, and sets the imagination at work; whereas, the finished picture, if a good one, leaves the spectator nothing to do.
>
> (Hawthorne 1995, 110)

Henry James was another writer much admired by Lee and known to her personally. In his early story 'Travelling Companions' (1870), his narrator describes the condition of Leonardo's fresco *The Last Supper* at Milan, which, in its ravaged state, has about it something akin to the sketch:

> Another secondary source of interest lies in the very completeness of its decay. The mind finds a rare delight in filling each of its vacant spaces, effacing its rank defilement, and repairing, as far as possible, its sad disorder. Of the essential power and beauty of the work there can be no better evidence than this fact that, having lost so much, it has yet retained so much. An unquenchable elegance lingers in those vague outlines and incurable scars; enough remains to place you in sympathy with the unfathomable wisdom of the painter.
>
> (James 1962, 171)

We have already seen in Chapter 2 how Pater characterised Leonardo's *Last Supper*, 'finished or unfinished, or owing part of its effect to a mellowing decay', as enhanced by its evanescence: 'the head of Jesus does but consummate the sentiment of the whole company – ghosts through which you see the wall, faint as the shadows of the leaves upon the wall on autumn afternoons. This figure is but the faintest, the most spectral of them all' (Pater 1980, *Ren* 95).[23] In 'Symmetria Prisca', Lee herself mentions Leonardo, famous for the incomplete state of his artworks, as one 'who could make an imperfect figure, beckoning mysteriously out of the gloom, more fascinating than the finest drawn Florentine Madonna' (Lee 1884a, 1.207).

Lee's supernatural seems to me to have its roots in the sublime in that it shuns sharp definition and finds its expressive means in obscurity and the lack of confining boundaries. Remembering how Burke identifies obscurity as a precondition for the sublime, we might turn again to Lee's indicative word for the supernatural: 'vague'. For example, Alice Oke and her atmospheric home are repeatedly described in terms of the vague: we note 'her vague, absent glance'; she shares with the portrait of her ancestress 'the same vague eccentricity of expression'; the house has 'a vague sense of rose-leaves and spices, put into the china bowls by the hands of ladies long since dead'; and she sits in her drawing room 'confronting, as it were, that vague, haunting something which seemed to fill the place' (Lee 2006, 136, 118, 112, 130). In 'Faustus and Helena', writing of our 'transient delight in the impossible and the vague', Lee explains how 'We moderns seek in the world of the supernatural a renewal of the delightful semi-obscurity of vision and keenness of fancy of our childhood' (Lee 2006, 312). Relating the supernatural to a remembered fullness of imaginative vision, she sets up a Post-Romantic version of Wordsworth's Intimations

23 Pater's image is perhaps echoed by Lee in her description of the faded tapestry in 'Prince Alberic': 'the figures seemed like ghosts, sometimes emerging then receding again into vagueness' (Lee 2006, 186).

Ode in which epiphany is always experienced as a haunting, a relic of the past. The already-mentioned counter-chronological boundary-breaking tendencies of Lee's revenants inevitably evoke the boundlessness of sublimity, and the elusive revenants themselves are all characterised by a beauty which is dangerous and disturbing, moving out of the contained, domestic beautiful into the unlicense of the sublime. The identity, character or nature of these ghosts also manifests itself as flexible and unstable, partaking of the fluctuation Lee ascribed to the perception of divinities in earliest times, which depended on

> the effect on the imagination of certain external impressions, . . . impressions brought to a focus, personified, but personified vaguely, in a fluctuating ever-changing manner; the personification being continually altered, reinforced, blurred out, enlarged, restricted by new series of impressions from without, even as the shape which we puzzle out of congregated cloud-masses fluctuates with their every movement.
>
> (Lee 2006, 296–7)

Like the sublime, Lee's supernatural imaginative projections are cued or triggered by blurring, breaks, gaps, fissures, ruins, relics, and fragments. The Preface to *Hauntings* intimates that her ghosts are born out of suggestions, mental oddments, mnemonic bits and pieces: 'They are things of imagination, born there, bred there, sprung from the strange, confused heaps, half-rubbish, half-treasure, which lie in our fancy, heaps of half-faded recollections, of fragmentary vivid impressions, litter of multi-coloured tatters' (Lee 2006, 39). Two of Lee's narratives – 'Amour Dure' and 'Dionea' – indeed have a somewhat fragmentary appearance in that they are pieced together out of letters and diary entries, but the narrators of all the *Hauntings* stories seem alive to suggestion, to cues and associations which trigger imaginative recreation.[24] Disappointed by Rome, Trepka discovers in Urbania a place already formed by art, streets peopled by characters who look as if they were painted by Signorelli or Raphael, and of whom he writes: 'I do not talk much to these people; I fear my illusions being dispelled' (Lee 2006, 43). Later, a witness at an olive pressing which features 'vague figures working at pulleys and hurdles', he notices how it all 'looks, to my fancy, like some scene of the Inquisition' (Lee 2006, 62). His impressions recorded in the form of diary entries will, he thinks, console him with their imaginative reconstruction when he returns to Berlin: 'these scraps will help . . . to bring to my mind . . . these happy Italian days' (Lee 2006, 44). As we have seen, De Rosis in 'Dionea' describes the way in which natural effects and phenomena can so combine as to suggest to sensitive imaginations the

24 The original title of the French translation of 'Amour Dure', published in the *Revue Politique et Littéraire* in 1888 (a year after its first English publication), is 'Fragments du journal du Professeur Spiridion Trepka'.

presence of numinous presences. The painter in 'Oke of Okehurst' reports himself 'very susceptible' to the 'imaginative impression' of the house at Okehurst, especially 'the yellow room, where the very air, with its scent of heady flowers and old perfumed stuffs, seemed redolent of ghosts' (Lee 2006, 112, 142), while Magnus in 'A Wicked Voice', examining Zaffirino's portrait, finds himself recalling the *femmes fatales* described by Swinburne and Baudelaire and, responding to a subconscious cue, brings about his fateful encounter with Zaffirino at Mistrà.

In 'Faustus and Helena', meditating on what she calls the 'real supernatural', Lee gives us embedded at the heart of her essay a magnificent example of synecdoche, the rhetorical figure of part-for-whole, which most often conveys imaginative suggestion by projecting vision from intimation: 'The real supernatural was . . . in the contagious awe of the crowd sinking down at the sight of the stained napkin of Bolsena; in that soiled piece of linen was Christ, and God, and Paradise; in that and not in the panels of Angelico and Perugino, or in the frescoes of Signorelli and Filippino' (Lee 2006, 303–4). In other words it is the bloodstain on a scrap of material that conjures up the vastness and sublimity of godhead and not the glorious artworks of the great painters. This superb encapsulation of the 'infinite within the finite' to use Browning's phrase (Browning 1996, 257) is another of Lee's ingenious renovations of the sublime as the supernatural.

In an essay published much later in 1925, 'Out of Venice at Last', Lee would sum up the motivating force of her aesthetic. The sensory excess of Venice, she believes, overloads the mind with too many associations: 'Venice is always too much and too much so. I cannot cope with it, it submerges me' (Lee 2006, 340). While some might describe that kind of cumulative overload as a type of the sublime, albeit one that is painful to experience, it is not the kind favoured by Lee, who contrasts it with her own preferred aesthetic strategy dependent on 'The virtue of paucity, the stimulus of the insufficient and the unfinished, the spell of the fragment, forcing us to furnish what it lacks out of our own heart and mind' (Lee 2006, 340). Lee's supernatural sublime, projected by 'the spell of the fragment', borrows heavily, as I have shown, from Romantic and Post-Romantic writers, as well as from various Renaissance artists such as Leonardo and Michelangelo, themselves mediated by Romantic accounts such as Pater's, as we saw in Chapter 2. Leonardo was famous for failing to bring his works to completion and, in his *Treatise on Painting* (*c.* 1550), urged would-be painters to stimulate their powers of invention by seeing the germ of a picture in a stain on a wall, while the Michelangelo sculptures known as the *non-finiti* deliberately seem to lack finish or show the sculptural form in the process of emerging from the stone. Lorenzo de' Medici, one of the Renaissance poets Lee admired (Lee 1884a, 1.153–65), included in his 'Ambra' a description of a pursued nymph who is metamorphosed into stone, a description which has been seen as a verbal equivalent of Michelangelo's *non-finiti*. In her essay 'The Outdoor Poetry' in *Euphorion*, Lee is rather cool about the storyline of this poem, preferring the beautifully observed natural detail of its opening stanzas, but she duly notes the nymph's transformation and the rock 'dimly showing her former woman's shape' (Lee 1884a, 1.162). Yet Lorenzo's stanzas of naturalistic description serve in their own way as 'the spell of the fragment' in that, to Lee's mind (which is here the mind of a literary historian), they prelude the shift from medieval romance to the Renaissance 'eye for the bolder, grander, more solemn sights of Nature' (Lee 1884a, 1.166). Some of Lorenzo's details, which 'are a good deal more than details, things little noticed till recently' (Lee 1884a, 1.163), even hint at the impressionistic style – 'a picture which you might call almost impressionistic' (Lee 1884a, 1.163) – that will become popular in the late nineteenth century and be adopted by Lee herself. Lorenzo's stanzas thus summon up not only the spirit of the Renaissance to come but something of Lee's contemporary modernity as well. But perhaps with regard to those aspects of her aesthetic that specifically celebrate the 'virtue of paucity, the stimulus of the insufficient', of working with limited materials and of making much from little, Lee had an example that was much closer to home.

Eugene Lee-Hamilton's *Imaginary Sonnets*

Eugene Lee-Hamilton, a fine poet who has been even more neglected than his remarkable half-sister, now seems now be receiving a little more of the attention he richly deserves. Although admired by George Macbeth, who included him in his anthology of Victorian poetry, and in spite of other similar select appearances, Lee-Hamilton has remained until recently not so much a marginal as an almost unknown figure.[25] This is undoubtedly because, apart from piecemeal inclusions in anthologies, it has been difficult for readers to get hold of editions of his verse. In 1984 Garland published a one-volume reprint that included *Gods, Saints, and Men* (1880), *The New Medusa, and Other Poems* (1882), and *Sonnets of the Wingless Hours* (1894). However, this Garland reprint is now difficult to come by and does not include *Imaginary Sonnets* (1888), a collection which is perhaps more likely to appeal to modern taste and which MacDonald P. Jackson has called 'among the most innovative, idiosyncratic, and imaginative of all nineteenth-century sonnet sequences' (Jackson in Lee-Hamilton 2002, 17). In 2002 Jackson published his valuable edition

25 See Macbeth 1969, 27, 314–19; Fletcher 1987, 152–7; Ricks 1987, 527–9; Karlin 1997, 663; Collins and Rundle 1999, 1055–75; Cunningham 2000, 883–7; O'Gorman 2004, 545–56. I am grateful to MacDonald P. Jackson (Lee-Hamilton 2002, 23) for his listing of the first four of these selections. Collins and Rundle provide the largest and best selection, and O'Gorman the best annotated selection.

Selected Poems of Eugene Lee-Hamilton (1845–1907): A Victorian Craftsman Rediscovered, allowing modern readers with no access to original editions of his work to get a full sense of his range and abilities. Jackson's excellent introduction to this volume provides a thoughtful, informative overview of Lee-Hamilton's life and achievement. However, his edition does not include annotation on individual poems, an addition which does seem necessary with regard to works such as the *Imaginary Sonnets*, where the historical background and significance of many of Lee-Hamilton's dramatic speakers are likely to be obscure to many modern readers. More recently Francis O'Gorman's inclusion in his anthology *Victorian Poetry* (2004) of five of Lee-Hamilton's poems, four taken from *Imaginary Sonnets*, demonstrates how effective notes and commentary can show his work to its best advantage. Meanwhile the growing interest in Vernon Lee has meant that her brother has also become more visible. The details of his life and illness have been reexamined by Vineta Colby in her biography of Lee (2003), while both the recent English and Italian essay collections on Lee include an essay on Lee-Hamilton. My own essay in *Vernon Lee: Decadence, Ethics, Aesthetics* (Maxwell and Pulham 2006a) examines the complex personal and creative relationship that existed between brother and sister, while Alex R. Falzon's short essay, in *Vernon Lee e Firenze settant'anni dopo* (Cenni and Bizzotto 2006), on the late-nineteenth-century vogue for the sonnet and Lee-Hamilton's meta-sonnets (or sonnets on the sonnet), usefully sets him in context with other previous and contemporary sonneteers. Patricia Pulham and I also included Lee-Hamilton's Venus torso sonnets and his dramatic monologue 'The Mandolin' among the contextual documents that form the Appendices to our Broadview edition of Vernon Lee's *Hauntings and Other Fantastic Tales* (Lee 2006, Appendices F and H).

As Eugene Lee-Hamilton's admirers have noted, one of the recurrent themes of his poetry is imprisonment. His poetic speakers continually find themselves imprisoned, trapped, or confined, and eloquently lament their condition. In many of these poems such as the sonnets that comprise the *Sonnets of the Wingless Hours* (1894), the 'I' of the speaker is clearly intended to be identified with Lee-Hamilton himself, a man confined by his illness, speaking of the particular pains and frustrations of his condition: 'The cage is narrow and the bars are strong / In which my restless spirit beats its wings' ('Lost Years', in Lee-Hamilton 1894, 9). Yet we should note that this apparently autobiographical form of address is hardly unmediated in that it relies on a form of persona, heavily determined by poetic and cultural conventions. Lee-Hamilton himself admitted that 'but for my illness, I should never have existed at all as an artist', and declaring 'Perhaps, too, there's a sort of connection between physical disability and specialised intelligence. Think of all the work that's been done in the world by infirm people and invalids! We'll let Homer slide; but look at Milton, Beethoven, Heine, Leopardi, Keats, Darwin, Mrs. Browning' (Duclaux 1907,

936). Lee-Hamilton does not include in this list Rossetti whose shattered nerves and constitution kept him confined to his home, although the older poet is his nearest and arguably most influential precursor, being not merely the author of the most famous late Victorian sonnet sequence, but also, in his final decade, a paradigm of the Romantic and Post-Romantic hypersensitive male poet. In constructing himself as a suffering artist, Lee-Hamilton clearly draws on the mythic conception of the stricken male poet, a man more responsive to both pleasure and pain than ordinary men, wounded, castrated even, but endowed with exceptional powers of vision by way of compensation. This inner imaginative and visionary world and the world of art, of artifice, often seen as vastly superior to the everyday world of humdrum human activity, achieves an added intensity in a poet who is by his very nature debarred from participating in the business of normal life. Yet to Lee-Hamilton, bed-bound for twenty years and so thrown back on his imaginative talents for daily occupation, this intense inner world at times seems far from superior, being often claustrophobic or tormentingly phantasmagorical, while the ordinary life of other people with its normal activities, pleasures, and rewards becomes tantalisingly desirable. It is hard, he says, in the first sonnet of *Sonnets of the Wingless Hours*,

> To keep through life the posture of the grave,
>   While others walk and run and dance and leap . . .
>
> In summer's heat no more to breast the wave;
>   No more to wade through seeded grasses deep;
> Nor tread the cornfield where the reapers reap;
>   Nor stretch free limbs beneath a leafy nave.
>
> ('To the Muse', in Lee-Hamilton 1894, 3)

But poetry, although it cannot take away what is for him a real and not merely a symbolic feeling of blight and castration – 'And now my manhood goes where goes the song / Of captive birds, the cry of crippled things' ('Lost Years', in Lee-Hamilton 1894, 9) – does provide him with a craft, something with which to occupy himself, and, very occasionally, a sense of release: 'the pure height / Of sky within us, when the soul upgoes / To spheres of higher self, from clods and night' ('On an Illustration in Doré's Dante' II, in Lee-Hamilton 1894, 40).

The other voices that bewail their imprisonment in Lee-Hamilton's poetry are those of his many dramatis personae, these being either completely fictional, his own invention, or, alternatively, known historical, mythical, or legendary characters whose utterance he imagines. Some of these prisoners inhabit the prisons of mental derangement or of the troubled or guilty conscience; for example, the narrators of 'The New Medusa', 'The Raft', and 'The Mandolin', dramatic monologues from *The New Medusa, and Other Poems* of 1882. While Browning arguably perfected and made the dramatic monologue his own, Lee-Hamilton's use of the form put him in the company of those other Victorians – Tennyson, Dante Gabriel Rossetti, and Augusta Webster – who brilliantly exploited its potential for complex psychological portraiture and confessional exposition. Moreover, Lee-Hamilton carried something of the form over and adapted it into what became his own form: the imaginary or dramatic sonnet, an invented sonnet monologue, spoken by a particular character, real or mythical, which is an exposition of his circumstances and related frame of mind and is addressed to or apostrophises either another person or a creature, object, natural force, or abstraction. Lee-Hamilton's *Imaginary Sonnets* (1888), a hundred mini-soliloquies, each titled, assigned a date, and ordered chronologically, took their collective title from the famous *Imaginary Conversations* (1824–29) of Walter Savage Landor (1775–1865), short imaginary prose dialogues between famous historical or legendary persons that were much admired during the Victorian period but attract little attention now. Walter Pater's *Imaginary Portraits* (1887), impressionistic tales of four different personalities, published the year before Lee-Hamilton's sequence, may also have had an impact. George Macbeth, in one of the very few critical articles published on Lee-Hamilton, suggests that 'The kernel of the idea may have come from the *Hortorum Deus* group of sonnets in [José Maria de] Hérédia's collection *Les Trophées*, which Lee-Hamilton could have read in French magazines or in MSS before their publication in book form [in 1893]' (Macbeth 1962, 148). But, while Hérédia's sonnets delineate a cultural and artistic history from classical to modern times, they are not voiced by dramatic speakers. English poetry provides better analogues in Mary 'Perdita' Robinson's sequence *Sappho and Phaon* (1796), where Sappho voices her hopes, fears, and desires in a series of sonnet monologues, or in 'After Death' and 'A Pause', those strange dramatic sonnets by Christina Rossetti, in which a female speaker describes how, following her death, her corpse is visited by the man she formerly loved. But Robinson's sonnets are spoken by one person only while Christina Rossetti's examples differ from Lee-Hamilton's in that her speakers are anonymous, and the scenes and events described of personal rather than of historical significance. In fact the closest analogue I can find is Dante Gabriel Rossetti's Italian and English 'Proserpina' sonnets, discussed in Chapter 1, which must have struck a responsive chord with their portrayal of a melancholy speaker imprisoned against her will in the Underworld and tantalised by the earthly light which momentarily lightens the gloom. The influence of Rossetti's sonnet seems all the more likely as Lee-Hamilton named Rossetti along with Dante, Petrarch, and Shakespeare as one of the great sonneteers in his own sonnet titled 'What the Sonnet Is', first published in the *Academy* in August 1889 and afterwards included in *Sonnets of the Wingless Hours*.

During the worst of his illness, Lee-Hamilton was so incapacitated that he had to lie in a darkened room, unable to bear more than a few words addressed to him at any one time. For a long period he was unable to hold a pen himself or to read on his own, relying on others to read to him or take dictation. Poetry was one of the very few activities he could undertake, as when confined to his bed he could work his verses over and over in his mind till he had got them to his satisfaction before dictating them, sometimes, on account of his weakness, just a few lines at a time. The sonnet, being a short, highly compressed, and concentrated form, ideally suited this type of composition and Lee-Hamilton became an expert sonneteer; as Jackson has commented, 'From 1885 onwards virtually all his worthwhile poems were sonnets' (Lee-Hamilton 2002, 16).

'We'll build in sonnets pretty rooms', says the speaker of John Donne's 'The Canonization' to his mistress (Donne 1971, 48), and Wordsworth, although he compared the confined space of 'the Sonnet's scanty plot of ground' to the 'convent's narrow room' and the hermit's cell, insisted that such limited space offered recreation to those oppressed by 'too much liberty' (Wordsworth 1997, 137). But Keats writes of the 'Sonnet sweet / Fettered' (Keats 1970, 521), and for writers like Lee-Hamilton, restricted by circumstance and not by choice, the concentrated space of the sonnet is a natural analogue to the claustrophobic sickroom or the gaol. Yet the Petrarchan sonnet, the type used by Lee-Hamilton, may have its own innate therapy, not simply because it allows the expression of painful ideas and emotions, but because within its structure, its structure contains a mechanism of compression and release which pivots at its 'volta', or turning point, between octave and sestet. In the late nineteenth century many poets and critics applauded the description of the sonnet's flow and ebb as described by Theodore Watts-Dunton in his sonnet titled 'The Sonnet's Voice', originally printed in the *Athenæum*, and then much anthologised.[26] In this sonnet he declares:

Yon silvery billows breaking on the beach
   Fall back in form beneath the starshine clear,
   The while my rhymes are murmuring in your ear
A restless lore like that the billows teach;
For on these sonnet-waves my soul would reach
   From its own depths and rest within you, dear,

26 Watts-Dunton lists as those who have accepted his 'wave theory': D. G. Rossetti, Mark Pattison, J. A. Symonds, Hall Caine, and William Sharp (Watts-Dunton 1916b, 185). For comments by the last two writers see the prefatory essays to their sonnet anthologies Caine 1882b, xxii–xxiv, and Sharp 1886, li–liii. I use the larger *édition de luxe* of Sharp's text, which has an expanded preface. For remarks by Watts-Dunton on the sonnet see Chapter 5 in his expanded essay 'Poetry' (1916b, 171–88), posthumously published in 1916, but originally written for the *Encyclopædia Britannica*, 9th ed. (1887a). The essay incorporates comments from his entries on the sonnet written for the *Encyclopædia Britannica*, 9th ed. (1887) and *Chambers's Encyclopædia* (1891).

As through the billowy voices yearning here
Great nature strives to find a human speech.

A sonnet is a wave of melody:
From soundless gulfs of the impassioned soul
A billow of heart-music music one and whole
Flows in the 'octave;' then, returning free,
Its ebbing surges in the 'sestet' roll
Back to the deeps of Life's tumultuous sea.

(Watts-Dunton 1881, 361)[27]

While the model proposed in the sestet suits the surf-rolling wash of Lee-Hamilton's Venus torso sonnets, the kinds of analogy proposed by a modern critic like Paul Fussell are much more appropriate to the dynamic of many of Lee-Hamilton's other sonnets. Of the Petrarchan sonnet, Fussell writes:

> The octave and sestet conduct actions which are analogous to the actions of inhaling and exhaling, or of contraction and release in the muscular system. The one builds up the pressure, the other releases it; and the turn is the dramatic and climactic center of the poem, the place where the intellectual or emotional method of release first becomes clear and possible.
>
> (Fussell 1979, 116)

The octave traditionally rehearses a situation, question, problem, or circumstance that the sestet reflects on, pronounces on or answers. Although the conclusions of the sestet may not provide an easy solution, the rhythm of an accumulative build-up, followed by release may, in its own way, take the pressure out of the situation and allow a necessary emotional catharsis. Fussell also remarks:

> We may even suggest that one of the emotional archetypes of the Petrarchan sonnet structure is the pattern of sexual pressure and release. Surely no sonnet succeeds as a sonnet that does not execute at the turn something analogous to the general kinds of 'release' with which the reader's muscles and nervous system are familiar.
>
> (Fussell 1979, 116)

27 Theodore Watts-Dunton, 'The Sonnet's Voice (A Metrical Lesson by the Sea-shore)', in *The Athenæum* (17 September 1881), 361. With regard to sonnet anthologies, Watts-Dunton's sonnet was cited in variant form in the prefatory essays of Hall Caine 1882b, xxi, and Sharp 1886, lii. Also cited in Prins 2004, 55, and Phelan 2005, 138. It was not included in either the first or later editions of Watts-Dunton's only published poetry collection *The Coming of Love: Rhoda Boswell's Story and Other Poems* (1897). Although most commentators adopted the flow followed by ebb model proposed by his sonnet, Watts-Dunton himself was less rigid, arguing that the 'sestet . . . must always act as a response by way of *either* ebb or flow to the metrical billow embodied in the octave' (Watts-Dunton 1916b, 172; my emphasis).

Unsurprisingly, during his illness, Lee-Hamilton did not write many amatory sonnets (although there are several fine examples in *Imaginary Sonnets*, of which the dazzling 'Venus to Tannhäuser' is by far the loveliest). That sexualised rhythm described by Fussell may itself be absorbed into and find expression within the larger dynamic of pressure and release in the Petrarchan sonnet structure, allowing Lee-Hamilton and his confined speakers some outlet for their tensions within the compact cell of the sonnet.

Unable to generate material from his own impoverished daily life, Lee-Hamilton, a highly cultivated *littérateur* with a passion for history, was forced back upon the resources of his memory, education, and intellect. A virtual prisoner, he had to work with what he had to hand, in a manner reminiscent of the poet Chatterton, whom Browning described in an essay of 1842, as

> setting sometimes to work with the poorest materials; like any painter a fathom below ground in the Inquisition, who in his penury of colour turns the weather-stains on his dungeon wall into effects of light and shade, or outlines of objects, and makes the single sputter of red paint in his possession go far indeed!
> (Browning 1971, 3.179)

Many of the *Imaginary Sonnets* feature characters who are prisoners: some of these are literally confined in gaol: Carmagnola, La Balue, Lady Jane Grey, Sir Walter Raleigh, Arabella Stuart, Latude imprisoned in a dungeon at the Bastille, the captive of Fenestrelle, Napoleon on St Helena. While not actually in gaol, Pia dei Tolomei is locked up by her husband in a tower in the marshland of the Maremma, while Alexandra Selkirk is a virtual prisoner shipwrecked on a deserted island. In contrast, Christopher Columbus, now free, keeps with him the fetters that once bound him. Other speakers are on the verge of captivity: Tannhäuser willingly submits to Venus' enchantment; Francesca da Rimini pledges herself to Paolo Malatesta, even if it means they are afterwards trapped in Hell; Savonarola, Sir Thomas More and Chastelard anticipate their arrest and subsequent death by execution. Some speakers are prisoners of circumstance such as the Duke of Milan, driven mad by strange shadows and sounds, and the legendary Wandering Jew. Some, not prisoners themselves, are concerned with the captivity of others: the singer Blondel seeks the gaoled Richard Coeur-de-Lion, Queen Eleanor meditates her entrapment of Rosamund Clifford, a voice lambastes Charles VII for his cowardly abandonment of Jeanne d'Arc, burnt at the stake by the English, while Domingo Lopez ghoulishly imprisons in the cellar Jew a whom he can crucify as a living model for his painting of Christ. Other speakers, as we shall see, use metaphors and images of imprisonment incidentally to convey some pent-up energy or force. All these diverse experiences of imprisonment bring an intensity and urgency to the utterances of the speakers concerned, concentrating mind and expression to epitomise the situation in which they find themselves.

In his prefatory sonnet to *The House of Life* (1882), Rossetti, a poet much admired by Lee-Hamilton, declared that a sonnet was 'a moment's monument, – / Memorial from the Soul's eternity / To one dead deathless hour' (Rossetti 1911, 74); the condensation of the sonnet form is the means by which the poet crystallises either epiphanies, moments of peak experience, or crises, determining fateful moments in each individual's life. In his 'Introductory Sonnet' to *Imaginary Sonnets*, Lee-Hamilton imagines his spirit standing 'Beside the great abyss where seethes the Past', catching and treasuring up the 'wild voices of despair and fear, / Of love and hate' emanating from figures he sees below 'Sucked down forever in the whirlpool's maw' (Lee-Hamilton 1888, 1). These 'appeals' the poet then puts into rhyme. These sonnet monologues are thus epitomes, small synecdochic fragments or snatches of utterance which, characterising each individual speaker and his situation, temporarily rescue him from the abyss of the past and bring him into view. Moreover, some of the sonnets incorporate further imagistic synecdoches, which have the extraordinary capacity of opening out an expansive sublimity of vision within the tightly bound limits of both the sonnet and the immediate situation presented. I have restricted myself to discussing three that I find particularly effective: 'Stradivarius to an Unfinished Violin', 'James Watt to the Spirit of His Kettle', and 'The Captive of Fenestrelle to his Flower'.

Stradivarius to an Unfinished Violin
(1710.)
The roar and gurgle of the ocean cave
Are in thy fibres, and the sob of man,
And moans that through a haunted cloister ran,
And every murmur that the beech-woods have.

Ay, and the wild bee's hum, where red pines wave;
The carol of the gipsy caravan;
The song that's uttered by the dying swan;
The warning growl that brooding Etna gave.

All this is in thy fibres – Ay, and more,
If men but care to have it, and set free
The quivering soul that only waits to soar.

Thy voice shall be as thrilling as the plea
Of caverned spirits, gathering to implore
The gloomy Powers of Eternity.

(Lee-Hamilton 1888, 82)

Just as the word 'lyric' recalls the lyre with which classical poets would have accompanied their verses so, too, the sonnet has an inherent relationship with music. As Theodore Watts-Dunton and other nineteenth-century commentators noted, the word 'sonnet' is connected with the Italian verb 'suonare' meaning 'to play upon an instrument',[28] a connection particularly pertinent to this sonnet in which a violin-maker imaginatively projects the playing of his violin. The speaker of this sonnet is Antonio Stradivarius (1644–1735), the most famous member of the best-known of the violin-making families of Cremona, Italy. Stradivarius refined the geometry and design of the violin, and his instruments are universally prized as the most perfect and desirable of their kind. All violins have a distinctive voice of their own, but the violins of Stradivarius sang like no others with a special purity of tone that made them seem almost alive in the hands of a great violinist. This sonnet tries to communicate something of that voice, as yet unformed, through the ventriloquising voice of Stradivarius himself, maker, in more than one sense, of that purer voice. The violin is crucially unfinished, *non-finito*, emergent, in the process of being fully formed like a sculpture from a stone. For Stradivarius, the violin is not just a creation, but a living creature in embryo which, when completed, will have a spirit of its own.[29] To its voice as yet unformed, Stradivarius imputes a natural origin: 'All this is in thy fibres'. The 'fibres' that compose a violin are traditionally pine, maple wood, and sheep-gut; 'fibres' being a marvellously chosen word which does duty for both wood and strings, but also hints anthropomorphically at 'the fibres of one's being'. Composed from natural fabrics – wood and sheep-gut – the violin has within its fibres a compendious memory, a natural history of sounds which it absorbed in its pre-infancy when it was a tree in the forest or a grazing animal. But equally that rich range of sounds is also its projected future history, the sounds it holds *in potentia*, to be released by the skilful musician who knows how to use it to its best advantage. The catalogue of sound includes peaceful lullabies – the 'murmur of the beech-woods', the 'wild bee's hum'; hymns of joy – the 'carol of the gipsy caravan'; and haunting pain fugues – 'the sob of man' and the spectral 'moans' from the cloister. The last two sounds listed – 'The song that's uttered by the dying swan; / The warning growl that brooding Etna gave' – have a particular intensity. In legend 'swan song' is the last

28 See Watts-Dunton, 'Poetry', 1916b, 176.

29 Lee-Hamilton may recall his sister's phrase 'violin of flesh and blood' (Lee 2006, 154) to describe the castrato singer Zaffirino. If Lee's Magnus makes the singer into an instrument, Lee-Hamilton's Stradivarius makes the instrument into a singer. Coleridge's 'The Aeolian Harp' is another possible influence. Coleridge compares the sound of the wind-blown harp to 'some coy Maid half-yielding to her Lover', but then compares himself, the poet, to the harp, played by his 'phantasies'. Finally he imagines 'all of animated nature' as harps played by 'one intellectual Breeze, / At once the Soul of each, and God of all' (Coleridge 1974, 52–3).

and finest song sung by the bird, while the warning growl of Etna is the prelude to a volcanic eruption, a manifestation of previously hidden fire or energy. This final image hints at the gathering or cumulative power of the violin's so-far repressed song. It is with this final image of accumulation that the sonnet reaches its volta, a moment of high tension which will pivot into release and which Lee-Hamilton here exploits brilliantly.

Stradivarius sees the voice and spirit of the violin as attendant on the musician who can then 'release' its latent power: 'The quivering power that only waits to soar'. 'Quivering', like 'thrilling' in line 11, besides suggesting the vibrating strings and body of the violin and the vibration of air that makes music, also suggests a hypersensitive creature trembling with nervous anticipation. The image recalls Shakespeare's 'airy spirit' Ariel, imprisoned in a 'cloven pine' for a dozen years, until released by the magician Prospero (*The Tempest* 1. 2.274–9, in Shakespeare 1974, 1615). Once free, the violin's voice and spirit have the poignant vibrancy of pleading 'caverned spirits', perhaps suggesting that its song is particularly suited to charm and win over obdurate powers, gaining release for others. The allusion here may be to the poet Orpheus who, by his song, charmed his way into the Underworld and won over its ruler Pluto, who released the poet's wife Eurydice from death. In Gluck's opera *Orfeo ed Euridice* (1762), an opera much loved by Vernon Lee, the shades of the Underworld join with Orpheus in petitioning the release of Eurydice. Moreover, Orpheus – like Apollo, the god of music – is usually pictured with a lyre, but from the Renaissance onwards both figures are occasionally represented as playing a violin, seen as the lyre's modern equivalent.[30]

Stradivarius' unfinished violin is thus a synecdoche for the voice it will one day embody, and the compact, but skilfully shaped body of the sonnet, like the compact, beautifully fashioned body of the violin, contains within it a concentrated, artfully focused power, a sublime 'infinite within the finite', with extraordinary qualities of visionary expansion and emotional range. Stradivarius through his suggestive language is the voice for that other properly unspeakable voice. In this sonnet, as in his early dramatic monologue 'The Mandolin', Lee-Hamilton, like Vernon Lee in her story 'A Wicked Voice', manages to suggest what words cannot convey: the sound of music. We don't actually hear that music but through the speaker's evocative list of properties and effects, we are tantalised by a kind of pre-echo, anticipatory ghost or spirit of the violin's voice – 'Heard melodies are sweet, but those unheard / Are sweeter' (Keats 1970,

30 In her essay 'Apollo the Fiddler', Lee discusses the representation of Apollo with a violin in Raphael's fresco in the Signature Room of the Vatican (1887, 165–218). The Victorian painter Frederic Leighton pictured Orpheus with a violin in his painting *The Triumph of Music* (1856).

534–5) – the 'unheard' melody, symbolically represented by visual symbols, perhaps forming an analogue to Lee's 'sketch'.

James Watt to the Spirit of His Kettle
(1765.)

I sit beside the hearth, and for an hour,
I watch the steam that shakes the kettle's lid,
Like some live thing that struggles hard to rid
Its limbs of bondage, and assert its power.

Yea, like some fiend that Solomon made cower,
And who, for countless centuries was bid
Dwell in a bottle which the deep sea hid
Where, tight compressed, it panted still to tower:

What if this vapour were a stronger thing
Than all the genii cast into the sea
And curst for ever by the Wizard King?

And what if I one day should set it free,
And break the seal of Solomon's own ring
And make the Daemon do my drudgery?

(Lee-Hamilton 1888, 86)

The Scottish engineer James Watt (1736–1819), whilst not, as is sometimes said, the inventor of the steam engine, certainly perfected its design, making significant improvements to Thomas Newcomen's earlier model. In 1865, while working for the University of Glasgow, Watt was given one of Newcomen's atmospheric engines to repair. Noting the deficiencies of the machine, he came up with the idea of a separate condenser, and a cylinder sealed at the top that made a far more efficient use of steam pressure, resulting in a huge increase in power. The image of Watt watching the boiling kettle, inspired by the power of steam, relates to a story told by the French mathematician and physicist Dominique Arago (1786–1853) in his early and influential biography *Eloge de James Watt*, given as a lecture to the French Academy of Sciences in December 1833, translated as the *Historical Eulogium of James Watt*, and probably published in 1834.[31] Arago tells how, in 1750, at the age of fourteen, Watt amused himself by experimenting with the steam given off by his aunt's kettle (Arago [1834], 4).[32] In this sonnet Lee-Hamilton

31 This first translation is undated but gives the impression of being published shortly after the lecture.

32 The first translation actually uses the word 'teapot', but the next translation of 1839, *Historical Eloge of James Watt*, by James Patrick Muirhead, sets the trend by using the word 'kettle' (Arago 1839, 7).

uses the image of the boiling kettle, which supposedly induced the young Watt's interest in steam, to suggest to the adult Watt his improvement of the sealed cylinder in 1765.

What is interesting, however, is that the language of the sonnet, far from being scientific and functional, is highly romantic and visionary. The steam trapped within the boiling kettle is its 'spirit', like the voice or spirit latent within Stradivarius' violin. While the action of bowing the violin makes air vibrate as sound, here compressed water vapour makes its presence felt by shaking the kettle's lid. Again the image of the imprisoned 'airy spirit' Ariel is pertinent, especially as Ariel, left in confinement, 'did vent [his] groans' till Prospero heard and released him, and made him his own servant. On this occasion, however, Watt sees himself as a Prospero, a modern magician who usurps the position of the wise King Solomon of Biblical fame. Less well known is the fact that Solomon also appears in the Qur'an as King Suleimen, able to understand the language of birds and ants, and to see some of the hidden glory of the world not accessible to ordinary human beings. The Qur'an tells how Suleiman ruled not only over his people, but also over a host of *jinn*, an Arabic word, commonly anglicised as 'genie', or 'genii' in the plural. The word *jinn* has connotations of concealment, invisibility, seclusion, and remoteness, and refers to magical beings, spirits, or demons who, in Islamic-associated mythology and Middle-Eastern folk stories, can be controlled by magically binding them to objects, the famous example of this being the genie in Aladdin's lamp in the *Arabian Nights.* Suleiman possessed this power, having in his possession a magic ring, known as the 'seal of Solomon', which gave him power over demons.

Lee-Hamilton's sonnet, with its reference to 'genii', evokes an intense atmosphere of enchantment: Solomon, the 'Wizard King', is seen as a skilled sorcerer, able to trap a malevolent spirit or 'fiend' in a bottle. But Watt is a latter-day rival who thinks he sees a way to overcome Solomon's control. It is the convention that, once unbound, a genie is obliged to carry out the wishes of the person who releases him. The limited or circumscribed nature of this 'release', which, in fact, commits the genie to be the slave of his liberator, is mirrored in Watt's meditative monologue. If he ends the confinement of the 'Daemon' or steam spirit, he does so, like Prospero or Aladdin, only to bind it to his own purposes and to make it serve his own advantage – 'do my drudgery'. Traditionally a daemon is a spirit occupying a middle place between gods and men. It can be a good spirit, but is more often thought of as a bad one, with the capacity, like fiends or genii, to harm men. Steam, like a vaporous genie, is, when Watt first perceives it, a power that defies man's ability to chain it. In literal terms, steam is potentially dangerous, especially in large quantities when, if mishandled, it can fatally scald or burn. In order to make it serviceable, steam, like a daemon or a genie, must be carefully controlled; in fact, confinement or 'tight compression' is the very means of making it most effective, building up a head of steam whose force of pressure can power an engine. Such steam-powered engines can do the work of many people in a fraction of the time, thus saving them from hours of unrelenting toil or 'drudgery'.

Watt's language, though apparently fanciful, is a highly effective compression of literal and figurative meanings. Moreover, the language of enchantment or magical romance he uses to describe the mental process of invention is, at root, an uncompromising self-assertion, showing that he conceives invention in terms of mastery, subjection, and bondage, and reminding us of Romantic language used by colonisers or explorers who, in a similar manner, see peoples and territories as forces to be claimed and mastered. Yet in this sonnet, there is also the sense that the steam spirit, animated by Watt's lively mind, also represents the power of his own mental conception as it steadily comes to boiling point and lifts the lid on new ideas. Rather than let this remain all so much hot air, which will vaporise and vanish, Watt tries to arrest the nascent thought, to pin it down and concentrate it so that it gains in effective forcefulness. If he succeeds, he may eventually make a breakthrough that will shatter conventional, centuries-old wisdom – 'the seal of Solomon's old ring'. The steam spirit in the kettle is thus a synecdoche for the power of steam, which Watt will bind and harness to make a more efficient modern steam engine, but it is also a synecdoche for the mental process, showing the glimmer of an idea which, efficiently contained and concentrated, will eventually turn into a fully formed theory with both a powerful and power-saving application.

The economy of this dual-system is, of course, effected by the brilliant economy of the sonnet itself which, like the kettle, is a compact mini-steam engine, compressing meanings for better effectiveness. Trapped within the confined space of the sonnet is an expansive vision of supernatural power merged with the potential of natural power and the conceptual mind, all of which must be encapsulated, concentrated as 'an infinite within the finite', to be of any use. Again Lee-Hamilton deploys sonnet structure to maximum effect: at the mid-point of the sonnet, just before the volta, we find the greatest pressure with the mighty force of the genie trapped inside the bottle, 'panting' to break free and 'tower'. The sestet, allowing release, gives us Watt's reflections on what he has just seen and imagined, providing the germ of an inventive solution, which will release his mind from its creative tension, and himself and others from drudgery. Like the previous sonnet, this sonnet has a dual chronological perspective. Stradivarius looked back at the prehistory of the violin but also forward to its singing future; Watt reviews the history of romance to furnish himself with images of how people have struggled to control and contain apparently insuperable powers, and these Romantic images give him a clue as to how he might deal with the power he wishes to control.

The Captive of Fenestrelle to His Flower
(1805.)

Pale plantlet that hast sprouted up between
The loosened flagstones of my prison floor
When I well-nigh could recollect no more,
What meant on earth the very colour green;

Thou tiny sweetheart that hast never seen
The sun, nor felt the breezes of the shore;
I kneel in silent rapture and adore
Thy beauty, like the lover of a queen.

Thou art the murmurous woods, the waving corn,
The seeded grass, where babbling streamlets run,
The rosary of dewdrops on the thorn;

Thou art all Nature, with her charms each one,
When least expected, suddenly new-born
In this dull cell, to fill my heart with sun.

(Lee-Hamilton 1888, 99)

The Fortress of Fenestrelle is a virtually impregnable fortification in the upper Chisone valley, in northernmost Italy. It is the largest single military construction after the Great Wall of China. Replacing earlier fortifications, it was commissioned by the Savoyard King Vittorio Amedeo in the 1720s, and designed and constructed by the engineers Antonio and Ignazio Bertola. Work began in 1728 and continued for many years. That part of the Fort known as the Officers' Pavilion, constructed between 1780 and 1789 to the design of Count Lorenzo Bernardino Pinto, on the instructions of Vittorio Amedeo III, had the function of state and military prison. It is historically the most significant building within the Fortress, and is the setting for this sonnet. Used by both Napoleon and the Savoyards as a maximum security gaol, the Fortress was feared for the harshness of its conditions. During the nineteenth century, many important figures were confined in the Fortress, the most famous being Cardinal Pacca, Secretary to Pope Pius VII. However, the imprisoned speaker of this sonnet is not a real-life figure, but Count Charney, a fictional character from a best-selling novel published in 1836. Written by the French novelist Xavier Boniface Saintine, this popular romance, titled *Picciola*, translated into English in 1837, describes the imprisonment of Count Charles Veramont de Charney for anti-Napoleonic activities.[33] Isolated in his cell for most of the time, Charney is allowed to take two hours' daily

33 *Picciola or Captivity Captive* (1837). As Lee-Hamilton's title for his sonnet uses the word 'flower', he may have known a later translation 'Picciola; or, the Prison Flower. A Tale', in *Masterpieces of Foreign Literature* (1866), 289–339.

exercise in a small paved court where he sees a little plant grow from a seed blown in and lodged in a crack between the paving stones. As it grows, it becomes his friend and he speaks to it as if it were a companion, giving it the name 'Picciola', an affectionate Italian feminine diminutive meaning 'dear little one'. Ludovico, a friendly prison warder, helps him tend the plant, which flourishes and develops beautiful flowers. However, as the plant grows bigger, the Count becomes anxious lest it should die from lack of sustenance around its roots and asks if the crack could be enlarged. The Governor of the Fortress refuses, but Teresa Gerhardi, the visiting daughter of a fellow prisoner, takes pity on Charney and tries to help by taking his request to Josephine, wife of Napoleon, who was a keen gardener. After a series of events, a letter arrives from Napoleon in the nick of time instructing that the plant, which is about to be cut down, should be saved. Finally, after Charney's release, he and Teresa marry.

Lee-Hamilton, a fluent French speaker, may have read this story in the original or in translation. As he dispenses with most of the plot of the novel to concentrate on its central motif, he may be recalling it from memory or he may not have actually read it at all, simply referring to a received idea of a well-known text. Previous to the sonnet, he had earlier referred to the story in the poetic 'Introduction' to his collection *The New Medusa, and Other Poems* (1882), which, when reprinted in the later collection *Dramatic Sonnets, Poems, and Ballads* (1903), was retitled 'Picciola'. In this 'Introduction', Lee-Hamilton narrates the story of the plant's growth, before declaring that his 'prison-nurtured Poetry' has been itself another Picciola:

> This book is all a plant of prison growth,
> Watered with prison water, not sweet rain;
> The writer's limbs and mind are laden both
> By heavy chains.
>
> (Lee-Hamilton 1882, 8)

In the sonnet, as in this 'Introduction', the small plant has grown up from a crack in the flagstones of the Captive's cell floor rather than in the outer courtyard. For the Captive, presumably unable even to see anything of his external surroundings from his window, and reduced to the narrow grey world of his cell, this little living thing is a tiny token and reminder of natural beauty. Even though, as a fellow prisoner sharing his gloomy conditions, it, too, is pale, it none the less manages to bring a shred of vital colour into his life. Reminded of the significance of green, a colour ordinarily assumed by healthy plants exposed to the sun and other elements, the Captive finds himself revivified. In the presence of the plant, he is transformed; no longer is he a sense-deprived prisoner languishing in gaol, but a Romantic poet who worships in a religious cult of natural beauty. At this point in the poem, the plant increasingly personified, becomes a 'she', and, exquisitely, a 'tiny sweetheart', Lee-Hamilton's endearing synonym for 'Picciola', a name that otherwise does not appear in the poem. Adopting the chivalric language of the courtly lover who prostrates himself before his 'queen', his adored beloved, the Captive is filled with tender devotion as the plantlet reminds him how to love, keeping alive his powers of empathy. We might remember Shelley's pronouncement in his essay 'On Love', that 'Hence in solitude, or in that deserted state where we are surrounded by human beings and yet they sympathise not with us, we love the flowers, the grass and the waters and the sky. . . . Sterne says that if he were in a desart he would love some cypress' (Shelley 1977, 474), and Freud's complementary statement in 'On Narcissism' (1914) that 'in the last resort we must begin to love in order not to fall ill' (Freud 1984a, 11.78). Perhaps, too, for readers of Saintine's novel, the Captive's love of his plant, Picciola, is part of a natural prelude to and prefigurement of his love for Teresa, his eventual bride. Unlike the violin and the steam spirit, which are animated by the brilliant inventive minds of Stradivarius and Watt, the plant is naturally a living creature, and, as such, has an inbuilt capacity to stand in or do duty for other larger natural creations.[34]

Like his Captive, and unlike many Decadent poets of the late Victorian period, Lee-Hamilton did not feel the need to downgrade or transcend the Nature of woods and fields, and cultivate instead hot-house flowers, because to him ordinary natural beauty becomes exotic by virtue of being out of reach. As a result of this, his evocations of the beauty of Nature have a startlingly pure, unembarrassed lyrical power that at its best reminds one of Shakespeare and Tennyson. The attitude of prayerful rapture assumed by the Captive at the conclusion of the octave, a heightened moment of intensity, gives way to the sestet's release in which his consciousness is renovated and solaced by a soothing, hypnotic vision of natural beauty, which he hymns in a song of praise. The courtly lover is also something of a medieval mystic, prepared for vision by a rigorous asceticism. His powers of imagination, roused, no doubt by 'the virtue of paucity and the stimulus of the insufficient', as well as by 'the spell of the fragment', use the plant as a synecdoche, connecting him to the unseen natural world by making it a visionary symbol and thus a gateway to that world. In this way, through a visionary condensation which is also an expansion, the infinite beauties of the natural world contained within the finite body of the plant; the limits of the Captive's 'dull cell' are bypassed as the plantlet rewards his devotion, giving him access to the litany of lovely sights and sounds he catalogues. In his final acknowledgement and an ultimate radiant Blakeian epiphany, the plantlet is 'all Nature', her charms 'When least expected, suddenly new-born',

34 Lee-Hamilton may also be influenced by Shelley's poem 'The Sensitive Plant' (composed 1820), in which the Plant (often interpreted as a figure for the poet) loves and is sustained by love, but perishes when the Lady, the nurturing spirit of the garden, dies (Shelley 1977, 210–19).

filling the Captive's heart with sun. The simple, emphatic monosyllables of the final line make this a movingly matter-of-fact miracle.

The ideas Lee-Hamilton plays with in this ending evoke by association reminiscences of Donne's love poetry. In Donne's 'The Good Morrow', the speaker declares 'For love, all love of other sights controls, / And makes one little room, an every where' (Donne 1971, 60); that is, the exclusive nature of amatory passion inhibits pleasure in all other sights, making the room where lovers meet their only world. The outside world shrinks to the peripheral limits of the space in which they see each other. But in Lee-Hamilton's sonnet, the Captive's love of the plant and, kindled by her, his love of Nature, miraculously expands a world which before was lamentably contracted. He cherishes the plant, but shares the Romantic poet's desire to 'always seek in what I see the manifestation of something beyond the present & tangible object' (Shelley 1964, 2.47). In Donne's 'The Sun Rising', the lover as speaker demands that the sun fulfil its duty to warm the world by 'warming us': 'Shine here to us, and thou art everywhere; / This bed thy centre is, these walls, thy sphere' (Donne 1971, 81). In Lee-Hamilton's sonnet, no assertion or demand is necessary, because the outer natural world is necessarily linked to the Captive's inner world. Thus the visionary beauties of the outside world, projected into his shadowy 'dull cell', cannot but help but illuminate his inner world.

If, as in the 'Introduction' to *The New Medusa*, the plant also in some way represents poetry, then it may be that here it specifically signals the sonnet form, indicating that it is possible to contain within the 'prison cell' of the sonnet a range of visionary expansiveness more naturally associated with other 'freer' verse forms. The sonnets examined in this final section seem particularly moving and absorbing because they offer images of the creative mind which manages to find its way out of limitation into a wider expansiveness. Although Lee-Hamilton mourned the paralysis of his body, his sonnets have a vigorous ingenuity that stretches the minds of both his speakers and his readers. The unfinished violin, the as-yet inadequately harnessed steam spirit, and the growing plantlet, are all types of the *non-finito*, conjuring up a formative and informing power. In one of his gloomier sonnets from *Sonnets of the Wingless Hours*, Lee-Hamilton imagined himself as a funerary monument: 'Make me in marble after I am dead; / Stretched out recumbent, just as I have lain' (Lee-Hamilton 1894, 21). In the light of his eventual recovery in 1896, he might have imagined his monument as made after the manner of Michelangelo's 'Day' in the Medici Chapel, a sculpture whose face is famously unfinished. As his own Michelangelo would put it in the imaginary sonnet monologue 'Michael Angelo to His Statue of Day (1535.)':

> Therefore I give thee neither face nor eyes
> But leave thy head unhewn, until such time
> As Freedom burst her slumber and shall rise . . .
>
> (Lee-Hamilton 1888, 45)

4

Theodore Watts-Dunton's *Aylwin* and the reduplications of Romanticism

For most modern readers of Victorian literature, the name Theodore Watts-Dunton carries little weight, and he is registered, if at all, as a peripheral figure – a friend of the Pre-Raphaelites and the companion of Swinburne in his latter years. Few know that he was regarded as one of the most important critics of his generation or that he achieved considerable fame late in his career with the publication of his best-selling novel *Aylwin* (1898), which was one of the literary successes of its year. Although *Aylwin* went into an Oxford World's Classics imprint in 1904 well within its author's lifetime, had sold over a hundred thousand copies by the time of his death in 1914,[1] and was still in print in 1950, it is now almost unknown and has received virtually no academic attention. Yet *Aylwin* is a fascinating work with many features which might prove attractive to modern readers.

Influenced by the sensation fiction of Wilkie Collins, and in part a *roman à clef* featuring members of Watts-Dunton's own literary and artistic circle including his close friend Dante Gabriel Rossetti, the novel is a strange amalgam of gypsy lore, the occult, mesmerism, and Romanticism. The occult and Romantic elements help constitute that pervasive aspect of the book which Watts-Dunton called 'the Renascence of Wonder', basically a reaction to the growing materialism of the later nineteenth century, and a revival of belief in the redemptive powers of Nature and the imagination. With its strong commitment to a spiritual realm and life beyond death, and its refusal of materialism and positivistic values, the novel should recommend itself to anyone interested in the growth

1 In his 'Introduction' to an anthologised selection of poems by Watts-Dunton, Mackenzie Bell states that, 'in a comparatively short time', *Aylwin* reached its twenty-sixth edition and had sold upwards of a hundred thousand copies (Bell 1915, 262). The twenty-sixth edition was in press at the time of Watts-Dunton's death in 1914. There were also American editions and a Tauchnitz edition. The Oxford World's Classics reprint of 1950 is the latest edition I have traced. The novel, widely and cheaply available second-hand, can also be downloaded from Project Gutenberg.

of non-orthodox religious belief or spirituality in the late Victorian period; however, other elements such as the novel's intimately drawn characterisation of Rossetti, its generic debts to sensation fiction and Romantic poetry, its observations on the contemporary medical treatment of hysteria, and its positive portrayal of the best aspects of gypsy life deserve to win it a larger audience.

My own interest in the novel lies in its restatement of certain Romantic values at the turn of the nineteenth century. It is the contention of this chapter that, by explicitly associating key aspects of the narrative with Coleridge's visionary poetry, the novel participates in a strategic late Victorian revival of Romanticism. I propose that repetition and reduplication – structural devices which are integral to the organisation, movement, and symbolic and thematic matter of *Aylwin* – are also part of the novel's larger purpose to communicate its transmission and reproduction of a visionary Romanticism which is itself founded on repetition.

Some preliminary words of introduction about Watts-Dunton, his interests, and the circumstances in which he came to write his extraordinary novel are in order. Walter Theodore Watts (1832–1914), or Watts-Dunton as he became after 1896, first made acquaintance with two of the most famous poets of the Victorian era through his professional legal expertise. A trained and skilful solicitor, he handled the sometimes delicate affairs of both men, advising Rossetti over a forged cheque and helping extricate Swinburne from a potential blackmail at the hands of his unscrupulous publisher John Camden Hotten. However, it was not merely for his professional tact and discretion that Watts-Dunton was valued. His passionate love of art and literature and his lively conversational manner, together with great personal warmth, loyalty, and generosity were among those qualities which caused Swinburne to describe him as 'closer than a brother' and made Rossetti declare 'Watts is a hero of friendship'.[2] Indeed, Rossetti's 'friend of friends' was one of the few people outside of his own family whom the poet continued to see during the last reclusive years of his life.[3] At one point Watts would make a round trip each week to spend a day and night with Rossetti at 16 Cheyne Walk, would then visit the

2 Swinburne's words are taken from the dedicatory sonnet that prefaces his epic poem *Tristram of Lyonesse* and bears the sub-epigraph 'The Pines', April 1882' (Swinburne 1904, 4.iii). His *Collected Poetical Works* are dedicated to Watts-Dunton and are prefaced by a 'Dedicatory Epistle' addressed to him (Swinburne 1904, 1.iii, v–xxix). Rossetti's remark is reportedly one of his last, made at Birchington where he died on 9 April 1882, to Thomas Hall Caine (Caine 1882, 75).

3 The phrase 'friend of friends', often used to describe Watts-Dunton's relation to Rossetti, derives from his own long poem 'Christmas at the Mermaid' where it denotes the young man beloved by Shakespeare who was the dedicatee of many of his sonnets (Watts-Dunton, 10th ed., n.d., 119). This edition is undated but the ninth edition dates to 1913.

poet John Leicester Warren, Lord de Tabley (another recluse), before returning to Putney and 'The Pines' to resume his guardianship of Swinburne. Rossetti dedicated his last volume, *Ballads and Sonnets* (1881), to Watts-Dunton, who was among the close friends and family present at the poet's death in April 1882, and supported the dying man in his arms.[4]

But Watts-Dunton was more than just a friend to poets. After settling in London in the early 1870s, he began to write journalistic articles on literature and eventually became the leading critic of poetry for the *Examiner* and, from 1876, the *Athenæum*. These articles clearly had an important educative function, a writer for *Poetry Review* stating 'There are middle-aged men who have learnt all they knew about poetry from Mr. Watts-Dunton's delightful and profound criticisms in the *Athenæum*'.[5] Certainly this was the view of Arthur Strong, Librarian of the House of Lords, who named these articles as the source of his literary education (Douglas 1904, 1). But Watts-Dunton's critical work was also valued by poets themselves: Robert Browning and James Russell Lowell (who was also American Minister in London) were among his admirers and Swinburne described him as 'the first critic of our time – perhaps the largest-minded and surest-sighted of any age' (Swinburne 1894, 135–6). Hyperbole apart, there is no doubt that his opinions were generally held in the highest regard and that he was an influential and supportive figure for many aspirant young poets and writers. Augusta Webster and the Native Canadian poet E. Pauline Johnson ('Tekahionwake')[6] were among many writers whose work he championed and he was a familiar figure on the London literary and artistic scene, rubbing shoulders with Tennyson, George Eliot and George Henry Lewes, R. H. Horne, James McNeill Whistler, Henry Irving, and William Bell Scott, to give but some of the better-known names. Beside Rossetti and Swinburne, his close friends included William Morris, Ford Madox Brown, George Meredith, the blind poet Philip Bourke Marston, and the physician Dr Thomas Gordon Hake, known as 'the parable poet', through whom he came to know Rossetti.

Yet Watts-Dunton's prominence as a critic is now hardly recognised, partly owing to the fact that he failed to bring out collections of his essays during his heyday. This failure to seize the moment and publish in book form recurred throughout his life, and was due to a number of reasons. These included his

4 The dedication reads 'To Theodore Watts, the Friend whom my verse won for me, these few more pages are affectionately inscribed' (Rossetti 1881, iii).

5 *Poetry Review* 5, 3, cited in Graham 1930, 319.

6 He reviewed various of Webster's verse collections in the *Athenæum*, where his obituary (Watts-Dunton 1894, 335) for her also appears. See also his Preface to *Flint and Feather: The Complete Poems of E. Pauline Johnson (Tekahionwake)* (Watts-Dunton 1912, vii–xvi).

tendency to spread himself too thinly. He had, as will be seen, a diverse set of interests and, in his business and personal life, tended to take on too many commitments. Moreover, the engrained habits of journalism – the production in fairly swift succession of short articles exploring just one or two particular aspects of a subject – militated against the larger all-consuming commitment to monographs. Well-placed to write biographies on Rossetti and Swinburne and widely expected to produce definitive 'lives' of both poets, his characteristic procrastination, ethical over-scrupulosity, and reticence to disclose personal information made him reluctant to write biographical accounts of either of them. The chapter on Rossetti in the posthumously published collection *Old Familiar Faces* (1916), a compilation of two earlier articles from the *Athenæum*, seems an exercise in evasion, giving little direct personal information about the poet and recording instead the problems faced by the biographer in giving an authentic portrait of his subject (Watts-Dunton 1916a, 69–119). For insight into Swinburne's later years and the domestic life of 'The Pines', we have to turn not to Watts-Dunton but to his young wife Clara (*née* Reich), whom, after a long bachelorhood, he married in November 1905 when she was twenty-nine and he was seventy-three, having first met her when she was a school girl of sixteen. Clara Watts-Dunton's *The Home Life of Swinburne*, published in 1922 some years after her husband's death, paints an affectionate, though some might say rather banal, picture of the daily routines of the Swinburne–Watts-Dunton household. Constant deferral, anxiety about finalising and perfecting his work, and, it would seem, a diffidence or lack of interest in promoting himself and cultivating a lasting reputation all contributed to Watts-Dunton's failure to see book projects come to fruition.

In 1885 Watts-Dunton was asked to contribute the definitive entry on 'Poetry' for the ninth edition of the *Encyclopædia Britannica*, a substantial piece which became celebrated, to use Thomas Hardy's words, as 'that masterly essay on Poetry' and was still used in the eleventh edition of 1911 (Letter of 26 February 1899; Hardy 1978–88, 2.16). According to James Douglas, Watts-Dunton's earliest biographer, the poet Richard Le Gallienne bought the complete set of the *Encyclopædia* just so that he could possess this essay (Douglas 1904, 1). 'Poetry', along with another much-admired piece called 'The Renascence of Wonder in Poetry', the opening entry of the third volume of *Chambers's Cyclopædia of English Literature* (1903), were eventually collected and published in book form in 1916, two years after Watts-Dunton's death, but by that time the essays had lost their moment and looked rather dated.[7] Alfred Richard Orage, the literary critic and editor of the journal *New Age*, commenting on Watts-Dunton's 'famous article on Poetry', is coolly contemptuous:

7 In the text of this collection, the second essay is titled 'The Renascence of Wonder in *English* Poetry' (my italics).

'What could have attracted our predecessors so greatly to this essay? It is not only painstakingly dull, but it is wrong upon matters in which to be wrong is almost a crime' (Orage 1935, 29–30). Actually 'Poetry' contains many interesting perceptions, although Watts-Dunton's overall style of argument – lots of sweeping statements and generalisation accompanied by a continual division of poets into ranks and classes – seems very old-fashioned. One of the notable features of the essay that its author, who is unusually well-read in Middle-Eastern and Indian literature, is able to range very widely, comparing Icelandic sagas with Persian epics. This is not always an advantage in that he often refers to texts that the average reader is not likely to know; however, it does attest to an interesting eclecticism, which can also be detected informing his creative work. *Aylwin*, for example, refers on a number of occasions to religious traditions and spiritual and mystic beliefs other than those of Christianity.

In spite of his later involvement in literary matters, Watts-Dunton's initial education had been in the sciences, and natural history remained a life-long preoccupation. Thomas Gordon Hake's sequence *The New Day* (1890) is dedicated to Watts-Dunton, and various of the sonnets commemorate his love of the outdoors and the beauty of the natural world. Natural beauty had a mystical, quasi-religious significance for him that he celebrated in his own creative writing, most of which at that point was known only to his immediate circle of friends. 'You are loved Nature's best biographer', writes Hake of Watts-Dunton in Sonnet 51, while Sonnet 55 asks, 'And what is poetry but Nature's song . . .?' (Hake 1890, 51, 52). Nature stimulated another passion, his intense interest in British gypsy life and culture, again conspicuous in his creative work. As a young man he had learnt Romany and spent time with the gypsies. Frances Hindes Groome, the writer and scholar of Gypsy life, was a friend and associate, as was that other authority on the gypsies, George Borrow, whose autobiographical texts *Lavengro* (1851) and *Romany Rye* (1857) Watts-Dunton edited and introduced in 1893 and 1900 respectively. However, most of his gypsy romancing went into his own creative work.

In 1897 he published a long-awaited and well-received collection of poems, *The Coming of Love*, which had appeared piecemeal in the *Athenæum* from 1882 onwards. The most important poems in this collection tell the story of a young upper-class poet and sailor, Percy Aylwin, and his love for a gypsy girl, Rhona Boswell. Thwarted by his family, Percy is temporarily separated from Rhona, but the couple are eventually married. When Rhona is murdered, the anguished Percy retreats to live alone in the Alps, where he experiences mystical visions and, finally, a consoling dream of his lost love. We are told that it is the poem about this dream, titled 'The Promise Again Renewed', which, many years before it was collected in *The Coming of Love*, inspired Rossetti to meet Watts-Dunton. Staying at Kelmscott with Morris and Rossetti, Watts-Dunton's good friend, Thomas Gordon Hake recited the poem, which concludes with the lines: 'But when again upon my neck she fell / Her hair smelt sweet of whin and woodland spice' (Watts-Dunton n.d., 106). The poem is said to have moved Rossetti so deeply that his eyes filled with tears and he said, 'I must know that man' (Nicoll 1898, 800–1). Clearly the poem spoke to his own experience of loss and bereavement, although he seems to have combined his desire with expediency, as, needing to consult a solicitor, he wrote to Watts asking for his help.

The following year, 1898, saw the appearance of what the writer Rupert Croft-Cooke has called 'that curious, so nearly splendid best-selling novel *Aylwin*', which Watts-Dunton had been working on for over twenty-five years (Croft-Cooke 1967, 89). His biographers Thomas St E. Hake and Arthur Compton-Rickett tell us that he read versions of the first few chapters to Thomas Gordon Hake and his sons in 1872. Proofs were set up and corrected in 1885 and were evidently circulated among Watts-Dunton's friends and associates, but he found it impossible to let go and kept revising it and adding to it for another thirteen years (Hake and Compton-Rickett 1916, 1.70–2, 305–6).[8] Croft-Cooke's qualification 'so nearly splendid' is probably prompted by the commonly held belief that the novel is overlong and would have been better if cut by a third, a view strongly supported by Hake and Compton-Rickett (Hake and Compton-Rickett 1916, 1.312). Even so, Watts-Dunton admitted that the original version of the novel was considerably longer: 'the story was much too long for market purposes. Its length appalled me, and I was impelled to cut out some thousands of words of description and symbolical suggestions' (Sharp 1904, 142).

Aylwin, a prequel or parallel narrative to *The Coming of Love*, tells the story of Henry Aylwin of Raxton Hall, Percy's cousin, the son of a famous family and 'heir of one of the largest landowners in England' (Watts-Dunton 1914, 59), who falls in love with his childhood sweetheart, Winifred Wynne, the daughter of the local church organist and custodian.[9] Brought up since infancy by her aunt in Wales, Winifred comes to visit her alcoholic father every year and begins a friendship with Henry that ripens into love. Henry's mother, mindful of her son's status, does not approve, and after a succession of tragic events, the couple are separated, Winifred disappears, and the novel narrates Henry's long

8 See the warm letter dated 1885 from William Sharp, in Hake and Compton-Rickett 1916, 1.307–10. See also the heartfelt letter of praise by Swinburne's mother, Lady Jane Swinburne, dated 11 August 1889, in Swinburne 1962, 5.271. It is clear that Lady Jane has read only part of the novel because she indicates that she is 'longing for the rest'.

9 I use throughout the World's Classics edition of 1914 as this usefully collects various prefaces by Watts-Dunton as well as two important Appendices, which provide information about the events and personalities mentioned in the novel.

and frustrating search to find her, aided by his close friend, a young gypsy woman, Sinfi Lovell. Both the poetic narrative *The Coming of Love* and *Aylwin* illustrate, in Watts-Dunton's own words, 'love's warfare with death', and were written to show 'how terribly despair becomes intensified when a man has lost – or thinks he has lost – a woman whose love was the only light of his world' (Watts-Dunton 1914, xviii, xix).

Aylwin became the publishing sensation of 1898. Brought out in October, it had gone into nine editions by December and was deemed by G. P. Gooch in *The Annals of Politics and Culture, 1492–1899* to be first among the three most important books published that year.[10] It was reviewed admiringly in Britain and on the continent and there were many requests for its translation, although Watts-Dunton again hung fire, doubting that the translators possessed the necessary fluency.[11] Those parts of the North Norfolk coast and North Wales where a large part of the action of the novel is set were immediately claimed by their inhabitants as 'Aylwin-land'. 'I wonder', commented the poet William Sharp, 'if any other first romance has ever had so swift and so great a success' (Sharp 1904, 127).

Why was the novel so popular? It is likely that the non-sectarian generalised and positive religious message of the book attesting to the spiritual power of Nature, life beyond the grave, and a love that defies death appealed to a large number of readers who may no longer have felt able to believe in orthodox Christianity. This religious element is skilfully and sensitively handled, being in the words of *Primitive Methodist Quarterly Review* 'felt rather than seen, . . . not so much an assertion as an unmistakeable presence' (Eccles 1900, 108). The supernaturalism of *Aylwin*, another attraction, is deftly handled by the narrative so that, on careful examination, the discriminating reader can see much, if

10 According to Hake and Compton-Rickett (1916, 1.319), *Aylwin* reached its seventeenth edition in six months. ('Edition' here seems to mean 'impression'.) The publisher's advertisements in the *Athenæum* for the last three months of 1898 trace sales of the various 'editions', indicating that the novel was prepared in batches of one thousand copies at a time. An advertisement appearing on 31 December 1898 (p. 918), declares that the twelfth edition is now ready, 'making 12,000 copies of the English edition' and that the thirteenth edition is in the press. See Gooch 1901, 469 (item 3737).

11 *The Bookman* (December 1898), 310–11, gives a useful digest of some leading reviews of what it calls 'Mr Watts-Dunton's fascinating romance, which is the book of the moment in England' (310). See also the large advertisement for the US third edition of *Aylwin* in *The Bookman* (February 1899) which contains positive comment by the following British newspapers and periodicals: *Daily Chronicle, The Daily News, Athenæum, Lloyd's Weekly Newspaper, Literature, London Echo, The Star, The Daily Telegraph.* On proposed translations see Hake and Compton-Rickett 1916, 1.321, and 'Literary Gossip', in *Athenæum* (12 November 1898), 679.

not all, of it as the work of unconscious suggestion in the minds of the characters. Oddly such a discovery does not seem to diminish lessons learnt or the novel's power in that, in its own way, a psychologically determined supernaturalism is made to seem just as marvellous. Other allurements include the romance of star-crossed lovers who succeed against the odds, an excitingly sensationalistic plot, a cast of interesting idiosyncratic characters (some of whom, it seemed, might be based on real-life personages), and curiosities such as gypsy beliefs and customs and French mesmeric therapy. Oscar Wilde's sometimes repeated throwaway comment – 'a capital book to give to one's parents at Christmas time' – takes on a somewhat altered appearance when read in context. Wilde reveals in a letter to Robert Ross of 3 December 1898 that he has just read Watts-Dunton's novel for the second time – although *Aylwin* had been in print for only two months and is nearly five hundred pages long. Clearly Wilde was sufficiently interested by the novel and its popular success to make a second reading. 'Of course,' he writes, 'it is old-fashioned in style, but the tone is nice, and the plot romantic' (Wilde 2000, 1106). As the speedy reprints of the novel suggest, Watts-Dunton's publishers were more than aware of the novel's appeal to the general reading public and its likelihood of doing well in the Christmas market.

Moreover, the author had made a concerted effort to make the novel accessible to a wide audience. Although we learn that *Aylwin* was first of all written in a much more elaborate literary style, Watts-Dunton wisely altered it to something much plainer and clearer. This 'flawless English' as Francis Hindes Groome called it, may owe something to the admirably direct style of George Borrow, one of Watts-Dunton's literary heroes (Groome 1898, 39). However, as the reviewer for the *Athenæum* noted, Watts-Dunton retained, as examples of 'deliberate eloquence' in the high style, passages spoken by those characters who expound the novel's spiritual philosophy (Anonymous, 22 October 1898, 561).

This same *Athenæum* review also speaks of the novel's strong pull on its readers' sympathy and identification. Somehow merging, I think, Watts-Dunton with his narrator Henry Aylwin – an interesting conflation as Henry is undoubtedly part-based on his author – the reviewer remarks how Watts-Dunton's readers 'identify themselves, to an almost painful degree, both with him and with his creations' (Anonymous, 22 October 1898, 561). Certainly the affective experience of reading the novel can be powerful. Henry's passionate despair at losing his lover and his sensation that she is always just beyond his reach becomes in the second half of the narrative a kind of frustrated delirium, and, through their continued involvement with the feverish intensity of his point of view, readers may begin to feel oddly disorientated and destabilised as they experience the peculiarly heightened, almost hallucinatory unfolding of the narrative.

Romantic repetitions

If the novel manages to transmit or transfer to the reader something of Henry's delirium, this would seem to be a characteristic it has itself absorbed from its own Romantic sources, and these influences help the novel determine and strengthen its structure of repetition and transference. In his treatment of Nature and the imagination Watts-Dunton is primarily influenced by the Romantic poets, in particular Coleridge, whom he called 'the great Lord of romance', and whose 'Christabel', 'Ancient Mariner', and 'Kubla Khan' he rated as the supreme works of Romanticism (Watts-Dunton 1916b, 260, 271).

Coleridge himself seems to be a writer determined and motivated by repetition, as can be seen in his own theorising in the *Biographia Literaria*, where the primary imagination is 'a repetition in the finite mind of the eternal act of creation in the infinite I AM', while the secondary imagination is 'an echo of the former' (Coleridge 1975, 167). But repetition is integral to his own creative work. The supernatural poems 'Christabel', 'The Ancient Mariner', and 'Kubla Khan' so admired by Watts-Dunton are all poems which figure compulsive repetition as well as listeners or viewers who find themselves compelled or spell-bound, such as the Wedding-Guest, arrested and hypnotised by the tale of the Ancient Mariner, Christabel entranced by Geraldine, Bard Bracy haunted by his ominous dream, and the speaker of 'Kubla Khan', who, mesmerised by his vision of the Abyssinian maid, longingly imagines himself as a visionary with the power to mesmerise his auditors. Moreover, these poems seem to exert their own compulsive repetitions on both their author and his readers. Stephen Bygrave points out that there were six published versions of 'The Ancient Mariner', 'a poem Coleridge continued to revise, sometimes radically, throughout his life', adding that he seemed 'restlessly compelled to revise a poem within which the Mariner is similarly compelled to repeat and tell his story' (Bygrave 1997, 1). Watts-Dunton himself in his essay 'The Renascence of Wonder in English Poetry' repeats the story of how Sir Walter Scott's 'friend Stoddart, having heard Coleridge recite the first part of *Christabel* while still in manuscript, and having a memory that retained everything, repeated the poem to Scott. The seed fell upon a soil of magical fertility. Scott at once sat down and produced *The Lay of the Last Minstrel*' (Watts-Dunton 1916b, 270–1). 'Christabel', a poem which will play an important part in *Aylwin*, is thus established even before its publication as a compulsive and entrancing poem with the power to beget other texts.

In *Aylwin*, Watts-Dunton also follows Coleridge in tying repetition to devices such as curses and states of enthralment, which demand that individuals compulsively act out or repeat specific behavioural scripts. Coleridge's Ancient Mariner, doomed by a curse for shooting the albatross, has to work out his salvation and then finds himself periodically compelled to repeat his story by way of atonement. Enchanted by Geraldine, Christabel finds herself forced to mimic the daemonic woman's look of hate, while Edward, Mary, and Ellen in Coleridge's unfinished poem 'The Three Graves' – a poem which, like 'Christabel', is directly mentioned in *Aylwin* (Watts-Dunton 1914, 89) – are traumatised by and, thus cannot help themselves fulfilling, the curse of Mary's wicked mother. In his Preface to 'The Three Graves', Coleridge said that the subject matter interested him as 'a striking proof of the possible effect on the imagination, from an idea violently and suddenly impressed on it' (Coleridge 1974, 144).

Ideas suddenly or violently impressed on the imagination and the tendency to repeat or duplicate them, a tendency characteristic of obsession or trauma, are, as we shall see, defining features of *Aylwin*. Repetition is present from the very beginning of the novel, whose opening paragraph is a quotation, taken from a spiritualist text named by the narrative as *The Veiled Queen*,[12] itself a product of obsessive mourning for a lost love. This text, the work of Henry Aylwin's father, Philip Aylwin, and inspired by the bereavement of his first wife, acts as the novel's strange shadow-self. Henry, a rationalist and Darwinian, is initially sceptical of his father's beliefs, but after enduring, like his father, the loss of the woman he loves, gradually finds that he comes into sympathy with his views. The 'Veiled Queen' of the title is the mystical spirit of Nature, whose true aspect and body are but glimpsed through the material veil, yet she is also the spirit of the lost woman, glimpsed through the veil of mortality or the material screen. The text *The Veiled Queen* thus acts as a primer of belief and a script which Henry comes to repeat or follow and, presented as the philosophical message of the novel, is a book within a book, a partly buried or veiled subtext which comes to double with the novel itself. Watts-Dunton opens his Preface to the World's Classics edition of the novel with the statement that 'The heart-thought of the book [is] the peculiar doctrine in Philip Aylwin's *The Veiled Queen*, and the effect of it upon the fortunes of the hero and the other characters' (Watts-Dunton 1914, xi), and, in the 1904 Arvon illustrated edition of the novel (the twenty-second edition), and in subsequent editions, he restored some passages from *The Veiled Queen* which he had felt obliged to cut when the book first went to press from fear of their being too long.[13]

It should be noted that this gradual replication in Henry of his father's views is prompted, in good Coleridgean style, by the pressure of a curse, also emanating from his father. The action of the novel stems from a precious

12 The title *The Veiled Queen* is, of course, another distorted repetition, evoking Helena Blavatsky's theosophical treatise *Isis Unveiled*, published in two volumes in 1877. *Aylwin* refers specifically to Nature as the figure of Isis on a number of occasions. See, for example, Watts-Dunton 1914, 205, 209.

13 These excerpts, included in all subsequent editions, occur at the ends of Chapter 12: 'The Revolving Case of Circumstance' and Chapter 13: 'The Magic of Snowdon' (Watts-Dunton 1914, 359–60 and 383–4). See Douglas 1904, 445–50.

Gnostic jewelled cross that carries a curse. Henry's father Philip Aylwin, mystic and author of *The Veiled Queen*, is devoted to the memory of his first wife with whom he believes himself to be in direct communication. Before his death he shows Henry, his son by his second marriage, the cross he gave his first wife as an engagement present and which he always wears in memory of her. He makes Henry promise to bury the cross with him when he dies and places a curse on whoever might attempt to steal it: a curse which would also descend on the thief's children who would be forced to live as vagabonds and beg their bread. The cross, inevitably, is stolen, and by none other than by Tom Wynne, the father of Henry's fiancée who dies in a landslip almost immediately afterwards and whose shattered corpse, still bearing the cross, is later discovered by his horrified daughter. Henry, who knew Tom was the thief, has feared for Winifred's discovery of her father's crime: 'Her sweet soul would pine under the blazing fire of a curse real or imaginary; her life would be henceforth but a bitter penance. Like the girl in Coleridge's poem of "The Three Graves," her very flesh would waste before the fires of her imagination' (Watts-Dunton 1914, 89). The hideous shock of the actual discovery, 'an idea violently and suddenly impressed' on the imagination of the suggestible Winifred, traumatises the girl and eventually causes her to take flight in her madness. Winifred's implicit belief in the transmission of the curse from father to child, which effectively incriminates her, also thus entangles Henry in the action of the curse, finally rendering him responsive to the transmission of his father's spiritual legacy.

While Coleridge's poems act as a structuring influence on *Aylwin*, something I shall return to later on, a more immediate but complementary influence is the sensation novelist Wilkie Collins, and principally his two best novels.[14] If the cursed jewelled cross recalls the cursed diamond of Collins's *The Moonstone* (1868), Sinfi Lovell, the resourceful young gypsy woman who helps Henry in his search for Winifred and is clearly in love with him, recalls the courageous Marian Halcombe in *The Woman in White* (1860), who, although drawn to the hero Walter Hartwright, helps him recover his beloved, Laura Fairlie – another woman, like Winifred, whose fate seems to hover between death and madness. Having been friends with Winifred from childhood, Sinfi regards her as a sister and feels bound to help her, just as Marian Halcombe, the half-sister of Laura, makes her welfare and interests paramount. While Winifred is a considerably more attractive character than the insipid Laura Fairlie, Sinfi, like Marian, will be seen by most readers as the real heroine of the novel.[15]

14 See Hake and Compton-Rickett 1918, 184, concerning Swinburne and Watts-Dunton's admiration for Collins's novels. Swinburne preferred *The Woman in White* and Watts-Dunton *The Moonstone*.

15 This was undoubtedly the case with the novel's first readers. See James Douglas – 'It is quite certain that Sinfi is the reader's heroine' (Douglas 1904, 363).

If Sinfi bears a superficial likeness to Marian in terms of her resilient strength and the role she plays in the novel, Watts-Dunton's treatment of her is distinct and original. Her gypsy background means that he can dispense with all the proprieties that usually attend on the portrayal of Victorian heroines. Fiercely independent, strong-minded, and forcefully spoken, Sinfi is a tall, powerful, handsome woman, a talented musician, skilled in gypsy lore, who drinks ale, smokes a pipe, and is capable of decking a man in a fight. Henry's cousin Cyril, a bohemian artist, calls her 'The finest girl in England' (Watts-Dunton 1914, 218), and his admiration was shared by many of the novel's readers including Swinburne, Ford Madox Brown, and George Meredith, who professed himself in love with her (Hake and Compton-Rickett 1916, 2.68, 126). In common with the novel's other key characters, Sinfi is also referred to as possessing 'magnetic' or 'mesmeric' power, exercised semi-consciously 'partly through her gaze and partly through her voice' (Watts-Dunton 1914, 236). She also claims to be able to summon either the person or the 'livin' mullo' ('living wraith') of the lost Winifred, if she is still alive, by the 'magnetic' power of her *crwth* or Welsh fiddle (Watts-Dunton 1914, 336). This ritual she performs on a number of occasions (Watts-Dunton 1914, 161–3, 190–1, 400), miraculously producing for Henry his lost love or her seeming image.

Although Henry, wholly absorbed by his obsession with Winifred, is quite unaware of Sinfi's feelings for him, he has a strong affinity with her and adapts easily to gypsy life while carrying out his search. The narrative has prepared for this affinity and adaptation by indicating another kind of genealogical transmission. It is explained earlier that Henry's paternal great-grandfather had married Fenella Stanley, a 'famous Gypsy beauty' and seeress, whose portrait, painted by Reynolds, hangs in the picture gallery at Raxton Hall, and whose papers and diaries show her to be what Henry at first declares to be 'the very embodiment of the wildest Romany beliefs and superstitions' (Watts-Dunton 1914, 33, 256, 34). This gypsy ancestry, visible in Henry's dark complexion, can be seen to condition his love of nature and the outdoor life, and, although his rationalism makes him initially unsympathetic to any mystical beliefs, this prejudice will gradually give way during the course of the narrative. It is also explained that Fenella Stanley had previously been married to a gypsy named Lovell who had died after she had a child by him. Fenella is thus Sinfi's great-grandmother too (Watts-Dunton 1914, 250), making Henry and Sinfi blood relatives and increasing the bond between them. When Henry revisits the picture of Fenella Stanley, whom Reynolds has portrayed as a Sybil, he notices 'The likeness to Sinfi was striking' (Watts-Dunton 1914, 256). Like Fenella, Sinfi has various psychic gifts and a believer's respect for the curse, and urges the sceptical Henry to replace the cross, recovered from Tom Wynne's body, in his father's tomb. When he views Fenella's portrait, he observes how 'The face seemed to pass into my very being, and Sinfi's voice kept singing in my ears,

"Fenella Stanley's dead and dust, and that's why she can make you put that cross in your feyther's tomb, and she will, she will"' (Watts-Dunton 1914, 256). Finally bowing to Sinfi's advice, he is fearful on opening the coffin lest he find his father's face distorted by the curse:

> I looked into the coffin. The face (which had been left by the embalmer exposed) confronted mine. 'Fenella Stanley!' I cried, for the great transfigurer Death had written upon my father's brow that self-same message which the passions of a thousand Romany ancestors had set on the face of her whose portrait hung in the picture-gallery.
>
> (Watts-Dunton 1914, 284)

In an important review of the novel, Robertson Nicoll noted that 'One point will specially strike the reader of "Aylwin" – the influence of heredity which, since the vogue of Ibsen's dramas, has permeated imaginative literature' (Nicoll 1898, 807). Like many of the sensation novels which predate it and like more contemporary novels such as Hardy's *Tess of the D'Urbervilles* (1891), *Aylwin* shows a fascination with genealogy, with the unveiling of hidden family relations and with family characteristics, likenesses, beliefs, and burdens passed from one generation to another. Henry later reflects on the 'prepotency of transmission in descent' (Watts-Dunton 1914, 474), and the legacy of Fenella Stanley's blood which he shares with Sinfi. Elsewhere, pondering the curse which she believes to be all the stronger because it is a paternal curse, Sinfi sagely observes of the oedipal legacy: ' "There's nobody can't hurt you and them you're fond on as your own breed can. As my poor mammy used to say, 'For good or for ill you must dig deep to bury your daddy' " ' (Watts-Dunton 1914, 159).

Aylwin also shares with Coleridge and Collins's novels a profound interest in mental strain and hysteria. As in *The Moonstone*, there is something contagious about heightened emotions and hysteria which are communicated like electric shocks between the lead characters. While *The Moonstone* starts off by attributing hysteria to its female characters but then finds it is a displaced effect of male unconsciousness, mutability, and irrationality, key male characters in *Aylwin* such as Henry, his father Philip Aylwin, and the artists Wilderspin and D'Arcy whom we meet later in the novel, are immediately shown as emotionally susceptible and prone to nervous disturbance. Each man suffers because of the loss of a beloved woman with that loss defining his character and subsequent actions. In each case, the bereaved man will turn to mystical belief to allay his grief.[16] Moreover, the mourning process has the effect of softening him, even feminising him. Henry himself speaks of 'the unmanning effect of the

16 See D'Arcy's response to Henry's query about when he became a mystic: ' "When? Ask any man who has passionately loved a woman and lost her" ' (Watts-Dunton 1914, 239–40).

sorrowful brooding' (Watts-Dunton 1914, 381), and, in his case, grief brings out a stronger resemblance to his lost love.

The close identity between the unstrung heroine Winifred Wynne and her anguished lover Aylwin is immediately signalled in the similarity or partial *twinning* of their names, reminding us of both their unity as a couple and that the larger part of the narrative is about the winning of Winifred so that she will eventually become Winifred Aylwin. The Old English word 'wynne' or 'wine', signifying 'friend' or 'object of love', acts as Winifred's surname while her first name means 'friend of peace'. 'Aylwin' means appropriately 'noble or formidable friend'. Winifred also has two other symbolic namesakes in the novel. As a child, she visits St Winifred's Well at Holywell in Wales, whose waters she hopes will heal the lameness that afflicts Henry as a child (Watts-Dunton 1914, 21). She also shows her belief in the power of a curse by telling him the story of the wicked Sir John Wynn (Watts-Dunton 1914, 93), whose spirit is imprisoned by a curse at the bottom of the famous cascade known as Swallow Falls and whose wail can be heard in the noise of the cataract. Other echoes of the couple's names occur perhaps in the natural things beloved by both Winifred and Henry Aylwin. As children they share an unusual love of the wind – 'I can't be quite happy without wind, can *you*? I love to run up hills in the wind and sing to it' says Winifred (Watts-Dunton 1914, 19) – and one notices also the 'whin' (Watts-Dunton 1914, 475) or gorse, which forges a link to the poem 'The Promise Again Renewed' from *The Coming of Love* and the line about the dream recovery of the dead Rhona that so moved Rossetti: 'Her hair smelt sweet of whin and woodland spice'. (The novel *Aylwin*, of course, repeats the plot of loss and recovery experienced by Percy Aylwin in *The Coming of Love*, although in *fictional* time the poetic romance follows on from or repeats the novel – we might say they are 'twinned' works).

The twinning of Winifred and Henry, seen in their shared love of Nature, is strongly indicated in Henry's increasing resemblance to his lost love. As a boy, Henry's lameness rouses Winifred's tenderness. As he notes, 'She loved me because I was lame! Those who say that physical infirmity does not feminise the character have not had my experience' (Watts-Dunton 1914, 27). The vulnerability and greater sensitivity, which he develops as a result of this disability, evidently deepens Winifred's attraction to him. Henry, however, later recovers from his lameness, and, when the couple first meet again as adults and rekindle their love for each other, Winifred admits she misses 'the pathos and tenderness and yearning' of his voice and gaze (Watts-Dunton 1914, 74). Yet, although the adult Henry is a strong vigorous young man, readers do not really experience him as such because for the greater part of the narrative, while he is vainly searching for Winifred, his highly wrought mental state seems at times akin to the mania that afflicts his beloved. Thus mental rather than physical infirmity feminises Henry, and restores his former look of 'pathos and tenderness and yearning'. Moreover, his frantic pursuit of Winifred, his haunting of the places of frequented by her such as St Winifred's Well and Swallow Falls, his ever-present consciousness of what she might be suffering – '"Oh Sinfi", I said, . . . "she is starving – starving on the hills – while millions of people are eating, gorging, wasting food. I shall go mad!"' (Watts-Dunton 1914, 172) – means that he experiences the curse just as much as she does, becoming through sympathetic identification a kind of version of her. The epipsyche or 'reflecting beloved' of visionary Romantic poetry, best defined in Shelley's essay 'On Love' and his poem 'Epipsychidion' (Shelley 1977, 473–4; 371–88), is typically a woman who mirrors back to her male lover the best or purified aspects of himself, but in Watts-Dunton's version of this figure it is the woman who exacts from the man a mimicry, repetition, or emulation of herself.[17]

But much of this is a repetition of a pattern previously enacted by Henry's father. Earlier in the narrative we learn that Philip Aylwin, who helplessly watched his first beloved wife, a Swiss governess, drown before his eyes, manifests in his bereavement an obsession with his dead partner: 'He was a monomaniac, and all his thoughts were in some way clustered round the dominant one' (Watts-Dunton 1914, 48). This obsession develops into a form of mimicry. He wears the jewelled cross he gave his wife as a betrothal gift on a cord made of her hair, and studies amulets 'because the "Moonlight Cross" had been cherished by her' (Watts-Dunton 1914, 47, 48). Although previously uninterested in books, he becomes a savant through emulating her love of reading and study, takes up brass rubbing because it was one of her hobbies, and once a year, travels to Switzerland 'to revisit the old spots made sacred to him by reminiscences of his romantic love' (Watts-Dunton 1914, 36, 48, 37). Finally he becomes a mystic, joins a sect founded by Lavater, and believes himself to be in direct communication with his dead wife's spirit (Watts-Dunton 1914, 37, 38). His book *The Veiled Queen*, thus arising from his bereavement, is a testimony to the realm beyond the grave. His curse allows the same paradigm of mimicry to be repeated in Henry and Winifred, and Henry to double as versions of both his own father and his own beloved. At a turning point in the novel, Henry remembering his father's words '"Should you ever come to love as I have loved, you will find that materialism is intolerable – is hell itself – to the heart that has known a passion like mine"' (Watts-Dunton 1914, 276), falls into a waking dream. On coming to, he is taken aback:

> I gave a start of horror, and cried, 'Whose face?' Opposite to me there seemed to be sitting on a bed the figure of a man with a fiery cross upon his breast. That strange wild light upon the face, as if the pains of the heart were flickering up through the flesh – where had I seen it?
>
> (Watts-Dunton 1914, 276).

17 For a discussion of the epipsyche see Maxwell 2001, 53–7.

Momentarily he recalls his father showing him the jewelled cross, but then realises he has been looking at his own reflection in the mirror.

The theft of the amulet which sets the curse in action immediately sets up a number of uncanny repetitions. Tom Wynne's horrible shriek, uttered as he falls to his death in the landslip after robbing Philip Aylwin's tomb, brings both Henry and Winifred to the beach. That unearthly sound reminds Winifred, as she tells Henry, of the cry of the wicked spirit of Sir John Wynn which haunts Swallow Falls (Watts-Dunton 1914, 93), an association which suggests her unconscious link between Wynn and her father, who is, like Wynn, also the subject of a curse. To Henry, 'It was like a shriek coming from a distance . . . and yet it seemed to come from *me!* It was though *I* was witnessing some dreadful sight unutterable and intolerable. And then it seemed the voice of Winifred, and then it seemed her father's voice, and finally it seemed the voice of my own father struggling in his tomb' (Watts-Dunton 1914, 89–90). Here the shriek, voicing the anguish of both fathers, also carries within it fore-echoes of cries that will be uttered both by Winifred, when she finds her father's corpse, and Henry, when he later hears of her discovery which he has vainly tried to forestall (Watts-Dunton 1914, 129, 130). Indeed another repetition is triggered on the moonlit beach by Henry's attempt to prevent his fiancée seeing Tom Wynne's mangled body. Cut off by the tides in Mousetrap Cove, the couple very nearly suffer the death by drowning which was the fate of Philip Aylwin's first wife at the same spot. Henry recalls how, increasingly aware of the growing danger, he felt that 'A fiery photograph of the cove was burning within my brain' (Watts-Dunton 1914, 107), and afterwards he finds that 'not only had the physiognomy of the cove, but every circumstance of our lives together, been photographed on my brain in one picture of fire' (Watts-Dunton 1914, 114). Here the 'fiery photograph' marks Henry's initial trauma, 'an idea violently and suddenly impressed' on his sympathetic imagination. It presages what will be Winifred's own mark of trauma, absorbed not from her surroundings, but, as we shall see, from the sight of her dead father's face. In such ways the theme of doubling and reduplication, present in key poems by Coleridge, the Romantic epipsyche, and novels such as Collins's *The Woman in White*, is replayed in *Aylwin*'s uncanny and elaborate structure of mimicry, repetition, and transference.

Repetition and the gaze

One of the principal ways in which the novel dramatises repetition is through the power of looking and the gaze. From the very start of the novel, the young Henry is described as enthralled by Winfred's 'quivering, glittering, changeful eyes' – 'yet it was not her beauty perhaps, so much as the look she gave me, that fascinated me, melted me' (Watts-Dunton 1914, 8). Those glittering eyes recall

Coleridge's Ancient Mariner, who fixes the Wedding-Guest with his 'glittering eye', and Geraldine in 'Christabel' whose eyes ''gan glitter bright' (Coleridge 1974, 173, 200). The young Winifred is repeatedly described as an object of 'wonder' (12), irresistible (15), 'bewitching' (16), absorbing (17), and 'fascinating' (24). The boy Henry is the object of Winifred's own beguiled gaze. She admires what she calls his 'love-eyes' and, when adult, explains on meeting her former companion again: '"It is impossible for me even now . . . to put into words that expression in your eyes which won me as a child. All I knew at the time was that it fascinated me"' (Watts-Dunton 1914, 26, 74). Although Winifred remarks '"That expression . . . will . . . never return to you now"' (Watts-Dunton 1914, 74), it is precisely that saddened wistful look that will characterise the bereft Henry Aylwin, as Winifred inadvertently makes him reproduce the look she longs for.

However there are other looks which are much more formidable. Earlier Henry Aylwin's disapproving mother, coming across the lovers in the churchyard, directs a baleful glare of hatred at Winifred that brings terror to her eyes (Watts-Dunton 1914, 57). But even more powerful is the traumatic and petrifying look of horror that is passed from one character to another. This look is first passed from the corpse of Tom Wynne to his daughter Winifred, who finds his corpse on Raxton Sands, standing in the fallen earth, 'Bolt upright . . . , staring with horribly distorted features, as in terror, the crown of the head smashed by a fallen gravestone' (Watts-Dunton 1914, 104). She is discovered squatting in front of the body 'and on her face was reflected and mimicked, in the most astonishing way, the horrible expression on the face of the corpse, while the fingers of her right hand were . . . closely locked around the cross' (Watts-Dunton 1914, 130). Winifred suffers a hysterical attack which the physician Dr Mivart, a man who has studied with the famous clinical neurologist Jean-Martin Charcot at the Salpêtrière Institute in Paris, describes as 'a seizure brought on by terror in which the subject's countenance mimics the appearance of the terrible object that has caused it' (Watts-Dunton 1914, 129).[18] As Henry tries to track down Winifred in Wales, he is haunted by her eyes, whose expression fluctuates between this appalled and 'appalling' look of trauma and a state of innocent dreamy unconscious trance which he refers to as 'the witchery of the gaze!' (Watts-Dunton 1914, 153, 164). On the two occasions he manages to encounter her (Watts-Dunton 1914, 150–4, 163–9), her entranced dream state is broken by recollections from the past, 'the awful mimicry of her

18 Mivart may be partly based on the physician and poet Thomas Gordon Hake, although the name 'Mivart' might be a conscious or unconscious repetition of St George Jackson Mivart (1827–1900), a prominent zoologist and biologist, who tried to integrate a version of evolutionary theory with Catholic theology. His son Frederick St George Mivart was also a distinguished medical man.

father's expression spread over her face' (Watts-Dunton 1914, 168), and, terrified, she flees so swiftly that Henry is unable to stay her.

During her subsequent dazed and amnesiac wanderings, Winifred is found and looked after by Mrs Gudgeon, a working-class woman who takes her to London and later brings her to pose for a Pre-Raphaelite painter called Wilderspin, a spiritual follower of Henry's father, Philip Aylwin. Wilderspin, a ' "Visionary" ' (Watts-Dunton 1914, 196) who lost his beloved mother when he was a child, and who paints only women, sees Winifred as the perfect face he has been searching for, and believes her sent by his mother to be the subject of his masterwork. He paints Winifred as Aylwin's 'Veiled Queen', and the resulting picture, *Faith and Love*, becomes famous throughout London. Yet strangely Winifred has already taken this role before, when, as a child, the young Henry persuaded her to pose for a photograph on Raxton Sands wearing a crown of sea-flowers and draped in a long white veil of his mother's. Henry's father, charmed by the image, adorns the title-page of the third edition of his book *The Veiled Queen* with a woodcut based on this photograph (Watts-Dunton 1914, 39), an association which eerily prefigures the identity Winifred will assume when she is lost and presumed dead, and Henry, following in his father's footsteps, comes to see her as 'the Veiled Queen'. We learn that it is the title-page woodcut that first enticed Wilderspin to buy Philip Aylwin's book, by means of which he became a mystic. His instinctive decision that Winifred should be his model for his painting is thus already determined by an unconscious suggestion that makes him replicate the original woodcut more accurately than he realises.

Having first met Wilderspin in Wales, Henry meets him later in London and finds out that he has also painted his mother's portrait. He accompanies his mother to Wilderspin's studio to view *Faith and Love*, the famous painting of his father's 'Veiled Queen', recognises Winifred as the subject and frantically questions Wilderspin about her. Wilderspin, who had not realised that his model was the same person as Henry's lost love, relates how he found the girl selling matches, tracked her to her lodgings, and asked the working-class woman he presumed to be her mother if her daughter could model for him. In her daily life as match-girl and model, Winifred bears the dreamy entranced look that makes her Wilderspin's ideal subject, but the painter tells how she suffered a seizure when she came across the portrait of Henry's mother which he was working on in his studio: 'Her face became suddenly distorted by an expression of terror such as I had never seen and never imagined possible. . . . She revived and tried to run out of the studio. Her mother and I seized her, and then she fell down insensible' (Watts-Dunton 1914, 302). The look of terror that the girl has on her face inspires Wilderspin to paint another picture of her as Coleridge's Christabel, and he unconsciously uses Henry's mother as model for Geraldine (Watts-Dunton 1914, 306), the enchantress who causes such terror. On viewing with her son Wilderspin's painting of *The Lady Geraldine and Christabel*, Henry's mother, who has remained unsympathetic to his sufferings, swoons away at the recognition or reflection of herself and her own cruelty (Watts-Dunton 1914, 306).

As mentioned earlier, 'Christabel', one of Watts-Dunton's favourite poems, is centred on a transferred or transmitted look. Christabel, in thrall to Geraldine, is induced 'by forced unconscious sympathy' to replicate her look of hatred and so alienate her father:

> I know not how, in fearful wise,
> So deeply had she drunken in
> That look, those shrunken serpent eyes,
> That all her features were resigned
> To this sole image in her mind:
> And passively did imitate
> That look of dull and treacherous hate!
>
> (Coleridge 1974, 208–9, ll. 600–6)

However, in Watts-Dunton's novel, Winifred imitates or mimics her father's petrified expression rather than that of Mrs Wynne's hatred, although it is the recollection of Mrs Wynne's baleful glare that triggers her traumatised recall of her former life, her father's sin, and his death, apparently the result of the curse. Thus, like the inauspicious unearthly shriek heard by Henry at Tom Wynne's death which contains other cries within it, looks in *Aylwin* always carry within them and reduplicate the memories of other looks, carry the condensed histories of tangled family romances.

Wilderspin's painting depicts the scene from 'Christabel' in which the daemonic Geraldine undresses in Christabel's chamber, revealing, it is hinted, some terrible sight to the innocent maiden:

> Her silken robe, and inner vest,
> Dropped to her feet, and full in view
> Behold! Her bosom and half her side –
> A sight to dream of, not to tell!
> O shield her! shield sweet Christabel!
>
> (Coleridge 1974, 200, ll. 250–4)

In trying to account for his model's horror, Wilderspin unconsciously recreates an analogue for the unspeakable locus of trauma: 'A sight to dream of, not to tell!' The Coleridgean picture at the heart of the novel depicts Winifred's temporary traumatic recovery of memory, but it is also a painful recognition scene for Henry and his mother, a scene that will prompt Mrs Wynne to remorse and repentance for her treatment of Winifred.

During the latter stages of the novel's composition, Freud, exploring the treatment of hysteria, was making his first steps towards developing psychoanalysis or 'the talking cure' in which patients were encouraged to explore the root causes of their psychically determined physical symptoms in the course of a specially directed dialogue with their physician. Such patients, then, were explicitly invited to revisit the psychical origins of a possible trauma which they were encouraged to 'tell'. In *Aylwin* Winifred's friends and allies feel that in order to cure her she must 'forget' and so obliterate the cause of her trauma; it must not be 'told'. Indeed the techniques eventually used for her treatment are those immediately pre-dating Freud's and draw on mesmeric practices involving magnets.

Magnetic transmission

We know by from a Postscript to the novel added by Watts-Dunton himself that the practices he describes in the novel, however strange or incredible they may seem, were derived from accounts of psychological experiments undertaken in France during second half of the 1880s. In his Postscript Watts-Dunton quotes from an article in the *Quarterly Review* for July 1890, which, when examined in full, turns out to be a detailed unsigned review article, examining six of the latest academic texts on mesmerism and hypnotism by French physicians, published between 1888 and 1890 (Anonymous 1890, 234–59). (Only one of these texts, *Animal Magnetism* by Alfred Binet and Charles Féré, had been translated into English.) In the novel we are told that Winifred's treatment is based on a series of magnetic experiments made by a friend of Dr Mivart's, a French medical man called Marini, at the Salpêtrière Hospital in Paris. Mivart, explaining these procedures, reads out an account taken from the British newspaper the *Daily Telegraph* (Watts-Dunton 1914, 464) an account which in his Postscript Watts-Dunton states to be an authentic source with only the names changed (Watts-Dunton 1914, 488). A footnote to the narrative explains that the experiments were 'mostly effected by M. Babinski of the Salpêtrière. They excited great attention in Paris' (Watts-Dunton 1914, 465).

So what are the mesmeric or magnetic means of Winifred's cure? True to the novel's own logic, if Winifred gained her agonised looks from mimicking someone else, then she can be cured by passing them to another party who mimics her. Her hysterical symptoms are transferred by the aid of a magnet to a much stronger patient who has been placed in a hypnotic trance and who, it is understood, will experience the transferred symptoms only temporarily, although there is a risk if she has a strong imagination. That patient is Sinfi Lovell, who volunteers to undergo magnetic transmission when she learns that Winifred's seizures are increasing in strength and liable to become fatal. Sinfi undertakes the experiment believing that she is transferring the curse from Winifred to herself. A witness reports that 'the seizure was transmitted in a way that was positively uncanny – she passed into a paroxysm so severe that Mivart was seriously alarmed for her. Her face assumed the same expression of terror which I had seen on Miss Wynne's face, and she uttered the cry, "Father!" and then fell back into a state of rigidity' (Watts-Dunton 1914, 468).

Possessing a strong and fertile imagination, Sinfi is painfully afflicted and takes a long time to recover, and when she re-encounters Henry, who has not been party to the magnetic transmission, he startles her by approaching her from behind, prompting a fit which exactly replicates Winifred's seizures. Astonished, Henry decides that 'Long brooding over Winnie's dreadful fate had unhinged her mind' and tells her ' "You are suffering through sympathy, Sinfi" ' (Watts-Dunton 1914, 393), which is, after a fashion, true in that the magnetic transmission or transference of symptoms represents an oddly literalised or physicalised form of sympathy. Sinfi, the woman who is also Henry's closest sympathiser, his own kin and a close friend of his beloved's, a woman with the apparent ability to conjure up his beloved's likeness, finally gives him back his lost lover by taking on her trauma. (It is however, possible, that in sacrificially taking on her friend's symptoms, and thus taking on, as she believes it, the curse, Sinfi is also unconsciously making herself into a version of Winifred, the woman beloved by Henry.) Meanwhile Winifred makes a full recovery and is able to recall all the events prior to finding her father's corpse but has no memory of that grisly spectacle or of anything after that event. The interval between her first lapse into madness and her cure is a complete blank to her, nor do her friends seek to enlighten her.

It appears that in his description of Winifred's cure Watts-Dunton is drawing on experimental techniques of magnetic transmission developed by Charcot's student, Joseph Babinski, which Babinski described in an influential report of 1886 (Babinkski 1886). As Anne Harrington explains in an article of 1988 published in *Psychological Medicine*, Babinski 'conceived the idea of transferring hysterical disorders, not just from one side of the body to another, but from one patient to another. By means of magnets, Babinski said, he had caused one hemi-anaesthetic patient, A, to take up the half sensibility of another hemi-anaesthetic patient, B, making A fully sensible and B fully anaesthetic. The transfer had then reversed itself; B taking back not only her own sensibility but that of A, leaving A now anaesthetic on both sides of her body' (Harrington 1988a, 32).[19] Harrington comments that Barbinski 'would eventually repudiate his researches in this area, but his 1886 report became and remained a paradigm for a certain branch of the metalloscopy and transfer experimental enterprise that sought to develop the work along lines best characterised as

19 See also Harrington's 'Hysteria, Hypnosis, and the Lure of the Invisible: The Rise of Neo-Mesmerism in *fin-de-siècle* French Psychiatry', in particular pp. 234–5 (Harrington 1988b). My thanks to Forbes Morlock for alerting me to this second essay.

"fluidist" or "bio-metallic"'. She goes on to discuss in more detail the work of Jules Bernard Luys, who directed the school of hypnotism at the La Charité hospital, and claimed in a report of 1888 that 'it was possible to transfer between individuals, not only diseases (as Babinski had done) but also mental states. The emotions in question were artificially induced using magnets' (Harrington 1998a, 32, 33).[20]

The description Harrington provides of Luys's magnetic experiments concerning physiological and psychological transfer between individuals, experiments usually conducted on hysterical patients, bears a strong resemblance to the kind of procedure Mivart applied to Winifred and Sinfi. An interesting footnote to this episode in psychological medicine is that the young Freud spent the period from October 1885 to March 1886 at the Salpêtrière observing Charcot's clinical practice and possibly could have witnessed magnetic transference. He was certainly aware of the experiments, for a review written by him in 1888 when he was still enthusiastic about hypnotism refers to 'the famous experiment of Babinski with Charcot, where a suggestion was transferred from one hypnotized person to another by means of a magnet'.[21] Freud's enthusiasm for hypnotism subsequently waned and a later article by him is evidently sceptical about magnetic transference.[22] As stated above, he went on to develop a therapeutic practice that was in many ways a reversal of these techniques in that he abandoned hypnosis to have his patients consciously recall and recount their troubled histories. However, it is possible that the idea or metaphor of symptoms transferred from one patient to another which lies at the heart of magnetic therapy may have conditioned his own later account of

20 See also Luys 1890, 39–48, published in his own journal *Revue d'Hypnologie Théorique et Practique.* For a contemporary British article that examines Luys's work in more detail see Robertson 1892, 494–531. Section IV (pp. 522–8) deals with Luys's treatment by transference. See pp. 523–4 in particular. George Robertson was the Senior Assistant Physician at the Royal Edinburgh Asylum, Morningside.

21 Freud's review of Heinrich Obersteiner's *Der Hypnotismus* (1887), which appeared in the *Szentralbatt für Physiologie* on 4 February 1888 (1: 632–3), is translated and discussed by Mark Solms in his article 'A Previously-untranslated Review by Freud of a Monograph on Hypnotism' (Solms 1989a, 401–3). I am most grateful to Forbes Morlock for alerting me to this article.

22 Another article by Mark Solms, 'Three Previously-untranslated Reviews by Freud from the Neue Freie Press', includes Freud's 1904 Note on 'Magnetische Menschen' [Magnetic Man]. Freud writes: 'Man always longs for a key with which to unlock all secrets. Magnetism has ever appeared to be such a key-word. It has been, and still is, a word of great suggestive significance. It also seems understandable that the mysterious power of the magnet to act at a distance has not failed to have an effect on phantasy. There can naturally be no question of the magnet having an actual [physical] effect upon a person, or a person upon the magnet' (Solms 1989b, 398).

the transference which is central to the psychotherapeutic process and in which patients transfer on to the analyst feelings and ideas that reflect their earlier relationships with their parents.

Clearly then, Watts-Dunton, as he stated in his Postscript, did base his notion of Winifred's cure on what he believed to be an innovative medical procedure. Indeed examination of the original *Daily Telegraph* report which inspired him and which he transcribed in *Aylwin*, a report I have dated to 12 November 1886, reveals other interesting snippets of text surrounding the extract that may have prompted him to see Babinski's experiments as a narrative solution for Winifred's illness. The columnist introduces the account thus: 'In these days when mesmeric, hysteric and other pathological phenomena are made to play so large a part in fiction, it must be consoling to the practical mind, to find them for once connected with fact.' And the account concludes: 'Luckily for [M. Babinski's] healthier patients, however, their borrowed pains and symptoms did not last long, and they were saved from a calamity almost similar to that which befel Doctor Jekyl [*sic*] when he swallowed too much salts, and irrevocably became Mister Hyde.'[23] Moreover, the original *Daily Telegraph* leading article, also alluded to by the narrative as accompanying the report from Paris (Watts-Dunton 1914, 464), and printed on the same page of the newspaper, expands on the report's reference to contemporary fiction in some detail, mentioning in addition to Robert Louis Stevenson's ' "Doctor Jekyll" ', a novel '"Elsie Venner"' by the American writer Oliver Wendell Holmes, *Creatures of Impulse* (1871), a one-act musical play by W. S. Gilbert, Edward Bulwer-Lytton's tales 'A Strange Story' (1863) and 'The House and the Brain' (1857), and the 'romances' of Edgar Allan Poe.[24] Noting that works by these last two authors feature 'magnetic force', the leader continues: 'It did not occur, however, even to these great fantastic geniuses, or to the gifted literary godfathers of the "materialised spirit" who occupies so distinguished a position in several popular fictions of the day, to conceive the possibility of transferring dangerous illnesses from one living person to another by magnetic agency.'[25] The suggestive juxtaposition of mesmeric therapy with contemporary fiction's use of pathology and medical cure – Stevenson's novel, incidentally, had been published earlier that same year, 1886 – together with the leader's hint that magnetic transference could potentially be the subject of literary treatment

23 'Paris Day by Day', *Daily Telegraph*, 12 November, 1886, p. 5, column 8.

24 Interestingly, like *Aylwin*, *Elsie Venner: A Romance of Destiny* (1861) also features a strange transmission or transference in that the mother of the eponymous heroine is bitten by a rattlesnake while pregnant and dies some months later shortly after giving birth. Her daughter Elsie grows up with some strangely disturbing serpentine characteristics. Moreover, Coleridge's 'Christabel' with its references to the snake-like Geraldine is also a presence in the novel.

25 *Daily Telegraph*, 12 November 1886, p. 5, columns 3–4.

seem likely to have helped motivate Watts-Dunton's choice of magnetic therapy as a means of returning his heroine to her normal self.

However, the recourse to magnetic therapy is primarily interesting to me not because of its contemporary resonances (fascinating though those are), but because of the way it beautifully enacts or dramatises a pattern of replication which is integral to the novel as a whole. What the novel calls the 'magnetic transmission of the seizure' and 'transmission of hysterical symptoms from one patient to another' has much in common in that other form of transmission, what Henry elsewhere terms 'prepotency of transmission in descent' (Watts-Dunton 1914, 220, 465, 474), an especially effective blood legacy. Genealogy or heredity, a significant theme of the novel, might well make us aware that the novel's repetitions are ultimately determined by its genealogical kinship to a certain strain of Romanticism and its devices. The complex pattern of replication in *Aylwin* which I have sketched only briefly here is itself a replication of key structures in Romantic and Post-Romantic poetry which I have identified elsewhere whereby certain awesome figures – Medusas, Sapphos, hermaphrodites – have the power to repeat themselves, or reflect or mirror themselves in their beholders (see Maxwell 2001, 213). These repetitions typically occur in response to loss, just as in *Aylwin* the lost woman continually repeats herself in her bereaved mate or impresses herself on his consciousness. Moreover, Henry Aylwin's effective re-enactment of his father's bereavement under the influence of his curse is strongly reminiscent of the way in which poets act out their own versions of the scripts of loss and compensation they inherit from their poetic forefathers.[26]

Poetic transmission and the Romantic Image

The Victorian poet whom Watts-Dunton would have seen as acting out a script given by Coleridge is Dante Gabriel Rossetti, who appears in the novel as the painter D'Arcy, a colleague of Wilderspin's, who befriends Henry while he is searching for Winifred in London. We know that Watts-Dunton regarded Coleridge as the most important of the Romantic poets for his visionary poetry, a poetry which most potently conveyed an awe for natural supernaturalism or what Watts-Dunton would call 'The Renascence of Wonder', a renovating imaginative energy roused by Nature's mystic sublimity. Watts-Dunton's entry on Dante Gabriel Rossetti in the ninth edition of the *Encyclopædia Britannica* sees Rossetti's writing as the flowering of a visionary poetic tradition which has its roots in Coleridge, and especially Coleridge's 'Christabel':

26 See my discussion of the ways poets respond to the Miltonic paradigm in Maxwell 2001.

> We must turn . . . to the most perfect efflorescence of the poetry of wonder and mystery – to such ballads as the 'Demon Lover,' to Coleridge's 'Christabel' and 'Kubla Khan' . . . for parallels to Rossetti's most characteristic designs. . . . It is perhaps with Coleridge alone that Rossetti can be compared as a worker in the Renascence of Wonder. Although his apparent lack of rhythmic spontaneity places him below the great master as a singer (for in these miracles of Coleridge's genius poetry ceases to appear as a fine art at all – it is the inspired song of the changeling child 'singing, dancing to itself'), in permanence of the romantic feeling, in vitality of belief in the power of the unseen, Rossetti stands alone. Even the finest portions of his historical ballad 'The King's Tragedy' are those which deal with the supernatural.
>
> (Watts-Dunton 1886, 20.858, 860)[27]

Modern critics have seen Rossetti as influenced by Keats or Shelley, but, when it comes to the question of affinity, William Michael Rossetti in the Preface to his edition of his brother's collected works informs us that 'In the long run he perhaps enjoyed and revered Coleridge beyond any other poet whatsoever' (W. M. Rossetti 1911b, xv).[28] In his *Recollections of Rossetti*, Thomas Hall Caine noted that he and Rossetti 'were on common ground . . . in the worship of Coleridge: "The three greatest imaginations," he said, "are Shakespeare, Coleridge, and Shelley," and he never tired of extolling the beauties of "Christabel" '. Recalling a trip with the ailing Rossetti to the Lakes, Hall Caine recorded that 'not even Borrowdale, the supposed scene of the second part of "Christabel," could draw him to the cliffs that had been rent asunder in the passage he liked best of the poet he admired most' (Caine 1990, 74, 116). More recently the critic Florence Boos has detailed how Rossetti's 'Rose Mary' resembles Coleridge's 'Christabel' with regard to its rhythms, narrative, theme, and imagery (Boos 1976, 167–71). Watts-Dunton noted that Rossetti shared with Coleridge an unusual method of composition: 'Like Coleridge, he had the singular habit of "cartooning," as he used to say, a poem in prose. It is difficult to imagine a poem thus written, but so it was with two of the greatest poets of the nineteenth century' (Watts-Dunton 1908–9, 323–32). Both poets used a strategy which involved them repeating or translating the same ideas into a different form. But Watts-Dunton suggests that this habit of cartooning may be responsible for both poets on occasion finding themselves unable to complete poems inasmuch as 'a full prose expression of the subject-matter' can impede poetical

27 The same remarks can be found in the revised entry reprinted in the 11th edition of 1911 (Watts-Dunton 1911b, 23.749, 750). See also Watts-Dunton's comment made in 1887 in his *Athenæum* review of the newly published two-volume edition of *The Collected Works of Dante Gabriel Rossetti*: 'in poetical atmosphere he seems to us to stand next to Coleridge' (Watts-Dunton 1887b, 346).

28 For modern critics on Rossetti's influences see Bloom 1973, 2.1402–3; Riede 1983, 122–33.

treatment in that when 'the poet tries to rise on his winged words, his wingless words are likely to act as a dead weight' (Watts-Dunton 1916a, 95). Experiencing difficulties of this kind when working on his poem 'The King's Tragedy', Rossetti was directly reminded, presumably by Watts-Dunton himself, of Coleridge's similar blockage: 'the remark was made to him with regard to Coleridge's "Wanderings of Cain," that . . . the matchless fragment . . . might have passed nearer towards completion, . . . had it not been for those elaborate and beautiful prose notes which he has left behind' (Watts-Dunton 1916a, 95).

Watts-Dunton was by no means the only critic to connect the two poets. In an article of 1887, William Sharp declared of Rossetti that 'In the domain of the supernatural he is the sole worthy inheritor of Coleridge. This note of what is known as supernaturalism – this note of the mysterious, of the weird – is of modern emphasis; it is the sign of the projection of the soul, stifled with the conventionalities and growing materialism of civilisation, into the region of romance' (Sharp 1912, 46). Yeats's friend the poet and critic Arthur Symons observes in his essay 'Dante Gabriel Rossetti' (1904) that 'Only Coleridge among English poets has anything like the same definite grasp upon whatever is essential in poetry' (Symons 1916, 201), adding in his later work, *Studies in Strange Souls*: 'Next after Coleridge, his vision, lifted into its higher ecstasies, possessed and was possessed by the supernatural' (Symons 1929, 13). Yeats himself casts Rossetti and Coleridge in the image of the Romantic poet who suffers for his art in his *Autobiographies*: 'But Coleridge of the *Ancient Mariner*, and *Kubla Khan*, and Rossetti in all his writings, made what Arnold has called that "morbid effort", that search for "perfection of thought and feeling, and to unite this to perfection of form", sought this new, pure beauty, and suffered in their lives because of it' (Yeats 1955, 313).

We have already seen in Chapter 1 how Watts-Dunton's memorial sonnets for both poets cast them as hypersensitive artists in isolation, brilliant but thwarted by their own fatal flaws, and it is the case, from a purely biographical point of view, that Rossetti replicates some striking features of Coleridge's life – the consuming love for a married woman, the harrowing drug addiction, the physical and mental breakdown – that may have helped secure the connection in Watts-Dunton's mind. Both poets were frequently described as talkers and personalities who had a 'magnetic' or spellbinding effect on those who met them. Richard Holmes talks of Coleridge's 'almost hypnotic effect on new acquaintances' (Holmes 1990, 71), while Henry Nelson Coleridge describes how one evening his uncle's speech, which had been 'particularly brilliant and enchanting', left him 'so thoroughly *magnetized*, that I could not for two or three days afterwards reflect enough to put anything on paper' (cited in Perry 2002, 105). As Seamus Perry has pointed out, Coleridge's auditors repeatedly compared him to the mesmeric power of his own most famous narrator; in the words of Leigh Hunt: 'Like his own bright-eyed marinere; he had a spell in his voice that would not let you go' (cited in Perry 2002, 112). As mentioned in Chapter 1, friends and associates frequently remarked on Rossetti's own magnetic temperament. We recall that, in his 'Autobiographical Notes', Watts-Dunton described Rossetti's face as possessing 'an imperious magnetism', while his voice 'awakened an eagerness on the part of the listener to catch the sound; it seemed to draw one towards him' (cited in Hake and Compton-Rickett 1916, 1.82). Watts-Dunton's portrait of D'Arcy in *Aylwin* repeats the phrase 'imperious magnetism', while we are told that the 'indescribable resonance' of D'Arcy's voice 'marked it off from all other voices, and . . . made the ear of the listener eager to catch the sound' (Watts-Dunton 1914, 222). In the second of the two Appendices attached to the 1914 edition of the novel, Watts-Dunton's biographer, Thomas St E. Hake, assures the reader that 'in *Aylwin*, Rossetti lives as I knew him; it is impossible to imagine a more living picture of the man. I have stayed with Rossetti at 16 Cheyne Walk for weeks at a time, and at Bognor also, and at Kelmscott' (Watts-Dunton 1914, 500). In the first of the Appendices (which is unattributed but probably by Hake or Watts-Dunton himself), the writer, dilating on the 'magnetism' of Rossetti, describes it as a benign (because unconscious) 'demonic power – the power of shedding quite unconsciously one's personality upon all brought into contact with it' (Watts-Dunton 1914, 496).

D'Arcy then, although depicted as a painter rather than a poet, is a type of Rossetti, who is himself a Victorian version of Coleridge. He is another of the novel's male characters stricken by the loss of a beloved woman – a loss that echoes Rossetti's bereavement of his wife Elizabeth Siddal who died of an overdose of laudanum in 1862. D'Arcy plays more than an incidental role in the novel in that his experience of loss helps him establish a bond with Henry, to whom he gives important advice. Later on he effectively rescues Winifred and, through Dr Mivart, engineers her cure. We know from Watts-Dunton's admission to his biographer James Douglas that large portions of the narrative about D'Arcy replicate details from Rossetti's life.[29] D'Arcy's house, garden, and menagerie are faithful reproductions of 16 Cheyne Walk, while Hurstcote, the other house he owns in the country, is a depiction of Kelmscott Manor in Oxfordshire, rented by Rossetti and Morris in the early 1870s. D'Arcy himself reproduces Rossetti's 'magnetism' (Watts-Dunton 1914, 222) through his animation, his musical voice, his humour and lively conversation, as well as his melancholy and superstition.[30]

29 For details about Rossetti see Douglas, 1904, 140–5, 165; Watts-Dunton 1914, Appendix 2, 493–7.

30 The inclusion of Rossetti as D'Arcy in *Aylwin* is part of a larger strategy of real-life replication. We know from other sources that a number of the characters in the

Shortly after Henry has visited D'Arcy's house and encountered in his garden various members of his menagerie, the painter remarks that 'Has it ever occurred to you how fascinating a beautiful young girl would be if she were as unconscious as a young animal?' Henry immediately thinks of Winifred in her 'waking dream', her unconscious entranced state, and thinks, '"How he would have been fascinated by a sight like that!"' (Watts-Dunton 1914, 166, 233). When Winifred is glimpsed at a London street corner singing and selling matches, she is described by Henry's aunt as 'quite unconscious apparently of the bustle and confusion around her', and Wilderspin first sees her at the corner of Essex Street, 'gazing before her, murmuring a verse of Scripture, perfectly unconscious whether she was dressed in rags or velvet' (Watts-Dunton 1914, 242, 292).

This image of the unconscious woman, Winifred's chief guise in the novel, can easily be seen as a version of what Frank Kermode identified as the Romantic Image, a master trope of Modernism and a key Yeatsian figure, which offers us as the emblem of the work of art a beautiful woman with a 'speaking body and . . . face devoid of intellect', passive, self-involved or absorbed in movement, typically a dancer, but predominantly unified in body and soul (Kermode 1986, 57, 58). The image reconciles opposites; as Kermode puts it: 'emblematic of the mysterious resolution between outward and inward . . . the dancer turns in her narrow luminous circle, still but moving, dead but alive' (Kermode 1986, 59). He also demonstrates the continuity between this figure and 'the inward-looking or expressionless face' which recurs in Romantic painting and poetry, although he tries to distinguish what he sees as the modern version of the Image from what he identifies as its 'pathological' aspect, as seen in the *femme fatale* (Kermode 1986, 60, 61). As Cassandra Laity has pointed out in a recent re-examination of the Romantic Image, this distinction is by no means as clear as Kermode would like (Laity 1996, 25–6).

What is interesting is that, in tracing Yeats's version of the Image, Kermode explicitly signals a debt to Rossetti: 'When an English reader contemplates such faces, he will probably find himself thinking first of Rossetti'. He then quotes

Footnote 30 *(Cont.)*

book have real-life correlates: D'Arcy is first seen dining in a Haymarket restaurant in the company of De Castro based on the raconteur and swindler Charles Augustus Howell whose preposterous stories and scams Rossetti found extremely entertaining. Sinfi Lovell and Rhona Boswell are based on young gypsy women known to Watts-Dunton, Philip Aylwin on his uncle, James Orlando Watts, and Cyril Aylwin on his brother, Alfred Eugene Watts who died in 1870. Wilderspin is based on the painter James Smetham, and Mrs Gudgeon, the grotesquely tragic-comic working-class woman who takes care of Winifred, on a cockney coffee-stall holder who lived in the Lincoln's Inn Fields area of London. Henry Aylwin seems to have certain of his author's characteristics including his dark complexion, while Winifred, presumably some time after 1890, got tinged with some traits of Clara Reich's.

from Rossetti's sonnet 'Body's Beauty', in which Lilith is described as 'subtly of herself contemplative', and also the sonnet 'Heart's Hope': 'Lady, I fain would tell how evermore / Thy soul I know not from thy body' (Kermode 1986, 61–2; Rossetti 1911, 100, 76).[31] But one is also reminded of Coleridge's short poem 'Phantom' whose female subject's expressionless yet radiant face is illuminated by her soul:

> there seem'd no Trace
> Of Aught upon her brighten'd Face
> Uprais'd beneath the rifted Stone,
> Save of one Spirit, all her own
> She, she herself, and only she
> Shone in her body visibly.
>
> (Coleridge 1974, 293)

When the distressed Wilderspin tells him that he has found his favourite model lying dead in a squalid room at Mrs Gudgeon's house, D'Arcy, who does not know that she is Henry's beloved Winifred, goes at once to view the body, determined that the girl should not be buried by the parish. On examining Winifred, he realises that she is not dead but suffering an extreme form of seizure and, when she comes to, he takes her to Hurstcote and places her in his housekeeper's care. Thereafter, as she remains under his protection, he comes to experience the charm of her unconscious self, which he recalls in a letter to Henry:

> do you remember my saying that the most fascinating creature in the world would be a beautiful young girl as unconscious as a child or a young animal, if such a combination of charms were possible? Such a young girl as this it was whom I was now seeing every day and all day. The charm exercised over me was no doubt partly owing to my own peculiar temperament – to my own hatred of self-consciousness and to an innate shyness which is apt to make me feel at times that people are watching me, when they most likely are doing nothing of the kind.
>
> (Watts-Dunton 1914, 461–2)

What D'Arcy here calls 'unconsciousness', Freud will call 'narcissism':

> The charm of a child lies to a great extent in his narcissism, his self-contentment and inaccessibility, just as does the charm of certain animals which seem not to concern themselves about us, such as cats and the large beasts of prey.
>
> (Freud 1984a, 11.83)

Interestingly D'Arcy's male voyeurism is also a form of identification as he sees in Winifred the unconsciousness or narcissism he would wish for himself. The

31 The full quotation from 'Heart's Hope' is 'Lady, I fain would tell how evermore / Thy soul I know not from thy body, nor / Thee from myself, neither our love from God' (Rossetti 1911, 76). In *Lady Lilith*, the painting by Rossetti that partners 'Body's Beauty', Lilith looks at her reflection in a mirror.

narcissistic, self-involved self-containment of the female Romantic Image has a kind of integrity which the male artist desires for himself and perhaps possesses vicariously through his art, or in D'Arcy's case, his guardianship. While Henry imitates his beloved throughout his mourning for her, he subsequently discovers that the men closest to him, artists whose experiences of loss most resemble his own, turn out inadvertently to have meditated upon, identified with, or imitated her image. In certain cases – one thinks here of Philip Aylwin as well as D'Arcy and Wilderspin – creative meditation on the lost woman or her Romantic Image seems to be an intrinsic part of the making of the man as a writer or artist. Henry, too, initially inspired by the young Winifred (Watts-Dunton 1914, 52), desires to be an artist, and, in the conclusion of the novel where he is reunited with her, voices that desire which she then urges him to fulfil by using her as a model (Watts-Dunton 1914, 484–5).

Certainly D'Arcy's charge of Winifred gives him the prolonged pleasure of surveying an incarnated Romantic Image but, as Winifred continues periodically to suffer the seizures with each more serious than the last, he realises further action is necessary. When Sinfi, who has sat for D'Arcy before, turns up to model for him at Hurstcote, she immediately recognises Winifred and reveals her identity to the painter. D'Arcy, believing Henry to be travelling abroad, consults Dr Mivart, who has been treating him for insomnia, and the cure is effected using Sinfi as the object of transfer. When Winifred is cured, the Image disappears. As D'Arcy writes, 'and charming as she is now, restored to life and consciousness . . . the inexpressible witchery I have tried to describe has vanished, otherwise I don't know how I should have borne what I have now brought myself to bear, parting from her' (Watts-Dunton 1914, 462).

After Winifred's cure, Sinfi takes her to Wales, and Henry, who had believed she was dead, is reunited with her in a magical scene on the slopes of Snowdon. He has experienced, like D'Arcy and his father, 'the tragedy of tragedies . . . the death of a beloved mistress, or a beloved wife', but with a saving grace. As D'Arcy's letter, which he reads after meeting with Winifred, tells him: 'All that death has to teach the mind and heart of man you have learnt to the very full, and yet she you love is restored to you and will soon be in your arms' (Watts-Dunton 1914, 470).

The larger part of the narrative, which thus charts Henry's spiritual education, takes place while he believes that his beloved is dead, or dying, or living precariously on the borders of life and death, and, indeed, Winifred in her somnambulistic unconsciousness has the kind of death-in-life typical of the Romantic Image. It is also surely indicative that when D'Arcy, a celebrated late Romantic painter, finds her apparently dead, he recognises that she has life-in-death, takes her away for safe-keeping and cherishes her as the living embodiment of a master trope. But for all D'Arcy's domestication of Winifred, his tender nurture of her as a bewitching Romantic Image, he still cannot prevent the other – what we might, after Kermode, call the extreme pathological aspect – of the Image breaking through in Winifred's seizures, in that petrified and petrifying look of horror which she absorbs from her dead father, has reinforced by the terrible recollection of Henry's mother, and will pass on in turn to Sinfi by mesmeric transmission. In this narrative the unconscious benign side of the Romantic Image cannot be had without and thus must co-exist with its malign aspect, which preserves the traces of the trauma which gave it birth.[32] Thus *Aylwin* shows us another genealogical transfer or transmission, this time a cryptic literary one, whereby the dual-natured Romantic Image – an Image associated with Coleridge in both its pathological and ideal aspects – is transmitted to Rossetti, Coleridge's inheritor, indicating, in Watts-Dunton's eyes, a powerful continuity between Romantic and a certain strand of late Victorian visionary literature; for, to recall Watts-Dunton: 'It is perhaps with Coleridge alone that Rossetti can be compared with as a worker in the Renascence of Wonder.'

Moreover, from our much later own vantage point, we can see that the novel, which so strangely manages to occupy the last quarter of the nineteenth century that went into its making, also encompasses a large and crucial part of the transition to literary Modernism as the Romantic Image transmitted to Rossetti will, in turn, be taken up by Yeats and other modernists. Far from being a curious Victorian relic, *Aylwin* is a highly complex meditation on and dramatisation of the making of visionary artists and their images, offering us in 1898 an unusually privileged viewpoint into a key moment in literary history.

32 Watts-Dunton's poetic sequence *The Coming of Love*, while not precisely featuring a Romantic Image, shows that he none the less understood how there could be an coincidence of opposing aspects within a single body, as his paired sonnets 'Natura Maligna' and 'Natura Benigna' respectively picture the mystical body of Nature as a cruelly alluring *femme fatale* and as a magical, sweet maternal presence (Watts-Dunton n.d., 103–4, 112–13).

5

Thomas Hardy's poetry: 'the intenser stare of the mind'

> Dreamed of being in Verona, or in some place that was and wasn't Verona. Met an Englishman, who said 'he had been staring at things'. I said I was glad to hear it – to stare was the right thing, to *look* only was no use.
>
> (Ruskin, *Diaries* (1958), 2.685)

Much contemporary work on vision and visuality in Victorian poetry is still dominated by a preoccupation with particulars, with the material and phenomenal world and with material practices. This chapter tries to readdress that bias by re-examining the work of the poet Thomas Hardy (1840–1928), who may, at first sight, seem to be a strange choice for such a project in that he has been popularly understood as a chronicler or recorder of finely observed naturalistic detail ('a man who used to notice such things', 'Afterwards'; Hardy 1976, 553). To read the list of titles in the contents of *The Complete Poems* is apparently to be faced by a world of material objects, concrete in its insistence even to the point of banality: 'The Levelled Churchyard', 'The Torn Letter', 'Logs on the Hearth', 'The Whitewashed Wall', 'The Pat of Butter'. Lytton Strachey, reviewing *Satires of Circumstance, Lyrics and Reveries* (1914) in the *New Statesman* (19 December 1914) wrote: 'what gives Mr Hardy's poems their unique flavour is their utter lack of romanticism, their common, undecorated presentments of things' (Hardy 1993, 133). Ezra Pound, too, admired what appeared to be the simple clarity of Hardy's verse, observing in his *Guide to Kulchur* (1938): 'When a writer's matter is stated with such entirety and with such clarity there is no place left for the explaining critic. Where the matter is of so stark a nature and so clamped to reality, the eulogist looks like an ass . . . poem after poem of Hardy's leaves one with nowt more to say' (Pound 1960, 285). Although such clarity is meant to suggest an admirable economy and spareness when voiced by critics like Pound (who apparently saw in Hardy's poetry a version of his own Imagism), it tends to ignore the symbolic dimension and all too easily converts into a criticism which banalises the verse, seeing it as an uncomplicated reflection of life. This is the view of Samuel Hynes, editor of Hardy's poems, and the author of an influential early critical work on the poetry, who opines that 'He is neither a symbolic nor a metaphorical writer; in his poems things remain intransigently things' (Hynes 1961, 66). Yet Hardy's thought and art are saturated in visionary Romanticism, and a close look at the poems and his own stated thoughts on the writing of poetry give a different picture. Hardy declared his dissatisfaction with photographic representation as a model for literary representation (Hardy 1962, 153, 351), and the form of realistic reproduction he favoured was not a concentration on externals but to see into 'the *heart of a thing*' (January 1881; Hardy 1962, 147), a statement which specifically echoes Wordsworth in the epiphanic 'Tintern Abbey' (1798), where he describes the visionary trance-like state in which the eye is 'made quiet by the power / Of harmony, and the deep power of joy', and 'We see into the life of things' (Wordsworth 1997, 58, ll. 48–50). Hardy describes this technique as 'realism, in fact, though through being pursued by means of the imagination . . . confounded with invention' (Hardy 1962, 147). A substantial number of his poems work by a process of defamiliarisation in which the prosaic object, presented to view, is suddenly resituated or reviewed by the speaker in such a way that it ceases to be its banal everyday self but is permeated, or even subsumed and displaced, by the history, memories, impressions, or associations that it evokes. Such objects lose their matter-of-fact solidity and identity as they become uncanny; estranged from their everyday reality, they function as potent relics or catalysts which activate or stimulate what Hardy called 'the intenser / Stare of the mind' ('In Front of the Landscape'; Hardy 1976, 304) in which they are further 'exalted' – that 'intenser stare' being synonymous with Ruskin's 'spiritual or second sight' which 'exalts' visible objects (Ruskin 1903–4, 5.355).

As preliminary illustration of this process, my discussion of Hardy opens with an examination of three poems. I choose the first, 'The Lodging-House Fuchsias', a poem from his last and posthumously published collection *Winter Words* (1928), partly because it is a poem singled out by Hynes for criticism as 'An example of a mechanical reversal which doesn't work' (Hynes 1961, 51):

Mrs Masters's fuchsias hung
Higher and broader, and brightly swung,
  Bell-like, more and more
Over the narrow garden-path,
Giving the passer a sprinkle-bath
    In the morning.

She put up with their pushful ways,
And made us tenderly lift their sprays,
  Going to her door:
But when her funeral had to pass

They cut back all the flowery mass
    In the morning.

(Hardy 1976, 855)

I make no great claims for what is essentially a modest poem, yet it seems to me that even here Hardy manages to lift a commonplace subject into something above the ordinary. When Mrs Masters, the landlady of the lodging house, is alive, her prized fuchsias, like favourite children, are allowed to express themselves at their exuberant, excessive, unruly best, even at the inconvenience of dew-sprinkled passers-by and incoming and outgoing guests who are instructed to lift gently the flower sprays aside. The flowers effectively become her sign, express something of her character and will; but on her death, when she is no longer master in her own house, they are cut back – a thing she would have hated – to allow her funeral cortège to pass through. We sense that something of the tender indulgence Mrs Masters felt towards her flowers is carried through in the speaker's feeling towards the landlady herself as he faithfully replicates her feeling for the flowers as animate: 'She put up with their pushful ways, / And made us tenderly lift their sprays, / Going to her door'. Hynes complains that there is no 'clear significance in the repetition of "in the morning"; the phrase ties the two stanzas together in a mechanical way, and asserts an ironic relationship between them which does not in fact exist' (Hynes 1956, 52). But surely this is where Hardy's delicate artistry is uppermost – the homophone 'mourning' making its ghostly presence felt in the repeated 'morning' of the second stanza, at once introducing a stark contrast between the innocent past and the sadness of the present moment; and with this repetition, the depleted flowery mass, roughly cut back to allow the coffin by, becomes a sign of loss and sorrow.

If cut flowers evoked sadness for Hardy, then a felled tree called forth an even stronger expression of regret and was a topic he treated on a number of different occasions. Like his hero Jude, Hardy 'could scarcely bear to see trees cut down or lopped, from a fancy that it hurt them' (Hardy 1974a, 36), and, in a symposium in the *Fortnightly Review*, he singled out a passage from Carlyle's *The French Revolution* about the felling of an ancient tree as a memorable example of 'excellence of style' (Hardy 1993, 313, 314). We see from its subtitle 'A Memory of a Sister' and appended date – December 1915 – that 'Logs on the Hearth', from *Moments of Vision* (1917), is an elegy for Hardy's shy schoolteacher sister Mary. But there is the sense that is also an elegy for the felled apple tree that has provided the logs, and for a remembered childhood when the speaker and his sister climbed the tree.

  The fire advances along the log
    Of the tree we felled,
Which bloomed and bore striped apples by the peck
  Till its last hour of bearing knelled.

The fork that first my hand would reach
  And then my foot
In climbings upward inch by inch, lies now
  Sawn, sapless, darkening with soot.

Where now the bark chars is where, one year,
  It was pruned, and bled –
Then overgrew the wound. But now, at last,
  Its growings all have stagnated.

My fellow-climber rises dim
  From her chilly grave –
Just as she was, her foot near mine on the bending limb,
  Laughing, her young brown hand awave.

(Hardy 1976, 489–90)

There is certainly a feeling of regretful sympathy for the tree, which seems callously treated by its human guardians, who 'wound' it and make it 'bleed' with pruning, and finally fell it; an act which seems like a cruel execution as, remaining generously fruitful till its death, the tree is innocent of any blame that might have brought about its demise. Moreover, its once vital body is quickly chopped up into logs, 'Sawn, sapless, darkening with soot', and burnt on the family hearth. But out of this scene of destruction comes creation. As Hardy, a classicist, would have known, the word for hearth in Latin is 'focus', and what this poem does is to intensify the speaker's gaze so that the hearth, and what it holds, becomes a place for 'the intenser stare of the mind'. As the tree is consumed by fire, the mind rekindles the flames of memory so that the speaker sees again in the burning logs the tree he used to climb with his sister, and, phoenix-like, 'My fellow-climber rises dim / From her chilly grave'. Tree and girl are resurrected, but this is, in a special sense, a 'family tree', recording the speaker's private history of affiliation and alliance, and the log on the hearth becomes a personal record of remembered childhood moments. Hardy's poems perpetually offer us such visual images for preserving memory.

A prime example of such a visual analogue is 'Under the Waterfall' (Hardy 1976, 335–7), from *Satires of Circumstance, Lyrics and Reveries* (1914), a poem based on Hardy's courtship of his first wife Emma, though not included in his much-praised commemorative sequence *Poems of 1912–13* included in this same volume. The poem was sparked by a description in Emma's memoir *Some Recollections*, which Hardy discovered and read after her death in 1912:

> We sketched and talked of books; often we walked down the beautiful Valley to Boscastle harbour where we had to jump over stones and climb over a low wall by rough steps, get through by narrow pathways to come out on great wide spaces suddenly, with a sparkling little brook going the same way, into which we once lost

> a tiny picnic-tumbler, and there it is to this day no doubt between two small boulders.
>
> (E. Hardy 1979, 35)

Reproduced opposite this page in the published memoir is a pencil sketch by Hardy, depicting Emma crouching by a small waterfall with her arm in the current. The sketch is annotated 'E. C. G. by T. H. Aug 19, 1870', and titled underneath 'Searching for the glass – (watercolour sketching in Valency [*sic*] valley)' (E. Hardy 1979, 34).[1] Emma's recollection of this incident became the germ for Hardy's poem (Hardy 1976, 335–7) for which he considered two alternative titles – 'The Lost Glass' and 'The Glass in the Stream' – before fixing on 'Under the Waterfall'. Yet the poem is no simple transcription of the event as Emma told it, nor the lost glass a clear and simple 'thing'. Indeed it becomes a mnemonic image, containing and preserving untainted memories of the couple's early love; and, moreover, caught and held in the flowing current, it is, for the imaginative speaker, necessarily 'opalized', its opacity testifying to the passage of time etched on its surface.

One of the many interesting things about the poem is that it starts with a physical memory which then gives way to a stream of reflective consciousness. The speaker, in conversation with a friend, asserts:

> 'Whenever I plunge my arm, like this,
> In a basin of water, I never miss
> The sweet sharp sense of a fugitive day
> Fetched back from its thickening shroud of gray.'

This opening is reminiscent of the physical sensation described by Pater in the Conclusion to *The Renaissance*: 'the moment . . . of delicious recoil from the flood of water in summer heat' (Pater 1980, *Ren* 186). That physical sensation, here described as 'the sweet sharp sense', and later as 'throbs' and 'a throe from the past', merges with the memory of a similar sensation and a revived ripple of sexual excitement and desire, enlivening an episode from the otherwise dull and distant past.[2] Like Pater, Hardy does not remain with the initial sensation but moves from outer to inner life, his speaker extracting from memory the particular day, scene, and emotion associated with the sensory stimulus. Unsurprisingly the recollected stream and 'purl of a little valley fall' mimes the flow of consciousness and memory, a confluence already hallowed by poets

1. Hardy reproduced Emma's account in his *Life* (Hardy 1962, 71) inserting the word 'Vallency' before 'Valley'.
2. The word 'throbs' is explicitly associated with sexual excitement by Hardy in an earlier poem, the well-known short lyric 'I Look into My Glass', in which the speaker laments how his ageing body is still shaken 'With throbbings of noontide' (Hardy 1976, 81).

such as Shelley, Tennyson, Swinburne, and Rossetti, and by Pater who, in turning away from sensation to 'the inward life of thought and feeling', traces a similar current conspicuous in 'the race of the midstream, a drift of momentary acts of sight and passion and thought' (Pater 1980, *Ren* 187).[3] However, Hardy's speaker directly associates 'the purl of a runlet that never ceases' with poetry, asserting that the brook, connected with these memories of first romance, is the best rhythmic 'love-rhyme / That I know by heart'. This natural love poetry is apparently prized by the speaker above all human song, but of course Hardy's poetic rendering of the description of the stream necessarily ensures that the purl of the 'little valley fall' can't be anything other than poetry, perhaps thereby implicitly transferring the speaker's accolade to his own verse to make it a superlative 'love-rhyme'.

In the second part of the poem the speaker responds to the interlocutor's questions as to why the stream's song has become the authentic 'love-rhyme', and why plunging an arm into a basin of cold water is such a powerful stimulant to memory. The story of the lovers' picnic lunch on a burning August day is told along with the detail of the rinsed glass that falls into the stream and cannot be recovered, 'Though we stooped and plumbed the little abyss / With long bared arms'. This much is factual. What happens next, however, starting with the confident assertion 'There the glass still is', is another matter. Although we may read with perfect belief and acceptance the lovely account of the glass preserved under the waterfall, held safe in a cleft of the rocks, it is the speaker's own desire and imagination which has projected this symbolic wholeness. In reality there can be no assurance that the glass did not break and shatter when it first fell into the pool or that, subsequently dislodged by the current, it did not get smashed against stones or other water-borne debris. Whether broken or out of reach, the glass is completely invisible, yet it is the speaker's intensity of conviction that miraculously makes it appear to us. Like the speaker, we want to believe in the continuing presence of the glass, perhaps because, as the poem says, 'its presence adds to the rhyme of love', and also because Hardy has subtly infused the poetry with mythic and other associations that help crystallise the central luminous image of the glass and foster our belief in it:

> 'By night, by day, when it shines or lours,
> There lies intact that chalice of ours,
> And its presence adds to the rhyme of love
> Persistently sung by the fall above.
> No lip has touched it since his and mine
> In turns therefrom sipped lovers' wine.'

3. See, by way of example, Shelley's 'Mont Blanc', Tennyson's 'The Brook', Swinburne's 'Before the Mirror', Rossetti's 'The Stream's Secret'.

Clearly the image of the chalice and the shared wine-drinking conjures up the notion of a eucharist or holy communion sacralising the lovers' bond and signifying not the 'real presence' of Christ, but the real presence of their love which at that time seemingly had the potential to endure for ever unbroken. Another Biblical echo might be the cup that 'runneth over' from Psalm 23 expressing excess of joy (v. 5). But I suspect Hardy also presses us delicately towards the legend of Tristram and Iseult, who accidentally drink from a chalice containing enchanted wine and fall passionately and irrevocably in love with one another. We know that this Celtic legend, set in Cornwall, had been in his mind since his courtship of Emma in her Cornish homeland, also the setting for the incident that inspired this poem. In his *Life*, Hardy recorded that, in August 1870, the month when he was staying with Emma's family and the glass was lost,

> His hosts drove him to various picturesque points on the wild and rugged coast near the Rectory, among others to King Arthur's Castle, Tintagel, which he now saw for the first time. . . . [A]fter it had been smouldering in his mind for between forty and fifty years, he constructed *The Famous Tragedy of the Queen of Cornwall* from the legends connected with that romantic spot. Why he did not do it sooner, while she was still living who knew the scene so well, and had frequently painted it, it is impossible to say.
>
> (Hardy 1962, 78)[4]

The poem's evocation of Tristram and Iseult, tender but ill-fated lovers whose alliance brings much suffering, also strengthens the hint that the preserved glass testifies to the initial purity and sincerity of the modern-day lovers' affection for one another, even though their lives and love may have been damaged by subsequent events. The memory and symbol of first love and affection endures even if their later relationship was fraught with pain and difficulty. The 'opalizing' of the glass reflects the misting of time, but also, by association with the precious stone, suggests that, as time has gone by, the treasured memory has become increasingly more valuable to the speaker.[5] It is possible that this memory also evokes an Edenic time of virginal longing and idealised desire before the 'fall' of sexual consummation and knowledge. The chalice, which remains 'intact', recalls the eroticised language of the Biblical Song of Songs where, in the wooing courtship address of the lover, the beloved woman's mouth 'is like the best wine' (Ch 7 v. 9) and her 'navel' – the word is a poetic euphemism for her sex – is 'a rounded goblet that never lacks mixed wine' (Ch 7 v. 2).

4. *The Famous Tragedy of the Queen of Cornwall* (1923) is included in *The Complete Poetical Works of Thomas Hardy*, 5 (1995), 257–329; explanatory notes 361–5.
5. It also perhaps suggests the culminating 'hard, gem-like flame' of Pater's Conclusion (Pater 1980, *Ren* 189).

Other associations also pervade the pool into which the water falls:

'And, as said, if I thrust my arm below
Cold water in basin or bowl, a throe
From the past awakens a sense of that time,
And the glass we used, and the cascade's rhyme.
The basin seems the pool, and its edge
The hard smooth face of the brook-side ledge,
And the leafy pattern of china-ware
The hanging plants that were bathing there.'

Hardy sets up the strangest of metamorphoses whereby, at the prompting of an evocative physical sensation, a common Victorian domestic object, a patterned china basin, is transformed into the pool the lovers plumbed with their arms. In his novels Hardy shows he is adept at uncanny scenic transformations which occur at moments of extremity: in *A Pair of Blue Eyes* (1873), Stephen Knight, clinging perilously to the cliff-face, sees pass before his eyes a telescoped history of evolution (Ch 22), while in *The Well-Beloved* (1897), Jocelyn Pierston, reading the letter relating Avice's death at a London dinner-party (Bk 2, Ch 3), finds his immediate surroundings melting into a coastal view of the Isle of Slingers, his dead love's home and the scene of his courtship of her. In this poem the physical stimulus of cold water provokes 'the intenser stare of the mind' that makes the basin into a pool, and the pool into the place where we see the visionary chalice of the couple's love. In Ovid's *Metamorphoses*, the pool in the mythic stories of Narcissus and Hermaphroditus is a place of transformation. It can also suggest, as it does in Rossetti's 'Willowwood', a depth model of the reflecting mind in which submerged memories can float up, or, as here, be sounded out.

Reading the poem for the first time (especially if one has no knowledge of Emma's memoir), the reader might well assume that the speaker is male till the very end of the piece where one meets the qualification 'his and mine'. Proportionally more of Hardy's dramatic poems are written in a masculine voice and, where a woman's voice is used, it is generally signalled in the title or quickly made explicit in the poem. In 'Under the Waterfall', the assumption of masculinity seems borne out by the first line with the word 'plunge' and the later 'thrust' which have a suggestive virility that one might not so easily associate with a young Victorian woman. Although, in retrospect, it is perhaps more common to use the word 'lover' of a man than a woman and although the domestic detail of rinsing the glass may be thought more feminine than masculine, these are not immediately self-evident signals. This unsettling ripple across gender might be attributed to the fact that Hardy, a man, is ventriloquising a woman and perhaps, in creating her viewpoint, inadvertently leaves traces of his own masculine voice behind. However, rather than regarding this slippage as an 'accident', it would be more interesting, in this poem about hallucinatory preservation, to preserve the hallucinatory marks of a reading where an apparently masculine voice transforms into a feminine one, as Hardy, plumbing the depths of consciousness, plunges through the more immediately evident upper strata of masculine identity in an attempt to reach and capture the elusive delicate vessel of the woman's fantasy; in such a reading the poem does, in fact, become something like the pool of Hermaphroditus, fusing male and female experience.[6]

In my exploration of these three poems, I hope to have shown that the things they treat – the fuschias, the logs, the basin and glass – all lose their everyday identity and, illuminated by 'the intenser stare of the mind' or 'second sight', become uncanny, quasi-ghostly versions of themselves, haloed by the imagination and radiant with symbolism. This is what Hardy means by the 'real': 'the material is not the real – only the visible, the real being invisible optically . . . it is because we are in a somnambulistic hallucination that we think the real to be what we see as real' (13 February 1887; Hardy 1962, 186). The imaginatively contemplative mind, a mind which naturally expresses itself in poetry, sees as 'real' what is normally regarded as metaphysical, abstract, supernatural, or unconscious. If material things can have a supernatural aspect, then they vary only in degree and not in kind from those spectres and visions more generally regarded as supernatural and which, as we shall see, play a dominant role in Hardy's poetry. The rest of this chapter will attempt to elucidate what Hardy calls the 'abstract imaginings' underlying the visible and to show how ghostliness is germane to his best verse.

'Abstract imaginings'

In *The Life of Thomas Hardy*, which he ghosted in the name of his second wife, Florence, Hardy recorded journal entries which show how naturalistic verisimilitude practised for its own sake left him cold. He made it clear that for him the interest of a scene depends on its human associations:

> An object or mark raised or made by man on a scene is worth ten times any such formed by unconscious Nature. Hence clouds, mists, and mountains are unimportant besides the wear on a threshold, or the print of a hand.
>
> (28 September 1877; Hardy 1962, 116)

The marks man imposes on Nature when he makes an artistic representation are also important. Commenting on contemporary painting and his growing

6. Hardy knew well Swinburne's 'Hermaphroditus', lines from which he inscribed in his 'Studies, Specimens &c' Notebook, a record mainly of his poetry reading in the late 1860s (Hardy 1994, 50). His editor Tim Armstrong detects an echo of 'Hermaphroditus' in 'Neutral Tones' (Hardy 1993, 54).

interest in Turner's late style, Hardy declares that 'the "simply natural" is interesting no longer', and continues:

> The exact truth as to material fact ceases to be of importance in art – it is a student's style – the style of a period when the mind is serene and unawakened to the tragical mysteries of life; when it does not bring anything to the object that coalesces with and translates the qualities that are already there, – half hidden, it may be – and the two united are depicted as the All.
>
> (January 1887; Hardy 1962, 185)

This entry is prefaced by the remark

> I don't want to see landscapes, *i.e.*, scenic paintings of them, because I don't want to see the original realities – as optical effects, that is. I want to see the deeper reality underlying the scenic, the expression of what are sometimes called abstract imaginings.
>
> (January 1887; Hardy 1962, 185)

This distinction broadly corresponds to the phenomenon Vernon Lee calls 'the lie of the land', by which she means

> the real, individual landscape – the landscape one actually sees with the eyes of the body and the eyes of the spirit – *the landscape you cannot describe*. . . . Yes, *lie of the land* is what has mattered to us since we were children, to our fathers and remotest ancestors; and its perception, the instinctive preference for one kind rather than another, is among the obscure things inherited with our blood, and making up the stuff of our souls.
>
> (Lee 1897, 45, 47)

Hardy's comments on landscape, written in response to the modernity of Turner, are informed by a latent Romanticism: Wordsworth's 'eye and ear' which 'half-create' and 'perceive' ('Tintern Abbey', ll. 107–8; Wordsworth 1997, 60), Coleridge's cry that 'in our life alone does nature live' ('Dejection Ode', l. 48; Coleridge 1974, 281), and Shelley's declaration in the *Defence* that 'All things exist as they are perceived: at least in relation to the percipient' (Shelley 1977, 505). It is apparent from comments dating from the very beginning of Hardy's career, such as 'The poetry of a scene varies with the minds of the perceivers. Indeed, it does not lie in the scene at all' (August 23 1865; Hardy 1962, 50), that Hardy was in line with the Romantic belief which still underpins much poetic writing in the period. In trying to distinguish with unnecessary rigour between Romantic and Victorian literatures, we have down-played similarities. For the Romantic belief that it is the viewer's subjective power which colours and charges what is viewed remains constant throughout the period, and culminates with the late Decadent assertion of the priority of the imagination over Nature. While certain Victorian commentators alarmed by their ever-more complex sense of 'the world's multitudinousness' (Arnold cited in

Christ 1975, 35, 65) may have sought objective standards of truth, as in Arnold's behest 'to see the object as in itself it really is' and Ruskin's unease with the pathetic fallacy, they were countered by those like Hardy who believed poetry's mission was 'to record impressions, not convictions' (Hardy 1962, 377).

As Dennis Taylor points out, Hardy's '"notion of impression" came from a number of traditions, that of English skepticism particularly from Hume to Spencer, the aesthetic tradition from Keats to Pater, . . . and nineteenth-century impressionist painting' (Taylor 1993, 41). The quotations about landscape, 'material fact', and 'abstract imaginings' cited above date from a period when Hardy was observing impressionist painterly techniques in the galleries and exhibitions he attended. In *The Expressive Eye* (1986), his study of perception in Hardy's fiction, J. B. Bullen discusses the impact of impressionist painting on his novel *The Woodlanders* (1887), while Tom Paulin in *The Poetry of Perception* (1975; 2nd ed., 1986) makes a good case for the late poem 'The High-school Lawn' from *Human Shows* (1925) as 'impressionist' in the painterly sense, with its blur of colour, 'shimmering, ephemeral qualities of surfaces' and evocation of 'a passing mood' (Paulin 1986, 34). But Hardy's observations on impressionist technique are not essentially new but are recognisably a development of his earlier Romantic tenets such the Wordsworthian impulse to see into 'the *heart of a thing*' (January 1881; Hardy 1962, 147). Thus, discussing impressionism in art and literature, he sees it as '*what appeals to your own individual eye and heart in particular*' (December 1886; Hardy 1862, 184). Pater seems to me the crucial figure in mediating this development as, for example, in his own cunning transumption of Arnold in the Preface to *The Renaissance*: '"To see the object as in itself it really is," has been justly said to be the aim of all criticism whatever; and in æsthetic criticism the first step towards seeing one's object as it really is, is to know one's impression as it really is, to discriminate it, to realise it distinctly' (Pater 1980, *Ren* xix). In the Conclusion to *The Renaissance*, Pater also describes how, although, as perceivers, we, at first, feel ourselves buried under 'a flood of external objects, pressing upon us with a sharp and importunate reality', 'reflexion' dissipates those objects, suspending their 'cohesive force', so that 'each object is loosed into a group of impressions' (Pater 1980, *Ren* 187). These Paterian processes of reflective dissipation of the object and discrimination of one's impression seem to me intriguingly close to that defamiliarising review of the object which I have described Hardy as undertaking in so many of his poems. Hardy would almost certainly agree with Pater's follower, Lee 'that *seeing* is a business of the mind, the memory and the heart, quite as much as the eye' (Lee 1927b, 251) and that 'the life of all art goes on in the mind and heart, not merely of those who make the work, but of those who read it' ('The Lie of the Land'; Lee 1897, 59). In 'Alike and Unlike', his short poem about a couple's shared viewing of a particular scene (the 'Great

Orme's Head' of the subtitle), Hardy's metaphor of pictorial engraving is an evident synonym for 'impression':

> We watched the self-same scene on that long drive,
> Saw the magnificent purples, as one eye,
> Of those near mountains; saw the storm arrive;
> Laid up the sight in memory, you and I,
> As if for joint recallings by and by.
>
> But our eye-records, like in hue and line,
> Had superimposed on them, that very day,
> Gravings on your side deep, but slight on mine! –
> Tending to sever us thenceforth alway;
> Mine commonplace; yours tragic, gruesome, gray.
>
> (Hardy 1976, 788–9)

When the couple recall this incident afterwards, they have different impressions of 'the self-same scene' because of the different emotions they experienced on 'that very day'. From the perspective of hindsight, different emotions connected with the scene or with some aspect of their relationship, emotions perhaps not fully conscious or recognised at the time, prepare the ground for future dissension.

Hardy's awareness of how different emotions shape one's impression of a scene is obvious in both his novels and his poems. He appears to have first read Ruskin's *Modern Painters* (1843–60) around 1862 (Paulin 1986, 18), and his poems show a strong interest in what Ruskin termed 'the pathetic fallacy' (*Modern Painters* 3 (1856), Ch. 12) which, in its now common debased form, is understood as the imputation of human character and feeling to natural objects, but which is properly the imputation of human character and feeling to natural objects by the perceiving subject when under the influence of strong emotion. While Ruskin sanctions certain manifestations when they appear to him to be caused by genuine emotion, he remains at heart uneasy about the fallacy which, for him, is essentially based on false appearances and deceit and, as such, a perversion of the book of nature which is the revelation of the Divine Mind. His exposition of the fallacy makes it clear that he prefers those poets of the first rank who avoid the fallacy by making analogies, similes, and comparisons using words such as 'like', 'as', or 'seems'; for him, 'The temperament which admits the pathetic fallacy, is . . . that of a mind and body in some sort too weak to deal fully with what is before them or upon them' (Ruskin 1903–4, 5.208). As one of the best-known descriptive devices for representing the sympathy of the perceiving subject with Nature and vice versa, the pathetic fallacy is a master trope of Romantic and Post-Romantic poetry. Among those who use the fallacy are Wordsworth, Keats, and Tennyson who, thus tainted by weakness, immediately constitute Ruskin's second order of poets. Hardy clearly rejected Ruskin's deprecation of the fallacy with its degradation of users to a second order or below, judging emotional vision, and thus the fallacy, as implicit to acts of intense perception. While Ruskin saw the perceiver as subordinate to nature and praised Sir Walter Scott for this very thing (Ruskin 1903–4, 5.341), Hardy typically sees nature as subordinate to the perceiver.[7]

Hardy must have balked at Ruskin's charge of deceit and false appearance in the pathetic fallacy, for the anthropomorphic element of the fallacy was part of an imaginative animism which was habitual with him: 'In spite of myself I cannot help noticing countenances and tempers in objects of scenery, *e.g.* trees, hills, houses'; 'I sometimes look upon all things in inanimate Nature as pensive mutes' (10 February 1897; 30 May 1877; Hardy 1962, 285, 114). His writings are full of minor animations, as inanimate things or natural objects such as roads, rooms, trees, buildings, places, landscapes, the elements, are personified, and, typically, are given characters or faces, as in these examples from *The Woodlanders* and *The Mayor of Casterbridge*: 'the physiognomy of a deserted highway', 'the features of the town', 'the bleared white visage of a sunless winter's day'.[8] Often, when it is a face that comes to view, that face solicits or demands interpretation:

> These bridges had speaking countenances.
>
> (*Mayor*, Hardy 1974c, 247)

> Her own bedroom wore at once a look more familiar than when she had left it, and yet a face estranged.
>
> (*Woodlanders*, Hardy 1974d, 77)

> The smooth surfaces of glossy plants came out like weak lidless eyes; there were strange faces and figures from expiring lights.
>
> (*Woodlanders*, Hardy 1974d, 326)

This animism might be regarded as 'primitive' form of the imagination which is none the less a vital constituent in poetic perception. After citing remarks made by his friend Edward Clodd about the primitive temperament, Hardy commented, 'This "barbaric idea which confuses persons and things" is, by the way, also common to the highest imaginative genius – that of the poet' (18 December 1890; Hardy 1962, 230). Clearly animism also pervades his own poetry, as in, for example, 'The weakening eye of day' and 'The land's sharp features', from 'The Darkling Thrush'; 'the frigid face of the heath-hemmed pond' in 'At Rushy Pond'; or, in 'On the Esplanade', where 'The broad bald moon

7. Poems that directly explore the fallacy are 'Seasons of Her Year' (originally titled 'The Pathetic Fallacy'), 'The King's Experiment', and 'The Difference'.
8. *Woodlanders*, Hardy 1974d, 35; *Mayor*, Hardy 1974c, 60; *Woodlanders*, Hardy 1974d, 54.

edged up where the sea was wide, / Mild, mellow-faced' (Hardy 1976, 150, 713, 715). In 'Nature's Questionings', a poem which puts the speaker on the receiving end of Nature's philosophical queries, he tells how

> When I look forth at dawning, pool,
> Field, flock, and lonely tree,
> All seem to gaze at me
> Like chastened children sitting silent in a school.
>
> (Hardy 1976, 66)

The ensuing questions about existential origins, which the speaker is unable to answer, are, we assume, his own. In Hardy's poetry, 'the intenser stare of the mind' can seem like a version of Hopkins's 'what you look hard at seems to look hard at you' (Hopkins 1959, 204); that is, as in the pathetic fallacy's projection of identity through strong emotion, the experience of being looked at is the result of a reflection. In the second stanza of the poem 'Moments of Vision' which opens the 1917 verse collection of the same name, the speaker asks

> That mirror
> Whose magic penetrates like a dart,
> Who lifts that mirror
> And throws our mind back on us, and our own heart,
> Until we start?
>
> (Hardy 1976, 427)

One way of responding to this question might be that we (and, more specifically, Hardy) are the ones who have unconsciously or half-consciously positioned that mirror in Nature or our surroundings to 'throw our mind back' on ourselves. However, there might be another explanation if we consider Hardy's animism (which, as we have seen, he associates with his creative vision as a poet) in connection with the remarks of the psychoanalyst Marion Milner on the relation between the painter and his world. In *On Not Being Able to Paint* (1950), her personal investigation of painting and drawing, Milner came to the conclusion that

> the relationship of oneself to the external world is basically and originally a relationship of one person to another, even though it does eventually become differentiated into relations to living beings and relations to things, inanimate nature. In other words, in the beginning one's mother is, literally, the whole world. Of course, the idea of one's first relationship to the outside world being felt as a relationship to persons, or parts of persons, was one I had frequently met with in discussions of childhood and savage animism. But the possibility that the adult painter could be basically, even though unconsciously, concerned with an animistically conceived world, was something I had hardly dared let myself face.
>
> Looked at in these terms the problem of the relation between the painter and his world then became basically a problem of one's own need and the needs of the

'other', a problem of reciprocity between 'you' and 'me'; with 'you' and 'me' meaning originally mother and child.

(Milner 1957, 116)

Hardy's animism then might be a relic or remnant of his original relationship with his mother, a relationship we know was a strong one. When at home in Dorset, Hardy visited her at Bockhampton every Sunday till her death at the age of ninety in April 1904. Hardy's biographer Michael Millgate calls Jemima Hardy 'the single most important influence in his life, and the source, together with his father, of so much of that local and traditional material which formed the groundwork of his fiction and poetry alike' (Millgate 1985, 20–3, 435). The traces of this relationship then reveal themselves through his representations of his surroundings, especially his personalised recreation of Wessex, his cherished motherland. In the psychoanalytic theory of D. W. Winnicott, the mother is the first person who, by offering the infant a mirror in herself (that is, in her face and expressions), reflects the infant back to himself and gives him a sense of self.[9] So the mother is behind the original mirroring which 'throws us back' on ourselves, and the 'reflection' provided by animistic perception is a relic of this original process. Thus a landscape that takes over this function, that perpetually reflects and reinforces a sense of identity, is in a real sense a motherland.

As theorists of child development have proposed, one of the infant's major tasks is to separate himself gradually from his mother. In 'Beyond the Pleasure Principle' (1920), Freud famously introduced the figure of his one-and-a half-year-old grandson playing with a wooden reel on a piece of string. Holding the string, the child would throw the reel into his curtained cot, noting its disappearance with what sounded like the German word '*fort*' meaning 'gone', and then pulling it back into view would greet 'its reappearance with a joyful "*da*" ["there"]'. Freud determined that through this game the child was miming his mother's departures from him, along with her subsequent returns, in order to gain mastery over his loss of her (Freud 1984b, 11.283–6). Later Winnicott theorised that children used playthings such as toys as transitional objects to aid them in the process of weaning themselves away from their mother. Adult versions of these transitional objects might be art objects, which may thus carry marks of that original primary relation between mother and child.[10] Hardy's own art objects are, of course, his novels and poems. He regarded his poetry as his real creative work and thought that it was much more personally revealing than his novels, writing to Clive Holland on 25 August 1923 that, 'If you read the thin paper volume called "Collected Poems", . . . you will gather more personal particulars than I could give you in an interview, circumstances not being so veiled in the verse as in the novels' (Hardy 1978–88, 6.206–7).

9. See Adam Phillips's account of this process (Phillips 1988, 128–33).
10. For a recent excellent discussion of this in relation to Vernon Lee see Pulham 2008.

One can't help but notice that Hardy is obsessed with the idea of the lost woman. Indeed, as repetition is fundamental to his writing, we should not be surprised to find the loss of the woman endlessly repeated.[11] His 1897 novel *The Well-Beloved* (*The Pursuit of the Well-Beloved* in the 1892 serial version), which in its opening chapters shows the inconstant Jocelyn Pierston allured by a succession of different women, satirises a temperament Hardy knew only too well. In life he was perpetually fixing on female strangers met casually, or glimpsed in the street, or on buses and trains, and falling in love with them.[12] Robert Gittings calls him 'A perpetual adolescent even into his eighties' and Hardy himself confessed to Florence, his second wife, that 'he thought he had never grown up' (Gittings 1978, 66, 159).[13] One wonders if it is not the very transient nature of these experiences, the fact that such women will swiftly and inevitably be removed from view, which makes them so exciting to him and the women so attractive. He looks everywhere for 'reflecting' female faces, but he also perhaps relies on their disappearance and his mastery of his loss. If the Romantic epipsyche or reflecting female beloved of male poets can be deemed an adult substitute for the reflecting mother, then more than most poets, Hardy seems reconciled to her loss, perhaps because he knows he will continue to see her refracted in the landscape and in the intense stare of his mind's eye. As we know, Hardy's feelings for Emma, his first wife, which had fallen into abeyance towards the end of her life, were rekindled only after her death, his powerful emotions of yearning and regret finding expression in some of his best poems. These poems, and indeed many other of his poems which are about lost women, can be read as Hardy's repeated version of the *fort / da* game, signifying his attempt to compensate for and master a separation that echoes that primary separation. In a similar vein U. C. Knoepflmacher suggests that 'The female shades who stimulated Hardy's imagination were, like the living women in his life, versions of the mother he could not afford directly to impersonate or appropriate' (Knoepflmacher 1993, 124).[14] Robert Gittings comments that

11. See Miller 1982.
12. See Millgate 1985, 296–8, 329–30, 336, 365, 453–4, 465, 535; Hardy 1962, 210, 212, 220, 235, 224.
13. For the complete text of Florence's letter of 7 April 1914 in which she records this see Millgate 1996, 97. Hardy put a slightly more flattering public spin on the matter when he recorded in the *Life*: 'I was quick to bloom; late to ripen. . . . I was a child till I was 16; a youth till I was 25; a young man till I was 40–50' (13 November 1917; Hardy 1962, 378).
14. Knoepflmacher's thoughtful essay 'Hardy Ruins: Female Spaces and Male Designs' (1993), an earlier version of which appeared in *PMLA* 105 (1990), 1055–70, also proposes the significance of the mother to Hardy's verse. One of his footnotes (Knoepflmacher 1993, 129) refers to Ruth Perry's use of Winnicott in the Introduction to *Mothering the Mind* (Perry 1984, 7).

the death of Hardy's childhood sweetheart, Louisa Harding, in September 1913 'made him realize that all dead women had a mysterious attraction for him, though Emma was still "the elect one"' and that 'The death of a woman remained the most powerful and lasting factor in his creative life' (Gittings 1978, 158, 66). Of the poems that commemorate Emma, Michael Millgate observes: 'It is perfectly clear that, as on many previous occasions, what gave Hardy pain was precisely what provided the fuel for his art'; and he also remarks: 'it is clear from the verbal and rhythmic control of these poems that Hardy remained very much in control of his emotions at this period, that he cherished his melancholy rather than surrendered to it' (Millgate 1985, 488). In a number of the poems about Emma, the return to Cornwall – her birthplace, native terrain, and the scene of the couple's courtship – identifies her with the landscape she inhabited, a displaced or extended version of Hardy's motherland. In these poems about lost women, the woman's ghost, which may appear after her death, might also be the enacted maternal return of the *fort / da*, a return carefully staged and controlled by the poet.

Ghosts

Hardy was to call one of his most celebrated verse collections *Moments of Vision* (1917). Evoking the Wordsworthian entranced subject 'who had passed alone / Beyond the visible barriers of the world / And travelled into things to come' ('The Borderers', 4.2.143–5; 1797–99 version; Wordsworth 1982, 238), much of his poetry celebrates 'The visioning powers of souls who dare / To pierce the material screen' ('The House of Silence'; Hardy 1976, 474). For Hardy, who told the interviewer William Archer that he 'cheerfully would have given ten years of my life to see a ghost . . . I should think I am cut out by nature for a ghost-seer' (Archer 1904, 37), poetry is a domain especially sympathetic to phantoms. 'Half my time – particularly when writing verse – I "believe" (in the modern sense of the word) . . . in spectres, mysterious voices, omens, dreams, haunted places, etc. etc.' (Hardy 1962, 370). Many of Hardy's poems are about ghosts or the experience of being haunted, something that that has been fully acknowledged only relatively recently in monographs by Tim Armstrong (2000) and Sven Bäckman (2001). That the treatment of this subject is by no means self-evident or predictable is shown by the widely divergent approaches of these writers. Armstrong's monograph, heavily informed by post-structuralist theory, is primarily interested in 'the construction of history as a discourse (often a haunted discourse) in Hardy's poetry . . . above all about the entry into history, the trauma of *becoming-historical* which is central to nineteenth-century conceptions of the human' (Armstrong 2000, 2), while Bäckman's discusses 'the use Hardy the poet makes of various supernatural elements – i.e. motifs, themes, and phenomena connected with the world beyond what he once referred to as "the material screen"' (Bäckman 2001, 1–2). Moreover, when dealing with the supernatural in Hardy's poetry, these differing views of what constitutes the ghostly or the spectral result in noticeably different selections of poems, and, while any selection is likely to be determined by personal preferences, Hardy's *œuvre* of some 950 poems allows for considerable variation in choice. My own position is different from both of these critics in that I see Hardy's phantasmal leanings as a more accentuated flowering of his visionary imagination, nurtured by Romantic and Post-Romantic writers, and by his own inner life in so far as it contributes to his shaping as a poet.

As indicated above, Hardy acknowledged that writing and especially the writing of verse opened him up to the supernatural. Poetry in particular for him has the potential to accommodate ghosts and other phantasmal things, to make space for forms of consciousness or unconsciousness which he might not so easily entertain in everyday life. We know that Hardy often had a sense of his poems as a particular space or shape before they took actual form in words; that is, they existed as 'verse skeletons' (Hardy 1962, 301). Of these Samuel Hynes writes: 'The notion of the empty poetic mold, waiting to be filled with words, may seem naïve . . . but they do show Hardy's lively interest in the technical aspects of his chosen art' (Hynes 1961, 20). Dennis Taylor's monograph on Hardy's metrical experiments, *Hardy's Metres and Victorian Prosody* (1988), suggests his approach was anything but naive, but, to put the issue of metre to one side, it is possible to think of these demarked or designated spaces as waiting for the appropriate form to inhabit them. These outlined gaps are reminiscent of the kind of gap in consciousness that occurs when searching for a forgotten name, as described by William James in his *The Principles of Psychology*:

> The state of our consciousness is peculiar. There is gap therein; but no mere gap. It is a gap that is intensely active. A sort of wraith of the name is in it, beckoning us in a given direction, making us at moments tingle with the sense of our closeness, and then letting us sink back without the longed-for term. If wrong names are proposed to us, this singularly definite gap acts immediately so as to negate them. They do not fit into its mould. And the gap of one word does not feel like the gap of another, all empty of content as both might seem necessarily to be when described as gaps. . . . The rhythm of a lost word may be there without a sound to clothe it; or the evanescent sense of something which is the initial vowel or consonant may mock us fitfully, without growing more distinct. Everyone must know the tantalizing effect of the blank rhythm of some forgotten verse, restlessly dancing in one's mind, striving to be filled out with words.
>
> (James 1901, 251, 252)

As the psychologist Anton Ehrenzweig has suggested with reference to this passage, James's '"gap" which . . . "beckons" us into a given direction is akin to the guiding vision of the creative artist or thinker which accepts or rejects the formative ideas' (Ehrenzweig 1975, 10). In Chapter 53 of *Tess of the D'Urbervilles* (1891), Hardy memorably described Angel Clare on his return from South America as whittled him down by mental agony to an excruciated core: 'You could see the skeleton behind the man, and almost the ghost behind the skeleton' (Hardy 1974b, 417). Likewise Hardy's verse skeletons allow us to speculate on the ghosts of poems that lie behind them which take shape and form in the act of writing. They direct us toward that region which the philosopher Maurice Blanchot indicates in his essay 'The Book to Come':

> Nothing is created and no discourse can be creative except through the preliminary exploration of the totally vacant region where language, before it is a set of given words, is a silent process of correspondences, or a rhythmic scansion of life. Words exist only to signify the area of correspondence, the space onto which they are projected.
>
> (Blanchot 1982, 237)

If, for Hardy, the writing of poetry is the taking shape and the taking over of a ghostly space, then within the poems ghost space is also important in that his spectres have specific territories or haunting grounds. Houses, in particular, are prime sites for accumulating spirits. In the poem 'The Two Houses', the older house, responding to the newer house's insults about his dilapidations, retorts, 'A new house has no sense of the have-beens. / Void as a drum / You stand', and after listing the many spectres who people his rooms, declares

> 'Where such inbe
> A dwelling's character
> Takes theirs, and a vague semblancy
> To them in all its limbs, and light, and atmosphere.'
>
> (Hardy 1976, 596)

Cowed by this speech, the newer house tentatively asks if the day will come when he, too, will '"with such spectral guests become acquaint"', to which the older replies with magisterial patronage:

> 'That will it, boy;
> Such shades will people thee,
> Each in his misery or, irk, or joy,
> And print on thee their presences as on me.'

That sense of the 'printed presence', akin to 'impression', is what makes places, especially houses, paradoxically 'vital' to Hardy. When, in the poem 'The Self-unseeing' (Hardy 1976, 166–7), the speaker visits his childhood home, the 'ancient floor / Footworn and hollowed and thin' bears tangible marks of former inhabitants, but he also sees with his mind's stare the phantom imprinted presences of his own self, mother, and father enjoying his father's fiddle music, but unaware, so it seems to him now, of the full extent of their happiness. It is this sense of a continuously printed presence that perhaps enables Hardy to make the observation in the *Life* dated 10 June 1923: 'Relativity. That things and events always were, are, and will be (*e.g.* Emma, Mother and Father are still living in the past)' (Hardy 1962, 419). This review of the past that makes it live on, that enables the reviewer to see even the ghost of his former self, seems to be something that Hardy specifically identified with poetry.

Hardy's perception of the printed presence corresponds well with Vernon Lee's sense, in her essay 'In Praise of Old Houses' (1892), 'which to many of us has grown into a cherished habit – the sense of being companioned by the past, of being in a place warmed for our living by the lives of others' (Lee 1897, 29). None the less for the sensitive subject such an experience can on occasion feel oppressive. In his *Life* Hardy complains feelingly that 'The worst of taking a furnished house is that the articles in the rooms are saturated with the thoughts and glances of others' (28 April 1893; 1962, 254). It is telling that Hardy's mother seemed to have felt something similar about her own inherited furniture; he noted that 'My mother says she looks at the furniture and feels she is nothing to it. All those belonging to it, and the place, are gone, and it is left in her hands, a stranger. (She has, however, lived there these fifty-three years!)' (31 August 1892; Hardy 1962, 249). The speaker of the poem 'Old Furniture' is one of those sitting 'amid relics of householdry / That date from the days of their mothers' mothers', who can

> see the hands of the generations
> That owned each shiny familiar thing
> In play on its knobs and indentations,
> And with its ancient fashioning
> Still dallying:
>
> Hands behind hands, growing paler and paler,
> As in a mirror a candle-flame
> Shows images of itself, each frailer
> As it recedes, though the eye may frame
> Its shape the same.
>
> (Hardy 1976, 485–6)

In 'The House of Silence' (Hardy 1976, 474), we find out that the house of the title, which seems to the observing child 'a quiet place', but is said to teem with phantasmal life, is actually 'a poet's bower', the implication being that the poet is one who has 'The visioning powers of those who dare / To pierce the material screen', but also that the phantoms are of his perception and creation, the products of the 'brain' that 'spins there till dawn'. The 'ghost space' of the house is here directly linked to the ghost space of poetry writing and perhaps poetry reading where 'Figures dance to a mind with sight'. The printed presences that haunt the house and the poet's creative consciousness are those that will eventually find their way into print, and thereafter impress themselves on the minds of sensitive readers. However the last two lines of this poem's first stanza – 'Why a phantom abides there, the last of its race, / And a brain spins there till dawn' – suggest that the 'phantom' and the spinning 'brain' are one, and thus that the poet, who necessarily inhabits ghost space, may be considered to be a phantom himself.[15] As Hardy recorded in his *Life*, 'For my part, if there is any way of getting a melancholy satisfaction out of life it lies in dying, so to speak, before one is out of the flesh; by which I mean putting on the manners of ghosts, wandering in their haunts, and taking their views of surrounding things' (July 1888; Hardy 1962, 209–10).

So what for Hardy is a ghost and what does it mean to be a ghost? If a ghost is a printed presence, it is also a 'visible essence', a phrase that, as we have seen in Chapter 2, has a strong Paterian ring. Hardy first used the phrase in *The Return of the Native* (1878) where, in Chapter 5 – a chapter in which critics have felt Pater's influence at work – he gives his famous portrait of Eustacia Vye: 'Assuming that the souls of men and women were visible essences, you could fancy the colour of Eustacia's soul to be flame-like'.[16] He used it again in a note of 4 March 1888 on novel-writing reproduced in his *Life*: 'Novel-writing as an art cannot go backward. Having reached the analytic stage, it must transcend it by going still further in the same direction. Why not by rendering as visible essences, spectres, etc., the abstract thoughts of the analytic school?' (Hardy 1962, 177). Underneath this entry, he added in the form of a later commentary: 'This notion was approximately carried out, not in a novel, but in the more appropriate medium of poetry, the supernatural framework of *The Dynasts* as also in smaller poems' (Hardy 1962, 177). An abstraction, virtually synonymous with the spectre, and inherently more suited to poetry, the 'visible essence', as in Paterian alchemy, is something condensed to its characterising essentials and an essential likeness. It also evokes Ruskin's statement in the second volume of *Modern Painters* that 'The virtue of the Imagination is its reaching, by intuition and intensity of gaze (not by reasoning but by its authoritative opening and revealing power), a more essential truth than is seen at the

15. The description of the phantom as 'the last of its race' suggests Hardy himself who, much to his regret, remained childless, and whose house, the rather gloomy Max Gate, is signified by 'That house in the trees with the shady lawn' (Hardy 1976, 474). Florence Hardy confirms this in a letter to John Cowper Powys of 26 October 1930. See Millgate 1996, 308.
16. David J. DeLaura and J. B. Bullen have pointed out that Hardy's description of Eustacia evokes Pater's Mona Lisa from his essay on Leonardo (DeLaura, 1967, 382–3; Bullen 1986, 103), but the adjective 'flame-like' is also Paterian, hailing from the Conclusion to *The Renaissance*: 'This at least of flame-like our life has' (Pater 1980, *Ren* 187).

surface of things' (Ruskin 1903–4, 4.284). If a ghost is a visible essence, to be a ghost is to be one's essential self or self-in-essence, to cast off extraneous matter, or superficial trappings and conventions, and to see beyond the immediate and the obvious. We can see why Hardy might well then readily identify the phantom with the writer and, especially, the poet. T. E. Lawrence evidently thought the elderly Hardy had succeeded in becoming a ghost, writing to Robert Graves in September 1923: 'Hardy is so pale, so quiet, so refined into an essence' (Lawrence 1964, 429–30). Hardy's ghost-making, whether of persons or objects, is also poetry-making, implying a kind of death in which the inessential is lost. If the imagination or intenser stare of the mind is what brings visible essence into view, loss or death is the pre-condition for the distillation or condensation of essence that activates the imaginative impulse. Thus in the poem 'When Dead' the speaker announces:

> It will be much better when
> I am under the bough
> I shall be more myself, Dear, then;
> Than I am now.
>
> (Hardy 1976, 721)

Robert Gittings has said that for Hardy 'Death . . . proved a stimulant whose effects did not so easily wear off' (Gittings 1978, 66), to which I would add that, as we shall see, death is also the imaginative stimulant that makes 'visible essence' or essential character appear.

Shades and silhouettes

> May 18 [1870]. Royal Academy. No. 118. 'Death of Ney', by Gérôme. The presence of Death makes the picture great.
>
> No. 985. 'Jerusalem', by the same. The *shadows only* of the three crucified ones are seen. A fine conception.
>
> (Hardy 1962, 76)

It is Hardy's imaginative belief in the visionary and the supernatural, a world that lies beyond optical verisimilitude, which occupies me in this conclusion where the poems I wish to explore are forms of cryptic portraiture which chart relations between the phenomenal and the visionary. Noticeable in most of these poems is Hardy's use of the silhouette which Tom Paulin has referred to as a mnemonic device (Paulin 1986, 107–20); an outline which calls to mind the familiar features of a well-known personage. Silhouettes occur naturally when individuals are seen, often from a distance, outlined against the sky or a lighter background, but they also constitute an important form of eighteenth- and nineteenth-century portraiture in which a profile view of the subject's head and shoulders is depicted either by a black paper cut-out or in black ink. Most fashionable in the period 1750–1850, these silhouette portraits were also, according to the *OED*, known as 'shades'; a word which is a particular favourite of Hardy's and which, like its Latin antecedent *umbra*, has the advantage of meaning both 'shadow' and 'ghost'. While the shade or silhouette recalls to memory the personage it represents, it is interesting for what it leaves out as much as for what it includes. An evocative outline which excludes the particularity of individual features, the silhouette is like a draft or sketch, a ghost of a drawing – that form of delineation also favoured by Vernon Lee in her re-routing of the sublime into the supernatural. The partial portraiture of the silhouette brings the subject to mind but, repressing the fullness of her presence, reminds us that she is not there. Thus, although as I have argued elsewhere (Maxwell 1997) all portraiture has a link with death, the silhouette has an even stronger relation in that it figures absence more graphically, so that where the subject of the representation is in fact dead, the silhouette becomes the shade of a shade. An archetypal female silhouette associated with death was imprinted early on Hardy's mind in August 1856. In a letter to Lady Hester Pinney of 20 January 1926, he recalls

> that unhappy woman Martha Brown [*sic*], whom I am ashamed to say I saw hanged, my only excuse being that I was but a youth, & had to be in the town at the time for other reasons . . . I remember what a fine figure she showed against the sky as she hung in the misty rain, & how the tight black silk gown set off her shape as she wheeled half-round & back.
>
> (Hardy 1978–88, 7.5)

In this gruesome but compelling recollection, Hardy literally watches Browne turning into a shadow of herself. But in this undoubtedly sexualised reminiscence she also seems to become the essence of nubile womanhood; for, if the empty outline of the shade figures absence, it can be also thought to offer a greater degree of visionary or imaginative potential in that it offers the sensitive observer the opportunity of projecting more freely his own memories, impressions, fantasies, and associations into the charged blank space of the silhouette; that is, it sums up what is important to him, or, as Hardy put it in his discussion of impressionism, '*what appeals to your own individual eye and heart in particular*' (Hardy 1962, 184). According to this view, the shade has the potential for a plenitude lacked by a more visually exacting resemblance as it functions as, to use Hardy's phrases, a 'visible essence' and not 'a photograph in words, that inartistic species of literary produce' (Hardy 1962, 177, 351).

The suggestive fragment or part-for-whole which prompts a fuller because *imaginative* vision is a staple of a visionary trend in nineteenth-century literature. Hardy habitually practised a synecdochic vision, declaring that 'The art of observation' lay in 'the seeing of great things in little things, the whole in the part – even the infinitesimal part' (Hardy 1962, 248), and that 'the would-be storyteller' required an 'intuitive power' that allowed him 'To see in half and quarter views the whole picture, to catch from a few bars the whole tune' (Hardy 1966b, 137). In his essay 'The Profitable Reading of Fiction' (1888), Hardy proposed that 'the appreciative, perspicacious reader' is one who is skilled at such synecdochic reading: 'He will see what his author is aiming at, and by affording full scope to his own insight, catch the vision which the writer has in his eye, and is endeavoring to project upon the paper, even while it half eludes him' (Hardy 1966d, 117). In her essay 'Thomas Hardy's Novels' (1928), Virginia Woolf sees Hardy employing in his fiction a kind of latent synecdochic appeal to the reader: 'It is as if Hardy himself were not quite aware of what he did, as if his consciousness held more than he could produce, and he left it for his readers to make out his full meaning and to supplement it from their own experience' (Woolf 1986–94, 4.510). In Hardy, as in other nineteenth-century writers such as Browning, Vernon Lee, and Lee-Hamilton, synecdoche is the figure that leads sight to vision, that tutors perception not just to register or document, but to make visible that which is normally unseen. It is well illustrated by Ruskin, commonly associated with more precisionist modes of representation, in the following moving passage from *Modern Painters* 3:

> It follows evidently from the first of these characters of the imagination, its dislike of substance and presence, that a picture has in some measure even an advantage with us in not being real. The imagination rejoices in having something to do, springs up with all its willing power, flattered and happy; and ready with its fairest colours and most tender pencilling, to prove itself worthy of the trust, and exalt into sweet supremacy *the shadow that has been confided to its fondness.* And thus, so far from its being at all an object to the painter to make his work look real, he ought to dread such a consummation as the loss of one of its most precious claims upon the heart. So far from striving to convince the beholder that what he sees is substance, his mind should be to what he paints as the fire to the body on the pile, burning away the ashes, leaving *the unconquerable shade* – an immortal dream.
> (Ruskin 1903–4, 5.184–5; my italics)

Ruskin describes the valuable nature of the sketch which, in complicity with the imagination, best preserves a cherished subject matter, but the deeply charged nature of his words and figures implies that the most desirable subject matter is a memorial likeness of a dead or absent beloved. If Ruskin unconsciously links the sketch or shade-drawing with a poignant play of absence and presence, then this too is present in an apocryphal history of representation where the drawn silhouette importantly foreshadows the evolution of painting. Pliny's *Natural History* (Bk 35) provides two accounts, the first being of a more general nature:

> The question as to the origin of the art of painting is uncertain and it does not belong to the plan of this work. The Egyptians declare that it was invented among themselves six thousand years before it passed over into Greece – which is clearly an idle assertion. As to the Greeks, some of them say that it was discovered at Sicyon, others in Corinth, but all agree that it began with tracing an outline round a man's shadow and consequently that pictures were originally done in this way.
> (Pliny 1961, 10.271)

In a second account, also set at Sicyon, Corinth, the first artist appears to be a woman, but her achievement is overshadowed by that of her father who subsumes her work into his claim to be the first sculptor:

> Enough and more than enough has now been said about painting. It may be suitable to append to these remarks something about the plastic art. It was through the service of that same earth that modelling portraits from clay was first invented by Butades, a potter of Sicyon, at Corinth. He did this owing to his daughter, who was in love with a young man; and she, when he was going abroad, drew in outline on the wall the shadow of his face thrown by a lamp. Her father pressed clay on this and made a relief, which he hardened by exposure to fire with the rest of his pottery; and it is said that this likeness was preserved in the Shrine of the Nymphs until the destruction of Corinth by Mummius.
> (Pliny 1961, 10.371–3)

David Allen's painting *The Origin of Drawing* (1775), in the National Gallery of Scotland, chooses to regard the woman as originary artist and shows her seated on her lover's knee while tracing his profile as it is shadowed on the wall. What is particularly interesting about this story is that the young woman captures her lover's likeness as a memorial likeness which will compensate her for his absence while he is abroad.

Shades and silhouettes evoke the forms of lost loved ones or absent individuals in a number of poems by Hardy. All the poems I shall discuss were written after the death of Emma Hardy in 1912, and the first two, 'The Figure in the Scene' and 'Why Did I Sketch' from *Moments of Vision* (Hardy 1976, 476, 477), have a special connection with drawing as the speaker describes sketches he has made of a woman who has since been 'called hence'. Biographical evidence can supply an actual sketch (Pinion 1968; Plate facing 339) which Hardy produced of Emma at Beeny Cliffs on a rainy August day in 1870, but it would be wrong to see the poem as a transcript of the sketch, for 'The Figure in the Scene' gives the woman a prominence which the sketch does not. She is clearly centre-stage in this drama as she seems confidently to organise the scene, electing to take a role whose importance her partner does not recognise at the time:

> It pleased her to step in front and sit
>   Where the cragged slope was green,

While I stood back that I might pencil it
  With her amid the scene; . . .

Yet the sketched woman, though immediately and painfully recognisable, is screened at three removes – by the cloak which protects her from the elements, by the curtaining drizzle of the rain, and by the stains watermarks have imposed on the drawing:

  And thus I drew her there alone,
    Seated amid the gauze
Of moisture, hooded, only her outline shown,
  With rainfall marked across.

The gauze metaphor was one that Hardy had used before in August 1876 when he noted, 'Rain: like a banner of gauze waved in folds across the scene' (Hardy 1978, 19). Joan Grundy has remarked on his fascination with the Victorian use of theatrical gauzes to obscure outline on stage, noting how he 'recommends them at the end of his Preface to *The Dynasts* as suitable to be used to "blur outlines" and thus "shut off the actual" in the "plays of poesy and dream" he surmises may be produced in the future', and she comments: 'Gauzes are for Hardy an intrinsic part of the human stage. Physically, in the form of mist or rain, they obscure or diminish vision' (Grundy 1979, 103, 105). Yet I would suggest that the gauze – in this poem 'the gauze / Of moisture' – while it obscures physical sight, intensifies vision. Together with the cloak, the blots on the paper, the gauze heightens the effect and impact of the woman's 'outline'. The gauze and other screening devices when viewed and read by the speaker stand in for what intervenes between him and the woman: the passage of time and death. Yet these things – time and death – do not detract from or diminish the figure but give it added emphasis. Death doubles the impact of the evocative outline giving it a power it did not possess when the speaker limned the woman's figure. Now a 'visible essence', the silhouette sums up and summons up the woman in all her ineffable power for the speaker so that

  her rainy form is the Genius still of the spot,
    Immutable, yea,
Though the place knows her no more, and has known her not
  Ever since that day.

Not only does she confront him with her own essential spirit but she becomes for him the *genius loci*, the tutelary divinity or presiding spirit of a place. The notion of the *genius loci* stems from classical mythology, but, as Hardy must have been aware, the attempt to capture the essence of a place in writing, something dear to his own heart, had recently been practised by writers such as Alice Meynell and Vernon Lee in short impressionistic essays gathered under titles such as *The Spirit of Place* (1896) and *Genius Loci: Notes on Places* (1899).[17] For the speaker, the woman comes before him not just as the essence of herself but as the essence of the place.

'Why Did I Sketch', the companion poem to 'The Figure in the Scene', returns compulsively to the sketch and 'a woman's silhouette'. This wryly ironic afterword is a half-hearted attempt at erasure as the speaker urges the reader not to repeat his mistake in thoughtlessly adding into his sketch a figure which will come to trouble him in the years thereafter:

> If you go drawing on down or cliff
>   Let no soft curve intrude
>   Of a woman's silhouette,
> But show the escarpments stark and stiff
>   As in utter solitude;
>   So shall you half forget.

But of course the speaker only adds to the power of the previous poem and the sketch it describes by retracing what he would erase or disfigure, thereby stressing its indelible impression; while the woman 'has ceased to be seen' in the phenomenal world, we know she dominates his imagination. His adjuration to the reader, evidently an adjuration to himself, shows that he can only 'half forget'; that is, he is doomed to remember. The defences he puts in place against the past, as suggested by the 'escarpments' of the projected sketch he recommends, serve merely to reinforce the sense of his vulnerability and bereavement, his 'utter solitude'. The poem becomes, in spite of itself, another testimony to Hardy's words about the mark of man on a landscape, its title ghosted by the realisation 'How could I not sketch?'

Hardy draws a different kind of sketch, that of a woman he has never seen, in his poem 'The Sunshade' (Hardy 1976, 490). Like the piece that precedes it, 'The Logs on the Hearth', this poem seems to be about resurrection. Here the speaker muses on the rusty spokes of an old parasol, which he discovers in a cleft in the rocks at the seaside. This skeleton-form acts as a trigger to the speaker's imagination and is reclothed and resurrected in his fantasy in a way that tacitly parallels Biblical narratives of divine creating power such as Ezekiel's vision of the renuited and refleshed bones (Ezekiel 37).[18]

> Ah – it's the skeleton of a lady's sunshade,
>   Here at my feet in the hard rock's chink,

17. Lee's *Genius Loci* went into a second (1907) and third edition (1908). In 1905 she brought out *The Enchanted Woods, and Other Essays on the Genius of Places*, which went into a second edition in 1910. See also her *The Spirit of Rome* (1906) and *The Sentimental Traveller: Notes on Places* (1908).
18. This Biblical allusion also lies behind Browning's accounts of the poet as resurrectionist in *The Ring and the Book*, 1.706–79, which Hardy may recall here.

Merely a naked sheaf of wires! –
Twenty years have gone with their livers and diers
Since it was silked in its white and pink.

Noonshine riddles the ribs of the sunshade,
No more a screen from the weakest ray;
Nothing to tell us the hue of its dyes,
Nothing but rusty bones at it lies
In its coffin of stone, unseen till to-day.

The deftly handled analogy of the parasol as 'skeleton' – the speaker refers to its 'ribs', its 'bones' and its 'coffin' – prepares the way for a process of embodiment as the speaker conjures up a version of the past. Such is the persuasive force of the speaker as he plunges headlong into his tale, it is hard not to see this as a genuine act of recovery rather than a flight of fancy. The recovered sunshade leads to speculations about its owner – we are asked to picture a pretty young woman with coquettish tendencies plotting her conquests at this fashionable seaside town:

Where is the woman who carried that sunshade
Up and down this seaside place? –
Little thumb bent against its stem,
Thoughts perhaps bent on a love-strategem,
Softening yet more the already soft face!

Then as a final *coup de grâce*, we are asked to speculate on the woman's possible death, on her once-attractive body, now too a skeleton:

Is the fair woman who carried that sunshade
A skeleton just as her property is,
Laid in the chink that none may scan?
And does she regret – if regret dust can –
The vain things thought when she flourished this?

The process of embodiment is inverted as the sunshade becomes abruptly a *memento mori* and the woman so vividly evoked is now consigned to the grave. A touch of the morality play enters as the innocent scene of the woman's flirtation is somewhat melodramatically reviewed as Vanity Fair and matter for her regret – 'if regret dust can'. The poem moves between light and dark as Hardy forces our attention upon the separate but juxtaposed 'sun' and 'shade' constituents of his title. From the gloom of the 'coffin of stone' that hides the parasol, we move to the sunlit idyll of the woman's careless youth and then back again to the darkness of the grave.

But, if we pause for reflection, we may also become aware that the woman herself is a 'sun-shade', a phantom and a sketch drawn by the speaker's daydreaming fantasy. Indeed we are reminded of the creative writer's ability to manipulate his fictions and his audience by the slightly sadistic way in which the speaker animates this girl only to kill her off, and by the calculated way in which he pulls at our heart-strings. No sooner have we been led to take an interest in this attractive new figure than we are rudely bereaved of her. Moreover the poem insists we accept its highly conjectural fantasy as a truth, a historical vignette with a moral; it allows us no space to demur with objections: that the owner of the parasol might have been other than the speaker describes her, older, plainer, with no interest in 'love-stratagems', or that, even as he dilates on her possible demise, she might be sitting comfortably at home, fair, fat, and forty, with a brood of children about her. Such prosaic alternatives are refused by the poem's masterful and masterly narrative, which presses ineluctably towards its desired conclusion. The poem, which works on the typical Hardy stratagem of a vision produced by a visual cue, testifies to the power of fictions and the way they are able to assume a reality of their own. The fleshing out of the skeleton-form of the parasol also acts as a kind of allegory of the fleshing out of the skeleton-form of the poem, a process that can reincarnate ghosts or make resurrections out of things that never existed. Although the grave is apparently a 'chink that none may scan', poetry and the poet do have the power to scan, to essentialise and capture phantoms in metrical form. In just such a way in 'After a Journey' does the substance of the verse allow the bereaved speaker to see his dead love 'Scanned across the dark space wherein I have lacked you' (Hardy 1976, 349).

The shade as a fiction of another sort occurs in Hardy's 'The Shadow on the Stone' (Hardy 1976, 530), another poem from *Moments of Vision*. A note by Hardy records that he began the poem in 1913 and finished it in 1916, and it is clearly one of many writings touched by the death of his first wife. The mysterious Druid stone mentioned in the first line of the poem had a biographical counterpart which Hardy found buried in his garden at Max Gate and had raised to ground level. Around the buried stone the excavators discovered 'a quantity of ashes and half charred bones' (Hardy 1962, 234). Clive Holland, a visitor to Max Gate in 1898, recorded that Hardy showed him the stone with the remark '"Do you believe in ghosts? . . . If you do you ought to see such manifestations here, on a moonlight night."' Ghosts and burnt offerings of a more personal nature may also have imprinted the stone on Hardy's memory, for the second Mrs Hardy reported to Irene Cooper Willis that '"Hardy found his wife burning all his love-letters to her behind that stone"' (Bailey 1970, 412). However, intriguing though they are, the poem does not need these biographical details. The stone, one of the most ancient marks of man on a landscape, brings with it a halo of associations concerning burial, sacrifice, and regeneration. It evokes the primitive, removing us from the polite middle-class Christianity of Hardy's day to a place where other beliefs are tolerated. The stone personified as 'brood[ing] . . . white and lone' gently intimates the speaker's own meditative emotion, yet simultaneously reminds us of the 'animism' of Hardy's use of the pathetic fallacy, a 'primitive' form of the imagination '"confusing persons and things" . . . common to the highest imaginative genius – that of the poet' and a vital constituent in poetic perception. The stone serves as a monument to a certain kind of imaginative vision exercised in the poem.

The poem's preoccupation with shadows also recalls the Druidic use of large standing-stones as sundials, shadow-clocks, and calendars. This primitive chronology suggests that the speaker experiences the time of the imagination, which is outside of ordinary time and keeps its own calendar. Certainly the shadow that falls on the stone hearkens back to an earlier time, which mysteriously gets printed on the present moment. The poem shows us the imagination in the process of ghost-making whereby a shadow is made into a shade. The undifferentiated shadows playing on the Druid stone are 'shaped in [the speaker's] imagining' into the shadow the lost woman was wont to cast: 'the shade that a well-known head and shoulders / Threw there when she was gardening'. 'Shade' here, evidently meaning shadow and ghost, also evokes silhouette drawing, typically of a head-and-shoulders view.

If the power of the speaker's imagination makes him see the shadow as a resemblance, the resemblance – the shade of a shade – makes him imagine that the woman he has loved and lost stands behind him. The speaker, determined to prolong this belief, protects this visionary image by refusing to look at it directly: 'I would not turn my head to discover / That there was nothing in my belief.' This encounter evokes the myth of Orpheus and Eurydice; Tom Paulin remarks of the speaker – 'Like Orpheus he wants to look back' (Paulin 1986, 59). But Paulin doesn't note how the speaker corrects Orpheus' misadventure. Orpheus, who has charmed his way through the Underworld in order to retrieve his dead wife, is allowed to take her home on the condition that he doesn't look back at her until she has safely followed him to the earth above. Orpheus should properly believe that his wife follows behind him, but, doubting, has to look to make sure and so loses her; Hardy's speaker should properly know that his lost love is not behind him, but, in order to preserve her imagined presence, forgoes the desired backward glance. It is his not looking at her which keeps her 'alive', defended from rational objectifying scrutiny. The poem testifies to the recreative power of imaginative vision over and against the empirical proofs of optical sight.

> Yet I wanted to look and see
> That nobody stood at the back of me;
> But I thought once more: 'Nay, I'll not unvision
> A shape which, somehow, there may be.'
> So I went on softly from the glade,

And left her behind me throwing her shade,
As she were indeed an apparition –
My head unturned lest my dream should fade.

The speaker does not see a genuine apparition face to face. Arguably then this is not a genuine visionary poem like Milton's Sonnet 23, also part inspired by Orpheus myth, in which the speaker beholds the transfigured likeness of his dead wife (see Maxwell 2001, 57–61). Seemingly Hardy's speaker cannot attain to this full vision and can only fabricate it by hints, guesses, and make-believe. But Hardy is not quite so clear-cut. The language of the final stanza is equivocal about the woman's presence, suggesting she is both provisional and real. The attribution of agency to her gives her a kind of authenticity even as it suggests that she is not a 'true' spectre: 'So I went on softly from the glade, / And left her behind me throwing her shade, / As she were indeed an apparition'. The poem might equally make us question if there is a real distinction between imagining and the visionary, or if they are simply points of degree on the same spectrum. Moreover, it tantalises the reader with that space at the back of the speaker's head – the space he won't look at with his corporeal eyes –which becomes aligned with the imaginative space in which he can produce images he chooses not to share with the reader. At the heart of the poem is a mysterious and intimate privacy, a withheld vision which the speaker can see and which we can't and which allures us by being ever out of reach.

The private vision that cryptically energises a poem and arrests the reader who is none the less able to register its latent presence is one of Hardy's special devices. Subliminally present in the 'The Figure in the Scene' and 'Why Did I Sketch' where only the speaker can properly recreate from the 'outline' the features of his dead love, it is most powerfully employed in the last poem I shall treat in this series. All the poems I have looked at are exercises in memorial shade or shadow-drawing, but, while the earlier poems draw the shades of dead women, this last one features a son mourned by his mother. The dedication of this particular woman's vision suggests that for Hardy the memorialising tendencies of the female gaze are no less potent than those of its male counterpart. Moreover this look of recovery is directed towards a shade which derives from Hardy's most literal and perhaps most fascinating rendering of the technique described by Pliny.

'The Whitewashed Wall' (Hardy 1976, 685–6), from *Late Lyrics and Earlier* (1922), is written in the form of a conversation in which two acquaintances of the woman cottager discuss her strange behaviour. One of them wants to know why her attention seems held by the chimney-corner wall, so the other explains that a friend drew her son's shadow-portrait there which the 'whitener' unthinkingly covered over when he came to whitewash the cottage wall. This second speaker also explains that the woman still intuits the presence of her son's portrait hidden underneath the paint and turns to it for consolation in his absence. That absence is implied to be terminal by the poem, which figures death in the reported apology of the whitener:

> 'Yes,' he said: 'My brush goes on with a rush,
>   And the draught is buried under;
> When you have to whiten old cots and brighten,
>   What else can you do, I wonder?'

The 'draught' is not simply erased but is 'buried under'; it lingers like a cadaver underneath the layering of paint, described by the second speaker as a shroud-like 'sheet of white'.

Hardy originally wrote the poem for *Reveille*, the government quarterly 'Devoted to the Disabled Soldier and Sailor'. The editor John Galsworthy had written to Hardy on 30 July 1918 to ask for a contribution. Hardy sent the poem in a letter dated 15 August 1918 and it was published in the November edition (Hardy 1985, 5.275–6). In the first published version, line 9 reads 'Well, her soldier-son cast his shadow there' (Hardy 1979, 686). But, when Hardy came to reprint the poem in *Late Lyrics and Earlier* (May 1922), he removed the obvious military reference as well as making one or two other smaller alterations. This emendation significantly alters the way we read the poem as it becomes impossible to age the son, who is defined solely by his relation to his mother. But, for those who know of its existence, the first version of Hardy's poem also lingers on buried under the later one. The word 'draught' is a Hardy variant on 'draft', the usual spelling for the word meaning both a rough sketch and military conscription. The 'draught / draft is buried under' becomes a beautifully subtle way of suggesting the son's demise in battle and also of alluding to the first *Reveille* version which lies inhearsed in the second, *Late Lyrics* poem.

The draught or shadow-drawing, the relic which conjures up the absentee, has precursors not only in Pliny but in Hardy's tender feeling for 'the mark of man' on a scene. In his commentary on 'The Whitewashed Wall', J. O. Bailey directs us to moments in *Two on a Tower* (Ch 28) and *The Woodlanders* (Ch 3) where Swithun's grandmother and Grace Melbury's father preserve marks and traces left by their loved ones (Bailey 1970, 494). I find another precursor to this poem in *Tess of the D'Urbervilles* (1891), which shows how affection can be aroused by the (albeit transitory) shadow of the beloved. Retty teases Izz about Angel Clare – '"I zid you kissing his shade' – and explains to Marian how, when Angel's shadow was cast on the wall close to Izz, she surreptitiously kissed 'the shade of his mouth' (Hardy 1974b, 175). Hardy seems to remember this scene when the woman, like a coy lover, turns in a 'shy soft way' to 'kiss to the chimney-corner wall' on which lies her son's submerged shadow-likeness. This shade-drawing, so cherished by the woman, is more than just a banal tracing; apparently it captures a 'lifelike semblance', a 'familiar look', and, just at the moment it disappears under the whitewash, it becomes, poignantly, 'a face'. The whitening, which becomes synonymous with death, has the strange effect of making the obliterated image more like and more powerful precisely because it can't be seen. But this is owing to the strength of the woman's determination to keep that face in view even if it is isn't actually visible. Although she was not the one who drew the shadow-drawing – that was the act of 'a friend' whose gender is not specified – it is her devotion which continually re-marks its presence and, refusing to abandon it, makes it a reality even to others. The speaker does not deride her belief as the hysterical fantasy of a bereaved woman but tenderly endorses it in the poem's last lines, when, as in earlier poems, the identity of the shade-portrait and the absent subject are merged – 'she knows he's there' – to suggest that the woman experiences an authentic vision of her son.

That vision, even when glimpsed at a remove, suggests the all-consuming nature of the woman's feeling for her son. As mentioned before, the *Late Lyrics* version does not specify whether the son is child or adult and the poem exploits this uncertainty in its last lines where Hardy delicately fuses eros, maternity, and mourning:

> But she knows he's there. And when she yearns
>   For him, deep in the labouring night,
> She sees him as close at hand, and turns
>   To him under his sheet of white.

Birth is figured in the 'labouring' night and the form beneath the sheet could be an infant's or, even more strangely, the body of a lover or mate. Thus embodied in the mother is the woman who tends to her infant, the woman who turns to her lover in the night, and the woman who lifts the shroud of her son in a perpetual wake that is his and her reawakening.

What is haunting about 'The Whitewashed Wall' is how the power of what is hidden charges the whole poem; a humble and prosaic interior is flooded by the strangest phantasmagoria. The wall, the site of the 'draught', lacks the mystery of the Druid stone, but it becomes just as uncanny under the intensity of a woman's visionary gaze. In the *Life*, Hardy records a notebook entry of 1886 in which he describes a process of revelation under conditions of extremity:

> *January* 2 . . . Cold weather brings out upon the faces of people the written marks of their habits, vices, passions, and memories, as warmth brings out on paper a writing in sympathetic ink. The drunkard looks still more a drunkard when the splotches have their margins made distinct by frost, the hectic blush becomes a

> stain now, the cadaverous complexion reveals the bone under, the quality of handsomeness is reduced to its lowest terms.
>
> (Hardy 1962, 177)[19]

This revelation of character is produced by a physical circumstance – intense cold – just as 'sympathetic' or invisible ink becomes visible when exposed to heat, but we realise that the kind of legibility which Hardy describes can be read only by an observer who has a particularly discriminating and penetrating way of looking. So too the poet inscribes the visionary ('the real being invisible optically') in a kind of 'sympathetic ink' which communicates only to an attuned sympathetic reader. In the *Life*, an entry adjoining the one quoted above shows that Hardy understands that the aesthetic revelation of the visionary essences of things must occur as a result of intensity: '*January* 3. My art is to intensify the expression of things, as is done by Crivelli, Bellini, etc., so that the heart and inner meaning is made vividly visible' (Hardy 1962, 177). Just as the press of mortality on Angel Clare makes him resemble the dead Christus of Crivelli, that intensely expressive painter – 'You could see the skeleton behind the man, and almost the ghost behind the skeleton. He matched Crivelli's dead *Christus*' (Hardy 1974b, 417) – so too in 'The Whitewashed Wall', as elsewhere in Hardy's poetry, death is the condition of extremity that acts as a stimulant, intensifying the stare of the mind or the imagination for writer and reader as much as for the woman in the poem. It is this kind of stare that activates the legibility of hidden draughts or 'sympathetic ink' which, in its gradual appearance on the page, looks as if it is emerging out of the paper, coming through from a 'beyond' on the other side. Just so the 'sheet' of paint that shrouds the son is permeated by the power of his image. Because the actual picture remains, like the son's familiar look, a family secret or familial property, we can't actually see the form of the dead as the woman can – 'She sees him close at hand' – but we sense the hint of a recovered outline, the image of an image, or shade of a shade, a presence shielded from direct view.

When sending his poem to Galsworthy, Hardy wrote 'The fact is that I cannot do patriotic poems very well – seeing the other side too much' (Hardy 1985, 5.275). Evidently 'the other side' means the enemy point of view or the death and destruction caused by war, but it also carries a ghostly meaning of the visionary world on the 'other side' of the 'material screen', the world which breaks into the phenomenal and alters its appearance, turning an attempt at a patriotic poem into a moment of vision. In such a way does Hardy achieve Shelley's aim to 'always seek in what I see the manifestation of something beyond the present & tangible object' (Shelley 1964, 2.47), and the words he

19. Compare the following entry in Rossetti's manuscript notebook: 'Days when the characters of men came out as strongly as secret writing exposed to fire' (Rossetti n.d. Ashley MS. 1410, Notebook 1, 4r, cited in McGann 1992, 169).

used to William Archer in an interview of 1901 are perhaps fitting ones with which to end this chapter and this book:

> But for my part I say in all sincerity, 'Better be inconvenienced by visitants from beyond the grave than see none at all.' The material world is so uninteresting, human life is so miserably bounded, circumscribed, cabin'd, cribb'd, confined. I want another domain for the imagination to expatiate in.
>
> (Archer 1904, 45)

References

Archives

The Rossetti Archive: www.rossettiarchive.org/.
Vernon Lee Papers, Colby College, Maine, Manuscript Collections.
Watts-Dunton Letterbooks, Rutgers University Special Collections.
Watts-Dunton. Proof of unpublished edition of poems. The British Library.

Primary Texts

Thomas Hardy

Hardy, Florence [and Thomas Hardy]. 1962. *The Life of Thomas Hardy 1840–1928.* London and Basingstoke: Macmillan.

Hardy, Thomas. 1966a. 'A Christmas Ghost-Story' (1899). In *Thomas Hardy's Personal Writings.* Ed. Harold Orel. Lawrence: University of Kansas Press. 201–2.

Hardy, Thomas. 1966b. 'The Science of Fiction' (1891). In *Thomas Hardy's Personal Writings.* Ed. Harold Orel. Lawrence: University of Kansas Press. 134–8.

Hardy, Thomas. 1966c. 'Memories of Church Restoration' (1906). In *Thomas Hardy's Personal Writings.* Ed. Harold Orel. Lawrence: University of Kansas Press. 203–18.

Hardy, Thomas. 1966d. 'The Profitable Reading of Fiction' (1888). In *Thomas Hardy's Personal Writings.* Ed. Harold Orel. Lawrence: University of Kansas Press. 110–33.

Hardy, Thomas. 1974a. *Jude the Obscure.* Intr. Terry Eagleton. Notes by P. N. Furbank. The New Wessex Edition. London and Basingstoke: Macmillan.

Hardy, Thomas. 1974b. *Tess of the D'Urbervilles.* Intr. P. N. Furbank. The New Wessex Edition. London and Basingstoke: Macmillan.

Hardy, Thomas. 1974c. *The Mayor of Casterbridge.* Ed. Ian Gregor. Notes by Bryn Caless. The New Wessex Edition. London and Basingstoke: Macmillan.

Hardy, Thomas. 1974d. *The Woodlanders.* Ed. David Lodge. The New Wessex Edition. London and Basingstoke.

Hardy, Thomas. 1976. *The Complete Poems.* Ed. James Gibson. London and Basingstoke: Macmillan.

Hardy, Thomas. 1978. *The Personal Notebooks of Thomas Hardy.* Ed. Richard H. Taylor. London and Basingstoke: Macmillan.

Hardy, Thomas. 1978–88. *The Collected Letters of Thomas Hardy.* Eds Richard Little Purdy and Michael Millgate. 7 vols. Oxford: Clarendon Press. Volume 1: *1840–1892* (1978); Volume 2: *1893–1901* (1980); Volume 3: *1902–1908* (1982); Volume 4: *1909–1913*

(1984); Volume 5: *1914–1919* (1985); Volume 6: *1920–1927* (1987); Volume 7: *1926–1927* (1988).

Hardy, Thomas. 1979. *The Variorum Edition of the Complete Poems*. Ed. James Gibson. London and Basingstoke: Macmillan.

Hardy, Thomas. 1985. *The Literary Notebooks of Thomas Hardy*. Ed. Lennart Björk. 2 vols. London and Basingstoke: Macmillan.

Hardy, Thomas. 1993. *Thomas Hardy: Selected Poems*. Ed. Tim Armstrong. Longman Annotated Texts. London and New York: Longman.

Hardy, Thomas. 1994. *'Studies, Specimens &c' Notebook*. Eds Pamela Dalziel and Michael Millgate. Oxford: Clarendon Press.

Hardy, Thomas. 1995. *The Complete Poetical Works of Thomas Hardy*. Ed. Samuel Hynes. 5 vols. Oxford: Clarendon Press. 1982–95. Volume 5 (1995).

Vernon Lee

Lee, Vernon. 1879. 'The Artistic Dualism of the Renaissance'. *Contemporary Review* 36 (September), 44–65. Reprinted as 'Symmetria Prisca' in *Euphorion: Being Studies of the Antique and Mediæval in the Renaissance*. 2 vols. London: T. Fisher Unwin. 1884. 1.167–214.

Lee, Vernon. 1880. 'Faustus and Helena: Notes on the Supernatural in Art'. *Cornhill Magazine* 42, 212–28. Reprinted in *Belcaro: Being Essays on Sundry Aesthetical Questions*. London: W. Satchell & Co. 1881. 70–105, and in *Hauntings and Other Fantastic Tales*. Eds Catherine Maxwell and Patricia Pulham. Peterborough, Ontario: Broadview Press. 2006. 291–319.

Lee, Vernon. 1881. *Belcaro: Being Essays on Sundry Æsthetical Questions*. London: W. Satchell & Co.

Lee, Vernon. 1884a. *Euphorion: Being Studies of the Antique and Mediæval in the Renaissance*. 2 vols. London: T. Fisher Unwin.

Lee, Vernon. 1884b. *Miss Brown: A Novel*. 3 vols. Edinburgh and London: W. Blackwood and Sons.

Lee, Vernon. 1884c. 'The Outdoor Poetry of the Middle Ages and the Renaissance'. *Contemporary Review* 45 (January), 25–42. Reprinted in *Euphorion: Being Studies of the Antique and Mediæval in the Renaissance*. 2 vols. London: T. Fisher Unwin. 1884. 1.109–66.

Lee, Vernon. 1885. 'A Dialogue on Novels'. *Contemporary Review* 48 (September), 378–401. Reprinted as 'On Novels' in *Baldwin: Being Dialogues on Views and Aspirations*. London: T. Fisher Unwin. 1886. 185–245.

Lee, Vernon. 1886. *Baldwin: Being Dialogues on Views and Aspirations*. London: T. Fisher Unwin.

Lee, Vernon. 1887. *Juvenilia: Essays on Sundry Æsthetical Questions*. 2 vols. London: T. Fisher Unwin.

Lee, Vernon. 1890. *Hauntings: Fantastic Stories*. London: William Heinemann.

Lee, Vernon. 1894a. *Au Pays du Vénus*. Preface by Frédéric Masson. Paris: Librairie de La Société des Gens de Lettres.

Lee, Vernon. 1894b. *Althea: A Second Book of Dialogues on Aspirations and Duties*. London: London: Osgood, McIlvaine.

Lee, Vernon. 1895. *Renaissance Fancies and Studies*. London: Smith, Elder, & Co.

Lee, Vernon. 1897. *Limbo and Other Essays*. London: Grant Richards.

Lee, Vernon. 1904a. 'The Nature of Literature'. *Contemporary Review* 86 (September), 377–91; 645–61. Reprinted in *The Handling of Words and Other Studies in Literary Psychology*. London: John Lane, The Bodley Head. 1923.

Lee, Vernon. 1904b. *Pope Jacynth and Other Fantastic Tales*. London: John Lane, The Bodley Head.

Lee, Vernon. 1905. 'Of Hardy and Meredith'. *Westminster Gazette* (20 July), 2–3.

Lee, Vernon. 1908a. *The Sentimental Traveller: Notes on Places*. London: John Lane.

Lee, Vernon. 1908b. *Limbo and Other Essays to which is now added 'Ariadne in Mantua'*. London: John Lane, The Bodley Head.

Lee, Vernon. 1909. *Laurus Nobilis: Chapters on Art and Life*. London and New York: John Lane, The Bodley Head.

Lee, Vernon. 1921a. 'Dionysus in the Euganean Hills: W. H. Pater In Memoriam'. *Contemporary Review* 120 (September 1921), 346–53.

Lee, Vernon. 1921b. 'Dom Sylvanus'. *English Review* 33 (November), 365–71.

Lee, Vernon. 1923. *The Handling of Words and Other Studies in Literary Psychology*. London: John Lane, The Bodley Head.

Lee, Vernon. 1924. Introduction. *Art and Man: Essays and Fragments*. By Clementina Anstruther-Thomson. With Twenty Illustrations. London: John Lane, The Bodley Head. 3–112.

Lee, Vernon. 1927a. *For Maurice: Five Unlikely Stories*. London: John Lane, The Bodley Head.

Lee, Vernon. 1927b. 'J. S. S: In Memoriam'. In *John Sargent*. Ed. The Hon. Evan Charteris, KC. London: William Heinemann. 233–55.

Lee, Vernon. 1937. *Vernon Lee's Letters*, with a preface by her executor Irene Cooper Willis. Privately printed.

Lee, Vernon. 2006. *Hauntings and Other Fantastic Tales*. Eds Catherine Maxwell and Patricia Pulham. Peterborough, Ontario: Broadview Press.

Eugene Lee-Hamilton

Lee-Hamilton, Eugene. 1878. *Poems and Transcripts*. Edinburgh and London: William Blackwood.

Lee-Hamilton, Eugene. 1880. *Gods, Saints, and Men*. London: William Satchell.

Lee-Hamilton, Eugene. 1882. *The New Medusa, and Other Poems*. London: Elliot Stock.

Lee-Hamilton, Eugene. 1884. *Apollo and Marsyas, and Other Poems*. London: Elliot Stock.

Lee-Hamilton, Eugene. 1886. Selection. *Sonnets of this Century*. Ed. William Sharp. London: Walter Scott. 92–5, 291.

Lee-Hamilton, Eugene. 1888. *Imaginary Sonnets*. London: Elliot Stock.

Lee-Hamilton, Eugene. 1894. *Sonnets of the Wingless Hours*. London: Elliot Stock.

Lee-Hamilton, Eugene. 1903. *Dramatic Sonnets, Poems, and Ballads: Selections from the Poems of Eugene Lee-Hamilton*. With an Introduction by William Sharp. London and Newcastle-on-Tyne: Walter Scott.

Lee-Hamilton, Eugene. 1909. *Mimma Bella*. Introduction by Annie Lee-Hamilton. London: William Heinemann.

Lee-Hamilton, Eugene. 1915. Selection introduced by John Addington Symonds. In *The Poets and the Poetry of the Nineteenth Century*. Ed. Alfred H. Miles. 11 vols. Volume 7: *Robert Bridges and Contemporary Poets*. London: Routledge. 241–56.

Lee-Hamilton, Eugene. 1928. Selection in *An Anthology of 'Nineties' Verse*. Ed. A. J. A. Symons. London: Elkin Mathews and Marrot. 104–8.

Lee-Hamilton, Eugene. 1969. Selection in *The Penguin Book of Victorian Verse.* Ed. George Macbeth. Harmondsworth: Penguin Books. 314–19.

Lee-Hamilton, Eugene. 1984. *Gods, Saints, & Men. The New Medusa. Sonnets of the Wingless Hours.* Degeneration and Regeneration Texts of the Premodern Era. Eds Ian Fletcher and John Stokes. New York and London: Garland Publishing.

Lee-Hamilton, Eugene. 1987a. Selection in *British Poetry and Prose 1870–1905.* Ed. Ian Fletcher. Oxford: Oxford University Press. 152–7.

Lee-Hamilton, Eugene. 1987b. Selection in *The New Oxford Book of Victorian Verse.* Ed. Christopher Ricks. Oxford and New York: Oxford University Press. 527–9.

Lee-Hamilton, Eugene. 1997. Selection in *The Penguin Book of Victorian Verse.* Ed. Daniel Karlin. London: Allen Lane, Penguin Books. 663.

Lee-Hamilton, Eugene. 1999. Selection in *The Broadview Anthology of Victorian Poetry.* Eds Thomas J. Collins and Vivienne J. Rundle. Broadview Anthologies. Peterborough, Ontario: Broadview Press.

Lee-Hamilton, Eugene. 2000. Selection in *The Victorians: An Anthology of Poetry and Poetics.* Ed. Valentine Cunningham. Oxford: Blackwell Publishers. 883–7.

Lee-Hamilton, Eugene. 2002. *Selected Poems of Eugene Lee-Hamilton (1845–1907): A Victorian Craftsman Rediscovered.* Ed. MacDonald P. Jackson. Lewiston and Lampeter: Edwin Mellen Press.

Lee-Hamilton, Eugene. 2004. Selection in *Victorian Poetry: An Annotated Anthology.* Ed. Francis O'Gorman. Blackwell Annotated Anthologies. Oxford: Blackwell Publishing. 545–56.

Walter Pater

Pater, Walter. 1873. *Studies in the History of the Renaissance.* Oxford: Macmillan.

Pater, Walter. 1883. 'Dante Gabriel Rossetti.' In *The English Poets: Selections with Critical Introductions by Various Writers.* Ed. Thomas Humphry Ward. London: Macmillan & Co., Vol. 4: W*ordsworth to Rossetti.* 631–41.

Pater, Walter. 1887. 'Vernon Lee's "Juvenilia"'. *Pall Mall Gazette* (5 August), 5.

Pater, Walter. 1889. 'Aesthetic Poetry'. *Appreciations.* London and New York: Macmillan, 213–27. Reprinted in *Selected Writings of Walter Pater.* Ed. Harold Bloom. A Signet Classic. New American Library: New York, Scarborough, Ontario, and London. 1974. 190–8.

Pater, Walter. 1892. Introduction. *The Purgatory of Dante Alighieri: An Experiment in Literal Verse Translation.* Tr. Charles Lancelot Shadwell. London: Macmillan. xiii–xxviii.

Pater, Walter. 1910. *The Library Edition of the Works of Walter Pater.* London: Macmillan.

Pater, Walter. 1961. *The Renaissance: Studies in Art and Poetry.* Ed. Kenneth Clark. Illustrated. The Fontana Library. London and Glasgow: Collins.

Pater, Walter. 1970. *Letters of Walter Pater.* Ed. Lawrence Evans. Oxford and London: Oxford University Press.

Pater, Walter. 1973. 'Coleridge's Writings' (1866). *Essays on Literature and Art.* Ed. Jennifer Uglow. Dent: London. 1–26.

Pater, Walter. 1974a. *Selected Writings of Walter Pater.* Ed. Harold Bloom. A Signet Classic. New American Library: New York, Scarborough, Ontario, and London.

Pater, Walter. 1974b. 'Poems by William Morris' (1868). *Pre-Raphaelitism: A Collection of Critical Essays.* Ed. James Sambrook. Chicago and London: University of Chicago Press. 105–17.

Pater, Walter. 1980. *The Renaissance: Studies in Art and Poetry: The 1893 Text.* Ed. Donald L. Hill. Berkeley, Los Angeles, and London: University of California Press.
Pater, Walter. 1985. *Marius the Epicurean.* Ed. Michael Levey. Penguin Classics. Harmondsworth: Penguin.
Pater, Walter. 1986. *The Renaissance.* Ed. Adam Phillips. World's Classics. Oxford and New York: Oxford University Press.
Pater, Walter. 1995. *Gaston de Latour.* The Revised Text. Ed. Gerald Monsman. Greenboro, NC: ELT Press.

Dante Gabriel Rossetti

Rossetti, Dante Gabriel. 1875. 'Proserpina'. *Athenæum* (28 August), 273.
Rossetti, Dante Gabriel. 1881. *Ballads and Sonnets.* London: Ellis and White.
Rossetti, Dante Gabriel. 1911. *The Works of Dante Gabriel Rossetti.* Ed. William Michael Rossetti. London: Ellis.
Rossetti, Dante Gabriel. 1961. *Poems.* Ed. Oswald Doughty. Everyman's Library. London and Toronto: J. M. Dent.
Rossetti, Dante Gabriel. 1965–67. *The Letters of Dante Gabriel Rossetti.* Ed. Oswald Doughty and John Robert Wahl. 4 vols. Oxford: Clarendon Press.
Rossetti, Dante Gabriel. 2002–. *The Correspondence of Dante Gabriel Rossetti.* Ed. William Fredeman et al. 6 vols to date. Cambridge: Boydell & Brewer. Volume 1: *1835–1854* (2002); Volume 2: *1855–1862* (2002); Volume 3: *1863–1867* (2003); Volume 4: *1868–1870* (2004); Volume 5: *1871–1872* (2005); Volume 6: *1873–1874* (2006).
Rossetti, Dante Gabriel. 2003. *Collected Poetry and Prose.* Ed. Jerome McGann. New Haven and London: Yale University Press.
Rossetti, Dante Gabriel. 2007. *The House of Life: A Sonnet-Sequence by Dante Gabriel Rossetti.* A Variorum Edition with an Introduction and Notes. Ed. Roger C. Lewis. Cambridge: Boydell & Brewer.

Theodore Watts-Dunton

Watts-Dunton, Walter Theodore. 1881. 'The Sonnet's Voice'. *Athenæum* (17 September), 361.
Watts-Dunton, Walter Theodore. 1882a. 'Heine' (later titled 'A Dead Poet'). *Athenæum* (25 March), 380. Reprinted in Caine, T. Hall. *Recollections of Dante Gabriel Rossetti.* London: Elliot Stock. 1882. 297.
Watts-Dunton, Walter Theodore. 1882b. Review of Eugene Lee-Hamilton's *The New Medusa and Other Poems. Athenæum* (16 December), 809.
Watts-Dunton, Walter Theodore. 1883. 'The Truth about Rossetti'. *The Nineteenth Century,* 404–23.
Watts-Dunton, Walter Theodore. 1885. 'Poetry'. *The Encyclopædia Britannica: A Dictionary of Arts, Sciences and General Literature.* 25 vols. 9th edition. Edinburgh: Adam and Charles Black, 1875–89. Vol. 19: *PHY to PRO.* 256–73.
Watts-Dunton, Walter Theodore. 1886. 'Rossetti'. *The Encyclopædia Britannica: A Dictionary of Arts, Sciences and General Literature.* 25 vols. 9th edition. Edinburgh: Adam and Charles Black, 1875–89. Vol. 20: *PRU* to *ROS.* 857–60.

Watts-Dunton, Walter Theodore. 1887a. 'Sonnet'. *The Encyclopædia Britannica: A Dictionary of Arts, Sciences and General Literature.* 25 vols. 9th edition. Edinburgh: Adam and Charles Black, 1875–89. Vol. 22: *SIB-SZO.* 261–3.

Watts-Dunton, Walter Theodore. 1887b. Review of *The Collected Works of Dante Gabriel Rossetti,* 2 vols. *Athenæum* (12 March), 346–8.

Watts-Dunton, Walter Theodore. 1891. 'Sonnet'. *Chambers's Encyclopædia: A Dictionary of Universal Knowledge. A New Edition.* 10 vols. London and Edinburgh and Philadelphia, William and Robert Chambers and J. P. Lippincott, 1888–92. Vol. 9: *Round to Swansea.* 571–2.

Watts-Dunton, Walter Theodore. 1892. 'Apparent Pictures: I. Coleridge; II. Life, The Khan'. *Athenæum* (19 March), 373.

Watts-Dunton, Walter Theodore. 1893. Introduction to George Borrow. *Lavengro: The Scholar, The Gypsy, The Priest.* Minerva Library of Famous Books. London: Ward, Lock & Co. vii–xxiv.

Watts-Dunton, Walter Theodore. 1894. 'Mrs Augusta Webster'. *Athenæum* (15 September), 335.

Watts-Dunton, Walter Theodore. 1897. *The Coming of Love: Rhoda Boswell's Story and Other Poems.* London: John Lane, The Bodley Head.

Watts-Dunton, Walter Theodore. 1900. Introduction to *The Romany Rye: A Sequel to 'Lavengro' by George Borrow.* London: Ward, Lock & Co. ix–xx.

Watts-Dunton, Walter Theodore. 1908–9. 'Rossettiana: A Glimpse of Rossetti and Morris at Kelmscott'. *The English Review* (December–March), 323–32.

Watts-Dunton, Walter Theodore. 1911a. 'Poetry' (Revised essay). *The Encyclopædia Britannica: A Dictionary of Arts, Sciences, Literature and General Information.* 11th edition. 29 vols. Cambridge and New York: Cambridge University Press. Volume 21: *PAYN to POLKA,* 877–890.

Watts-Dunton, Walter Theodore. 1911b. 'Rossetti' (Revised essay). *The Encyclopædia Britannica: A Dictionary of Arts, Sciences, Literature and General Information.* 11th edition. 29 vols. Cambridge and New York: Cambridge University Press. Volume 23: *REF to SAI.* 749–51.

Watts-Dunton, Walter Theodore. 1911c. 'Sonnet' (Revised essay). *The Encyclopædia Britannica: A Dictionary of Arts, Sciences, Literature and General Information.* 11th edition. 29 vols. Cambridge and New York: Cambridge University Press. Volume 25: *SHUV–SUBL.* 414–16.

Watts-Dunton, Walter Theodore. 1912. Preface. *Flint and Feather: The Complete Poems of E. Pauline Johnson (Tekahionwake).* Toronto: The Musson Book Company. vii–xvi.

Watts-Dunton, Walter Theodore. n.d. *The Coming of Love: Rhoda Boswell's Story and Other Poems,* 10th edition. London: John Lane, The Bodley Head, no date but after 1913.

Watts-Dunton, Walter Theodore. 1914. *Aylwin.* World's Classics. London: Humphrey Milford, Oxford University Press.

Watts-Dunton, Walter Theodore. 1915. Selection in *The Poets and Poetry of the Nineteenth Century: William Morris to Robert Buchanan.* Ed. Alfred H. Miles. London: George Routledge & Sons. 255–80.

Watts-Dunton, Walter Theodore. 1916a. *Old Familiar Faces.* London: Herbert Jenkins, Limited.

Watts-Dunton, Walter Theodore. 1916b. *Poetry and the Renascence of Wonder.* London: Herbert Jenkins Limited.

Secondary texts

Abraham, Lyndy. 1990. *Marvell and Alchemy*. Aldershot and Brookfield, VT: Scolar Press.

Abraham, Lyndy. 1998. *A Dictionary of Alchemical Imagery*. Cambridge, New York, and Melbourne: Cambridge University Press.

Anonymous. 1890. 'Mesmerism and Hypnotism'. *The Quarterly Review* 171 (July–October), 234–59.

Anonymous. 1886. 'Paris Day by Day'. *Daily Telegraph* (12 November), 5.

Anonymous. 1898. Review of *Aylwin*. *Athenæum* (22 October), 561–2.

Anonymous. 1898. 'Literary Gossip'. *Athenæum* (12 November), 679.

Anonymous. 1898. Review of *Aylwin*. *The Bookman* (December), 310–11.

Arago, Dominique. 1834. *Historical Eulogium on James Watt and an Essay on Machinery; considered in regard to the Prosperity of the Working Classes*. Read before the Academy of Sciences at Paris, on the 8th December, 1833 by M. Arago. Tr. Hyde Clarke, Esq. London: John Weal & R. Groombridge. n.d. [1834?].

Arago, Dominique. 1839. *Historical Eloge of James Watt by M. Arago*. Tr. James Patrick Muirhead. London: John Murray.

Archer, William. 1904. 'Conversation II with Mr. Thomas Hardy'. In *Real Conversations*. London: William Heinemann. 29–50.

Armstrong, Tim. 2000. *Haunted Hardy: Poetry, History, Memory*. Basingstoke: Palgrave Macmillan.

Arnold, Matthew. 1979. *The Poems of Matthew Arnold*. Ed. Kenneth Allott. 2nd edition. Miriam Allott. London and New York: Longman.

Austin, Alfred. 1970. 'Mr Swinburne' (1869). In *Swinburne: The Critical Heritage*. Ed. Clyde K. Hyder. London: Routledge & Kegan Paul. 92–111.

Babinski, Joseph. 1886. *Recherches servant à établir que certaines manifestations hystériques peuvent être transférées d'une sujet à une autre sous l'influence de l'aimant*. Paris: A. Delahaye & E. Lecrosnier.

Bäckman, Sven. 2001. *The Manners of Ghosts: A Study of the Supernatural in Thomas Hardy's Short Poems*. Gothenburg Studies in English 82. Göteborg: Acta Universitatis Gotheburgenisis.

Bailey, J. O. 1970. *The Poetry of Thomas Hardy: A Handbook and Commentary*. Chapel Hill: University of North Carolina Press.

Bann, Stephen (ed.). 2004. *The Reception of Walter Pater in Europe*. Athlone Critical Traditions Series. London and New York: Thoemmes Continuum, 2004.

Barolsky, Paul. 1987. *Walter Pater's Renaissance*. University Park and London: Pennsylvania State University Press.

Bates, Milton J. 1985. *Wallace Stevens: A Mythology of Self*. Berkeley, LA, and London: University of California Press.

Bell, Mackenzie. 1915. Introduction to Watts-Dunton selection. In *The Poets and Poetry of the Nineteenth Century: William Morris to Robert Buchanan*. Ed. Alfred H. Miles. London: George Routledge & Sons. 255–80.

Bentley, D. M. R. 1990a. 'From Allegory to Indeterminacy: Dante Gabriel Rossetti's Positive Agnosticism. Part 1'. *Dalhousie Review* 70.1, 70–106.

Bentley, D. M. R. 1990b. 'From Allegory to Indeterminacy: Dante Gabriel Rossetti's Positive Agnosticism. Part 2'. *Dalhousie Review* 70.2, 146–68.

Bickley, Pamela. 2001. '"How They Met Themselves": Rossetti and Yeats in the 1890s'. *Yeats Annual* 14: *Yeats and the Nineties*. Ed. Warwick Gould. Basingstoke: Palgrave. 50–103.

Bini, Benedetta. 2004. ' "The sterile ascetic of beauty": Pater and the Italian *fin de siècle*'. In *The Reception of Walter Pater in Europe*. Ed. Stephen Bann. Athlone Critical Traditions Series. London and New York: Thoemmes Continuum. 19–33.

Bizzotto, Elisa. 2004. 'Pater's Reception in Italy: A General View'. In *The Reception of Walter Pater in Europe*. Ed. Stephen Bann. Athlone Critical Traditions Series. London and New York: Thoemmes Continuum. 62–86.

Blanchot, Maurice. 1981. 'Two Versions of the Imaginary'. In *The Gaze of Orpheus and Other Literary Essays*. Ed. P. Adams Sitney. Tr. Lydia Davis. New York: Station Hill. 79–89.

Blanchot, Maurice. 1982. 'The Book to Come'. In *The Sirens' Song: Selected Essays by Maurice Blanchot*. Ed. Gabriel Jospovici. Tr. Sacha Rabinovitch. Brighton: Harvester. 227–48.

Blavatsky, Helena Petrovina. 1877. *Isis Unveiled: A Master-Key to the Mysteries of Ancient and Modern Science and Theology*. 2 vols. New York: J. W. Baton.

Bloom, Harold. 1973. 'Dante Gabriel Rossetti'. In *The Oxford Anthology of English Literature*. Eds Frank Kermode and John Hollander. 2 vols. Oxford University Press, New York. 2.1402–3.

Boos, Florence. 1976. *The Poetry of Dante G. Rossetti: A Critical Reading and Source Study*. The Hague and Paris: Mouton.

Boos, Florence. 2004. 'Dante Gabriel Rossetti's Poetic Daughters: *Fin de Siècle* Women Poets and the Sonnet'. In *Outsiders Looking In: The Rossettis Then and Now*. Eds David Clifford and Lauren Roussillon. London: Anthem Press. 253–81.

Borrow, George. 1893. *Lavengro: The Scholar, The Gypsy, The Priest*. With an introduction by Theodore Watts-Dunton. Minerva Library of Famous Books. London: Ward, Lock & Co. vii–xxiv.

Borrow, George. 1900. *The Romany Rye: A Sequel to 'Lavengro' by George Borrow*, with special introduction by Theodore Watts-Dunton. London: Ward, Lock & Co. ix–xx.

Brake, Laurel. 2006. 'Vernon Lee and the Pater Circle'. In *Vernon Lee: Decadence, Ethics, Aesthetics*. Eds Catherine Maxwell and Patricia Pulham. Houndmills, Basingstoke, and New York: Palgrave Macmillan. 40–57.

Brake, Laurel, and Small, Ian (eds). 1991. *Pater in the 1990s*. Greenboro, NC: ELT Press. 205–15.

Brake, Laurel, Higgins, Lesley, and Williams, Carolyn (eds). 2002. *Walter Pater: Transparencies of Desire*. Greenboro, NC: ELT Press.

Bronfen, Elisabeth. 1992. *Over Her Dead Body: Death, Femininity and the Aesthetic*. Manchester: Manchester University Press.

Brown, Oliver Madox. 1873. *Gabriel Denver*. London: Smith, Elder, & Co.

Browning, Robert. 1951. *Dearest Isa: Robert Browning's Letters to Isa Blagden*. Ed. Edward C. McAleer. Austin, TX and Edinburgh: University of Texas Press and Thomas Nelson & Sons Ltd.

Browning, Robert. 1966. *Learned Lady: Letters from Robert Browning to Mrs Thomas FitzGerald*. Ed. Edward C. McAleer. Cambridge, MA: Harvard University Press.

Browning, Robert. 1971. 'Essay on Chatterton'. Ed. Donald Smalley. In *The Complete Works of Robert Browning*. Gen. Ed. Roma A. King. 16 vols. Athens, OH and Waco, TX: Ohio University Press, 1969–98. 3.159–79.

Browning, Robert. 1981. *The Poems*. Ed. John Pettigrew. 2 vols. Harmondsworth: Penguin.

Browning, Robert. 1996. Exchange with Ruskin in Woolford, John, and Karlin, Daniel. *Robert Browning*. Studies in 18th and 19th Century Literature. New York and London: Longman. 252–9.

Browning, Robert. 2001. *The Ring and the Book*. Ed. Thomas J. Collins and Richard D. Altick. Peterborough, Ontario: Broadview.

Buchanan, Robert. 1871. 'The Fleshly School of Poetry: Mr. D. G. Rossetti'. *Contemporary Review* 18 (October), 334–50. Reprinted in *Critical Essays on Dante Gabriel Rossetti*. Ed. David G. Riede. New York: G. K. Hall & Co. 1992. 24–39.

Buchanan, Robert. 1872. *The Fleshly School of Poetry and Other Phenomena of the Day*. London: Strahan & Co.

Buchanan, Robert. 1887. 'A Note on Dante Gabriel Rossetti' (1883). *A Look Round Literature*. London: Ward and Downey. 152–61.

Bullen, J. B. 1981. 'Pater and Ruskin: Two Contrasting Views'. In *Walter Pater: An Imaginative Sense of Fact: A Collection of Essays*. Ed. Philip Dodd. London and Totowa, NJ: Frank Cass and Company. 55–73.

Bullen, J. B. 1986. *The Expressive Eye: Fiction and Perception in the Work of Thomas Hardy*. Oxford: Clarendon Press.

Bullen, J. B. 1997. *The Pre-Raphaelite Body: Fear and Desire in Painting, Poetry and Criticism*. Oxford: Clarendon Press.

Burke, Edmund. 1987. *A Philosophical Enquiry into the Origins of Our Ideas of the Sublime and the Beautiful*. Ed. James T. Boulton. Oxford: Basil Blackwell.

Bygrave, Stephen. 1997. *Samuel Taylor Coleridge*. Writers and Their Work. Plymouth: Northcote House.

Caine, T. Hall. 1882a. *Recollections of Dante Gabriel Rossetti*. London: Elliot Stock.

Caine, T. Hall (ed). 1882b. *Sonnets of Three Centuries: A Selection*. London. Elliot Stock.

Caine, T. Hall. 1990. *Recollections of Rossetti* (1928). Introduction by Jan Marsh. London, Sydney, Auckland, and Johannesburg: Century.

Carr, Comyns J. W. 1914. 'With Rossetti in Cheyne Walk'. In *Coasting Bohemia*. London: Macmillan & Co. 42–55.

Carson, Anne. 2002. *If Not, Winter: Fragments of Sappho*. New York: Vintage.

Cenni, Serena, and Bizzotto, Elisa (eds). 2006. *Vernon Lee e Firenze settant'anni dopo*. Consilio Regionale Toscana: Florence.

Chapman, Alison, 1999. 'Mesmerism and Agency in the Courtship of Elizabeth Barrett and Robert Browning'. *Victorian Literature and Culture* 27, 303–19.

Chapman, Alison, and Stabler, Jane. 2003. *Unfolding the South: Nineteenth-century British Women Writers and Artists in Italy*. Manchester: Manchester University Press.

Christ, Carol. 1975. *The Finer Optic: The Aesthetic of Particularity in Victorian Poetry*. New Haven and London: Yale University Press.

Christ, Carol, and Jordan, John O. (eds). 1995. *Victorian Literature and the Victorian Visual Imagination*. Berkeley, Los Angeles and London: University of California Press.

Clifford, David, and Roussillon, Lauren (eds). 2004. *Outsiders Looking In: The Rossettis Then and Now*. London: Anthem Press.

Colby, Vineta. 2003. *Vernon Lee: A Literary Biography*. Charlottesville and London: University of Virginia Press.

Coleridge, S. T. 1974. *Poems*. Ed. John Beer. Everyman's Library. London and Melbourne: Dent.

Coleridge, S.T. 1975. *Biographia Literaria*. Everyman's Library. London and Melbourne: Dent.

Collins, Thomas J., and Rundle, Vivienne J. (eds). 1999. *The Broadview Anthology of Victorian Poetry*. Broadview Anthologies. Peterborough, Ontario: Broadview Press.

Colvin, Sidney. 'Dante Gabriel Rossetti' (1921). *Memories and Notes of Poems and Places 1852–1912*. London: Edward Arnold & Co. 60–75.

Corrigan, Beatrice. 1962. 'Giovanni Ruffini's Letters to Vernon Lee 1875–9'. *English Miscellany* 13, 179–240.

Crary, Jonathan. 1990. *Techniques of the Observer: On Vision and Modernity in the Nineteenth Century*. Cambridge, MA: MIT Press.

Croft-Cooke, Rupert. 1967. *Feasting With Panthers: A New Consideration of Some Late Victorian Writers*. London: W. H. Allen.

Cunningham, Valentine (ed.). 2000. *The Victorians: An Anthology of Poetry and Poetics*. Oxford: Blackwell Publishers.

Curtis, Gregory. 2005. *Disarmed: The Story of the Venus de Milo*. Stroud: Sutton Publishing.

Daley, Kenneth. 2001. *The Rescue of Romanticism: Walter Pater and John Ruskin*. Athens, OH: Ohio University Press.

Daley, Kenneth. 2006. Review of *Nervous Reactions: Victorian Recollections of Romanticism* (2004), eds Joel Faflak and Julia M. Wright. *Victorian Studies* 34.2, 551–3.

Davies, Charles Maurice. 1875. *Mystic London; or, Phases of Occult Life in the Metropolis*. London: Tinsley Bros.

Dawson, P. M. S. 1986. '"A Sort of Natural Magic": Shelley and Animal Magnetism'. *Keats–Shelley Review* 1, 15–34.

DeLaura, David J. 1967. 'The "Ache of Modernism" in Hardy's Later Novels'. *English Literary History* 34, 380–99.

Dellamora, Richard. 1990. *Masculine Desire: The Sexual Politics of Victorian Aestheticism*. Chapel Hill and London: University of North Carolina Press.

Djikstra, Bram. 1986. *Idols of Perversity: Fantasies of Feminine Evil in Fin-de-Siècle Culture*. New York and Oxford: Oxford University Press.

Donne, John. 1971. *The Complete English Poems*. Ed. A. J. Smith. Harmondsworth: Penguin.

Donoghue, Denis. 1995. *Walter Pater: Lover of Strange Souls*. New York: Alfred A. Knopf.

Doughty, Oswald. 1960. *A Victorian Romantic: Dante Gabriel Rossetti*. 2nd edition. London: Oxford University Press.

Douglas, James. 1904. *Theodore Watts-Dunton: Poet Novelist Critic*. London: Hodder & Stoughton.

Drew, Rodger. 2007. *The Stream's Secret: The Symbolism of Dante Gabriel Rossetti*. Cambridge: The Lutterworth Press.

Duclaux, A. Mary F. Robinson. 1907. 'In Casa Paget: A Retrospect. In Memoriam Eugène Lee-Hamilton'. *Country Life* 28, 935–7.

Dunn, H. Treffry. 1904. *Recollections of Dante Gabriel Rossetti and His Circle*. Ed. Gale Pedrick. London: Elkin Matthews.

Eccles, Wilson. 1900. Review of *Aylwin*. *Primitive Methodist Quarterly* 22 (January), 99–109.

Ehrenzweig, Anton. 1975. *The Psychoanalysis of Artistic Vision and Hearing: An Introduction to a Theory of Unconscious Perception*. 3rd ed. London: Sheldon Press.

Eliot, T. S. 1920. *The Sacred Wood: Essays on Poetry and Criticism*. London: Methuen.

Eliot, T. S. 1932. *Selected Essays 1917–1932*. London: Faber.

Evangelista, Stefano-Maria. 2002. '"Outward Nature and The Moods of Men": Romantic Mythology in Pater's Essays on Dionysus and Demeter'. In *Walter Pater: Transparencies of Desire*. Eds Laurel Brake, Lesley Higgins, and Carolyn Williams. Greenboro, NC: ELT Press. 107–18.

Evangelista, Stefano-Maria. 2003. 'Walter Pater's Romantic Hellenism'. University of Oxford D.Phil.

Evangelista, Stefano-Maria. 2006. 'Vernon Lee and the Gender of Aestheticism'. In *Vernon Lee: Decadence, Ethics, Aesthetics*. Eds Catherine Maxwell and Patricia Pulham. Houndmills, Basingstoke, and New York: Palgrave Macmillan. 91–111.

Evangelista, Stefano. *Aestheticism and the Greeks*. Forthcoming from Palgrave Macmillan.

Faflak, Joel, and Wright, Julia M. (eds). 2004. *Nervous Reactions: Victorian Recollections of Romanticism*. Albany: State University of New York.

Falzon, Alex R. 2006. 'Eugene Lee-Hamilton, Violet Paget and the "Sonnet-mania" in Tuscany'. In *Vernon Lee e Firenze settant'anni dopo*. Eds Serena Cenni and Elisa Bizzotto. Florence: Consilio Regionale Toscana. 195–208.

Fletcher, Ian (ed.). 1987. *British Poetry and Prose 1870–1905*. Oxford: Oxford University Press.

Flint, Kate. 2000. *The Victorians and the Visual Imagination*. Cambridge: Cambridge University Press.

Fredeman, William. 1971. 'Prelude to the Last Decade: Dante Gabriel Rossetti in the Summer of 1872'. *Bulletin of the John Rylands Library* 53 (1970–71), 75–121; 272–328. Reprinted in part in *The Correspondence of Dante Gabriel Rossetti*. Ed. William Fredeman et al. 6 vols to date. Cambridge: Boydell & Brewer. 2002–. Volume 5: *1871–1872* (2005). 207–69.

Freud, Sigmund. 1888. Review of Heinrich Obersteiner's *Der Hypnotismus* (1887). *Szentralbatt für Physiologie* 1 (4 February), 632–3.

Freud, Sigmund. 1984a. 'On Narcissism: An Introduction' (1914). *The Pelican Freud Library*. 15 vols. Eds Angela Richards and Albert Dickson. Tr. James Strachey. Harmondsworth: Penguin, 1973–86. Volume 11: *On Metapsychology*. 59–97.

Freud, Sigmund. 1984b. 'Beyond the Pleasure Principle' (1920). *The Pelican Freud Library*. 15 vols. Eds Angela Richards and Albert Dickson. Tr. James Strachey. Harmondsworth: Penguin, 1973–86. Volume 11: *On Metapsychology*. 269–338.

Fulford, Tim. 2004. 'Conducting the Vital Fluid: The Politics and Poetics of Mesmerism in the 1790s'. *Studies in Romanticism* 43 (Spring), 57–78.

Fuller, Peter. 1980. *Art and Psychoanalysis*. London: Writers and Readers Publishing Cooperative.

Fussell, Peter. 1979. *Poetic Meter & Poetic Form*. Rev. edition. New York: Random House.

Gardner, Burdett. 1987. *The Lesbian Imagination (Victorian Style): A Psychological and Critical Study of 'Vernon Lee'*. New York and London: Garland.

Gelpi, Barbara Charlesworth. 1982. 'The Feminization of D. G. Rossetti'. In *The Victorian Experience: The Poets*. Ed. Richard A. Levene. Athens, OH: Ohio University Press. 94–114.

Getsy, David J. 2004. '"Hard Realism": The Thanatic Corporeality of Edward Onslow Ford's Shelley Memorial'. In *Body Doubles: Sculpture in Britain, 1877–1905*. New Haven and London: The Paul Mellon Centre for Studies in British Art/Yale University Press. 119–41.

Gittings, Robert. 1978. *The Older Hardy*. London: Heinemann.

Gooch, G. P. 1901. *The Annals of Politics and Culture, 1492–1899*. Introductory note by Lord Acton. Cambridge: Cambridge University Press.

Gosse, Edmund. 1882. 'Dante Gabriel Rossetti'. *The Century: A Popular Quarterly* 24. 5 (September), 718–26.

Gosse, Edmund. 1896. 'Walter Pater'. *Critical Kit-Kats*. London: William Heinemann. 239–71.

Graham, Walter. 1930. *English Literary Periodicals*. New York: Thomas Nelson & Sons.

Gregory, Eileen. 1997. *H.D. and Hellenism: Classic Lines.* Cambridge: Cambridge University Press.

Gregory, Horace. 1954. 'The Romantic Inventions of Vernon Lee'. Introduction to *The Snake Lady and Other Stories by Vernon Lee.* New York: Grove.

Gregory, William. 1877. *Animal Magnetism; or, Mesmerism and Its Phenomena.* 2nd edition. London: William H. Harrison.

Groome, Francis Hindes. 1898. Review of *Aylwin. The Bookman* 15 (November), 37–9.

Grundy, Joan. 1979. *Hardy and the Sister Arts.* London and Basingstoke: Macmillan.

Gunn, Peter. 1964. *Vernon Lee: Violet Paget 1856–1935.* London: Oxford University Press.

Hake, Thomas Gordon. 1890. *The New Day: Sonnets.* Ed. with a Preface by W. Earl Hodgson. The Rosslyn Series. London: Remington & Co.

Hake, Thomas Gordon. 1892. *Memoirs of Eighty Years.* London: Richard Bentley & Sons.

Hake, Thomas St. E. 1914. Appendix 2 to Watts-Dunton, Walter Theodore. *Aylwin.* World's Classics. London: Humphrey Milford, Oxford University Press. 493–7.

Hake, Thomas, and Arthur Compton-Rickett. 1916. *The Life and Letters of Theodore Watts-Dunton.* 2 vols. London: T. C. & E. C. Jack, Ltd.

Hake, Thomas, and Arthur Compton-Rickett. 1918. *The Letters of Algernon Charles Swinburne With Some Personal Recollections.* London: John Murray.

Hardy, Emma. 1979. *Some Recollections.* Introduction by Robert Gittings. Oxford: Oxford University Press.

Harrrington, Anne. 1988a. 'Metals and Magnets in Medicine: Hysteria, Hypnosis, and Medical Culture in fin-de-siècle Paris'. *Psychological Medicine* 18, 21–38.

Harrington, Anne. 1988b. 'Hysteria, Hypnosis, and the Lure of the Invisible: The Rise of Neo-Mesmerism in *fin-de-siècle* French Psychiatry'. In *The Anatomy of Madness: Essays in the History of Psychiatry.* Eds W. F. Bynum, Roy Porter, and Michael Shepherd. 3 vols. London and New York: Routledge. Volume 3: *The Asylum and its Psychiatry.* 226–46.

Hawthorne, Nathaniel. 1995. *The Marble Faun.* Ed. Malcolm Bradbury. The Everyman Library. London: Dent.

Heine, Heinrich. 1892. *The Gods in Exile.* In *The Works of Heinrich Heine.* Tr. Charles Godfrey Leland et al. 12 vols. London: William Heinemann, 1892–1905. Volume 6. 295–377.

Hersey, G. L. 1986. 'St. Cecily and the Lady of the Tomb: Rossetti's Double Works of Art'. In *The Pre-Raphaelite Poets.* Ed. Harold Bloom. Modern Critical Views. New York, New Haven, and Philadelphia: Chelsea House Publishers. 37–42.

Hobsbaum, Philip. 1996. *Metre, Rhythm and Verse Form.* The Critical Idiom. London: Routledge.

Holmes, John. 2004. 'Pursuing the Well-Beloved: Thomas Hardy, Jocelyn Pearston and the School of Rossetti'. In *Outsiders Looking In: The Rossettis Then and Now.* Eds David Clifford and Lauren Roussillon. London: Anthem Press. 237–51.

Holmes, John. 2005. *Dante Gabriel Rossetti and the Late Victorian Sonnet Sequence: Sexuality, Belief and the Self.* The Nineteenth Century. Aldershot and Burlington, VT: Ashgate.

Holmes, Richard. 1987. *Shelley: The Pursuit* (1974). Harmondsworth: Penguin.

Holmes, Richard. 1990. *Coleridge: Early Visions.* Harmondsworth: Penguin.

Holmes, Oliver Wendell. 1883. *Elsie Venner: A Romance of Destiny* (1861). Boston and New York: Houghton Mifflin and Co.

Hopkins, Gerard Manley. 1959. *The Journals and Papers of Gerard Manley Hopkins.* Ed. Humphry House and Graham Storey. London: Oxford University Press.

Hough, Graham. 1961. *The Last Romantics* (1947). University Paperbacks. London and New York: Methuen and Barnes & Noble.

Hunt, Chandos Leigh. 1876. *A Treatise on All the Known Uses of Organic Magnetism, Phenomenal and Curative.* London: James Burns.

Hyder, Clyde K. (ed.). 1970. *Swinburne: The Critical Heritage.* London: Routledge & Kegan Paul.

Hynes, Samuel. 1961. *The Pattern of Hardy's Poetry.* Chapel Hill: University of North Carolina University Press.

Inman, Billie Andrew. 1981. 'The Intellectual Context of Walter Pater's "Conclusion"'. In *Walter Pater: An Imaginative Sense of Fact: A Collection of Essays.* Ed. Philip Dodd. London and Totowa, NJ: Frank Cass and Company. 12–30.

James, Henry. 1962. 'Travelling Companions' (1870). In *The Complete Tales of Henry James 1864–1910.* 12 vols. Ed. Leon Edel. London: Rupert Hart-Davis, 1962–64. Volume 2: *1868–1872.* 171–225.

James, William. 1901. *The Principles of Psychology.* London: Macmillan & Co.

Joseph, Gerhard. 1992. *Tennyson and the Text.* Cambridge: Cambridge University Press.

Kane, Mary Patricia. 2004. *Spurious Ghosts: The Fantastic Tales of Vernon Lee.* Rome: Carocci.

Karlin, Daniel (ed.). 1997. *The Penguin Book of Victorian Verse.* London: Allen Lane, Penguin Books.

Keats, John. 1958. *The Letters of John Keats 1814–1821.* Ed. Hyder E. Rollins. Cambridge, MA: Harvard University Press.

Keats, John. 1970. *The Complete Poems.* Ed. Miriam Allott. London and New York, Longman.

Kermode, Frank. 1986. *Romantic Image* (1957). London: Ark Paperbacks.

Kintner, Elvan (ed.). 1960. *The Letters of Robert Browning and Elizabeth Barrett Barrett.* 2 vols. Cambridge, MA: The Belknap Press of Harvard University Press.

Knoepflmacher, U. C. 1993. 'Hardy Ruins: Female Spaces and Male Designs'. In *The Sense of Sex: Feminist Perspectives on Hardy.* Ed. Margaret R. Higgonet. Urbana and Chicago: University of Illinois. 107–31.

Kramer, Dale. 1999. *The Cambridge Companion to Thomas Hardy.* Cambridge: Cambridge University Press.

Laity, Cassandra. 1996. *H. D. and the Victorian Fin de Siècle: Gender, Modernism, Decadence.* Cambridge: Cambridge University Press.

Larkin, Philip. 1983. 'The Poetry of Hardy' (1968). *Required Writing: Miscellaneous Pieces 1955–1982.* London and Boston: Faber. 175–6.

Lawrence, D.H. 1986. *Study of Thomas Hardy and Other Essays.* Ed. Bruce Steele. Introduction by Melvin Bragg. London and Glasgow: Grafton Books.

Lawrence, T. E. 1964. *The Letters of T. E. Lawrence.* Ed. David Garnett. London: Spring Books.

Leask, Nigel. 1992. '"Shelley's Magnetic Ladies": Romantic Mesmerism and the Politics of the Body'. In *Beyond Romanticism: New Approaches to Texts and Contexts 1780–1832.* Eds Stephen Copley and John Whale. London and New York: Routledge. 53–78.

Leavis, F. R. 1952. *The Common Pursuit.* London: Chatto & Windus.

Leighton, Angela. 1992. *Victorian Women Poets: Writing against the Heart.* Hemel Hempstead: Harvester Wheatsheaf.

Leighton, Angela. 2003. 'Resurrections of the Body: Women Writers and the Idea of the Renaissance'. In *Unfolding the South: Nineteenth-century British Women Writers and Artists in Italy.* Eds Alison Chapman and Jane Stabler. Manchester: Manchester University Press. 222–38.

Luys, J. B. 1890. 'Du transfert comme methode thérapeutique dans le traitement des maladies nerveuses'. *Revue d'Hypnologie Théorique et Practique*, 39–48.

Lyon, Harvey T. 1955. 'The Deep Reverberation of a Bell: The Life and Poetry of Eugene Lee-Hamilton'. PhD dissertation, Harvard University.

Lyon, Harvey T. 1957. 'A Publishing History of the Writings of Eugene Lee-Hamilton'. *Papers of the Bibliographical Society of America* 51, 141–59.

Macbeth, George. 1962. 'Lee-Hamilton and the Romantic Agony'. *Critical Quarterly* 4, 141–51.

Macbeth, George (ed.). 1969. *The Penguin Book of Victorian Verse*. Harmondsworth: Penguin Books.

McGann, Jerome. 1974. 'Rossetti's Significant Details' (1969). In *Pre-Raphaelitism: A Collection of Critical Essays*. Ed. James Sambrook. Chicago and London: University of Chicago Press. 230–42.

McGann, Jerome. 1992. 'Dante Gabriel Rossetti and the Betrayal of Truth' (1988). In *Critical Essays on Dante Gabriel Rossetti*. Ed. David G. Riede. New York: G. K. Hall & Co. 169–90.

McGann, Jerome. 2000. *Dante Gabriel Rossetti and The Game That Must Be Lost*. New Haven and London: Yale University Press.

McGann, Jerome (ed.). 2003. *Dante Gabriel Rossetti: Collected Poetry and Prose*. New Haven and London: Yale University Press.

McGrath, F. C. 1986. *The Sensible Spirit: Walter Pater and the Modernist Paradigm*. Tampa: University of Florida Press.

Marsh, Jan. 2005. *Dante Gabriel Rossetti: Painter and Poet* (1999). A Phoenix Paperback. London: Orion Books Ltd.

Matthews, Samantha. 2004. *Poetical Remains: Poets' Graves, Bodies, and Books in the Nineteenth Century*. Oxford: Oxford University Press.

Maxwell, Catherine. 1993. 'Devious Symbols: Dante Gabriel Rossetti's Purgatorio'. *Victorian Poetry* 31.1, 19–40.

Maxwell, Catherine. 1997. 'From Dionysus to Dionea: Vernon Lee's Portraits'. *Word & Image* 13.3 (July–September), 253–69.

Maxwell, Catherine. 2001. *The Female Sublime from Milton to Swinburne: Bearing Blindness*. Manchester and New York: Manchester University Press.

Maxwell, Catherine. 2003. 'Vernon Lee and the Ghosts of Italy.' In *Unfolding the South: Nineteenth-century British Women Writers and Artists in Italy 1789–1900*. Eds Alison Chapman and Jane Stabler. Manchester: Manchester University Press. 201–21.

Maxwell, Catherine. 2004. '"It once should save as well as kill": D. G. Rossetti and the Feminine'. In *Outsiders Looking In: The Rossettis Then and Now*. Eds David Clifford and Lauren Roussillon. London: Anthem Press. 223–36.

Maxwell, Catherine. 2006a. *Swinburne*. Writers and Their Work. Plymouth: Northcote House.

Maxwell, Catherine. 2006b. 'Vernon Lee and Eugene Lee-Hamilton'. In *Vernon Lee: Decadence, Ethics, Aesthetics*. Eds Catherine Maxwell and Patricia Pulham. Basingstoke and New York: Palgrave Macmillan. 21–39.

Maxwell, Catherine and Pulham, Patricia (eds). 2006a. *Vernon Lee: Decadence, Ethics, Aesthetics*. Basingstoke and New York: Palgrave Macmillan.

Maxwell, Catherine and Pulham, Patricia. 2006b. 'Introduction'. In *Vernon Lee: Decadence, Ethics, Aesthetics*. Eds Catherine Maxwell and Patricia Pulham. Basingstoke and New York: Palgrave Macmillan. 1–20.

Meisel, Perry. 1980. *The Absent Father: Walter Pater and Virginia Woolf.* Yale University Press: New Haven and London.
Meisel, Perry. 1987. *The Myth of the Modern: A Study of British Literature and Criticism after 1850.* New Haven and London: Yale University Press.
Meredith, George. 1970. *The Letters of George Meredith.* Ed. C. L. Cline. 3 vols. Oxford: Clarendon Press.
Mermin, Dorothy. 1986. 'The Damsel, the Knight and the Victorian Women Poet'. *Critical Inquiry* 31 (Autumn), 64–80.
Michelangelo Buonarroti. 1950. *The Sonnets of Michelangelo.* Italian text with English Translation by John Addington Symonds. Plymouth: Vision Books.
Michelangelo Buonarroti. 1991. *The Poetry of Michelangelo.* Ed. James M. Saslow, New Haven and London: Yale University Press.
Miller, J. Hillis. 1982. *Fiction and Repetition: Seven English Novels.* Oxford: Basil Blackwell.
Millgate, Michael. 1985. *Thomas Hardy: A Biography* (1982). Oxford Paperbacks. Oxford: Oxford University Press.
Millgate, Michael (ed.). 1996. *Letters of Emma and Florence Hardy.* Oxford: Clarendon Press.
Millgate, Michael. 2004. *Thomas Hardy: A Biography Revisited.* Oxford: Oxford University Press.
Milner, Marion. 1957. *On Not Being Able to Paint.* 2nd edition. Oxford: Heinemann Educational.
Milton, John. 1971. *Paradise Lost.* Ed. Alastair Fowler. London: Longman.
Mourey, Gabriel. 1895. *Passé Le Detroit: La Vie et L'Art à Londres.* Paris: Paul Ollendorf.
Mourey, Gabriel. 1896. *Across the Channel: Life and Art in London.* Tr. Georgina Latimer. London: George Allen.
Munich, Adrienne. 1989. *Andromeda's Chains: Gender and Interpretation in Victorian Literature and Art.* New York: Columbia University Press.
Myers, F. W. H. 1883. 'Rossetti and the Religion of Beauty'. *Cornhill Magazine* 47, 213–24. Reprinted in *Essays Modern*, London: Macmillan & Co, 1885. 312–34, and in *Critical Essays on Dante Gabriel Rossetti.* Ed. David G. Riede. New York: G. K. Hall & Co. 1992. 46–57.
Nead, Lynda. 1988. *Myths of Sexuality: Representation of Women in Victorian Britain.* Oxford: Basil Blackwell.
Nead, Lynda. 1992. *The Female Nude: Art, Obscenity and Sexuality.* London: Routledge.
Nicholl, Charles. 1980. *The Chemical Theatre.* London, Henley, and Boston: Routledge & Kegan Paul.
Nicoll, LLD, Rev. W. Robertson. 1898. 'The Significance of Aylwin'. *Contemporary Review* (December), 798–809.
Notopoulos, James A. 1969. *The Platonism of Shelley: A Study of Platonism and the Poetic Mind.* New York: Octagon Books.
O'Gorman, Francis (ed.). 2004. *Victorian Poetry: An Annotated Anthology.* Blackwell Annotated Anthologies. Oxford: Blackwell Publishing.
Orage, Alfred William. 1935. 'A Self-Made Critic: Watts-Dunton'. In *Selected Essays and Critical Writings.* Eds. Herbert Read and D. Saurat. London: Allen. 29–31.
Østermark-Johansen, Lene. 1998. *Sweetness and Strength: The Reception of Michelangelo in Late Victorian England.* Aldershot and Vermont: Ashgate.
Østermark-Johansen, Lene. 2002. 'Serpentine Rivers and Serpentine Thought: Flux and Movement in Walter Pater's Leonardo Essay'. *Victorian Literature and Culture* 30.2, 455–82.

Ovid. *Metamorphoses*. 1946. Tr. Frank Justus Miller. Loeb Classical Library. 2nd edition. 2 vols. London and Cambridge, MA: William Heinemann and Harvard University Press.

Owen, Alex. 1990. *The Darkened Room: Women, Power and Spiritualism in Late Victorian England*. Philadelphia: University of Pennsylvania Press.

Paglia, Camille. 1991. *Sexual Personae: Art and Decadence from Nefertiti to Emily Dickinson* (1990). Harmondsworth: Penguin Books.

Paulin, Tom. 1986. *The Poetry of Perception*. 2nd edition. Basingstoke: Macmillan.

Pearce, Lynne. 1991. *Woman/Image/Text: Readings in Pre-Raphaelite Art and Literature*. Hemel Hempstead: Harvester Wheatsheaf.

Perry, Ruth. 1984. Introduction. *Mothering the Mind: Twelve Studies of Writers and Their Silent Partners*. Ed. Ruth Perry and Martine Watson Brownley. New York: Holmes. 3–24.

Perry, Seamus. 2002. 'The Talker'. In *The Cambridge Companion to Coleridge*. Ed. Lucy Newlyn. Cambridge: Cambridge University Press. 103–25.

Phelan, Joseph. 2005. *The Nineteenth-Century Sonnet*. Basingstoke and New York: Palgrave Macmillan.

Phillips, Adam. 1986. Introduction to Walter Pater. *The Renaissance*. World's Classics. Oxford and New York: Oxford University Press. vii–xviii.

Phillips, Adam. 1988. *Winnicott*. Fontana Modern Masters. London: Fontana Press.

Pinion, F. B. 1968. *A Hardy Companion*. London: Macmillan.

Plato. 1875. *The Dialogues of Plato*. Tr. Benjamin Jowett. 2nd edition. 5 vols. Oxford: Clarendon Press.

Plato. 1962. *The Statesman, Philetus, Ion*. Tr. Harold N. Fowler and W. R. M. Lamb. Loeb Classical Library. London and Cambridge, MA: William Heinemann and Harvard University Press.

Pliny. *Natural History*. 1961. Tr. H. Rackham. 10 vols. London and Cambridge, MA: William Heinemann and Harvard University Press. 1958–62. Volume 10.

Polidori, John. 1911. *The Diary of John William Polidori*. Ed. W. M. Rossetti. London: Elkin Mathews.

Potts, Alex. 2000. 'Pungent Prophecies of Art: Symonds, Pater, and Michelangelo'. In *John Addington Symonds: Culture and the Demon Desire*. Ed. John Pemble. Basingstoke and London: Macmillan Press. 102–21.

Pound, Ezra. 1954. *Literary Essays of Ezra Pound*. Ed. T. S. Eliot. Norfolk, CT: New Directions.

Pound, Ezra. 1960. *Guide to Kulchur*. London: Peter Owen.

Pound, Ezra. 1977. *Collected Early Poems of Ezra Pound*. Ed. Michael John King. London: Faber & Faber.

Praz, Mario. 1970. *The Romantic Agony*. Tr. Angus Davidson. 2nd ed. with a Foreword by Frank Kermode. Oxford and New York: Oxford University Press.

Prins, Yopie. 2004. 'Voice Inverse'. *Victorian Poetry* 42.1 (Spring), 43–60.

Psomiades, Kathy Alexis. 1997. *Beauty's Body: Femininity and Representation in British Aestheticism*. Stanford, CA: Stanford University Press.

Pulham, Patricia. 2006. 'Duality and Desire in *Louis Norbert*'. In *Vernon Lee: Decadence, Ethics, Aesthetics*. Eds Catherine Maxwell and Patricia Pulham. Basingstoke and New York: Palgrave Macmillan. 123–42.

Pulham, Patricia. 2008. *Art and the Transitional Object in Vernon Lee's Supernatural Tales*. Aldershot and Burlington, VT: Ashgate.

Rees, Joan. 1981. *The Poetry of Dante Gabriel Rossetti: Modes of Self-Expression*. Cambridge: Cambridge University Press.

Richardson, James. 1988. *Vanishing Lives: Style and Self in Tennyson, D. G. Rossetti, Swinburne and Yeats.* Charlottesville: University Press of Virginia.
Ricks, Christopher (ed.). 1987. *The New Oxford Book of Victorian Verse.* Oxford and New York: Oxford University Press.
Riede, David. 1983. *Dante Gabriel Rossetti and the Limits of Victorian Vision.* Ithaca: Cornell University Press.
Riede, David G. (ed.). 1992a. *Critical Essays on Dante Gabriel Rossetti.* New York: G. K. Hall & Co.
Riede, David. 1992b. *Dante Gabriel Rossetti Revisited.* Twayne's English Authors Series. New York and Toronto: Twayne Publishers and Maxwell Macmillan Canada, Inc.
Rilke, Rainer Maria. 1960. *Selected Works.* 2 vols. London: The Hogarth Press, 1954–60. Volume 2: *Poetry.* Tr. J. B. Leishman.
Robb, Nesca. 1935. *Neoplatonism of the Italian Renaissance.* London: Grant Allen & Unwin.
Robertson, M.B., M.R.C.P.E, George M. 1892. 'Hypnotism at Paris and Nancy: Notes of a Visit'. *The Journal of Mental Science* 38 (October), 494–531.
Roellinger, F. X. 1965. 'Intimations of Winckelmann in Pater's *Diaphaneitè*'. *English Language Notes* 2, 277–82.
Rosenberg, John. 2005. 'Walter Pater and the Art of Evanescence'. In *Elegy for an Age: The Presence of the Past in Victorian Literature.* London: Anthem Press. 187–215.
Rossetti, William Michael. 1870. Memoir. *The Complete Poetical Works of Percy Bysshe Shelley.* Ed. with Notes and a Memoir by William Michael Rossetti. 2 vols. London: E. Moxon, Son, & Co. 1.xxix–clxxix.
Rossetti, William Michael (ed.). 1895. *Dante Gabriel Rossetti: His Family Letters, With a Memoir by William Michael Rossetti.* 2 vols. London: Ellis and Elvey.
Rossetti, William Michael. 1911a. Preface. *The Works of Dante Gabriel Rossetti.* London: Ellis. vii–xxi.
Rossetti, William Michael. 1911b. Introduction. *The Diary of John William Polidori.* London: Elkin Mathews. 1–24.
Rothenstein, William. 1931. *Men and Memories: Recollections of William Rothenstein 1872–1900.* London: Faber & Faber.
Ruck, Carl A. P. and Staples, Danny. 1994. *The World of Classical Myth: Gods and Goddesses, Heroines and Heroes.* Durham, CA: Carolina Academic Press.
Ruskin, John. 1903–4. *The Works of John Ruskin.* Eds Alexander Cook and E. T. Wedderburn. 39 vols. London and New York: George Allen and Longmans, Green and Co., 1903–12. Volume 4: *Modern Painters* 2 (1903). Volume 5: *Modern Painters* 3 (1904).
Ruskin, John. 1958. *The Diaries of John Ruskin.* Ed. Joan Evans and John Howard Whitehouse. 3 vols. Oxford: Clarendon Press. 1956–59. Volume 2: *1848–1873.*
Saintine, Xavier Boniface. 1837. *Picciola, Or, Captivity Captive.* Tr. Mrs C. F. Gore [attrib.]. 2 vols. London: Henry Colburn.
Saintine, Xavier Boniface. 1866. 'Picciola; or, the Prison Flower. A Tale'. In *Masterpieces of Foreign Literature.* London: Charles Griffin & Co. 289–339.
Sambrook, James (ed.). 1974. *Pre-Raphaelitism: A Collection of Critical Essays.* Chicago and London: University of Chicago Press.
Santayana, George. 1968. 'The Poetry of Barbarism'. In *Selected Writings of George Santayana.* Ed. Norman Henfrey. 2 vols. Cambridge: Cambridge University Press. 1.84–116.
Schor, Naomi. 1987. *Reading in Detail: Aesthetics and the Feminine.* New York and London: Methuen.

Segal, Hannah. 1952. 'A Psycho-Analytical Approach to Æsthetics'. *International Journal of Psychoanalysis* 33, 196–207.
Segal, Hannah. 1975. 'Art and the Inner World'. *Times Literary Supplement* no. 3827 (18 July), 800–1.
Seiler, R. M. (ed.). 1987. *Walter Pater: A Life Remembered.* Calgary, Alberta: University of Calgary Press.
Shakespeare, William. 1974. *The Riverside Shakespeare.* Textual ed. G. Blakemore Evans. Boston: Houghton Mifflin Co.
Shakespeare, William. 1977. *Shakespeare's Sonnets.* Ed. Stephen Booth. New Haven and London: Yale University Press.
Sharp, William. 1882. *Dante Gabriel Rossetti: A Record and a Study.* London: Macmillan.
Sharp, William. 1894. 'Some Personal Reminiscences of Walter Pater'. *The Atlantic Monthly* 74.446 (December), 801–14. Reprinted in *Walter Pater: A Life Remembered.* Ed. R. M. Seiler. Calgary, Alberta: University of Calgary Press. 1987. 78–98.
Sharp, William. 1904. 'Aylwin-Land: Wales and East Anglia'. *Literary Geography.* London: Office of the 'Pall Mall Publications'. 125–45.
Sharp, William. 1912. 'Rossetti in Verse and Prose' (1887). *Papers Critical and Reminiscent.* Selected and edited by Mrs. William Sharp. London: William Heinemann.
Sharp, William (ed.). 1886. *Sonnets of this Century.* London: Walter Scott.
Shelley, Percy Bysshe. 1964. *The Letters of Percy Bysshe Shelley.* Ed. F. L. Jones. 2 vols. Oxford: Clarendon Press.
Shelley, Percy Bysshe. 1970. *Shelley: Poetical Works.* Ed. Thomas Hutchinson. Rev. G. M. Matthews. Oxford and New York: Oxford University Press.
Shelley, Percy Bysshe. 1977. *Shelley's Poetry and Prose.* Eds Donald H. Reiman and Sharon B. Powers. New York and London: Norton.
Shelley, Percy Bysshe. 1988. *Shelley's Prose.* Ed. David Lee Clark. London: Fourth Estate.
Smith, Lindsay. 1995. *Victorian Photography, Painting and Poetry: The Enigma of Visibility in the Nineteenth Century.* Cambridge: Cambridge University Press.
Solms, Mark. 1989a. 'A Previously-untranslated Review by Freud of a Monograph on Hypnotism'. *International Journal of Psycho-analysis* 70, 401–3.
Solms, Mark. 1989b. 'Three Previously-untranslated Reviews by Freud from the Neue Freie Press'. *International Journal of Psycho-analysis* 70, 397–400.
Stein, Richard. 1975. *The Ritual of Interpretation: Literature and Art in Ruskin, Rossetti, and Pater.* Cambridge, MA: Harvard University Press.
Stephens, Frederick. 1875. 'Pictures by Mr. Rossetti'. *Athenæum* (14 August), 219–21.
Stevens, Wallace. 1984. *The Collected Poems of Wallace Stevens.* Faber and Faber: London and Boston.
Stevenson, Lionel. 1972. *The Pre-Raphaelite Poets.* Chapel Hill: University of North Carolina Press.
Stillman, W. J. 1901. *The Autobiography of a Journalist.* 2 vols. London: Grant Richards.
Stokes, Adrian. 1955. 'Form in Art'. In *New Directions in Psycho-analysis: The Significance of Infant Conflict in Adult Behaviour.* Eds Melanie Klein, Paula Heiman and R. E. Money Kyrle. London: Tavistock Publications. 406–20.
Stokes, Adrian. 1972. *The Image in Form: Selected Writings of Adrian Stokes.* Ed. Richard Wollheim. Harmondsworth: Penguin Books.
Swinburne, Algernon Charles. 1875a. 'Notes on Some Pictures of 1868' (1868). *Essays and Studies.* London: Chatto & Windus. 358–80.

Swinburne, Algernon Charles. 1875b. 'Notes on Designs of the Old Masters at Florence' (1868). *Essays and Studies.* London: Chatto & Windus. 314–57.
Swinburne, Algernon Charles. 1894. *Studies in Poetry and Prose.* London: Chatto & Windus.
Swinburne, Algernon Charles. 1904. *The Collected Poetical Works of Algernon Charles Swinburne.* 6 vols. London: Chatto & Windus.
Swinburne, Algernon Charles. 1962. *The Swinburne Letters.* Ed. Cecil Y. Lang. 6 vols. New Haven and London: Yale and Oxford University Presses, 1959–62. 5: *1883–1890* (1962).
Sword, Helen. 2002. *Ghostwriting Modernism.* Ithaca: Cornell University Press.
Symons, Arthur. 1916. 'Dante Gabriel Rossetti' (1904). In *Figures of Several Centuries.* London: Constable & Co., Ltd. 201–6.
Symons, Arthur. 1925. 'The Decadent Movement in Literature' (1893). In *Dramatis Personæ.* London: Faber & Gwyer, Ltd. 96–117.
Symons, Arthur. 1929. *Studies in Strange Souls.* London: C. J. Sawyer.
Taylor, Dennis. 1981. *Hardy's Poetry, 1860–1928.* London and Basingstoke: Macmillan.
Taylor, Dennis. 1988. *Hardy's Metres and Victorian Prosody*, Oxford. Clarendon Press.
Taylor, Dennis. 1993. *Hardy's Literary Language and Victorian Philology.* Oxford: Clarendon Press.
Varty, Anne. 1991. 'The Crystal Man: A Study of "Diaphaneitè"'. In *Pater in the 1990s.* Eds Laurel Brake and Ian Small. Greenboro, NC: ELT Press. 205–15.
Wallen, Jeffrey. 1999. 'Alive in the Grave: Walter Pater's Renaissance'. *English Literary History* 66.4, 1033–51.
Warner, Eric, and Hough, Graham (eds). 1983. *Strangeness and Beauty: An Anthology of Aesthetic Criticism 1840–1910.* 2 vols. Cambridge: Cambridge University Press.
Watts-Dunton, Clara. 1922. *The Home Life of Algernon Charles Swinburne.* London: A. M. Philpotts.
Whalley, George. 1972. 'England/Romantic – Romanticism'. In *'Romantic' and Its Cognates: The European History of a Word.* Ed. Hans Eichner. Manchester, Toronto and Buffalo: Manchester University Press and University of Toronto Press. 159–262.
Wharton, Edith. 1996. 'The Sonnets of Eugene Lee-Hamilton'. *Bookman* 26 (November 1907), 251–3. Reprinted in *Uncollected Critical Writings.* Ed. Frederick Wegener. Princeton, NJ: Princeton University Press. 115–19.
Wilde, Oscar. 2000. *The Complete Letters of Oscar Wilde.* Eds Merlin Holland and Rupert Hart-Davis. London: Fourth Estate.
Wiley, Catherine. 2006. '"Warming me like a cordial": The Ethos of the Body in Vernon Lee's Aesthetics.' In *Vernon Lee: Decadence, Ethics, Aesthetics.* Eds Catherine Maxwell and Patricia Pulham. Basingstoke and New York: Palgrave Macmillan. 58–74.
Williams, Carolyn. 1989. *Transfigured World: Walter Pater's Aesthetic Historicism.* Ithaca and London: Cornell University Press.
Winter, Alison. 1998. *Mesmerized: Powers of Mind in Victorian Britain.* Chicago and London: University of Chicago Press.
Wood, Esther. 1894. *Dante Rossetti and the Pre-Raphaelite Movement.* London: Sampson Low, Marston and Co.
Woolf, Virginia. 1986–94. *The Essays of Virginia Woolf.* Ed. Andrew McNeillie. 4 vols. London: Hogarth Press. Volume 1: *1904–1912* (1986); Volume 2: *1912–1918* (1987); Volume 3: *1919–1924* (1988); Volume 4: *1925–1928* (1994).
Woolf, Virginia. 1976. *The Letters of Virginia Woolf.* Eds Nigel Nicolson and Joanne Trautman. 6 vols. London: Hogarth Press, 1975–80. Volume 2: *1912–1922.*

Woolford, John and Karlin, Daniel. 1996. *Robert Browning*. Studies in 18th and 19th Century Literature. New York and London: Longman.

Wordsworth, William. 1982. *The Borderers*. Ed. Robert Osborn. Ithaca and London: Cornell University Press.

Wordsworth, William. 1997. *Selected Poetry*. Eds Stephen Gill and Duncan Wu. Oxford World's Classics. Oxford and New York: Oxford University Press.

Wright, Thomas. 1907. *The Life of Walter Pater*. 2 vols. London: Everett & Co.

Yeats, W. B. Introduction. 1936. *The Oxford Book of Modern Verse 1892–1935*. Oxford: Clarendon Press. v–xlii.

Yeats, W. B. 1955. *Autobiographies*. London: Macmillan and Co., Ltd.

Yeats, W. B. *Collected Poems*. 1982. The Papermac Yeats. London and Basingstoke: Macmillan.

Yeats, W. B. 1989. *Essays and Introductions*. The Papermac Yeats. London and Basingstoke: Macmillan.

Zorn, Christa. 1997. 'Aesthetic Intertextuality as Cultural Critique: Vernon Lee Rewrites History through Walter Pater's "La Gioconda"'. *The Victorian Newsletter* 91, 4–10.

Zorn, Christa. 2003. *Vernon Lee: Aesthetics, History, and the Victorian Female Intellectual*. Athens, OH: Ohio University Press.

Index

Note: 'n' after a page reference indicates the number of a note on that page

Lightning Source UK Ltd.
Milton Keynes UK
UKOW01f1102290617
304320UK00004B/100/P

9 780719 071454